# PRISONS

*Today and Tomorrow*

# PRISONS

## *Today and Tomorrow*

**J**OYCELYN **M.** **P**OLLOCK
*General Editor*
**Southwest Texas State University**

**An Aspen Publication**

**Aspen Publishers, Inc.**
**Gaithersburg, Maryland**
**1997**

Cover photos come from a documentary called "Mom's in Prison . . . Again" produced by Annabella Chan, Ellen Halbert, Mary Willis, and Glen Ely. For more information, please write Box 101823, Fort Worth, TX 76185.

**About Aspen Publishers** • For more than 35 years, Aspen has been a leading professional publisher in a variety of disciplines. Aspen's vast information resources are available in both print and electronic formats. We are committed to providing the highest quality information available in the most appropriate format for our customers. Visit Aspen's Internet site for more information resources, directories, articles, and a searchable version of Aspen's full catalog, including the most recent publications: **http://www. aspenpub.com**

**Aspen Publishers, Inc.,** • The hallmark of quality in publishing
Members of the worldwide Wolters Kluwer group.

**Printed in the United States of America**

**1 2 3 4 5**

# Summary of Contents

# TABLE OF CONTENTS

**CHAPTER**

—— **1** ——

## THE PHILOSOPHY OF PUNISHMENT                              **2**

*Joycelyn M. Pollock*

**CHAPTER**

——— **4** ———

**THE CLASSIFICATION OF INMATES**    84

*David Spencer*

CHAPTER

—— 5 ——

# INDUSTRY, AGRICULTURE, AND EDUCATION    116

*William Stone*

CHAPTER

——— 7 ———

## THE SOCIAL WORLD OF THE PRISONER          218

*Joyceln M. Pollock*

Chapter

—— 8 ——

# MANAGEMENT AND ADMINISTRATIVE ISSUES

*Robert Freeman*

CHAPTER

—— 9 ——

## CORRECTIONAL OFFICERS: UNDERSTUDIED AND MISUNDERSTOOD

*Robert Freeman*

CHAPTER

—— 10 ——

## PRISONERS' RIGHTS: THE PENDULUM SWINGS

*John McLaren*

**CHAPTER**

—— **11** ——

## THE PRIVATIZATION OF PRISONS 382

*Ronald Becker*

CHAPTER

—— **12** ——

## JAILS                                                  414

*Dennis Giever*

CHAPTER
—— **13** ——

## THE FUTURE                                                            **466**

*Joyceln M. Pollock*

# PREFACE

Crime and the criminal justice system permeate every political race, every evening newscast, and every newspaper. Even though crime rates have been falling, "what to do about crime" is a stock element in politicians' platforms — from mayoral races to presidential elections. The answer to crime always seems to be "more" — more punishment, more police, and, of course, more prisons.

This text's underlying theme is that prisons do very little to solve the crime problems and that they sometimes do a great deal of damage to those who end up serving time. Prisons have many purposes: punishment, deterrence, rehabilitation, and incapacitation. It will become clear by the end of this book that the only goal that prisons accomplish quite well is incapacitation. Prisons now often serve as "human warehouses" where individuals are kept in captivity for short or long periods of time and then let loose again to pick up where they left off. While we incarcerate many more people than we have in the past, prison time isn't usually as painful. Physical punishment and severe conditions are no longer present, except in isolated situations, as prisons have become less oppressive and inhumane due to the recognition of legal rights of prisoners. Of course, the deprivations suffered in prison (of family, autonomy, and freedom) are painful, and, for some inmates, prison causes severe emotional trauma, even mental breakdowns. But for others, prison actually may be more comfortable and safer than living on the outside. It may provide a "home away from home" or just another place to "do business." For these types of inmates — some of whom consider prison a rite of passage — prison is hardly a deterrent. In fact, prison sentences have become as common as poverty for large segments of our society.

As to rehabilitation, we hardly even pay lip service to this goal anymore. There are attempts to provide education and vocational training, but no official rhetoric places much emphasis on the reformative goals of prison. Recidivism is high and hopes are low that anything we do "to" an offender will change his or her behavior once released. Actually, the only answer that seems to be offered by most politicians, policy makers, and the public at large is "more time." If a prisoner recidivates after a short sentence, let's give them a longer sentence; thus we have habitual sentence laws ("three strikes" laws) that have created the scenario where 24-year-old men are facing life sentences without parole. Whether we've actually thought through the effects of putting young men in prison for the next 60 years is another matter. Obviously some individuals are dangerous and need to be removed from society, and for those who break the law, there must be some consequence. The disagreement comes in answering the questions of who should be locked up and for how long. The chapter authors of this text do not necessarily agree with each other on these questions, but it becomes clear that at least on one thing there is agreement: Prisons have been a negative force in the lives of most of those who are touched by them, and if essential, they are essential evils in the society of humans.

In this text, the first three chapters introduce us to the concepts and realities of prisons. We look at the ideology that formed the rationale for their creation in Chapter 1, then we explore the history of prisons in Chapter 2. We see the repetition of cycles of great optimism and then inevitable neglect, corruption and overcrowding in prison history and find that present-day events are echoes of the past. In Chapter 3 the sentencing patterns that led to current overcrowding problems are examined with information also presented on the extent and effects of prison overcrowding. The next section of the book presents some of the basic operations and elements of prison life. We look at classification (Chapter 4), vocational programs, education, and industry (Chapter 5), rehabilitation programs (Chapter 6), and the prisoner subculture (Chapter 7). In each of the chapters, special attention has been given to the experiences (both historical and current) of minorities and women. We then turn to the other residents of the prison — the administrators and correctional officers. In Chapters 8 (management issues) and 9 (correctional officers), we look at prison from the "other side of the bars." In Chapter 10 we present the chronology of the recognition of legal rights of prisoners from the "hands off" era to the present court cases, which can be described as following a new "hands off" doctrine. In Chapter 11 we explore the growing presence of privitization in corrections, examining both practical and legal elements in the practice. Chapter 12 describes jails. For those who teach a course in penology and concentrate solely on prisons. Chapter 12 may easily be deleted from the reading assignment with no loss to the book's flow or integration. For those who teach a course on "incarceration" and include jails as a specific type of incarcerative facility, this chapter has been provided. It includes smaller sections on each of the elements discussed for prisons, including jail overcrowding, classification and program issues, subculture, management problems, and so on. Finally, in Chapter 13, we review, summarize, and present some projections for what might happen in the future.

The book may be used as a supplementary text in a Corrections class and presents much more detail than a survey text's chapters on prisons. Many curriculums now have upper division courses in penology or prison, for which this text would be ideal. We also suggest using smaller supplemental texts — many of which can be found in each chapter's source list — for highlighting specific elements of the prison experience. Finally, no course in prison is complete without the daily newspaper. The instructor must provide what we cannot — up-to-date, current events in the reader's own state. During any semester, one will read news announcing the opening of new prisons, erupting scandals involving corruption, escapes, private prisons contracting with the state to open new facilities, new programs, exposed brutality or sexual harassment by correctional officers, and, perhaps every so often, a "soft" news item of an offender who changes while in prison and creates a new crime- and drug-free life upon release.

*Joycelyn M. Pollock*

November 1996

# ACKNOWLEDGMENTS

The preparation of this book has been assisted by a number of people who deserve recognition. In many ways, an edited book is more difficult to complete than a book written by oneself. I thank all those who jumped in and completed their work quickly and competently. Dennis Giever and Bob Freeman deserve special mention — both gentlemen could be counted on to meet impossible deadlines. William Stone, my colleague here at Southeast Texas, has been gracious, patient, and, above all, knowledgeable about the intricacies of translating computer disks of various word processing programs into a format that my MacIntosh could read. (I should add that his help was offered despite his passionate allegiance to IBM and his predictions that the MacIntosh will soon be as obsolete as the Edsel.) Several graduate assistants have helped in a variety of ways, from preparing tables to discovering sources, helping make the task easier for me. Special thanks go to Daisy Sartor and Lance Hignite, who also provided some sources and thoughts for Chapter 7. Office staff also helped — thanks to Linda Staats and Rae Josey.

All reviewers were extremely helpful in improving the first draft of the manuscript. I speak for all chapter authors in thanking Jerry Armor, Calhoun Community College; Cliff Bryan, Idaho State University; Jack Curtin, San Francisco State University; Mary Finn, Georgia State University; Timothy Flanagan, Sam Houston State University; Ed Harver, University of Delaware; Bob Huckabee, Indiana State University; Joe Jimenez, Pima Community College; Fred Jones, Simpson College; Peter Kratcoski, Kent State University; Curt Kuball, Kings River Community College; Karol Lucken, University of Central Florida; Kevin Minor, Eastern Kentucky University; Barbara Owen, California State University-Fresno; Joan Petersilia, UCLA; Lori

Pompa, Temple University; John Wooldredge, University of Cincinnati; and Linda Zupan, Northern Michigan University.

Susan Beauchamp and Jessica Barmack of Little, Brown have been a pleasure to work with and have helped ensure the completion of the manuscript; Lisa Wehrle and Kurt Hughes have done an equally fine job of taking a raw manuscript and shaping and molding it into the final product you hold in your hands. I'd like to thank them all.

We would also like to thank the following copyright holder for permission to reprint:

Nichole Hahn Rafter, Partial Justice: Women, Prisons, and Social Control (2d ed. 1990). Reprinted by permission of Transaction Publishers, and the author. Copyright © 1990 by Transaction Publishers, all rights reserved.

Finally, I'd like to thank Glen Ely who provided the wonderful cover photos for this text. The video these photos came from, "Mom's in Prison . . . Again," can be ordered from Forest Glen Productions, P.O. Box 101823, Fort Worth, Texas 76185-1823.

# About the Contributors

**Ron Becker** is a graduate of Sam Houston State University, Texas A&M University, and St. Mary's School of Law. Recent publications include *Processing the Underwater Crime Scene,* a book published by Charles Thomas Publishing Co., and a chapter on teaching ethics in *Justice, Crime, and Ethics,* an ethics text published by Anderson Publishing Co. He is also under contract for a text on the use of scientific evidence in the courtroom.

**Robert M. Freeman** is an Assistant Professor in the Department of Criminal Justice at Shippensburg University in Shippensburg, Pennsylvania. He holds a B.A. in psychology (1970), an M.A. in clinical psychology (1974) from Indiana University of Pennsylvania, and a Ph.D. in criminal justice and criminology from the University of Maryland at College Park (1994). He was employed by the Pennsylvania Department of Corrections from 1970 to 1990. He was a psychologist and a corrections superintendent from 1980 to 1990. He is the author of *Strategic Planning for Correctional Emergencies* and "Public Perception and Corrections" in *Popular Culture, Crime, and Justice,* edited by Dr. Frankie Bailey and Dr. Donna Hale, and has published articles in *Corrections Today* and *American Jails.* He is a member of the American Correctional Association, Academy of Criminal Justice Sciences (Division of Corrections), and the American Society of Criminology. His research interests include discretion in rule enforcement, the evolution of correctional management, and the public perception of corrections.

**Dennis M. Giever** is an Assistant Professor of Criminal Justice at New Mexico State University. He received his Ph.D. in criminology from Indiana University of Pennsylvania in 1995. His most recent research involves an empirical assessment of Gottfredson and Hirschi's general theory of crime. He has co-authored an article in this area in *Justice Quarterly*. His teaching and research interests are in the areas of research methods, evaluation research, jails, corrections, and crime prevention through environmental design.

**Robert Johnson** is Professor of Justice, Law and Society in the School of Public Affairs at The American University in Washington, D.C. He holds a bachelor's degree in psychology from Fairfield University, and master's and doctoral degrees in criminal justice from the University of Albany, State University of New York. Dr. Johnson's books include *Culture and Crisis in Confinement, Condemned to Die,* and *Hard Time;* he co-edited and contributed to *The Pains of Imprisonment;* and he has published numerous articles in professional journals and anthologies. Professor Johnson received The American University Award for Outstanding Scholarship, and is a Distinguished Alumnus of the School of Criminal Justice, Nelson A. Rockefeller College of Public Affairs and Policy, University of Albany, State University of New York.

**John A. McLaren** is an Associate Professor in the Department of Criminal Justice at Southwest Texas State University. His scholarly interests are in criminal procedure and constitutional law, particularly as applied in institutional corrections, probation, parole, and community corrections.

**Alida V. Merlo** is an Associate Professor of Criminology at Indiana University of Pennsylvania. Professor Merlo previously taught in the Criminal Justice Department at Westfield State College in Westfield, Massachusetts. She was a Probation Officer and Intake Supervisor in Youngstown, Ohio. She co-edited *Women, Law, and Social Control* (1995) with Professor Joycelyn M. Pollock and *Corrections: Dilemmas and Directions in Corrections* (1992) with Professor Peter J. Benekos. Professor Merlo has authored chapters and articles on women offenders, ethical issues in corrections, and correctional policy. She serves on the editorial board of *Women and Criminal Justice* and *Journal of Crime and Justice.*

**Joycelyn M. Pollock** is the Chair of the Department of Criminal Justice at Southwest Texas State University. Her published works include *Ethics in Crime and Justice: Dilemmas and Decisions (Second*

*Edition); Women, Prison, and Crime; Sex and Supervision: Guarding Male and Female Inmates;* and chapters in *Women, Law, and Social Control.* Professor Pollock also has authored numerous articles in the area of ethics and women in the criminal justice system.

**David Spencer** graduated from the University of Texas at Austin, Texas, in 1966, with a B.A. in Political Science. He served four years as an officer in the U.S. Navy. In 1970, he returned to school a the University of Texas School of Law, graduating with a J.D. in 1972. He served as a prosecutor in the Travis County, Texas, District Attorney's office from 1973-1977, and was an attorney in private practice from 1977-1983. He became the General Counsel for the Texas Adult Probation Department from 1983-1989. He became the General Counsel for the Texas Adult Probation Department from 1983-1989. In 1988, he entered the graduate program in the Educational Psychology Department of the University of Texas at Austin. He received an M.A. in 1991 and is a candidate for a Ph.D. He has been a Lecturer in the Criminal Justice Department at Southwest Texas State University since 1991.

**William E. Stone** is an Associate Professor at Southwest Texas State University. He received his Ph.D. in Criminal Justice in 1975 from Sam Houston State University and has been teaching criminal justice for over twenty years. He has professional experience in both corrections and law enforcement. Professor Stone has published in numerous professional journals on subjects ranging from DWI treatment programs to handgun cartridge effectiveness.

# PRISONS

*Today and Tomorrow*

# THE PHILOSOPHY OF PUNISHMENT

*Joycelyn M. Pollock*

Could we all be put on prison fare, for the space of two or three generations, the world would ultimately be the better for it. Indeed, should society change places with the prisoners, so far as habits are concerned, taking to itself the regularity, and temperance, and sobriety of a good prison, then the grandiose goals of peace, right, and Christianity would be furthered. (Finley, cited in Rothman 1971, 561)

Abandon hope, all ye who enter here. (Carved into portal of prison, taken from Dante's *Inferno*)

*Chapter Overview*

—— **PHILOSOPHY OF PUNISHMENT**
      Retributive Rationale
      Utilitarian Rationale
      Methods of Punishment
—— **PHILOSOPHY OF IMPRISONMENT**
      Paradigms and Prison
            *Conservatism: Deterrence and Incapacitation*
            *Liberalism: Reformation and Rehabilitation*
            *Radicalism: Prison and Economics*
      The New Conservatism: Justice and "Just Deserts"
      Other Philosophical Approaches
—— **CONCLUSIONS**

Why prison? Why do we punish? Why do we imprison? Throughout this book prison is described — its exterior, its internal functions, the people who work and live within it, and the nature of their relationships. First, however, we should be concerned with the more abstract vision: Why does the prison exist at all?

In the quotes above, two extremes of prison are illustrated: Is it a utopia of orderliness and temperance, or a hell of hopelessness? In the United States, prison incarceration rates continue their upward spiral despite decreasing crime rates. "Getting tough" continues to be the battle cry of politicians, even though we are now imprisoning more people, for longer periods of time, with fewer programs to occupy their time productively. Punishment is a natural response to fear and injury, and prison seems to be our favorite punishment.

## PHILOSOPHY OF PUNISHMENT

Most people would agree that hurting someone or subjecting them to pain is wrong. However, punishment, by definition, involves the infliction of pain. Does this make punishment wrong? Philosophers are divided on this issue. One group believes that inflicting pain as punishment is fundamentally different than inflicting pain on innocents and therefore is not inherently wrong. Another group believes that punishment is a wrong that can only be justified if it results in a "greater good" (Murphy 1995).

The first view does not feel it necessary to justify punishment beyond the fact that the individual deserves it. This would be considered a *retributive* approach. The second view justifies punishment through the secondary rationales of deterrence, incapacitation, or rehabilitation. This will be called the *utilitarian* approach (Durham 1994).

### RETRIBUTIVE RATIONALE

The first philosophical approach (or rationale) is that punishment, strictly defined, is not evil. *Retribution* is a term that means balancing a wrong through punishment. While revenge is personal and not necessarily balanced, retribution is impersonal and balanced. Newman (1978), although recognizing the difficulty of defining punishment, presents it thus: Punishment is a pain or other unpleasant consequence that results from an offense against a rule and that is administered by others, who represent legal authority, to the offender who broke the rule (1978, 6-7). The supposition is that by strictly limiting what can be done, to who and by whom, the evilness of the action is negated. There are two equally important elements to this view: first, that society has a right to punish, and second, that the criminal has the right to be punished.

The right of society to punish is said to lie in the *social contract.* Although this idea dates back to the ancient Greeks, it gained its greatest currency during the Age of Enlightenment in the seventeenth and eighteenth centuries and is associated with Thomas Hobbes (*Leviathan* 1651), John Locke (*Two Treatises on Government* 1690), and Jean-Jacques Rousseau (*Du contrat social* 1762). Basically, the concept proposes that all people freely and willingly enter into an agreement to form society by giving up a portion of their individual freedom for the return benefit of protection. If one transgresses against the rights of others, one has broken the social contract, and society has the right to punish (Mickunas 1990).

One problematic element to the social contract theory of punishment is the fiction that everyone willingly plays a part or had a part in the agreement to abide by society's laws. Many authors have suggested that the legal system may not be "owned" by certain groups in society. To assume that such groups break a "contract" they had no part in creating (or receive benefit from) weakens the legitimacy of this theory.

> If persons are barred from such participation, then they are not bound to respect laws. This is to say, the reason for punishment rests on democratic grounds: The source of law is the individual, and the source of legality is based on agreement among individuals. Retribution is for breaking an *agreement* to uphold a law (emphasis in original). (Mickunas 1990, 81)

If we believe that our political process and even our justice system is operated for the benefit of only certain groups of citizens, then the social contract is a weaker rationale for punishment.

The second element of the retributive rationale is that the criminal *deserves* the punishment and, indeed, has a *right* to be punished. Only by forcing the individual to suffer the consequences of his actions does one accord them the rights of an equal citizen. Herbert Morris explains this view:

> [F]irst, . . . we have a right to punishment; second, . . . this right
> derives from a fundamental human right to be treated as a per-
> son; third, . . . this fundamental right is a natural, inalienable,
> and absolute right; and, fourth, . . . the denial of this right implies
> the denial of all moral rights and duties. (Morris, in Murphy
> 1995, 75)

To do anything other than to punish is to treat the person as less than
equal, perhaps even less than human. Under this view, correctional
treatment is infinitely more intrusive than punishment because it
doesn't respect the individual's ability and right to make choices. It
regards their behavior as "controlled" by factors that can be influenced by the intervention (Morris, in Murphy 1995, 83).

It is a primitive, almost instinctual, response of humankind to
punish wrongdoers, as noted by French sociologist Émile Durkheim
and cited in Durham (1994, 22). Punishment also is believed to be
an essential feature of civilization. The state takes over the act of
revenge and elevates it to something noble rather than base, something proportional rather than without bounds. Immanuel Kant
(1724-1804) supported a retributive rationale:

> Juridical punishment . . . can be inflicted on a criminal, never just
> as instrumental to the achievement of some other good for the
> criminal himself or for the civil society, but only because he has
> committed a crime; for a man may never be used just as a means
> to the end of another person. . . . Penal law is a categorical imper-
> ative. . . . Thus, whatever undeserved evil you inflict on another
> person, you inflict on yourself. (Kant, cited in Borchert and Stew-
> art 1986, 322)

In conclusion, the retributive rationale for punishment holds that
because of natural law and the social contract, society has the right
to punish, and the criminal has the right to be punished. It is not an
evil to be justified but rather represents the natural order of things.
According to Newman (1978, 287), "There is little grace in punishment. Only justice."

## UTILITARIAN RATIONALE

The utilitarian approach (or rationale) defines punishment as essentially evil and seeks to justify it by the greater benefits that result.
Under a utilitarian philosophical system, or *utilitarianism,* what is
good is that which benefits "the many." Thus, even if it is painful to

the individual, if the majority benefit from a certain act, then utilitarianism would define that act as good. In our discussion, if punishment did *deter* or *incapacitate* or facilitate *rehabilitation,* then "the many" (all of society) would benefit and punishment, by definition, would be good.

This rationale for punishment is ancient. Plato argued that punishment is a benefit to the person because it improves their souls or characters (cited in Murphy 1995, 17). Jeremy Bentham (1748-1832), the classical advocate of utilitarian punishment, believed that punishment could be calibrated to deter crime. His idea of a *hedonistic calculus* involved two concepts: first, that mankind was essentially rational and hedonistic (pleasure-seeking) and would seek to maximize pleasure and reduce pain in all behavior decisions; and second, that a legal system could accurately determine exactly what measure of punishment was necessary to slightly outweigh the potential pleasure or profit from any criminal act. Thus, if done correctly, the potential pain of punishment would be sufficient to outweigh the potential pleasure or profit from crime, and all people would rationally choose to be law-abiding.

Under the utilitarian rationale, punishment is evil, but it is justified when it accomplishes more good than the evil it represents. Cesare Beccaria (1738-1794), another utilitarian thinker, suggested that in some instances the benefits of punishment *do not* outweigh the evil.

> But all punishment is mischief: all punishment in itself is evil. Upon the principle of utility, if it ought at all to be admitted, it ought only to be admitted in as far as it promises to exclude some greater evil. . . . It is plain, therefore, that in the following cases punishment ought not to be inflicted.
>
> 1. Where it is groundless: where there is no mischief for it to prevent; the act not being mischievous upon the whole.
> 2. Where it must be inefficacious: where it cannot act so as to prevent the mischief.
> 3. Where it is unprofitable, or too expensive: where the mischief it would produce would be greater than what it prevented.
> 4. Where it is needless: where the mischief may be prevented, or cease of itself, without it: that is, at a cheaper rate.
>
> (Beccaria, cited in Murphy 1995, 24)

Situations in which punishment does not deter include *ex post facto* laws (because people cannot be deterred from some action they do not know to be illegal when they decide to do it), and infancy

**HIGHLIGHT 1-1**
**Philosophers of Punishment and Penology**

**Cesare Beccaria** (1738-1794). Beccaria was an Italian writer during the age of the Enlightenment, an historical era marked by great advances in political and social thought. He wrote a treatise on criminal law that was highly critical of the practices of the day and advocated major reforms that included ideas which were widely adopted, such as the right to defend oneself against one's accusers. The philosophical rationale for these reforms was utilitarianism. He believed that the objective of punishment should be deterrence and the effectiveness of punishment was based on certainty, not severity. He was largely responsible for major criminal law reforms in Europe and America.

**Jeremy Bentham** (1748-1832). Bentham was an English philosopher, economist, and theoretician. Among his many works was *The Rationale of Punishment* (1830), in which he proposed a utilitarian rationale for punishment. Mankind, according to Bentham, was governed by the pursuit of pleasure and the avoidance of pain. These two masters affected all behavior decisions and could be utilized to deter criminal behavior through a careful application of criminal law. He is also known for his design of the "Panopticon" prison.

**Immanuel Kant** (1724-1804). Kant was a German philosopher who wrote in the areas of metaphysics, ethics, and knowledge. He is the founder of "Kantianism," a philosophical tradition that explores the limits of human reason and establishes a philosophy of morality based on duty. His views on punishment would be considered purely retributive. He believed that the criminal deserved to be punished, but that to punish for other purposes, such as deterrence, was to violate the "categorical imperative," specifically, that one should not use others for one's own end.

or insanity (because people cannot be deterred if they cannot control their behavior). This approach views prevention of future harm as the only justifiable purpose of punishment, with retribution having no place because "what is done can never be undone" (Hirsch 1987, 361).

The *social contract* is also the basis for a utilitarian rationale for punishment. In this case, the social contract gives society the right to punish, not because of the offender's violation but rather to protect all members of society against future harms. The right of society to punish comes from the responsibility of society to protect. The utilitarian approach of punishment sees it as a means to an end — the end being either deterrence (general or specific), incapacitation, or rehabilitation (reform).

Utilitarian theory is forward-looking, it is consequentialist, and it is predictive. The goal of punishment is to prevent future harm. By making the criminal suffer, he, she, or others are deterred from criminal acts. The particular individual will be less likely to repeat the behavior (assuming he or she is rational), and others will be less likely to commit the behavior if they have observed the consequences. Deterrence theory presupposes rationality, free will, and logical consequences.

*Incapacitation* and *rehabilitation* are not really related to punishment at all. Incapacitation prevents an individual from inflicting further harm for at least as long as the individual is under control. Strictly speaking, it is not punishment because it does not necessarily imply pain. To put all criminals under a drug that induced sleep would be to incapacitate them, not necessarily to punish them. If one takes away the ability of the criminal to commit the crime, this also would be incapacitation; for instance, chemical castration has been discussed and, in some cases, inflicted on sexual offenders. This is obviously a punishment, but it could also be termed incapacitation because it takes away the ability to commit the particular crime. Note that there is no physical pain involved, only the incapacitative nature of the chemical. House arrest, electronic bracelets, or other means of monitoring the movements of criminals have all been suggested as less expensive alternatives to incapacitating criminals in prisons. Prison, of course, has become synonymous with incapacitation because as long as the person is incarcerated they cannot commit crimes against the rest of us. Of course, prisoners continue to commit crimes in prison against other inmates, and there is at least some limited ability to continue to commit some crimes, for instance, credit card abuse over prison phones or computer fraud using computers provided in vocational programs.

One issue of incapacitation is how long to hold the individual. There is little confidence in our ability to predict how long someone may be dangerous or even who may be a continued risk to society (Zimring and Hawkins 1995). Because incapacitation is forward-looking, it is assumed that the incapacitative period should last as long as the risk exists. This may be inconsistent with principles of justice, even assuming we could predict risk accurately. For instance, forgers have extremely high recidivism rates but are not especially dangerous; should we hold them longer than murderers who have better recidivism rates? Should the period of incapacitation be tied somehow to the seriousness of the risk (severity of the crime), as well as the extent of the risk itself (likelihood of recidivism)? Again, this discussion assumes that we can accurately predict risk, an extremely problematic assumption. Although strictly speaking incapacitation is not punishment, it usually does involve some deprivation of liberty and therefore is painful to those who value liberty and autonomy.

Neither is rehabilitation or reform punishment, although punishment may be used as a tool of reform. Rehabilitation is defined as internal change that results in a cessation of the targeted negative behavior. It may be achieved by inflicting pain as a learning tool (behavior modification) or by other interventions that are not painful at all (for example, self-esteem groups, education, or religion). Under the retributive philosophy described above, rehabilitation and treatment are considered more intrusive and less respectful of the individuality of each person than pure punishment because they attack the internal psyche of the individual. They seek to change offenders, perhaps against their will. This is probably more sophistry than reality as anyone who has worked with offenders can attest. Very few people enjoy the experience of being a drug addict or sex offender, and most prison programs have limited capacity to change individuals against their will anyway. In Chapter 6 we will explore the concept of rehabilitation and the various modes of individual change.

To conclude, the utilitarian rationale for punishment must determine that the good coming from punishment outweighs the negativity of the punishment itself. The beneficial aspects have been denoted as deterrence, incapacitation, and rehabilitation or reform.

## METHODS OF PUNISHMENT

Targets of punishment include one's possessions, one's body, or one's psyche. Most common punishments throughout the ages have attacked the body. *Corporal punishment* (meaning "to the body") included drawing and quartering, flaying, whipping, beheading, dismembering, and numerous other means of torture or death (Newman 1978). Fines and dispossession of property also have been common throughout history. Conley (1992) writes that fines were more common than physical torture during many time periods. Execution was an economic as well as a corporal punishment because the person's estate was forfeited to the monarch.

Economic and physical sanctions gradually have given way to imprisonment or lesser deprivations of liberty (probation or parole). We have reached the point today (at least in this country) where punishment is almost synonymous with imprisonment. Conley (1992) charts the slow growth of imprisonment as punishment. As early as the end of the fourteenth century, the purpose of imprisonment changed from custody until physical punishment was inflicted to custody as punishment itself. An increasing number of laws emerged with precisely defined prison sentences. The church also used imprisonment as a punishment for clerics. Gradually, imprisonment for crime became almost indistinguishable from the other institutions that developed for vagrants and idlers — the bridewells, workhouses, and gaols all were responses to the same class of citizens. Chapter 2 explains this progression more fully.

## PHILOSOPHY OF IMPRISONMENT

Of all the punishments described above, prison is perhaps the most complex. It affects the prisoner's material possessions because he can earn little or no income while incarcerated, may lose his job or livelihood, spend his life savings, and have his total lifetime earning capacity affected. It affects the prisoner's body because she is under the control of others. Imprisonment may result in actual physical harm, from attacks by correctional officers or other inmates or from illnesses or injuries left untreated. Prison also attacks the psyche — by its attempts at reformation and through the mental deterioration that occurs because of the negative environment of the prison. Prison is described by many as a "psychological punishment" (Mickunas 1990, 78). According to some, prison in its most severe form attacks "the soul"; it acts on the "heart, the thoughts, the will, the inclinations of the prisoner" (Howe 1994, 87). Prison critics allege that the most detrimental effects are not physical deterioration but mental and moral deterioration. "You are nothing!" is a theme that prison inmates live with during the course of their imprisonment, and the mental toll that prison takes on its population is very difficult to measure.

## PARADIGMS AND PRISON

A *paradigm* is a way of seeing the world or of organizing and making sense of knowledge. We can use the well-worn paradigms of conservatism and liberalism to illustrate the philosophy of imprisonment. The conservative ideology operates under the assumption that human beings have free will, can make rational choices, and deserve the logical outcomes of their choices. The liberal view of human behavior holds that behavior is influenced by upbringing, by affluence or poverty, by education, and life experiences in general. The radical paradigm calls into question the very existence of the social order; radicals reject private ownership of property and are in favor of restructuring socioeconomic relations (Durham 1994, 17-20).

With these elements in mind, it is clear that the *conservative approach* to imprisonment is one of deterrence and incapacitation. Prison life should be uncomfortable — even painful — and rational people will be deterred from committing crime to avoid being sent there again. If a short prison term doesn't work, the next sentence should be longer. The *liberal approach* embraces rehabilitation and reform. The purpose of prison should be to change the individual. Rehabilitative programs and reintegrative assistance, such as job placements, will help the person avoid future imprisonment by "solving their problems" of drug addiction, poor self-esteem, or no job skills. The *radical approach* would abolish prisons because it views them as tools of the powerful to enslave the powerless. The only solution to recidivism and crime, according to a radical perspective, is to reform law and society (Durham 1994, 28). At least two of these three perspectives can be roughly represented by different eras of prison history, each with a predominant philosophy of penalty.

***Conservatism: Deterrence and Incapacitation.*** The conservative approach characterized by views of deterrence and incapacitation was strong throughout pre-Jacksonian America and Europe. The philosophy of punishment in general, and of prison specifically, was to deter and punish.

> [C]learly the colonists relied on societal retribution as the basis for punishment and viewed the execution of punishment as a right of the society to protect itself and to wage war against indi-

vidual sin. Deviance was the fault of the offender, not the break-down of society or the community. . . . (Conley 1992, 42)

The use of prisons was seen as a more humane form of punishment than earlier corporal punishments, but it was not necessarily viewed as reformative. "Prisons at this point were merely a means to reform the law, not the individual, by providing an alternative form of punishment" (Conley 1992, 43). The individual was seen as evil, someone that society needed to protect itself against. Prison became a type of banishment. Earlier societies had banished wrongdoers to the wilderness; prisons (which were isolated far away from urban areas) became the "new wilderness." If individuals were not deterred by the thought of that punishment *(general deterrence),* then they might be after experiencing incarceration *(specific deterrence).* At the least, society was protected as long as the offender was away (incapacitation).

*Liberalism: Reformation and Rehabilitation.* At some point during the nineteenth century, the philosophy of imprisonment became more optimistic, that is, prison became viewed as more than an alternative to brutal corporal punishments. It was seen as redemptive and capable of changing the individuals within to become better persons (Conley 1992).

David Rothman (1971), one of the definitive authorities on the reformative origins of the prison, proposes that the idea of reforming the individual criminal was at odds with the Calvinist doctrine of original sin. Before the 1800s, punishment remained retributive and expiatory (a religious term meaning that personal redemption comes through suffering). People were not viewed as reformable. Once the possibility of individual change was born, the idea of prison developed as the site of the "reform" (Hirsch 1987).

Although the penitentiary might have been an idea born in Europe, its development was purely American. Hirsch (1987) describes a shift in penal philosophy as the concept developed in the United States and Europeans began to look to American models of penal institutions.

> The deluge of European delegations [to American prisons] in the 1830's masked a subtle shift in the intellectual center of penal reform. Before 1800, European theorists dominated the field of criminology, supplying the basic concepts and programs on which American facilities were built. (Hirsch 1987, 429)

Separation, obedience, and labor became the trinity around which officials managed the penitentiary (Crosley 1986). Convicts were "men of idle habits, vicious propensities, and depraved passions," who had to be taught obedience as part of their reformation (Rothman 1971, 579). By teaching convicts these virtues, prison officials reinforced their value for all of society. The penitentiary would "reawaken the public to these virtues" and "promote a new respect for order and authority" (Rothman 1971, 585).

The early reformative ideals, although corrupted by greed and coopted by practicality, evolved into the rehabilitative era of the 1960s. Reformation was the dominant theme of the 1870 Prison Congress, which laid out the principles of corrections, and it was endorsed again, almost without change, in the 1970 Prison Congress. The 1870 and 1970 Prison Congresses endorsed such philosophical principles as "respect for human dignity and worth with recognition that hope is essential to humane and just programs," "accused and convicted offender[s] shall be accorded the protection of recognized standards of safety, humaneness, and due process," "sanctions imposed by the court shall be commensurate with the seriousness of the offense," and "All offenders . . . shall be afforded the opportunity to engage in productive work and participate in programs . . . and other activities that will enhance self-worth, community integration, and economic status" (cited in Allen and Simonsen 1992).

Conley (1992) explains the difference between the early prison reformers (pre-1900s) and those who followed. He describes the Progressive Era (the first two decades of the twentieth century) as the time period during which educated professionals entered penology believing that science would aid in solving individual prisoners' problems. Indeterminate sentences and individualized treatment were the tools to accomplish this task. Scientific objectivity and professionalism replaced missionary zeal. The prison was no longer viewed as a utopia for society to emulate. It was viewed instead as a laboratory in which social work and psychiatry would work to help change people's behavior.

A natural outgrowth of the rehabilitative era was a concern for *reintegration,* or the process of reentering society. The philosophy behind reintegration, which was strongest during the early 1970s, was consistent with and somewhat parallel to the grassroots movement and the War on Poverty of the Johnson administration. Reintegration was born out of disillusionment that prison could ever be a productive tool of reform, combined with an emphasis on community sanctions and integration. The result was the development of halfway houses, work and school release, furloughs, and other means to assist the offender to reintegrate back into society (Allen and Simonsen 1989). Interestingly, the following quote from the 1700s parallels the concerns of those who championed reintegrative efforts in the late 1970s.

> A man shall be tried, sentenced, whipped and set at liberty; his character, if tolerable before, is now ruined; nothing is to be done but for him to go to the old trade of stealing, when he is again taken and goes through the same process, which instead of answering the least good purpose, serves only to harden him the more; and so he goes on stealing and being whipped, until death rids the community of him. (Newspaper, 1784, cited in Hirsch 1987, 398)

It has been an inevitable and persistent argument that deterrence in the form of imprisonment and reform cannot be good bedfellows.

***Radicalism: Prison and Economics.*** Rothman's (1971) view of penal philosophy accepted prison rhetoric at face value. That is, the writings of the time indicated that the motivation and purpose of prison was to reform offenders, and these goals are accepted as fact. Others see the rhetoric of early prison reformers as masking a more subtle, insidious philosophy of imprisonment, one based on economy rather than reformation or power rather than benevolence. Rusche and Kirchheimer (1939) are cited most often by those who present this approach. Rusche and Kirchheimer suggested that imprisonment emerged as the dominant method of punishment because of a desire to exploit and train captive labor. A scarcity of labor served as the impetus for the modern prison because of its role in training and exploiting labor reserves.

The so-called severity hypothesis of Rusche and Kirchheimer proposes that punishment becomes more severe when there is a surplus of labor and more lenient when labor is scarce and convicts are more valuable as labor. Some authors have supported this theory by using case histories of prison systems and comparing the treatment of prisoners to economic conditions. Other authors have not found any support to the theory, at least support measurable by standard methods (Gardner 1987). Gardner (1987), for instance, found in his study of New York prison history that harsher punishment often resulted from attempts to maintain and increase the production of essential commodities in overcrowded, tumultuous prisons.

However, even critics of the Rusche-Kirchheimer view mention economic elements in their explanations of motivations for the development of prison. Gardner (1987) proposes the idea that prisons would have developed much earlier in England and Europe if the Board of Trade in England had not been so vigorously opposed to their creation and the competition that would develop from prisoner labor. He also points out that in American prison history, the rhetoric of prison officials to make prisons self-supporting was belied by the low fees contractors were allowed to pay for leased labor, not to mention the economic boon of the prison itself to a local economy. In fact, he goes so far as to point to the economic benefits of the prison to certain interest groups as the reason for "the persistence and expansion of an otherwise politically and economically anachronistic form of punishment" (Gardner 1987, 106).

The earliest origins of the prison are tied to economics because prisons targeted the "idle poor" and were first cousins to the bridewells and workhouses, which were specifically designed for the vagrant classes of Europe and early American cities. Authors disagree, however, as to the meaning of labor within the prison. Some saw labor as a reformative element, helping the inmate take on the industriousness and good habits of a perfect citizen. Others describe prison labor as more purely punishment.

> Most institutions, rather than abandon convict labor, increasingly used it as a method of punishment. New Jersey legislators, concerned more with correction than with profit, instructed prison officials to institute "labor of the hardest and most servile kind, in which the work is least liable to be spoiled by ignorance, neglect or obstinacy." (Rothman 1971, 570)

There was no question that prison labor in southern prison systems was purely exploitive.

> [P]enal slaves were herded about the camps by armed guards, and at night they were shackled in "cribs." The lease-holders were interested in making as large a return as possible for the least outlay of money. (Crosley 1986, 21)

The radical view (one might say the Marxist view) sees economics as the central issue in all social relations. Those who have economic power also have legal and social power. The legal system, including the sanction of imprisonment, is viewed as a tool of those in power. The purpose is variously described as to capture and exploit the labor pool, to hold a portion of the labor class inactive to keep down labor costs, or to serve as a dumping ground for those who are expendable in a capitalist system. Theorists who advocate this philosophy of imprisonment point to the continued existence of an institution that seems to have failed miserably in its original goals of reformation. For instance, Reiman (1995, 4) says, "On the whole, most of the system's practices make more sense if we look at them as ingredients in an attempt to maintain rather than to reduce crime." According to this view, the criminal justice system maintains a "distorted image that crime is primarily the work of the poor." It keeps the public fearful and unsympathetic toward the disenfranchised and keeps attention away from economic powerholders who are the real perpetrators of most of the injury and loss in society.

Reiman (1995) points out that the latest crime bill passed by the legislature offers more prisons, longer sentences, and more law enforcement officers but does little for the widening gap between the rich and poor, which has increased during the 1980s and 1990s. The image of the offender as a poor, young, black male is created by a multitude of decisions throughout the whole criminal justice system, starting with police patrol decisions and ending with parole revocation decisions. The evidence seems to indicate that African Americans and Hispanics are less likely to be given probation, more likely to receive prison sentences, more likely to receive longer sentences, and more likely to serve a greater portion of their original time (Reiman 1995, 121).

Whether the system focuses on individual responsibility for crime (and therefore punishment) or individual deviance (and therefore treatment), the result is the same: The existing social order is excused from any charge of injustice. The radical theorists point out that this is the true reason why prisons fail to cure or deter. Even theorists who are not necessarily Marxist point out that imprisonment is futile without addressing social problems, such as unemployment, homelessness, poverty, discrimination, inadequate health care, and unequal education (Selke 1993).

Foucoult (1973) presented a slightly different view of prison, one based less on economics but still premised on the need of those in power to discipline and control the populace. In his history of the emergence of the prison, he sees the prison as one part of the institutionalization of society — the prison housed the ne'er-do-wells and criminals, the mental institutions housed the mentally ill, hospitals housed the physically ill, orphanages housed the young, and poorhouses housed those without economic means. All controlled and contained the class of people who were considered expendable. All normalized the idea of containment and deprivation of liberty as a natural right of society.

Although the radical view has had some support for many decades, it has never been the dominant penal philosophy. Nor are we in an era where liberalism or rehabilitation is the dominant correctional philosophy, despite the continuing theme of the popular press and politicians who advocate "getting tougher" as the answer to a "crime problem." There are two fallacies to this rhetoric. The first is that we are not "tough" enough. To the contrary, the prison-building frenzy that has occurred during the last several years has resulted in prison sentences and convictions that match or exceed previous time periods in history and contribute to this country's reputation as using prison as a first resort rather than a last resort. The second fallacy is that crime rates continue to go up because of this so-called soft on crime approach. The fact is that, except for certain specific population groups and certain crimes, crime rates have continued a steady decline for several years. Today, the dominant penal philosophy, which developed in the late 1970s and early 1980s, continues to be conservative and punitive.

## THE NEW CONSERVATISM: JUSTICE AND "JUST DESERTS"

Since the late 1970s and early 1980s there has been disillusionment and dissatisfaction with the idea of prison as a reformative tool. Whether one believes that the only purpose of prison should be punishment or that it should be treatment, which the negative environment of prison now makes impossible, most disagree with and oppose a penal philosophy of reform. Some of the first and most vocal critics of the rehabilitation ethic were von Hirsch (1976) and Fogel (1981). Although different in tone, both critiqued the idea that prison should be anything more than a measure of punishment. Their approach blends a curious mixture of utilitarianism and retributivism to form a "new retributivism." This philosophy is actually quite old and more similar to pre-Jacksonian deterrence and incapacitation than anything seen for the last 100 years. Von Hirsch justifies and limits the role of punishment by retributive proportionality:

1. The liberty of each individual is to be protected so long as it is consistent with the liberty of others.
2. The state is obligated to observe strict parsimony in intervening in criminals' lives.
3. The state must justify each intrusion.
4. The requirements of justice ought to constrain the pursuit of crime prevention (that is, deterrence and rehabilitation). (Von Hirsch 1976, 5)

The so-called *just deserts model* also views punishment as being justified solely by retributive ends rather than utilitarian ones. This view utilizes the "social contract" again to justify punishment for those who break the law. It promotes the idea that the only goal of the justice system should be justice, not reform of the individual (Fogel and Hudson 1981). This view advocates using determinate forms of sentencing rather than indeterminate, separating treatment options from release decisions, and circumscribing the goals of custody to retribution rather than reformation. It has found popular and political favor probably because it sounds punitive, although advocates of this philosophy were probably reacting to the abuses of power engendered by a utilitarian treatment ethic that allowed a great deal more control over the individual offender's body and mind "for their own good." There is a distinct difference between a penal philosophy that holds that we should do no more to the individual than she *deserves* (that is, not keep an offender imprisoned longer for treatment), and a penal philosophy that holds that the *only* thing an offender deserves is punishment. Despite their differences, both of these approaches have contributed to penal policies today.

## OTHER PHILOSOPHICAL APPROACHES

Two current alternative penal philosophies have emerged. The first view is the philosophy of redress offered by de Haan; the second is the feminine model of corrections and punishment, which has been pieced together by a number of theorists.

De Haan (1990) reviews and then criticizes those who advocate retributive philosophy for punishment. He believes that it is a fallacy that meting out punishment against injury "rights the wrong." The theory that sees the criminal as having gained some advantage by his crime which then must be neutralized by punishment to a like degree ignores the injury to the victim, which cannot be made right by punishment. True social equilibrium would only take place under some scheme of restitution or compensation. As he points out, "removal of the unfair advantage . . . [through punishment] is merely metaphorical" (de Haan 1990, 115). A philosophy of redress is preferable to one of punishment because of the following reasons.

1. Redress includes almost every conceivable reaction to an event — individual, collective, structural, material, or immaterial.
2. It implies that response is mandatory, without predefining the event as a crime, an illness, or anything else.
3. It invites analysis of the event before deciding or choosing a proper response.

4. As a concept with ancient origins, it invokes the consideration of historical and anthropological forms of dispute settlement and conflict resolution for possible clues to rational forms of response. (de Haan 1990, 158)

To summarize the philosophy: It is a reaction that sees the criminal act as an undesirable event that must be addressed through some course of action, although it carries no implications of what sort of reaction is appropriate. Because punishment does nothing to address the loss or injury of the victim, it may be the least desirable reaction to a criminal event.

This philosophy of punishment (which de Haan presents not as a philosophy but as a political alternative to punishment) is consistent with what has been termed a feminine correctional philosophy. Heidensohn (1986) and others have postulated an alternative to the "masculine" system of justice that is concerned with due process, rights, and responsibilities. The alternative "caring" model of morality and justice uses Carol Gilligan's (1982) work in moral development. The feminine correctional philosophy is more concerned with preserving and strengthening social relations. Unlike the treatment or medical ethic, it does not direct attention to the deviance of the individual in order to "fix" him or her. This philosophy is concerned with the needs of both victim and offender and the parallels between them. Rising from a concern with female offenders, for instance, theorists in this area note that very often female offenders in prison have been victims of incest and abuse, battering and rape. This needs-based philosophy does not view the offender as a subject to be worked on but as a person deserving the same amount of concern as the victim. Needs assessment is also directed to the victim, of course, but in this perspective, the lines may be blurred. Victims may be offenders, and offenders may be victims (for example, battered wives who kill).

The male model of justice is concerned with fair and equal treatment; the feminine view of justice is that legal equality does not necessarily meet needs, for the offender or the victim. Noddings (1989) critiques the whole Western philosophical tradition of rights-based justice by pointing out that the Greek philosophers who were the precursors to Kant and rights-based ethicists viewed women and slaves as unequal to free white males. While a rights-based system of justice may be able to reconcile these inequalities, a needs-based system of justice never would allow one group to be so disadvantaged. Noddings (1989) notes that a "caring ethic" finds its roots in such feminine relationships as between a mother and her child or a woman and her family. Obviously, these are mythical suppositions, but no more metaphorical than the idea that punishing an offender somehow balances the pain of the victim. This philosophy is termed feminine because it is emotional, relational, and other-directed — qualities that are associated with females. It is described as "feminine" rather than "feminist" because it is less concerned with political realities and social inequalities of females than the cultural differences in gender relations, concepts most feminists reject.

Neither of these philosophies have much support in correctional policies and practices today; they comprise no more than a footnote in a discussion of penal philosophy. However, the uniqueness of looking at a system of redress and recovery rather than meting out punishment may be a valuable addition to the development of penal philosophy.

## CONCLUSIONS

In this chapter we have surveyed some historical and current philosophies of punishment and prison. An implicit assumption of this chapter is that what we do has some relationship to what we believe. Is it important to review the motivations and purposes behind the prison? One benefit of this exercise is that we become more clear about what we expect from prison. For instance, many people, including many inmates, believe that the prison's main function is to rehabilitate. In reality, this has not been a major element in the philosophical basis of imprisonment for over a decade. Although we will discuss vocational training (Chapter 5) and correctional treatment programs (Chapter 6) in this book, much of the philosophical rationale for these interventions has been discarded by penologists and the politicians who fund the prison enterprise.

Another issue to consider is whether there is any evidence in support of the rationales for punishment discussed in this chapter. If one believes in a penal philosophy based on utilitarian deterrence, is it not important to have evidence that prison deters? Correctional treatment programs have been evaluated and found to be less than successful in reducing recidivism, but deterrence is harder to measure. How does one know whether prison has deterred someone from committing crime? To merely measure crime rates is not sufficient because other factors may affect the decision to commit crime. If one can never develop the means to measure the efficacy of deterrence, is it viable as a rationale for punishment?

What is probably most true about the penal enterprise is that it does not have one clearly defined, specific philosophy or rationale for existence. It is a slippery fish: If we criticize it for not rehabilitating, we are told it deters; if we ask for evidence of deterrence, we are told it is retributive. If the public is at all squeamish about locking their brethren up in cages, we are taken on tours of education buildings and carpentry apprentice programs. If the public rails against prison as the Holiday Inn for criminals, one can point to inmates sleeping next to toilets and 4:00 A.M. breakfasts before a long day in the cotton field. One prevailing aspect of penal philosophy may be its amorphous content. Prison can be all things to all people. The radical theorists may be right that the prison has been successful in diverting public attention away from the transgressions of the economically powerful by defining and reviling a "criminal" class, but they are less successful in any attempt to envision a society without prison.

## Vocabulary

corporal punishment
deterrence
*ex post facto* laws
general deterrence
hedonistic calculus
incapacitation
just deserts model

paradigm
rehabilitation
reintegration
retribution
social contract
specific deterrence
utilitarianism

## Study Questions

1. Explain the difference between the retributive rationale for punishment and the utilitarian rationale.

2. What is the social contract?

3. Discuss the three benefits of prison under the utilitarian rationale of punishment.

4. Discuss the differences between the conservative, liberal, and radical approaches to penal philosophy. What time period in history is associated with the conservative approach? The liberal approach?

5. What is the importance of "separation, obedience, and order"?

6. Explain the severity hypothesis and the economic theories of penal philosophy.

7. Discuss the elements of the new retributivism. What is the just deserts model?

8. What are the essential differences between the ethics of caring and a rights-based philosophy of justice?

## Sources Cited

— Allen, Harry, and Clifford E. Simonsen. 1992. *Corrections in America.* New York: Macmillan.

— Borchert, Donald, and David Stewart. 1986. *Exploring Ethics.* New York: Macmillan.

— Conley, John. 1992. "The Historical Relationship among Punishment, Incarceration, and Corrections." In *Corrections: A Introduction,* ed. Stan Stojkovic and Rick Lovell, 33-65. Cincinnati: Anderson.

— Crosley, Clyde. 1986. *Unfolding Misconceptions: The Arkansas State Penitentiary, 1836-1986.* Arlington: Liberal Arts Press.

— de Haan, Willem. 1990. *The Politics of Redress.* London: Unwin Hyman.

— DeLuca, H. R., T. J. Miller, and C. Wiedemann. 1991. "Punishment vs. Rehabilitation: A Proposal for Revising Sentencing Practices." *Federal Probation* 55(3): 37-45.

— Durham, Alexis. 1994. *Crisis and Reform: Current Issues in American Punishment.* Boston: Little, Brown.

— Fogel, David, and Joe Hudson. 1981. *Justice as Fairness.* Cincinnati: Anderson.

— Foucoult, Michel. 1973. *Discipline and Punish: The Birth of the Prison.* New York: Vintage.

— Gardner, Gil. 1987. "The Emergence of the New York State Prison System: A Critique of the Rusche-Kirchheimer Model." *Crime and Social Justice* 29: 88-109.

— Gilligan, Carol. 1982. *In a Different Voice.* Cambridge: Harvard University Press.

— Heidensohn, F. 1986. "Models of Justice: Portia or Persephone? Some Thoughts on Equality, Fairness, and Gender in the Field of Criminal Justice." *International Journal of the Sociology of Law* 14: 287-298.

— Hirsch, Adam. 1987. "From Pillory to Penitentiary: The Rise of Criminal Incarceration in Early Massachusetts." In *Police, Prison and Punishment: Major Historical Interpretations,* ed. Kermit Hall, 344-434. New York: Garland.

— Howe, Adrian. 1994. *Punish and Critique: Towards a Feminist Analysis of Penality.* London: Routledge.

— Lewis, Dan, and Cheryl Darling. 1987. "The Idea of Community in Correctional Reform: How Rhetoric and Reality Join." In *Police, Prison and Punishment: Major Historical Interpretations,* ed. Kermit Hall, 95-109. New York: Garland.

— McKelvey, Blake. 1987. "Penology in the Westward Movement." In *Police, Prison and Punishment: Major Historical Interpretations,* ed. Kermit Hall, 457-479. New York: Garland.

— Melossi, D., and M. Pavarini. 1981. *The Prison and the Factory: Origins of the Penitentiary System.* London: Macmillan.

— Mickunas, Algis. 1990. "Philosophical Issues Related to Prison Reform." In *Are Prisons Any Better? Twenty Years of Correctional Reform,* eds. John Murphy and Jack Dison, 77-93. Newbury Park: Sage Publications.

— Murphy, Jeffrie. 1995. *Punishment and Rehabilitation.* 3rd ed. Belmont, CA: Wadsworth.

— Newman, Graeme. 1978. *The Punishment Response.* New York: Lippincott.

— Noddings, N. 1989. *Women and Evil.* Berkeley: University of California Press.

— Reiman, Jeffrey. 1995. *The Rich Get Richer and the Poor Get Prison.* Boston: Allyn and Bacon.

— Rothman, David. 1971. *The Discovery of the Asylum: Social Order and Disorder in the New Republic.* Boston: Little, Brown.

— Rusche, G., and O. Kirchheimer. 1939. *Punishment and Social Structure.* New York: Russell and Russell.

— Selke, William L. 1993. *Prisons in Crisis.* Bloomington: Indiana University Press.

— von Hirsch, Andrew. 1976. *Doing Justice.* New York: Hill and Wang.

— White, Thomas. 1989. "Corrections: Out of Balance." *Federal Probation* 53(4): 31-35.

— Zimring, Franklin, and Gordon Hawkins. 1995. *Incapacitation: Penal Confinement and the Restraint of Crime.* New York: Oxford.

# 2

# RACE, GENDER, AND THE AMERICAN PRISON: HISTORICAL OBSERVATIONS

*Robert Johnson*

Emerging from my sequestered room, I was introduced into a spacious hall, where four-fifths of the convicts, eat their daily meals. Here were to be seen, people from almost every clime and country: Spaniards, Frenchmen, Italians, Portuguese, Germans, Englishmen, Scotchmen, Irishmen, Swedes, Danes, Africans, West-Indians, Brazilians, several Northern Indians, and many claiming to be citizens, born in the United States. (Coffey 1823, 105)

## *Chapter Overview*

—— **PENITENTIARIES**
> The Separate System
> The Congregate System
> Women and Minorities in the Penitentiary
> The Reformatory Era
>> *Women's Reformatories*
>> *Rhetoric and the Reformatory*

—— **THE BIG HOUSE**

—— **THE CORRECTIONAL INSTITUTION**

—— **CONTEMPORARY PRISONS**

—— **CONCLUSIONS**

The prison is an institution marked by great staying power but modest achievement. We have had prisons of one sort or another since at least biblical times (Johnson 1996). Though prisons have varied in their internal regimes and in their stated aims, the main achievement of the prison has been its most basic mandate — to contain and restrain offenders (Garland 1990). Rehabilitation has been a recurring aim of prisons, and at times this goal could be described as a grand dream. But it is a dream of reformers, not of the criminals who are to be its beneficiaries.

The use of prison as a sanction has grown steadily since the advent of the penitentiary at the turn of the nineteenth century (Cahalan 1979, 37) and indeed has come to dominate criminal justice. The growth in the use of prisons has been particularly pronounced for blacks and, more recently, women. It is thus telling that comparatively little attention has been paid to the prison experiences of minorities and women. Women, to be sure, have always been drastically underrepresented in our prisons, and this partly explains why limited attention has been paid to their prison experience. Even with the current accelerated rate of growth in rates of confinement for women, women comprise only 6 percent of the overall prison population (Johnson 1996 and Merlo and Pollock 1995).

The same cannot be said of minorities. Ethnic and, after the Civil War, racial minorities have *always* been well represented, and almost certainly overrepresented, in American prisons. Black women have been confined in disproportionate numbers in prisons for women; this trend is particularly evident in high-custody institutions, which traditionally are reserved for those female offenders seen by largely white officials as tough, manlike felons beyond the reach of care or correction (Rafter 1990). Similarly, black males, and especially young black males, have been grossly overrepresented in our nation's more secure prisons, once again settings reserved for those deemed least amenable to rehabilitation. The most recent statistics on these trends are nothing less than startling. As observed elsewhere,

> For black males, the 1992 incarceration rate was 2,678 per 100,000, which represents a rise of 141% since 1980 and is fully 7 times the incarceration rate of white males (372 per 100,000). The figures are lower for women, but the same racial disparities prevail. Thus, the incarceration rate for black women is 143 per 100,000; for white women, the rate is 20 per 100,000. Looking at the intersection of race and age, we see some especially disturbing figures. Figures for 1991, the most recent year for which

data are available for age and race, document incarceration rates for black men between the ages of 20 and 35 — the prime years of life — that range from 4,775 to 5,577 per 100,000. These rates are between 6 and 9 times the comparable rates for white males. (Johnson 1996, 12)

These racial disparities are long-standing and must be understood in historical context.

The first minorities in our prisons were European immigrants, with but a sprinkling of offenders of African descent; this is apparent from our opening quotation from Coffey, a penitentiary prisoner. Our current minorities are predominantly African Americans, together with a small but growing contingent of Latin Americans and, in some areas of the country, Native Americans. "Since 1850," notes Cahalan, "when the first [prison statistics] reports were published, the combined percentage of foreign-born persons, blacks and other minority groups incarcerated by the criminal justice system has ranged between 40 and 50 percent of all inmates present." It is almost as if the prison treats minorities as interchangeable commodities. "As the percentage of foreign-born in our jails and prisons has declined, the proportion of blacks and Spanish-speaking inmates has increased" (Cahalan 1979, 39). We have had, if you will, a steady overrepresentation of one minority or another since the advent of modern prison statistics. If anything, this trend is worsening for African Americans as we approach the close of the twentieth century. In what follows we will review the main lines of the history of modern prisons, with attention to the plight of minorities and women.

## PENITENTIARIES

The penitentiary was the first truly modern prison. In a sense, it was the template or model from which most, if not all, subsequent prisons were cast. Some authorities claim that the penitentiary was a uniquely American institution. There is some truth to this claim — America adopted the penitentiary with a more thoroughgoing passion than other countries — but it is important to note that penitentiaries did not exist in the original colonies. The first American penitentiary, the Walnut Street jail, was erected in Philadelphia in 1790. The construction of penitentiaries was not undertaken on a large scale, however, until the Jacksonian era, between 1820 and 1830. From the outset, penitentiaries were meant to be experiments in rational, disciplined living that combined punishment and personal reform.

In the most general sense, the penitentiary was meant to be a separate and pure moral universe dedicated to the reclamation of wayward men and women. It would isolate criminals from a corrupt and corrupting world, and it would reshape their characters through the imposition of a strict routine of solitude, work, and worship. Two distinct versions of this moral universe were offered, known respectively as the separate and congregate systems.

## THE SEPARATE SYSTEM

The *separate system* originated in Philadelphia at the Walnut Street jail and is sometimes called the *Philadelphia* or *Pennsylvania system*. The regime was one of solitary confinement and manual labor, a simple monastic existence in which the prisoners were kept separate from one another as well as from the outside world. Describing this system, Beaumont and Tocqueville observe that its advocates

> have thought that absolute separation of the criminals can alone protect them from mutual pollution, and they have adopted the principle of separation in all its rigor. According to this system, the convict, once thrown into his cell, remains there without interruption, until the expiration of his punishment. He is separated from the whole world; and the penitentiaries, full of malefactors like himself, but every one of them entirely isolated, do not present to him even a society in the prison. (1833/1964, 57)

Prisoners served time in a manner reminiscent of the monks of antiquity or the heretic of the early Middle Ages. Sentences were formally measured in loss of freedom, but the aim of punishment was penance resulting in purity and personal reform. At issue was a fundamental change of character, a conversion. Here the penitentiary was a place of *penance* in the full sense of the word. Even the prisoners' labors, essentially craft work, were intended to focus their minds on the simple things of nature and hence to bring ever to their thoughts the image of their Maker. For the prisoners of the separate system, there was to be no escape from their cells, their thoughts, or their God.

## THE CONGREGATE SYSTEM

The *congregate system* was first introduced at Auburn Prison, and is often called simply the *Auburn system*. Prisoners of this system slept in solitary cells. Though they congregated for work and meals, only their bodies mingled. Silence reigned throughout the prison. "They are united," observed Beaumont and Tocqueville, "but no moral connection exists among them. They see without knowing each other. They are in society without [social] intercourse." (1833/1964, 58) There was no communication and hence no contamination. Prisoners left their cells for the greater part of each day, primarily for work and sometimes also for meals. But they carried within themselves the sharp strictures of this silent prison regime. In the congregate penitentiary, "everything passes"

> in the most profound silence, and nothing is heard in the whole prison but the steps of those who march, or sounds proceeding from the workshops. But when the day is finished, and the prisoners have retired to their cells, the silence within these vast walls, which contain so many prisoners, is like that of death. We have often trod during night those monotonous and dumb galleries, where a lamp is always burning: we felt as if we traversed catacombs; there were a thousand living beings, and yet it was a desert solitude. (Beaumont and Tocqueville 1833/1964, 65)

Here, too, penance and purity were sought: solitary penance by night, pure labor by day, silence broken only by the sound of machines and tools. Throughout, prisoners had time to reflect and repent. The congregate system retained the monastic features of the separate system, in its solitary cells and silent labor, but blended them with a more contemporary lifestyle. A monastery at night; by day, a quasi-military organization of activities (all scheduled), movement (in unison and in lockstep), eating (backs straight, at attention), and work (long hours, usually at rote factory labor). The aim of this system was to produce docile, obedient inmates. Accordingly, regimentation was the cornerstone of congregate prison life. As is made abundantly clear in Beaumont and Tocqueville's description of the daily routine at Auburn, "The order of one day is that of the whole year. Thus one hour of the convict follows with overwhelming uniformity the other, from the moment of . . . entry into the prison to the expiration of . . . punishment." (1833/1964, 65-66)

The merits of these competing penitentiary systems were debated hotly and at great length. In the end, however, the details of the penitentiary regime and the practical definition of reform were determined as much by financial matters as by the merits of either penological perspective. Thus the congregate system became the model for the American penitentiary at least in part because workers were in short supply in nineteenth-century America, and hence the deployment of prisoners at factory labor provided an affordable quarantine against the dangers and corruptions of the larger world. Elsewhere, notably in Europe, workers were in greater supply. With no appreciable demand for prison labor, the solitary system was hailed in Europe as a more pure implementation of the penitentiary ideal and became the dominant form of the penitentiary.

## WOMEN AND MINORITIES IN THE PENITENTIARY

For the most part, women and blacks were excluded from the alleged benefits of the penitentiary. The penitentiary was considered a noble experiment in human reform; women and minorities were barely considered human — most blacks at this time were slaves, most women confined to subservient domestic roles — and hence these groups were not considered fit candidates for the penitentiary's rehabilitative regime. Women sentenced to penitentiaries were few in number. Even fewer were exposed to the penitentiary regime. Those who were confined to penitentiaries were warehoused, relegated to the unsupervised attics and kitchens and back rooms of these institutions.

> When the penitentiaries came into vogue, women, too, were sent to these institutions, but the level of their care dropped below that accorded to men. There were few female convicts. Sometimes there were but one or two, and in any case they were vastly outnumbered by men. To administrators, women were a great nuisance. They had to be isolated to prevent sexual mischief, but there were too few women to fill a wing of cells. Therefore officials locked them in large rooms above the guardhouse or messhall. To these officials, it seemed extravagant to hire a matron to supervise a small number of women. These prisoners were thus often left entirely on their own, vulnerable to attacks by one another and male guards. Secluded from the main population, women had less access than men to the physician and chaplain. Unlike men, they were not marched to workshops, messhalls, or exercise yards. Food and needlework were brought to their quar-

ters, where the women remained, day in and day out, for the years
of their sentences. (Rafter 1990, xxvi)

In these barren environments, women were allowed to mingle and
contaminate one another in the time-honored tradition of neglect
characteristic of prisons before the advent of the penitentiary.

The early penitentiaries held few African Americans because
most were essentially incarcerated on slave plantations. Exact figures
are unavailable because the early prison census figures did not even
include a category for blacks (Cahalan 1979). Beaumont and Tocqueville (1833/1964, 61) noted that "in those states in which there exists
one negro to thirty whites, the prisons contain one negro to four
white persons"; these prisoners were typically housed in regular, mass
confinement prisons, which made no effort at reforming prisoners
and served merely to warehouse them until release. Other minorities
such as immigrants were abundant in the penitentiaries, as made
clear in Coffey's quote introducing this chapter.

Paradoxically, the case can be made that women and African
Americans were inadvertently spared the considerable indignities of
the penitentiary. Putting rhetoric and intention to one side, penitentiaries offered at best only a deceptive facade of humanity. Pain, both
physical and psychological, was a central feature of the penitentiary
regime. Penitentiary prisoners often went hungry; firsthand accounts
report prisoners begging for food from the prison kitchen and being
punished for their temerity. Diseases ran rampant among poorly
nourished prisoners. Even for the healthy and well-fed, life in the
penitentiary was lonely and depressing and left no room whatsoever
for adult autonomy. There was also the crucible of fear; from the
outset penitentiaries were maintained by the threat and practice of
violence. Strict rules were routinely enforced with strict punishments,
including whippings and confinement to dark cells for weeks on end.
Looked at from the inside, as seen by the prisoners and not the reformers, the penitentiary was a profoundly inhumane institution.

Penitentiaries were born in a period of optimism about the prospects of reforming criminals. They reflected the Enlightenment faith
that people entered the world as "blank slates" on which environments, including reformative prison environments, would trace individual characters. This optimism persisted for decades, even as
experience proved these institutions to be unworkable. Indeed, from
early on, there was evidence that penitentiaries brutalized their
charges. Gradually, in the face of continuing failure, faith in the penitentiary waned.

## THE REFORMATORY ERA

To be sure, the men's *reformatory movement*, best exemplified in the famous Elmira Reformatory, dating from 1870, kept a version of the reform-oriented prison alive after the passing of the penitentiary as a setting of reform. But this was true only for young men and only briefly, in the context of some 20 institutions developed and devoted to the discipline and rehabilitation of wayward young men. The reformatory movement thrived on gender stereotypes. For men, military drills formed a key feature of the reformatory regime, which sought to produce disciplined "Christian gentlemen" (Pisciotta 1983, 1994); for women, as we will see, domestic pursuits were at the heart of the reformatory regime, which in this instance sought to produce "Christian gentlewomen." The men's reformatory as a prison type proved to be a brutal, punitive penal institution, an exercise in "benevolent repression" very much like the penitentiary and no more likely to reform its inhabitants (Pisciotta 1994).

*Women's Reformatories.* A notable departure from the masculine model of imprisonment for women was the reformatory. The women's reformatory movement, analyzed with great insight by Rafter (1990), lasted from roughly 1860 to 1935 and produced approximately 21 institutions. Reformatories, modeled on home or domestic environments, were an explicit rejection of the male custodial model of imprisonment.

> Unwalled institutions, women's reformatories architecturally expressed their founders' belief that women, because more tractable, required fewer constraints than men. Rejecting large congregate buildings, women reformatories came to adopt the "cottage" plan, holding groups of twenty or so inmates in small buildings where they could live with a motherly matron in a familial setting. (Rafter 1990, xxvii-xxviii)

The philosophy of reform that guided women's reformatories, again rejecting the male model, was premised on domestic training.

> Inmates were taught to cook, clean, and wait on tables; at parole, they were sent to middle-class homes to work as servants. Whereas men's reformatories sought to inculcate "manliness," women's reformatories encouraged femininity — sexual restraint, genteel demeanor, and domesticity. When women were disciplined, they might be scolded and sent, like children, to their "rooms." In-

deed, the entire regimen was designed to induce a childlike sub-
missiveness. (Rafter 1990, xxviii)

Perhaps the most distinctive feature of women's reformatories
was their "emphasis on propriety and decorum — on preparing
women to lead the 'true good womanly life.' " Rafter draws attention
to "the Thursday evening exercise and entertainment" offered at the
Detroit House of Shelter in the early 1870s.

> On this evening the whole family dress in their neatest and best
> attire. All assemble in our parlor . . . and enjoy themselves in con-
> versation and needlework, awaiting the friend who week by week
> on Thursday evening, never failing, comes at half past seven
> o'clock to read aloud an hour of entertaining stories and poetry
> carefully selected and explained. After exchange of salutations be-
> tween the "young ladies" and madam the visitor, and after the
> reading, tea and simple refreshments are served in form and man-
> ner the same as in refined society. (Quoted in Rafter 1990, 27)

Here we see what became "the hallmarks of the reformatory program: replication of the rituals of genteel society, faith in the reforming power of middle-class role models, and insistence that
inmates behave like ladies" (Rafter 1990, 27). One found nothing of
the sort in institutions for boys or men; as noted above, the men's
reformatories were modeled on the military, not on the home.

Indeed, women from custodial institutions might well have
found the domestic reformatory regime unappealing. One such
group of female felons, after being ostensibly saved from a corrupt
institution for men, were reportedly "indignant when . . . they found
they could no longer trade 'certain favors' for liquor and tobacco"
(Rafter 1990, 32). These offenders clearly preferred the old, custodial
regime, where they could trade sex for privileges, to the new reformatory program, with its genteel tea parties and ladylike sociability.

Women's reformatories were designed for young, minor offenders, especially those whose behavior contravened strict standards of
sexual propriety (Rafter 1990). The prototypical reformatory inmate
would be a young white girl of working-class background; her crime
might entail little more than sexual autonomy, though this would be
viewed as the earmark of prostitution. Black girls, even those convicted of minor offenses, would be routinely shunted off to custodial
prisons, including the brutal custodial plantation prisons of the
South, on the racist grounds that they were not as morally developed
as white girls. As with the original penitentiaries — described by

Rothman as geared to reclaim "the good boy gone bad, the amateur in the trade" (1971, 247) — reformatories were meant for novices in crime whose characters were presumed ripe for redemption. The object in both cases was to save those deemed valuable enough to warrant an investment of resources, not to reclaim hardened and essentially worthless criminals.

Significantly, black women, who "often constituted larger proportions within female state prisoner populations than did black men within male prisoner groups" (Rafter 1990, 141), were essentially excluded from the women's reformatory movement. They were seen by reformers as too much like men to be fully adapted to the domestic model that undergirded the women's reformatory. Black female offenders were sent to custodial prisons, including plantation prisons, in large numbers. In these settings, African American women were often treated as brutally as their male contemporaries.

With the demise of the reformatory movement, reformatory institutions became filled with common felons and returned, in varying degrees, to the (male) custodial model of imprisonment. It should be noted that custodial institutions for women "were more numerous [than reformatories] even after the reformatory movement had come to fruition" (Rafter 1990, 83). These custodial institutions for women, much like those for men, "were hardly touched by the reformatory movement. They continued along lines laid down in the early nineteenth century, slowly growing and in some cases developing into fully separate prisons" (Rafter 1990, 83). Certainly, it is the custodial prison, including its slave plantation variant, that has been the main prison reserved for minorities, both men and women.

***Rhetoric and the Reformatory.*** The rhetoric of the men's reformatory, promising differential classification and treatment but delivering heavy-handed control, had no discernible impact on the main lines of evolution followed by prisons for men (Johnson 1996, 66-68). Prisons that opened at the turn of the twentieth century reflected the demise of the penitentiary and reformatory. They were seen as industrial prisons in which inmates labored to defray operating costs and to fill idle time; little or no attention was given to the notion of personal reform. In effect, these "fallen penitentiaries" were settings of purposeless, gratuitous pain; increasingly, they were filled with devalued minorities, mostly African Americans. These prisons simply carried on the custodial warehousing agenda of the earliest prisons in a disciplined and regimented fashion. With the demise of prison labor in the early decades of the twentieth century — due primarily to resistance from organized labor — even the industrial prison passed from the prison scene. In its wake came the "Big House," in many ways the quintessential twentieth-century prison.

# THE BIG HOUSE

Maximum-security prisons throughout the first half of the twentieth century were colloquially known as *Big Houses*. If one were to think of prisons as having lines of descent, one would say that the Big House was the primary descendant and heir apparent of the penitentiary. In these prisons, a disciplined and often silent routine prevailed; prisoners worked, notably in such empty enterprises as the infamous rock pile, in which ax-wielding men broke rocks for no other reason than to show their submission to the prison authorities. The Big House prison, much like its rock piles, reflected no grand scheme or purpose; neither penance nor profit were sought. Routines were purposely empty. Activities served no purpose other than to maintain order.

To be sure, the Big House's lineage was not uniform. Many southern states bypassed the penitentiary entirely. The first prisons in Texas, for example, were essentially extensions of the slave plantation (Crouch and Marquart 1989). These plantation prisons were the agrarian equivalent of the industrial prison. The object was disciplined labor of the most servile, back-breaking sort; penance was never given a second thought. From these plantation prisons, the Big Houses of the South emerged, developed primarily to provide discipline and control for inmates incapable, due to age or infirmity, of working the fields and roads of the southern states (see Rafter 1990).

As the name would imply, plantation prisons contained a gross overrepresentation of black prisoners, both men and women. Newly emancipated African Americans would be incarcerated on the flimsiest pretexts and then put to hard labor in the fields of these prisons, often in chain gangs. Shackled groups of prisoners were also deployed to build various public works, notably roads and railroads. Other newly freed slaves would become indebted to white landowners and would be forced to work as peons to pay off debts or to sign restrictive contracts so that they could obtain food and housing. In these various ways, vast numbers of blacks were subjected to prison or prisonlike work regimes that drew their inspiration from slavery and offered none of the hope, however illusory, associated with the penitentiary (Franklin 1989 and Sellin 1977).

Significantly, southern prison chain gangs would include black female prisoners as well as black male prisoners. Though considerably fewer in number, the women would be subjected to the same harsh regime as the men (Rafter 1990). Work on the chain gang and at hard field labor was generally reserved for blacks and much less

---

**HIGHLIGHT 2-1**
**Investigation of Chain Gangs, Georgia**

*Q.* [Assemblyman Virgil Hillyer] Were there any women working on the Brunswick Railroad?

*A.* [prisoner witness] Yes, I think there were 19 or 20. They belonged both to the chain-gang and the Penitentiary. . . .

*Q.* Did you see any of them whipped?

*A.* Yes.

*Q.* Were they whipped on the bare skin?

*A.* Yes; I saw their bare skin myself.

*Q.* On what part of the body were they whipped?

*A.* On the butt.

*Q.* Were they whipped in the presence of the men?

*A.* Yes.

*Q.* How many licks did they receive?

*A.* About 20. . . .

*Q.* Were they kept in separate stockades?

*A.* In the same stockade, but in separate rooms.

*Q.* Out on the works, were they required to wait on the calls of nature in the presence of the men?

*A.* Yes; they were required to do their business right in the cuts where they worked, the same as the men did. It was taken out in the wheelbarrows and carts.

*Q.* [Mr. Turner, another assemblyman] Were the white and colored women mixed together?

*A.* There were no white women there. One started there, and I heard Mr. Alexander [the lessee] say he turned her loose. He was talking to the guard; I was working in the cut. He said his wife was a white woman, and he could not stand it to see a white woman worked in such places. (Reported in Rafter 1990, 150-151)

often meted out to whites. Comparatively few white men, and virtually no white women, were exposed to these brutal work regimes.

Parallels between slavery and prison can be striking. Thus, southern chain gangs drew on a heritage that spanned both the original slave plantations and the lockstep march of penitentiary discipline, as revealed in first-person accounts of this brutal institution.

> Just as day was breaking in the east we commenced our endless heartbreaking toil. We began in mechanical unison and kept at it in rhythmical cadence until sundown — fifteen and a half hours of steady toil — as regular as the ticking of a clock. (Burns, a prisoner, quoted in Franklin 1989, 164-165)

Burns wrote his account of the chain gang in the 1930s. For him, the German Army's goose step was the apparent inspiration for the disciplined character of the chain gang work routine. Clearly, however, American prison officials were not borrowing from German Army discipline; the lineage of this disciplined labor would be in the penitentiary *lockstep,* which in turn was a particular adaptation of factory discipline to the prison context (Johnson, 1996). Significantly, the labor routine Burns described was unchanged from plantation prison practices dating from the mid- to late-1800s. These practices, in turn, were rooted in slave labor practices dating from the early 1800s, the time of the first penitentiaries. It was at this point, at the birth of the penitentiary between 1800 and 1820, that southern plan-

---

**HIGHLIGHT 2-2**
**"Keeping the Lick"**

"A long steel rail," croons the leader.
"Ump!" grunt all the rest in chorus as pickaxes came down.
"An' a short cross tie," croons the leader.
"Ump!" grunt all the rest in chorus as pickaxes come up.
"It rings lik' sil-vah," croons the leader.
"Ump!" goes the chorus as the picks come down.
"It shin's lik' go-old," croons the leader.
"Ump!" and all the picks come up. And so it goes all day long, with the torrid rays of the blazing monarch of the skies adding their touch of additional misery. This working in unison is called "Keeping the lick." (Burns, a prisoner, quoted in Franklin 1989, 164-165)

tations first became formal business institutions marked by rigid discipline rather than family farming operations marked by more or less informal relations between keepers and kept (Franklin 1989). Ironically, then, the penitentiary, which originated in the North, may have found its first expression in the South in big business plantations. Only later was it expressed in plantation prisons and custodial prisons, never reaching fruition on its own in any of the southern states.

The historical lineage of the Big House is a mixed one. Yet one can fairly conclude that the Big Houses of northern states were more than gutted penitentiaries, and the Big Houses of the South were not merely adjuncts to ersatz slave plantations. The Big House, wherever it was found, was a step forward, however modest and faltering, in the evolution of prisons. Humanitarian reforms helped to shape its inner world, though these had to do with reducing deprivations and discomforts rather than establishing a larger agenda or purpose. Thus, whereas the penitentiary offered a life essentially devoid of comfort or even distraction, the Big House routine was the culmination of a series of humanitarian milestones that made these prisons more accommodating.

The first such advance was the introduction of tobacco, which was greeted by the prisoners with great relief. Officials report, without a hint of irony, that a calm settled over the penitentiary once the "soothing syrup" of tobacco was given to the formerly irritable and rambunctious prisoners. The second reform milestone was the abolition of corporal punishment. In Sing Sing, a fairly typical prison of its day, corporal punishment was abolished in 1871. Prior to that time, upwards of 60 percent of the prisoners would be subjected to the whip on an annual basis. Other prisons retained the practice of corporal punishment, but among prisons outside the South, whippings and other physical sanctions became an underground, unauthorized activity by the turn of the twentieth century. Tragically, regimes of corporal punishment, official and unofficial, remained in place in some southern prisons for much of this century.

The emergence of significant internal freedoms comprise the third and final reform milestone that paved the way for the Big House. These freedoms came in the wake of the lockstep march, which was abolished in Sing Sing in 1900. The daily humiliations of constrained movement implied in this shameful march soon gave way to freedom of movement in the recreation yard, first on Sundays (beginning in Sing Sing in 1912) and then, gradually over the early decades of the twentieth century, each day of the week.

There is no doubt that the Big House was more humane than the penitentiary, but similarities between these institutions are apparent. As in the penitentiary, order in the Big House was the result of threats and force, including, in the early decades of this century, clubs and guns, which line officers carried as they went about their duties. As in the penitentiaries, rules of silence prevailed in the Big House. Silence was both a cause and a consequence of order in the Big House and was a profound symbol of the authority of the keepers. This silence was, in the words of Lewis Lawes, a famous prison warden of the day, "the hush of repression" (1932, 34).

Though more comfortable than the penitentiary, prisoners of the Big House led spartan lives. Cells were cramped and barren; possessions were limited to bare essentials. Food was generally in good supply but was utterly uninspiring and was, in the eyes of the prisoners, fuel for reluctant bodies and nothing more. If the dominant theme of the penitentiary was terror, the dominant theme of the Big House was boredom bred by an endlessly monotonous routine. "Every minute of the day," said Victor Nelson, a prisoner, "all the year round, the most dominant tone is one of monotony" (Nelson 1936, 15). In the extreme, the Big House could be described as a world populated by people seemingly more dead than alive, shuffling where they once marched, heading nowhere slowly, for there is nothing of any consequence for them to do. In Nelson's words, "All about me was living death: anemic bodies, starved souls, hatred and misery: a world of wants and wishes, hungers and lusts" (Nelson 1936, 4). In the Big House, then, as in the penitentiary, the prison was a world circumscribed by human suffering.

Big House prisons contained an overrepresentation of minorities, though no accounts seem to exist describing the distinctive experience and adjustment of minority prisoners in these highly structured milieus. Certainly Big House prisons, like the larger society, were racially segregated, by policy in the early years and later by custom. Ethnic segregation of a voluntary sort was no doubt quite extreme, just as it was — and to some degree still is — in and out of prison (Carroll 1988). Early sociological discussions of northern prisons proceeded as if African American prisoners did not exist at all within Big House walls, though, of course, that is entirely untrue. Minority prisoners, invisible to white social scientists and even to white convicts, must have formed a world of their own, apart from that of white prisoners and white officials. Fictional accounts, written by black convicts, suggest that black inmates of Big House prisons led a more materially impoverished life than their white contemporaries. In one story, a white prisoner stumbles on an enclave of black prisoners far from the main prison living area in an area labeled "Black Bottom." In the story, it is as if the black prisoners are buried within the prison, residing at its bottom, left to suffer greatly in isolation from the larger white prison society (Himes 1934). In the typical Big House, it is white prisoners who rise to positions of considerable influence and even comfort due to their connections with the white power structure; few, if any, blacks have such an opportunity. Material from southern prisons, which during this era were of the plantation type, suggests that the harshest and most restrictive conditions within these prisons, particularly relating to labor, were reserved for blacks.

Big House prisons existed for women as well as for men. The origins of Big House prisons for women, like that of their male counterparts, can be traced to the penitentiary. As the numbers of women penitentiary prisoners grew, separate units within men's penitentiaries were developed for women. Eventually, these units were moved off the men's prison grounds to become completely separate and autonomous institutions. Most of these new separate institutions for women were run on a custodial model, which Rafter convincingly argues is an inherently masculine model of imprisonment.

> The custodial model was a masculine model: derived from men's prisons, it adopted their characteristics — retributive purpose, high-security architecture, a male-dominated authority structure, programs that stressed earnings, and harsh discipline. . . . [W]omen's custodial institutions treated inmates like men." (Rafter 1990, 21)

Confinement in custodial regimes was hard on the women, who were uniquely vulnerable in such settings. "Probably lonelier and certainly more vulnerable to sexual exploitation, easier to ignore because so few in number, and viewed with distaste by prison officials, women in custodial units were treated as the dregs of the state prisoner population" (Rafter 1990, 21).

Accounts by inmates of women's custodial prisons highlight the diversity of populations within these institutions (similar to the diversity within men's prisons). This 1930 description of entry into a women's prison offers a glimpse of a motley and diverse crew of women — petty thieves, addicts, prostitutes of varying ages and nationalities, lockstepping to meet a warden:

> Directly behind Red-frotz [the matron] walked Laura, the Candy Kid, seventeen year old shoplifter, prostitute and drug-addict, an inveterate thief, pretty as a picture.
>
> Then Rebecca, thirty year old Jewess, diseased, heavily sentenced after a fourth offence at shoplifting.

Next Old Lady Cuno, eighty-seven, arrested for begging, always swearing in German and smelling like a fish factory.

Following her, Stephanie, the Czechoslovakian girl, with swarthy complexion and large black eyes, with her deep guttural voice, an all-around crook and shoplifter.

Then back of her, Dora Conignsby, drug-addict and prostitute, with the needle-pocked body.

Next "Bugs," Big Bertha, a burly dark-complexioned drug-addict, with her mottled hair in curlers and skirts above her bare knees.

Then Pauline, the most beautiful girl in the prison, kleptomaniac, graduate of Vassar, with the background of a fine family, up the second time for cashing bad checks.

Behind her, Lillian Johnson, six feet tall, pretty but a badly diseased prostitute.

Then the Kid from Georgia, a nineteen year old girl taken from a sailor's dive, very badly diseased with red spots all over her body.

After her Rachel Endress, whose husband had framed her, then myself, followed by Ethel Kingsley, morose murderess, who had killed her husband in a row about another woman, and at the end of the rogue's gallery line Joan Barnum, bootleg queen, up for ten years for shooting a policeman.

Thus we lock-stepped down the iron stairs to the warden's office. (O'Brien 1938, 80-81, quoted in Franklin 1989, 171-172)

The warden proceeds to fondle the women as a part of their orientation to his prison regime, warning them that those who do not submit to their superiors will be punished:

"The first law of this prison," he continued, putting his hand on my shoulder, and gradually running it down my side, a smirk of sensual pleasure playing upon his leather-like countenance, ". . . is to obey at all times . . . to obey your superiors . . . to fit in to your surroundings without fault-finding or complaint. . . ." His hand had now progressed below my skirt, and he was pressing and patting my naked thigh . . . "because unruly prisoners are not wanted here and they are apt to get into trouble. . . ." (Quoted in Franklin 1989, 171-172)

Sexual abuse was disturbingly common in custodial prisons run by men. Women might well be fondled at intake, as in the preceding excerpt, and later raped in their cells by their male keepers. On other occasions, guards would make sport of their sexual encounters with their female captives (see, for example, Anonymous 1871). The impression one gains from this literature is that the women relegated to custodial institutions, from the penitentiary onward, had little or no choice but to submit to the predations of their keepers. In the harsh assessment of a nineteenth-century observer, criminal women were "if possible, more depraved than the men; they have less reason, more passion and no shame. Collected generally, from the vitiated sewer of venality, they are schooled in its depravity, and practised in its impudence" (Coffey 1823, 61). Coffey's views were shared by many early twentieth-century observers as well, at least through the period when custodial prisoners for women were run by men. As outright moral pariahs, women offenders in these prisons were presumed to be spoiled goods, there for the taking by their male keepers.

## THE CORRECTIONAL INSTITUTION

The correctional institution emerged gradually from the Big House, with the first stirrings of this new prison type manifesting themselves in the 1940s and 1950s. In correctional institutions, harsh discipline and repression by officials became less salient features of prison life. The differences between Big Houses and correctional institutions were real: Daily regimes at correctional institutions were typically more relaxed and accommodating. But the benefits of correctional institutions are easily exaggerated. The main differences between Big Houses and correctional institutions are of degree rather than kind. Correctional institutions did not correct. Nor did they abolish the pains of imprisonment. They were fundamentally more tolerable human warehouses than the Big Houses they supplanted, less a departure than a toned-down imitation. Often, correctional institutions occupied the same physical plants as the Big Houses. Indeed, one might classify most of these prisons as Big Houses "gone soft."

Correctional institutions were marked by a less intrusive discipline than that found at the Big Houses. They offered more yard and recreational privileges; more liberal mail and visitation policies; more amenities, including an occasional movie or concert; and more educational, vocational, and therapeutic programs, though these various remedial efforts seemed to be thrown in as window dressing. These changes made life in prison less oppressive. Even so, prisoners spent most of their time in their cells or engaged in some type of menial work. They soon discovered that free time could be "dead" time; like prisoners of the Big Houses before them, prisoners in correctional institutions often milled about the yard with nothing constructive to do. Boredom prevailed, though it was not the crushing boredom born of regimentation as in the Big House. Gradually, considerable resentment developed; officials had promised programs but not delivered them. The difficulty was that officials, however well intended they might have been, simply did not know how to conduct a correctional enterprise. Nor did they have the resources or staff to make a serious attempt at that task. The correctional institution promised to transform people, a claim reminiscent of the penitentiaries, but mostly these institutions simply left prisoners more or less on their own.

In the 1950s, Trenton State Prison in New Jersey was a fairly typical correctional institution for men, merging the disciplined and oppressive climate of the Big House with a smattering of educational, vocational, and treatment programs. Gresham Sykes's classic study, *The Society of Captives* (1958), describes Trenton State Prison. Significantly, Sykes describes the dominant reality at Trenton as one of pain. "The inmates are agreed," he emphasized, "that life in the maximum security prison is depriving or frustrating in the extreme" (Sykes 1958/1966, 63). To survive, the prisoner turned not to programs or officials but to peers. In essence, Sykes concluded that the prisoners must reject the larger society and embrace the society of captives if they are to survive psychologically. The prison society, however, promoted an exploitative view of the world. Weaker inmates were fair game for the strong. At best, prisoners "do their own time," to use an old prison phrase, and leave others to their predations, turning a deaf ear to the cries of victims.

Trenton State contained a substantial overrepresentation of minority offenders, no doubt a source of some conflict in the prison community. This salient fact is only mentioned in passing by Sykes (1958/1966, 81), who observes, "the inmate population is shot through with a variety of ethnic and social cleavages" that kept prisoners from acting in concert or maintaining a high degree of solidarity. Similarly, Irwin (1970) makes clear that during the 1950s Soledad Prison, also a correctional institution, was largely populated by groups called *tips*, or cliques that were largely defined in racial and ethnic terms; there, conflict simmered below the surface of daily life, erupting only occasionally, suppressed in large measure out of a vain hope that all inmates might benefit from correctional programs. In fact, however, treatment and the prospect of mature interpersonal relations were at best a footnote to the Darwinian ebb and flow of daily life in the prison yard of the correctional institution. The violence would come later, after the demise of the correctional institution.

Life in Trenton State Prison was grim. The plain fact is that prisons — whether they are meant to house men, women, or adolescents — are built for punishment and hence are meant to be painful. The theme of punishment is nowhere more evident than in the massive walls that keep prisoners both out of sight and out of circulation. Many of our contemporary prisons are built without those imposing gray walls, though these institutions usually feature barbed wire, which, ironically, is often a shade of gray. Almost all prisons feature a dull gray or other drab-colored interior environment. Colorful prisons — so-called pastel prisons, some built to resemble college dormitories — are few in number and are reserved for prisoners judged to pose little threat to one another, to staff, and to the public.

To the extent that such pastel prisons exist, they are likely to be reserved for women (Rafter 1990). Women's penal institutions more often resemble college campuses than prison compounds. Dorm rooms often replace cells; it is not uncommon to find vases of flowers in the rooms of confined female felons. Yet the ostensible comforts of women's prisons are belied by the custodial realities of daily life in these institutions, which are experienced by their inhabitants as prisons that, at best, offer too many rules and too few program opportunities. Those programs that exist, moreover, still follow stereotypical gender lines, focusing on domestic skills rather than job skills. Indeed, correctional institutions for women are of a piece with earlier women's prisons. The continuing theme is one of sexism and neglect.

## CONTEMPORARY PRISONS

Most of today's prisons are still formally known as correctional institutions, but this label can be misleading. One problem has been that, with the passing of the disciplined and repressive routines of penitentiaries and Big Houses, today's prisons are marked by more inmate violence than at any time since the advent of the penitentiary. This is most apparent in men's prisons. Prison uprisings, including such debacles as the infamous Attica and Santa Fe prison riots, occur with disturbing regularity. So, too, is inmate-on-inmate and inmate-on-staff violence more common today than was the case in earlier prisons (see generally Johnson 1996). While some staff members still abuse inmates, this grossly unprofessional behavior is considerably less in evidence in today's prisons than in earlier prisons, where staff-on-inmate violence was a routine feature of daily life.

Racial and ethnic imbalances, little-noted facts of prison history, are today more pronounced than ever and often give rise to inmate-on-inmate violence. Beginning in the correctional institution, when discontent with failed programs often followed racial lines, race forms perhaps the key fault line in today's prison community (Jacobs 1977, Carroll 1988, and McCall 1995). Prisons are balkanized along racial and ethnic lines; groups and gangs defined in terms of race and ethnicity are increasingly central sources of violence in today's prisons. It is only in the contemporary prison, between roughly 1965 and today, that a black prisoner can say with considerable confidence, "I was in jail, the one place in America that black men rule" (McCall 1995, 149). It is, to be sure, an exaggeration to say that African American men rule today's prisons, but a telling one; almost everywhere, minority groups comprising men of color — African American or Latin American or Native American — wield disproportionate power behind bars. Too often, that power is used to dominate and abuse whites, the despised minority group in many men's prisons. Racial and ethnic relations have been and remain more pacific in women's prisons, though anecdotal evidence from practitioners suggest that racial tensions may be rising in some women's prisons.

Over the last two or three decades, a fair number of American prisons have seemed out of control, with inmate violence reaching frightening proportions. Some evidence suggests that the worst of today's prison violence may be a thing of the past. The statistical trend in prisoner assaults and killings is down, at least over the last five years or so. This suggests that nonviolent accommodations are finally being worked out in our prisons, within and perhaps between inmate groups and the officials who run the prison (Johnson 1996).

## CONCLUSIONS

In some important respects, today's prisons represent a sharp and largely favorable departure from their predecessors. Prisons can never be returned to the days when officials ruled with an iron hand and prisoners marched, silently docile, at the command of their keepers. These regimes were themselves acts of violence and no doubt inflicted harms in great excess of today's penal institutions. It is widely recognized that prisoners today are no longer slaves of the state to be worked at will, often to the point of injury or death. Prisoners, no matter how serious their crimes, retain basic civil and human rights that were unheard of in earlier prisons. Today's prison officials must respect those rights. Accordingly, arbitrary or violent disciplinary practices are mere relics of a long-dead correctional past. Similarly, involuntary treatment programs, chosen for inmates by experts, are also a thing of the past.

Prisons are gradually and perhaps inexorably developing the *potential* to become decent institutions, which is to say, settings in which prisoners live like human beings, with a meaningful degree of autonomy. Today the prison world is a more collaborative venture than at any time in the history of prisons. Prison staff, especially line officers, increasingly must establish their competence in the delivery of a range of human services; they must prove themselves capable of running a responsive institution rather than falling back on the authority invested in their uniforms or on the power that emanated from their clubs, as in times past (see Johnson 1996, 197-248). From proven competence comes the authority and the capacity of the prison staff to maintain a more just and lawful social order behind bars. Rehabilitative programs, though often in terribly short supply, are now chosen voluntarily in most prison systems. Increasingly, staff are encouraged to see themselves as facilitators — as figures of authority who help inmates to see the need for programs rather than authoritarian figures who impose programs unilaterally. The growth of professional ideals in the corrections ranks means that more and more officials see themselves as role models of mature adjustment under the pressures of daily prison living. More than in times past, then, today's prisons explicitly aim to treat inmates as full-fledged human beings who have a right to a secure and responsive prison environment and a claim to choose from among a range of services and programs that offer them the opportunity to rebuild their lives.

We know more about prison life and prison reform than ever before, and we can point to successes on a number of discrete fronts. Yet the larger political picture is a grim one. Our prisons squander potential because they are too often overcrowded and underfunded. More perhaps than at any time in prison history, our penal institutions house grossly disproportionate numbers of minorities, mostly African Americans and Latin Americans. Incarceration of women is growing at an alarming rate, considerably above that of men. We are experiencing a minor rebirth of the worst excesses of Big House discipline in the form of maxi-maxi prisons. Though few in number, brutal institutions — maximizing control, minimizing autonomy — are on the rise.

The picture is a mixed one, and points to two strategies of reform. On the one hand, we can work to implement management and other reforms that accommodate the legitimate human needs of our captive criminals. On the other, we can work to reduce policies that promote the overuses of prison, particularly among minorities. Social justice — at a minimum, color-blind use of imprisonment — is a necessary if not sufficient condition of real prison reform. History teaches us that, in the absence of conscious, explicit, and continuing efforts at such reform, our prisons all too readily degenerate into warehouses for our least valued and most vulnerable fellow citizens.

## Vocabulary

chain gang                    reformatory movement
congregate system             separate system
lockstep                      tips
penance

## Study Questions

1. Distinguish between the early penitentiaries and the reformatories in terms of goals and philosophy.

2. Distinguish between Big Houses and correctional institutions in terms of programming and conditions.

3. What were the differences and similarities between the congregate system and the separate system of prisons?

4. What were the differences between prisons for men and women?

5. Discuss the use of prisons in the South.

## Sources Cited

—Anonymous. 1871. *An Illustrated History and Description of State Prison Life, by One Who Has Been There. Written by a Convict in a Convict's Cell* [Prison Life, 1865-1869]. New York: Globe.

— Barnes, H. E., and N. K. Teeters. 1952. *New Horizons in Criminology.* 2d ed. New York: Prentice-Hall.

— Beaumont, G. D., and A. de Tocqueville. 1833/1964. *On the Penitentiary System in the United States and Its Application to France.* Carbondale: Southern Illinois University.

— Cahalan, M. 1979. "Trends in Incarceration in the United States Since 1880." *Crime and Delinquency* 25(1): 9-41.

— Carroll, L. 1988. "Race, Ethnicity and the Social Order of the Prison." In *The Pains of Imprisonment,* ed. R. Johnson and H. Toch, 181-203. Prospect Heights, Ill.: Waveland.

— Coffey, W. A. 1823. *Inside Out: Or, An Interior View of the New York State Prison; Together with Bibliographic Sketches of the Lives of Several of the Convicts.* New York, printed for the author.

— Crouch, B. M., and J. Marquart. 1989. *An Appeal to Justice: Litigated Reform of Texas Prisons.* Austin: University of Texas Press.

— Foucault, M. 1977. *Discipline and Punish: The Birth of the Prison.* New York: Pantheon.

— Franklin, H. B. 1989. *Prison Literature in America.* New York: Oxford.

— Garland, D. 1990. *Punishment and Modern Society: A Study in Social Theory.* Chicago: University of Chicago Press.

— Himes, C. 1934. "To What Red Hell?" *Esquire* 2 (October): 100-101, 122, 127.

— Irwin, J. 1970. *Prisons in Turmoil.* Boston: Little, Brown.

— Jacobs, J. B. 1977. *Stateville: The Penitentiary in Mass Society.* Chicago: University of Chicago Press.

— Johnson, R. 1996. *Hard Time: Understanding and Reforming the Prison.* Belmont, CA: Wadsworth.

— Lawes, L. E. 1932. *Twenty Thousand Years in Sing Sing.* New York: Ray Long and Richard R. Smith, Inc.

— McCall, N. 1995. *Makes Me Wanna Holler: A Young Black Man in America.* New York: Vintage.

— McConville, S. 1981. *A History of English Prison Administration.* London: Routledge and Kegan Paul.

— Merlo, A., and J. Pollock. 1995. *Women, Law and Social Control.* Boston: Allyn and Bacon.

— Nelson, V. F. 1936. *Prison Days and Nights.* New York: Garden City.

— Pisciotta, A. W. 1983. "Scientific Reform: The 'New Penology' at Elmira." *Crime and Delinquency* 29(4): 613-630.

— Pisciotta, A. W. 1994. *Benevolent Repression: Social Control and the American Reformatory-Prison Movement.* New York: New York University Press.

— Rafter, N. H. 1990. *Partial Justice: Women, Prisons, and Social Control.* 2d ed. Boston: Northeastern University Press.

— Robinson, D., M. Grossman, and F. Porporino. 1991. *Effectiveness of the Cognitive Skills Training Program: From Pilot to National Implementation.* Research and Statistics Branch, Correctional Service of Canada: Research Brief No. B-07.

— Rothman, D. 1971/1990. *The Discovery of the Asylum: Social Order and Disorder in the New Republic.* Boston: Little, Brown.

— Sellin, J. T. 1977. *Slavery and the Penal System.* New York: Elsevier.

— Sykes, G. 1958/1966. *The Society of Captives.* Princeton: Princeton University Press.

— Toch, H. 1977. *Living in Prison: The Ecology of Survival.* New York: Free Press.

# THE CRISIS AND CONSEQUENCES OF PRISON OVERCROWDING

*Alida V. Merlo*

While we have prisons it matters little which of us occupy the cells.

— *George Bernard Shaw*
Man and Superman, *1903*

## *Chapter Overview*

From all indications, Americans love prisons. We willingly support legislation to increase their use and to extend the lengths of incarceration, with little regard for the resulting construction and maintenance costs, opportunity costs, or effects on other components of the system. With over 1.1 million offenders currently incarcerated in federal and state prisons and projections of over 2 million within the next ten years (*Corrections Digest* 1994b; *Corrections Today* 1996, 20), we are in the midst of a cycle that shows little sign of abatement. This chapter examines some of the reasons for prison overcrowding, the various strategies that have been attempted to address it, and the costs in both economic and social terms of a correctional policy that is heavily influenced by incapacitation and deterrence.

Overcrowding continues to be the number one problem challenging the correctional systems of America and their administrators (Vaughn 1993, 12). At the end of 1994, state prison systems were between 17 and 29 percent above capacity; the federal system was 25 percent above capacity (Furniss 1996, 38). Vaughn (1993) mailed questionnaires to the Commissioners of Corrections in all 50 states in the summer of 1990 to explore the factors that have played a part in the overcrowding of institutions and the various administrative strategies that correctional administrators used to deal with the problem. All 50 states were represented in the final sample, although the respondents varied from commissioners to researchers in the states' correctional systems. Each respondent was asked to complete the questionnaire in the manner that best reflected the ideology of the top administrator (Vaughn 1993, 15).

According to the administrators' responses, overcrowding affected 48 states (96 percent of the respondents); there were only two north central states that, according to their administrators, were not affected by overcrowding (Vaughn 1993, 15). News reports from states illustrate a strikingly similar picture. For example, at the Joseph Harp Correctional Center in Oklahoma, 980 inmates are being housed in a facility designed for 425. Cells that originally were intended to hold one inmate now house two (Walsh 1995, 28). Other state systems have been forced to employ dayrooms as makeshift dormitories, and some have even used tents to house the vast numbers of inmates.

When asked what contributed to the severe overcrowding, a consensus among administrators emerged. At least 44 administrators linked overcrowding to four factors: increased sentence length, the drug problem, the public's desire to get tough on crime, and the legislative response to that demand (Vaughn 1993, 15-16). Other factors like mandatory sentences, increases in minimum sentence

**TABLE 3-1**
**Prisoners under the Jurisdiction of State or Federal Correctional Authorities,**
**June 30, 1995, December 31, 1994, and June 30, 1994, by Region and State**

| Region and jurisdiction | Total[a] | | | Percent change from | | Incarceration rate on 6/30/95[b] |
| | 6/30/95 | 12/31/94 | 6/30/94 | 6/30/94 to 6/30/95 | 12/31/94 to 6/30/95 | |
|---|---|---|---|---|---|---|
| **U.S. total** | 1,104,074 | 1,055,073 | 1,014,670 | 8.8% | 4.6% | 403 |
| Federal | 99,466 | 95,034 | 93,708 | 6.1% | 4.7% | 31 |
| State | 1,004,608 | 980,039 | 920,962 | 9.1 | 4.6[a] | 372 |
| | | | | | | |
| **Northeast** | 158,184 | 153,072 | 150,702 | 5.0% | 3.3% | 295 |
| Connecticut[c] | 15,005 | 14,380 | 14,427 | 4.0 | 4.3 | 325 |
| Maine | 1,459 | 1,474 | 1,468 | (−.6) | (−1.0) | 112 |
| Massachusetts | 11,469 | 11,293 | 11,166 | 2.7 | 1.6 | 180 |
| New Hampshire | 2,085 | 2,021 | 1,895 | 9.0 | 2.2 | 180 |
| New Jersey | 25,626 | 24,632 | 24,471 | 4.7 | 4.0 | 323 |
| New York | 68,526 | 66,750 | 65,962 | 3.9 | 2.7 | 377 |
| Pennsylvania | 29,844 | 28,302 | 27,082 | 10.2 | 5.4 | 247 |
| Rhode Island[c] | 3,132 | 2,919 | 3,049 | 2.7 | 7.3 | 190 |
| Vermont[c,d] | 1,058 | 1,301 | 1,182 | — | — | 135 |
| | | | | | | |
| **Midwest** | 190,170 | 184,508 | 178,339 | 6.6% | 3.1% | 307 |
| Illinois | 37,790 | 36,531 | 35,614 | 6.1 | 3.4 | 320 |
| Indiana | 15,699 | 15,014 | 14,826 | 5.9 | 4.6 | 270 |
| Iowa | 5,692 | 5,437 | 5,090 | 11.8 | 4.7 | 201 |
| Kansas | 6,927 | 6,371 | 6,090 | 13.7 | 8.7 | 269 |
| Michigan | 41,377 | 40,631 | 40,220 | 2.9 | 1.8 | 434 |
| Minnesota | 4,764 | 4,575 | 4,573 | 4.2 | 4.1 | 103 |
| Missouri | 18,940 | 17,898 | 16,957 | 11.7 | 5.8 | 356 |
| Nebraska | 2,801 | 2,711 | 2,449 | 14.4 | 3.3 | 168 |
| North Dakota | 610 | 536 | 522 | 16.9 | 13.8 | 90 |
| Ohio | 43,158 | 43,074 | 41,156 | 4.9 | .2 | 387 |
| South Dakota | 1,780 | 1,708 | 1,636 | 8.8 | 4.2 | 245 |
| Wisconsin | 10,632 | 10,022 | 9,208 | 15.5 | 5.1 | 196 |
| | | | | | | |
| **South** | 446,498 | 422,455 | 395,491 | 12.9%[a] | 5.7% | 474 |
| Alabama | 20,082 | 19,573 | 19,098 | 5.2 | 2.6 | 459 |
| Arkansas | 8,825 | 8,643 | 8,916 | (−1.0) | 2.1 | 349 |
| Delaware[c] | 4,651 | 4,466 | 4,324 | 7.6 | 4.1 | 406 |
| District of Col.[c] | 10,484 | 10,949 | 11,033 | (−5.0) | (−4.2) | 1,722 |
| Florida | 61,882 | 57,168 | 56,052 | 10.6 | 8.4 | 437 |
| Georgia | 34,111 | 33,425 | 30,92 | 12.6 | 2.1 | 468 |
| Kentucky | 11,949 | 11,066 | 10,724 | 11.4 | 8.0 | 310 |
| Louisiana | 24,840 | 24,063 | 23,333 | 6.5 | 3.2 | 573 |
| Maryland | 21,441 | 20,998 | 20,887 | 2.7 | 2.1 | 398 |
| Mississippi | 12,446 | 10,930 | 10,631 | 17.1 | 13.9 | 447 |
| North Carolina | 26,818 | 23,648 | 22,650 | 18.4 | 13.4 | 357 |
| Oklahoma | 17,605 | 16,831 | 16,306 | 8.0 | 6.9 | 536 |

**TABLE 3-1** *(Continued)*

| Region and jurisdiction | Total[a] | | | Percent change from | | Incarceration rate on 6/30/95[b] |
|---|---|---|---|---|---|---|
| | 6/30/95 | 12/31/94 | 6/30/94 | 6/30/94 to 6/30/95 | 12/31/94 to 6/30/95 | |
| **South** *(cont.)* | | | | | | |
| South Carolina | 19,481 | 18,999 | 19,646 | (−.8) | 2.5 | 510 |
| Tennessee | 14,933 | 14,401 | 14,397 | 3.7 | 3.7 | 284 |
| Texas | 127,092 | 118,195 | 100,136 | 26.9 | 7.5 | 659 |
| Virginia | 27,310 | 26,968 | 24,822 | 10.0 | 1.3 | 412 |
| West Virginia | 2,438 | 2,332 | 2,244 | 8.6[a] | 4.6[a] | 134 |
| **West** | 209,756 | 200,004 | 196,430 | 6.8% | 4.9% | 348 |
| Alaska[c] | 3,031 | 3,292 | 3,128 | (−3.1) | (−7.9) | 293 |
| Arizona | 20,907 | 19,746 | 18,830 | 11.0 | 5.9 | 473 |
| California | 131,342 | 125,605 | 124,813 | 5.2 | 4.6 | 402 |
| Colorado | 10,757 | 10,717 | 9,954 | 8.1 | .4 | 287 |
| Hawaii[c] | 3,583 | 3,333 | 3,245 | 10.4 | 7.6 | 218 |
| Idaho | 3,240 | 2,811 | 2,801 | 13.2 | 15.3 | 278 |
| Montana | 1,801 | 1,764 | 1,654 | 8.9 | 2.1 | 207 |
| Nevada | 7,487 | 6,993 | 6,745 | 11.0 | 7.1 | 468 |
| New Mexico | 4,121 | 3,712 | 3,704 | 11.3 | 11.0 | 234 |
| Oregon | 7,505 | 6,936 | 6,723 | 11.6 | 8.2 | 199 |
| Utah | 3,272 | 3,045 | 2,948 | 11.0 | 7.5 | 166 |
| Washington | 11,402 | 10,833 | 10,650 | 7.1 | 5.3 | 210 |
| Wyoming | 1,308 | 1,217 | 1,174 | 11.4 | 7.5 | 271 |

0 Indicates a negative percent change.

— Not calculated.

[a] Includes inmates sentenced to more than 1 year ("sentenced prisoners") and those sentenced to a year or less or with no sentence. Prisoner counts may differ from previously published figures and may also be revised.

[b] The number of prisoners with a sentence of more than 1 year per 100,000 in the resident population.

[c] Prison and jails form one integrated system. Data include total jail and prison population.

[d] Data for 6/30/95 are custody counts only and are not comparable to previous counts.

*Source:* Bureau of Justice Statistics, U.S. Department of Justice (December 3, 1995).

length, and more effective law enforcement procedures and techniques were noted also, but not with the same level of consensus.

# PRISON INMATES

Unfortunately, there are two distinct groups that particularly appear to have been affected by the increased use of imprisonment: minorities and women. Their incarceration rate, both state and federal, has been especially dramatic. For African American males in 1992, the incarceration rate (to prison) was 2,678 per 100,000 black residents, which is more than seven times that of white males (Gilliard and Beck 1994, 9). For black females, the incarceration rate was 143 per 100,000 residents, while for white females it was 20 per 100,000 white residents (1994, 9). When jails are included in the incarceration rate, the differences are even more extreme, as shown in Table 3-2.

Of the 431,279 admissions to state prisons in 1992, African Americans comprised 47 percent and Hispanics 19 percent of all new court commitments: These two minority groups, therefore, comprised 66 percent of all new state court commitments to prison (Perkins 1994, 7). Not surprisingly, drug trafficking was the offense responsible for the largest percentage of men (18 percent) and women (24 percent) admitted to prison for the first time in 1992 (Perkins 1994, 7).

Furthermore, Gilliard and Beck (1994) note that although women comprised only 5.8 percent of all inmates in the United States at the end of 1993, their numbers increased at a faster rate (9.6 percent) than males (7.2 percent). This trend appears to be continuing. For the first six months of 1994, the number of female inmates increased 6.2 percent compared to a 3.9 percent increase for male inmates (Proband 1994, 4). There is no empirical evidence to suggest that an increase in women's criminal behavior can explain the surge

**TABLE 3-2**
**Number of Adults Held in State or Federal Prisons or in Local Jails per 100,000 Adult Residents in Each Group, 1984-1994**

| Year | White | | Black | |
|------|-------|---------|-------|---------|
| | *Males* | *Females* | *Males* | *Females* |
| 1984 | 490 | 24 | 3,309 | 166 |
| 1985 | 528 | 27 | 3,544 | 183 |
| 1986 | 570 | 29 | 3,850 | 189 |
| 1987 | 594 | 35 | 3,943 | 216 |
| 1988 | 629 | 41 | 4,441 | 257 |
| 1989 | 685 | 47 | 5,067 | 321 |
| 1990 | 718 | 48 | 5,365 | 338 |
| 1991 | 740 | 51 | 5,717 | 355 |
| 1992 | 774 | 53 | 6,014 | 365 |
| 1993 | 805 | 56 | 6,259 | 403 |
| 1994 | 860 | 60 | 6,753 | 435 |

*Source:* Bureau of Justice Statistics, Department of Justice (December 3, 1995).

in their imprisonment. On the contrary, the national data on women incarcerated found that the proportion of women in prison for violent offenses actually dropped in the 1980s (Chesney-Lind and Pollock 1995, 159). However, state statistics that have been compiled indicate that the "war on drugs" has adversely affected women (Chesney-Lind and Pollock 1995, 158).

Prison admission statistics are primarily comprised of two categories of offenders: new court commitments and *returnees* (parole violators, mandatory release offenders, or others released under some level of supervision). Both categories of admissions have increased dramatically. The evidence suggests that incarceration clearly has become the sentence of choice in the United States. For example, Langan, Perkins, and Chaiken (1994) found in their analysis of felony sentences in the United States in 1990 that state and federal courts imposed a prison sentence on 46 percent of convicted felons. An additional 25 percent of convicted felons were sentenced to jail. In short, their data reveal that 71 percent of all felons convicted in state and federal courts in 1990 were sentenced to incarceration.

By contrast, straight probation was the sentence imposed on only 29 percent of convicted felons. In fact, it was used most often for only fraud and embezzlement; more than half of these offenders were sentenced to probation (Langan, Perkins, and Chaiken 1994, 5). Although 54 percent of felons convicted of fraud and embezzlement were placed on probation in 1990, only 25 percent of those convicted of burglary and 36 percent of those convicted of larceny and auto theft were sentenced to probation (Langan, Perkins, and Chaiken 1994, 5). These data suggest that part of the prison overcrowding problem may be due to the incarceration of property offenders (especially burglars and thieves) who in previous years would have been placed on probation but are now being sentenced to prison.

In recent years, the number of released offenders who return to prison because they violate one or more conditions of their release has also significantly increased from 27,177 (17 percent of admissions) in 1980 to 141,961 (29.5 percent of admissions) in 1992 (Gilliard and Beck 1994, 7). The researchers contend that more than one-third of the growth in admissions to state prisons from 1980 to 1992 is due to the increase in the number of conditionally released offenders being returned to prison (Gilliard and Beck 1994, 7). A closer examination of these national data reveals distinct state differences. For example, in 1993, Texas reported that two-thirds of the prison admissions were probation and parole violators, while Nevada reported that only 10 percent of the prison admissions were returnees who had violated the conditions of their release (Austin 1995, 48). These offenders' readmission statistics help to explain the burgeoning prison population in the United States.

## SENTENCING REFORMS

In trying to understand the rationale for our increased reliance on prison as the primary method of crime control, it is useful to examine the sentencing changes that have occurred during the last 50 years. The federal government and the states employ various sentencing approaches. According to the U.S. Department of Justice, "the basic difference in sentencing systems is the apportioning of discretion between the judge and parole authorities" (1988, 91).

Shortly after World War II, the predominant approach was some type of an *indeterminate sentence*. These sentences meshed with the notion of prisons as correctional institutions (Irwin and Austin 1994, 9). In this kind of sentencing scheme, the judge imposed a minimum and a maximum sentence length. However, the actual time served was determined by some authority other than the judiciary, most typically the parole authority in the various states.

In some jurisdictions, *partially indeterminate* sentencing statutes existed. These statutes empowered the judge to set the maximum sentence that the offender could serve, but there was no minimum stipulated. Once again, the ultimate decision to release was in the hands of the parole authority (U.S. Department of Justice 1988, 91). These kinds of sentencing approaches reflected the rehabilitative ideal. Decisions to release an inmate were to be individualized and tailored to the specific offender's progress within the institution. They were very popular in the United States for most of the 1950s and 1960s.

Beginning in the 1970s, the indeterminate sentence came under attack from both liberals and conservatives. As discussed in Chapter 1, liberals, advocating for the rights of offenders (including war resisters and civil rights activists), contended that indeterminate sentencing adversely affected inmates and treated them unjustly and coercively (Goodstein and Hepburn 1985, 14). They also criticized excessive *judicial discretion* and *sentencing disparity* (Goodstein and Hepburn 1985, 18). Simultaneously, conservatives criticized the treatment ideal and found some empirical support for their position that rehabilitation was a failure (Goodstein and Hepburn 1985, 15).

Additionally, conservatives were anxious to make sentences tougher by restricting the judges' ability to impose lenient sentences (van den Haag 1975 and Wilson 1975, cited in Tonry and Hamilton 1995, 3). These two diverse groups agreed on at least one thing: The indeterminate sentence was unfair, albeit for very different reasons.

The *determinate sentencing* approach began to be viewed as more impartial and a greater deterrent to crime. In those states that adopted such statutes, the central feature was a fixed period of incarceration from which there could be no deviation. An offender served his full term less whatever good time credits he accrued while in prison. These kind of sentences effectively ended any parole discretion (U.S. Department of Justice 1988, 91). Proponents of determinate sentencing statutes contend that they physically restrain offenders from engaging in crime while deterring them from future criminal tendencies.

Determinate sentencing statutes affect overcrowding in three ways. First, offenders who previously might have been placed on probation or in other community-based settings are now sent to prison. Second, the average sentence length is increased so that offenders stay in prison longer. Third, some states abolished parole when they established determinate sentencing models, thereby eliminating a potential release mechanism to cope with overcrowding (Holten and Handberg 1994, 228; Singer 1993, 174).

Federal and state governments rely on a number of sentencing options in addition to the three basic approaches just discussed (indeterminate, partially indeterminate, and determinate) (U.S. Department of Justice 1988, 91). For example, at least 46 states now have *mandatory sentencing laws* (U.S. Department of Justice 1988, 91). The central feature of these laws is that judges are required to impose fixed periods of incarceration for offenders convicted of certain specific crimes. These very popular laws severely restrict the judges' discretion in sentencing.

Some states have adopted a determinate sentencing structure called *presumptive sentencing.* This system requires judges to sentence offenders convicted of certain offenses to a specified period of incarceration. Judges can deviate from these set terms if there are extenuating or mitigating circumstances, but judges must still conform to the legislative boundaries established. Any deviation usually requires the judge to stipulate in writing the rationale for the change in the sentence authorized (Holten and Handberg 1994, 222; U.S. Department of Justice 1988, 91).

Two other sentencing changes have occurred in recent years. The first involves the use of *sentencing guidelines,* which usually are drafted by a separate sentencing commission. They can be prescriptive, stipulating whether the judge is required to impose a prison sentence, or they can be advisory, providing information to the judge but not requiring a specific sentence (U.S. Department of Justice 1988, 92). These guidelines can be either incorporated in the statute or used selectively by the various states and the federal government (U.S. Department of Justice 1988, 91). For example, when Congress enacted the Comprehensive Crime Control Act of 1984, it included the Sentencing Reform Act of 1984 (Kennedy 1985, 113). This legislation established an independent U.S. Sentencing Commission that developed guidelines for all federal judges to use in the sentencing of convicted federal offenders (Kennedy 1985, 119). It abolished parole and mandated that offenders could only accrue good time credits not to exceed 15 percent of their total sentence or 54 days per year (Kennedy 1985, 119; Langan, Perkins, and Chaiken 1994, 8). This "truth-in-sentencing" law applies to offenders who committed crimes after November 1, 1987 (Langan, Perkins, and Chaiken 1994, 8).

A relatively simple strategy employed in some states is known as *sentence enhancements*. These statutes authorize judges to impose longer sentences or remove the parole possibility for chronic offenders (U.S. Department of Justice 1988, 91). Recently, these statutes (typically labeled *three strikes laws*) have become increasingly popular in the United States. For example, the recently enacted Violent Crime Control and Law Enforcement Act of 1994 authorizes mandatory life imprisonment for offenders convicted of a third violent or drug felony (Benekos and Merlo 1995, 4). Fourteen states have joined the federal system in passing these kinds of laws (Turner et al. 1995, 18).

The three strikes laws are popular for a variety of reasons. First, they are a manifestation of the public's penchant for the "get tough" rhetoric that has characterized criminal justice policy in recent years. Second, the baseball slogan is appealing because of its sound-bite appeal. Politicians are able to convey their message simply and quickly. Third, the laws are perceived as a deterrent to potential criminals. A poll conducted by the Wall Street Journal/NBC News found that 75 percent of Americans surveyed believe that passing such legislation would make a "major difference" in America's crime rate (*Criminal Justice Newsletter* 1994, 1). Last, these laws purport to take dangerous offenders off the streets for good, providing the public with a sense of safety and security.

Although the shibboleth is new, the legislative action is not. Habitual offender laws originated in the United States in the late 1700s in NewYork (Turner et al. 1995, 17). Other states followed NewYork's lead by enacting similar popular laws. Even as recently as 1968, 23 states had statutes that authorized life imprisonment for habitual offenders who had previously been convicted of certain specified offenses (Turner et al. 1995, 17).

Despite their appeal, these "new" sentencing laws have the potential to exacerbate already severely overcrowded prison conditions while simultaneously creating more problems for state and federal governments, criminal justice agencies, and prison administrators. The hidden costs of such policies will be borne ultimately by the public, whose penchant for the "quick fix" does not generally include a long-term commitment of public funding. If other states adopt the stance of the federal government and the 14 states that have enacted three strikes laws or some variation of them, the inmate population is expected to rise to 2.26 million within the next nine years (*Corrections Digest* 1994b, 1).

## Drug Offenders and Prison Overcrowding

In his survey of prison administrators, Vaughn (1993) found that, in addition to the increase in the length of sentences, the practice of incarcerating drug offenders was perceived as one of the explanations for prison overcrowding. To more clearly understand how the incarceration of drug offenders affects prison populations, it is useful to examine a few recent trends regarding criminal justice policy and drugs.

According to Zimring and Hawkins (1995), two categories of offenders are responsible for the majority of all sentences to prison in the United States: (1) drug users who have been convicted of drug or property offenses, and (2) recidivist property offenders (162). In examining new court commitments, Gilliard and Beck found that the number of offenders admitted to prison for drug offenses totaled 102,000 in 1992 and was second only to the number of persons admitted to prison for property offenses, which totaled 104,300 (1994, 7). Clearly, there are more drug and property offenders being convicted and sentenced to prison than violent offenders.

In their analysis of 1990 federal and state court data, Langan, Perkins, and Chaiken (1994) found that of the 14 offenses they studied, drug trafficking offenses were the most numerous (2). They accounted for 21 percent of the total number of convictions in the United States. Not surprisingly, drug crimes comprised 32 percent of the sentences to state prisons that were imposed and 62 percent of the federal sentences. Skolnick reports that one-fifth of the 90,000 federal inmates in 1994 were low-level drug offenders with no current or prior history of violence and no prior prison time (1995, 9). Clearly, American drug policy and law enforcement efforts have played a part in augmenting prison populations.

Unlike other categories of offenders, Zimring and Hawkins (1995) contend that the number of offenders arrested and convicted of drug offenses varies dramatically over time as policies change. These kinds of variations are not found for other serious crimes (Zimring and Hawkins 1995, 134-136). Not only has the number of drug arrests continued to increase, but "the proportion of prisoners being punished for drug crimes has increased more rapidly since the mid-1980s than ever before in United States history" (Zimring and Hawkins 1995, 162).

In 1980, 6.8 percent of all new court commitments to prison were drug offenders; in 1992, approximately 30.5 percent of all new court commitments were for drug offenses (Gilliard and Beck 1994, 7). For example, while the total number of inmates increased 4 times in 12 years in California, the number of offenders incarcerated for drug offenses increased 15 times (Zimring and Hawkins 1995, 162). In fact, they estimate that when offenders with drug crime convictions are added to those offenders who were dependent on drugs at the time of their offense, close to one-third of the California prison population has a significant involvement with illegal drugs (Zimring and Hawkins 1995, 162).

There is ample evidence that the War on Drugs initiated during the Reagan administration targeted cocaine rather than heroin. Cocaine first appeared to be the drug of wealthy Americans in the 1970s, but during 1985-1986 a new form of cocaine known as crack appeared (Kappeler, Blumberg, and Potter 1993, 153). It was this new "smokable" cocaine that was relatively inexpensive and widely available that prompted the criminal justice system to respond. With strong public support, the government aggressively investigated, apprehended, and incarcerated drug offenders.

For the most part, these policies have continued during the 1990s. Irwin and Austin (1994) contend that the war the government has waged against drugs has not only prompted a movement toward more punitive sentencing for drug offenders but has focused on crack cocaine, which primarily is sold and available in inner-city neighborhoods. It is the residents of these neighborhoods, African Americans and Hispanics who use the drug, that have been disproportionately incarcerated. In fact, two groups have been significantly impacted by the war on drugs: minorities and women.

With the Sentencing Reform Act of 1984 and the implementation of the U.S. Sentencing Commission's guidelines, the disproportionate representation of incarcerated African Americans has increased significantly. McDonald and Carlson (1994) examined all sentencing decisions in every federal district court between January 1, 1986, and June 30, 1990. Their research encompassed the period before and after the full implementation of the mandatory sentencing guidelines. They contend that after the full implementation of the guidelines, the sentencing disparities between African Americans and whites grew larger: African Americans' sentences were 41 percent longer (71 months on average) than whites (McDonald and Carlson 1994, 8).

The differences between the sentences of African Americans and whites were particularly apparent in three crime categories: drug trafficking, bank robbery, and weapons offenses. Although most of the sentencing differences for bank robbery and weapons offenses were fairly straightforward and were related to factors that would typically affect length of sentence (for example, prior criminal history), the sentences imposed for drug trafficking in cocaine were less straightforward (McDonald and Carlson 1994, 10).

In the federal system, cocaine trafficking is the most prevalent drug crime. When McDonald and Carlson examined the offenders sentenced for cocaine trafficking, they noted major differences between African American and white sentences. In particular, African Americans were sentenced to prison more often, and their sentences were longer (1994, 8). Furthermore, they found significant differences in the type of trafficking, which would account for most of the variation in sentencing: African Americans were more likely to be convicted of trafficking crack cocaine, and whites were more likely to be convicted of trafficking powdered cocaine (McDonald and Carlson 1994, 8-9).

When Congress enacted the Anti-Drug Abuse Act of 1986, it established minimum sentences for trafficking crack and powdered cocaine. However, the punishments for selling crack are greater than those for selling powdered cocaine. In short, "the punishments for selling or possessing crack (50 grams) are the same as those convicted of selling 100 times these amounts of powdered cocaine" (McDonald and Carlson 1994, 9). For example, if an offender is convicted of selling as little as five grams of crack (approximately a teaspoon), the sentence is a minimum of five years in prison (Isikoff 1995, 77).

The sentencing differences are especially problematic in view of prospective users. Crack is more likely to be used by African Americans than whites. As McDonald and Carlson (1994) point out, it may not be the case that African Americans prefer crack to powdered cocaine, but crack is more heavily promoted in minority neighborhoods.

For women, the effects of the drug war are even more pronounced. According to Bloom, Chesney-Lind, and Owen (1994), one out of three women in prison in the United States was serving a sentence for drug offenses in 1993. Even though the drug enforcement strategies have been theoretically targeted for the major drug dealers, Bloom et al. found that over 35 percent of the women who were incarcerated in prison for drug convictions were there for the crime of "possession" (1994, 1).

Self-report data gathered in 1991 on women offenders suggest that larger percentages of women than men report having used drugs in the month before their current offense, having used them daily in the month before their current offense, and being under the influence at the time of their offense (Maguire, Pastore, and Flanagan 1993, 627). The available data lend support to the research suggesting that female drug use is increasing and that it is a factor involved in women's criminal behavior (Merlo and Pollock 1995).

These trends are particularly disturbing when the paucity, duration, and intensity of drug treatment programs in prisons are well documented (Wellisch, Prendergast, and Anglin 1994). More women are being convicted and imprisoned for drug offenses than previously (one manifestation of mandatory sentencing laws), but there is little emphasis directed toward treating these women in the prison. Unfortunately, mandatory sentencing laws also foreclose the possibility of community treatment.

# RESPONDING TO OVERCROWDING

## THE EFFECTS OF PRISON OVERCROWDING

The research on prison overcrowding and its relationship to inmate violence, health, stress, prison disciplinary problems, and recidivism is not conclusive, probably for several reasons. First is the difficulty in finding comparable control groups. In the current correctional climate, few facilities are operating well below capacity. Second is the difficulty in comparing one inmate population with another. One institution might house more recalcitrant or violent offenders, thus affecting the impact of overcrowding (Durham 1994). Last, living in overcrowded conditions may have long-term effects that are not detectable until several years later (Durham 1994).

Despite these limitations, some research suggests "that prisons housing significantly more inmates than a design capacity based on sixty square feet per inmate are likely to have high assault rates" (Gaes 1985, 95). In their research, Clayton and Carr (1984) also found a strong relationship between crowding and inmate rule infractions, but not to recidivism. In their study of the Georgia prison system, age rather than crowding was related to recidivism (Clayton and Carr 1987).

Although overcrowding may not be a direct cause of stress, Gaes contends that it may exacerbate the many other sources of stress in prison, such as separation from family, loss of freedom, and fear of assault. Normally, crowding may intensify the effects of stress; however, when it reaches some as yet undetermined level it may act as a direct stress, rather than merely as a stress elevator (Gaes 1985, 141). There is little dispute among correctional staff. They contend that densely populated prisons are more difficult to control and to supervise.

Previous research has indicated that inmates who live in open areas (like dormitories) tend to use medical services more often and to have higher blood pressure levels than offenders in single cells (Crouch et al. 1995, 66). In recent years, there has been increased publicity about the incidence of HIV and tuberculosis infections among inmate populations. Although the risk of contracting HIV while in prison is minimal, the risk of spreading tuberculosis is a more serious concern (Durham 1994, 54). Tuberculosis is highly contagious, and housing inmates in densely populated institutions increases the likelihood of spreading the disease.

## STRATEGIES TO FIGHT OVERCROWDING

In his survey of state correctional administrators, Vaughn (1993) found that states employed a variety of strategies to deal with overcrowding. They ranged from constructing new prisons or increasing the size of existing prisons through expansion projects or double-bunking to the increased use of community-based correctional services (16-18). The most prevalent response is construction. Of the 50 state administrators who responded, 47 (94 percent) reported that their states were either building new prisons or increasing the size of their existing institutions. Additionally, 42 states (84 percent) reported that they were double- and triple-bunking inmates (Vaughn 1993, 16).

These responses typify the current correctional dilemma. Correctional administrators are in the unenviable position of trying to locate or construct additional space to cope with sentencing changes after they have been enacted by the legislature. Typically, these kinds of "get tough" sentencing laws are enacted without the accompanying funding for the additional prison space that will be required (Durham 1994, 45).

Court intervention compounds the dilemma. Despite all the construction, Marquart et al. (1994) report that 37 states were under some type of court order related to crowding. While the courts are concerned about crowding issues as they relate to violations of Eighth Amendment provisions regarding protection against cruel and unusual punishment, elected officials who fear being portrayed as "soft on crime" do not share their zeal. The result has been a somewhat acrimonious relationship in which the courts decree population limits, the remedies to be utilized, and the penalties (usually fines) to be invoked if the state refuses to comply (Cole and Call 1992).

The quickest method of dealing with overcrowding is the acquisition of space from within the institution. For example, the state may opt to convert a gymnasium into a dormitory. Simultaneously, additional facilities (either temporary or permanent) can be constructed. None of these space expansion projects comes cheaply in economic or social costs. During the 1980s, in many states prison budgets increased more rapidly than any other portion of the state budget (McGarrell 1993, 16).

Comparisons of states' corrections budgets between fiscal year 1994 and fiscal year 1995 illustrate sizable increases. For example, Proband (1995, 8) found that in 39 states, increases in corrections exceeded the expected rate of inflation. In fact, 14 states reported double-digit increases in their fiscal year 1995 corrections appropriations (Proband 1995, 8). Federal and state governments appropriated $5.1 billion for construction of additional prison space in fiscal year 1995 (McConnell Clark Foundation, cited in Furniss 1996, 40). Clark (1994) reports that while corrections spending has increased exponentially since 1970, state and local spending for such programs as welfare and health care have not kept pace.

## CALIFORNIA AND TEXAS: LEADERS
## IN INCARCERATION

To attempt to assess the costs of overcrowding, it is useful to examine California's experiences. California's prison population was 131,342 on June 30, 1995 (Furniss 1996, 39). It is the largest prison system in the country followed by Texas, where the population was 127,092 on June 30, 1995 (Corrections Today 1996, 20). Together, these two states account for 23 percent of all incarcerated inmates or more than one in five inmates in the United States (Furniss 1996, 38-39; Proband 1994, 4).

Since the early 1980s, California has spent more than $5 billion on the largest prison building program in the United States (Koetting and Shiraldi 1994, 2). Despite this massive effort, California facilities are operating at 177 percent of capacity (Hewitt, Shorter, and Godfrey 1994, 2). The California Department of Corrections estimates that it spends over $7 million per day to house its prison population (Clark 1994, 4).

The enormous expenses incurred due to prison construction and to longer incarceration periods might be worthwhile if they resulted in reduced crime rates. However, California has not demonstrated such a savings. Quite the contrary, California's total crime rate and violent crime rate were greater in 1993 than they were in 1983 (Koetting and Schiraldi 1994, 2). In fact, California data on crime substantiates national research that posits that there is no relationship between incarceration rates and rates of crime (Koetting and Schiraldi 1994, 3).

The Texas experience is not much different. Between 1980 and 1990, the state added 38,357 beds or 20 new prison units (Marquart et al. 1994, 518). The correctional budget for 1990-1991 was $2.02 billion, which represented a 39 percent increase over the previous two years. Most of these funds went to new prison construction (Marquart et al. 1994, 518). Between June 30, 1994, and June 30, 1995, Texas added another 34,000 inmates to its prison population (Montgomery 1995, A6). It is expected that the Texas prison population (up 27 percent to 127,092 on June 30, 1995) will soon reach 144,000 (Verhovek 1996, A10; Corrections Today 1996, 20). In recent projections, state officials indicate that with the 150,000 beds they will have in 1996, they should have enough space until the year 2000 (Ward 1996, A1). Not surprisingly, Texas also has the highest incarceration rate of all the states, 659 per 100,000 (Furniss 1996, 38).

The situation is remarkably similar, only on a somewhat smaller scale, in a number of other states. In Pennsylvania, four new prisons were authorized in 1994. In Georgia, legislators appropriated $43.5 million for 5,416 beds. The Florida legislature allocated funding for 17,000 new prison beds (Proband 1995, 8). From the available evidence, it appears that states that were primarily relying on utilizing existing space have had to resort to building new prisons to deal with overcrowding and projected increases in the adult prison population.

There is little optimism for the likelihood of constructing enough prison space to satisfy most of the states' demands. Although Florida's prison population reached 61,992 on June 30, 1995, it is expected to increase its current prison bed capacity by 18,000 in the next three years. Even that level of increase is not expected to satisfy demand. It is projected that Florida will need approximately 58,000 more beds in the next ten years at a cost of $1 billion to build (Furniss 1996, 40).

The only exception to this continual demand for new beds appears to have occurred recently in Texas. As already noted, this state may have satiated the public's demand for prison beds, at least for the time being. It was recently announced that there are more county jail beds than needed (Verhovek 1996, A1). Due to the prison building campaign in Texas, counties that built county jails to house "backed-up" state prisoners unable to be transferred to overcrowded state prisons now have empty institutions to fill. In true entrepreneurial fashion, Texas counties are now "selling" their product (prison beds) to other states. One thing seems certain — empty beds will be filled.

According to Gilliard and Beck (1994, 2) "the average growth in the number of sentenced state and federal prisoners was equal to a demand for 1,215 additional bedspaces per week". As a result, overcrowding will continue to plague correctional administrators. The search for alternative strategies has intensified.

## FRONT-END STRATEGIES TO FIGHT OVERCROWDING

In addition to new construction, the majority of states reported that they are utilizing front-end strategies to deal with overcrowding (Vaughn 1993). Typically, these include increased use of probation and other kinds of intermediate sanctions like intensive probation, house arrest, electronic monitoring, and shock probation or split sentences (Blumstein, cited in Clark 1994, 105). There is little doubt that the primary reason for the search for alternatives to incarceration is based primarily on economic rather than humanitarian motives.

Minnesota has been a leader in community corrections beginning with its Community Corrections Act enacted in 1973. That legislation authorizes annual state subsidies totaling approximately $31 million to local counties to help them in creating corrections programs including community service, electronic monitoring, and intensive supervision. These programs have flourished, seemingly without increased risk to the community (Wood 1996, 54).

Intensive supervision probation programs in Georgia and intensive supervision parole programs in New Jersey first became publicized in the early 1980s. They soon developed in every state. Similarly, house arrest and electronic monitoring were also a product of the 1980s. In the intervening years, these programs and shock incarceration programs have become increasingly utilized (Tonry and Hamilton 1995, 4-5).

Alternatives to incarceration are perceived as especially useful for nonviolent offenders. As previously noted, over 60 percent of new court commitments to prison in 1992 were drug offenders and property offenders, while violent offenders accounted for approximately 28 percent and public-order offenders accounted for approximately 8 percent (Gilliard and Beck 1994, 7). Using probation or some other type of community-based program for property offenders and drug offenders, particularly if it were coupled with some type of drug treatment and community service, might satisfy the public's demand to "get tough" while simultaneously saving much-needed capital for other public service projects. As in any community-based program, screening appropriate offenders is imperative.

There is some apprehension, however, that these kinds of alternatives will produce a *net-widening* effect. Having these alternatives available may prompt judges to sentence offenders who previously would have been diverted from the system or subject to a fine to intensive probation or shock probation. When this occurs, these alternatives simply become sentences rather than alternatives to incarceration.

## BACK-END STRATEGIES TO FIGHT OVERCROWDING

Using back-end strategies to cope with prison overcrowding generally necessitates the acceleration of early release, either through good time credits or parole (Blumstein, cited in Clark 1994, 105). These release procedures are extremely controversial. Consider the 1993 case of Polly Klaas, the 12-year-old girl who was abducted and murdered by Richard Allen Davis, a parolee who had served 8 years of a 16-year sentence for kidnapping and who had previous kidnapping, assault, and robbery convictions (*New York Times* 1993; Benekos and Merlo 1995). Media sensationalism and the fear of victimization by criminals who are released from prison prematurely discourage consideration of these kinds of approaches. Unfortunately, these kinds of cases prompt the public to demand tougher sentences, including life without the possibility of parole.

Typically, states will authorize emergency release mechanisms (for example, adding on extra good time credits) when they are under some type of court decree not to exceed a certain population ceiling. According to Durham (1994), in 1991, 14 states had emergency release procedures, and the vast majority of them were established by state legislatures (52).

Part of the reluctance to utilize early release programs may be due to the limited research on their effectiveness. Lane (1986) reported that a National Council on Crime and Delinquency (NCCD) evaluation of an early release program used by Illinois proved that the program did not jeopardize public safety or increase crime. Furthermore, he noted that the NCCD study found that the state saved millions of dollars by implementing a policy that prevented prison overcrowding and its attendant consequences (Lane 1986, 403). However, more research needs to be done to ascertain the effectiveness and safety of early release programs.

# FUTURE DIRECTIONS

## THREE STRIKES LAWS AND THEIR PROJECTED EFFECT

One of the more troubling aspects of the overcrowding phenomenon is whether most states will ever be able to overcome the problem. The public and elected officials seem to have an insatiable appetite for the increased use of incarceration. Recent changes in California legislation — the "three strikes" statute — are estimated to cost $5.7 billion a year and add 276,000 inmates to the prison system over the next three decades (Schiraldi 1994, 1; Skolnick 1995, 4). Additionally, California will need another $21 billion for prison construction (Mauer 1994a, 22).

California's zest for these new "three strikes and you're out" sentencing laws is not unparalleled (Benekos and Merlo 1995). As previously noted, 14 states and the federal government have enacted similar statutes. The National Council on Crime and Delinquency estimates that if other states continue to amend their sentencing laws, an estimated $351 billion will be needed by the federal government and the states in the next ten years (*Corrections Digest* 1994b, 1).

One of the more alarming aspects of these kinds of laws is their inability to deter crime. Skolnick's research suggests that the federal prison population will increase by 50 percent by the year 2000 (1995, 9). Furthermore, 60 percent of that population is expected to be drug offenders (Skolnick 1995, 9). This kind of selective incapacitation might be useful if it deterred drug-related crimes. There is no evidence that the public demand for cocaine and heroin has abated as a result of these criminal justice policies. In fact, there are an estimated 2 million hard-core abusers of these two drugs in the United States (Clark 1994, 103). Would incarcerating all of these abusers eliminate the demand for drugs in America?

Another distressing aspect of the laws concerns the likely targets. Schiraldi and Godfrey (1994) analyzed the effect of the new three strikes law in Los Angeles County in its first six months. Despite the fact that African Americans comprise 10 percent of the population of Los Angeles County, they comprised over 57 percent of those individuals charged under the third strike statute (1994, 1-2). In Los Angeles County, African Americans were charged with a third strike crime at 17 times the rate of whites (Schiraldi and Godfrey 1994, 2). Just as the War on Drugs has increased the incarceration of minorities disproportionately, there is grave concern that these three strikes laws will have a similar effect (Mauer 1994, 23).

The pessimism concerning minority overrepresentation and three strikes laws is augmented by the fact that 40 percent of African American males in their twenties in the state of California are under some type of criminal justice control (that is, prison, jail, probation, parole, house arrest). That is at least three times the number who are enrolled in four-year college degree programs in the state (Butterfield 1996, A8; Baum and Bedrick 1994, 9). The situation is not much different nationally. According to Mauer (1994), the number of African American males in prisons and jails in the United States (583,000) is greater than the number of African American males enrolled in higher education institutions (18).

## SOCIAL COSTS OF PRISON EXPANSION

There is little evidence that the massive expansion of federal and state prison beds has reduced crime. Given that fact and the enormous expenditures that these policies necessitate, there is little to justify such a position especially when the opportunity costs that these policies represent are considered. Zimbardo (1994) contends that, factoring in the interest paid for a construction bond debt, it costs $333 million to build one new prison in California. To build and maintain more prisons, states and the federal government have to forgo other programs. The funding has to come from other sources of public revenue, the consequences of which affect everyone long after the prison has been constructed, staffed, and filled with inmates.

The requisite funding for additional prison beds represents significant opportunity costs. Four months after Governor Wilson signed California's three strikes law, he "signed legislation which froze the state's educational expenditure for primary education at $4,217 per student. This represents one of the lowest per child K-12 educational allotments in the nation" (Hewitt, Shorter, and Godfrey 1994, 5). Unfortunately, the national trend with respect to state spending for public elementary and secondary schools is pretty dismal. Although states' share of the revenues for public elementary and secondary schools grew throughout most of the 1980s, that has changed now. More of the money for school funding is now coming from local sources, and there has been no significant increase in spending since 1989-1990 (U.S. Department of Education 1994, 45). Zimbardo (1994) estimates the opportunity costs of prison expansion by illustrating that one new prison is equal to 8,833 new teachers who could have been hired to teach the state's school children or equal to 89,660 children who could be supported to enroll in Head Start programs (7).

Consider the growth of California's corrections budget. Just ten years ago, higher education was allotted two and a half times as much money as corrections, but that was before the ramifications of the prison construction costs were realized (Zimbardo 1994, 7; Skolnick 1995, 4). In 1994, California's state corrections budget of $3.8 billion was equal to the entire budget for public higher education (Zimbardo 1994, 7; Baum and Bedrick 1994, 2). By the year 2002, corrections is predicted to consume 18 percent of the entire state budget while higher education will consume less than 1 percent (Zimbardo 1994, 7-8).

The trade-off is even more troubling when one considers Baum and Bedrick's (1994) projections. For what the state of California will spend to incarcerate one "third strike" burglar for 40 years, it could have provided 2-year community college educations to 200 students (Baum and Bedrick 1994, 5). Although Californians' share of these kinds of costs have been well documented, there are other costs that California and other states will have to address as a result of these policies.

Proband (1995) examined state appropriations for the Aid for Dependent Children (AFDC) program and for corrections. Not surprisingly, states are cutting their spending on poor children while increasing the money spent on prison spending (Proband 1995, 1). In America, more than half the states spend two times as much on prisons as they do on Aid for Dependent Children (Proband 1995, 8). Preliminary analysis of these data suggests that there is an inverse relationship between states' incarceration rates and AFDC spending. According to Proband (1995), "in general, states that invest little in AFDC have high incarceration rates and rankings." In six of the states, Arkansas, Idaho, Indiana, North Carolina, South Carolina, and Texas, $5.00 to $10.00 is appropriated for corrections for every dollar allocated for AFDC (Proband 1995, 1). The percentages of fiscal year 1995 state spending for AFDC when compared to corrections in these six states ranged from a low of 10.6 percent in North Carolina to 19.9 percent in Indiana (Proband 1995, 9). It makes more sense to adopt a proactive strategy and invest in early intervention in poor children's lives than to persist with a reactive strategy incarcerating large numbers of people and expending vast amounts of money after they have been involved in crime.

## CONCLUSIONS

It is unlikely that the excessive reliance on incarceration is likely to wane in the next ten years. Building prisons helps to enhance the illusion of their "incapacitative effect" (Sieh 1989, 49). As Zimring and Hawkins (1995) contend, incapacitating offenders is perceived as desirable because "restraint directly controls the behavior of the offender rather than leaving him or her any choice in the matter" (156). It is the ability to control an offender rather than simply influence her that makes incarceration of criminals so appealing to the public (Zimring and Hawkins 1995, 157).

Ironically, the vast amounts of capital and the increased number of prison beds have not solved the state's overcrowding problems, much less any perceived crime problem. Recent evidence suggests that the incidence of violent crime, particularly murder, may be decreasing in the larger cities. In fact, the murder rate in New York City was at its lowest level (during the first six months of 1995) in 25 years (Krauss 1995a, 1; Krauss 1995b, 1, 4). Crime also is decreasing in other cities like Detroit, Los Angeles, and Chicago (Krauss 1995a, 16). Although some public officials might quickly conclude that incarceration is the primary reason for the decline in the crime rate, no empirical evidence exists to support such a claim. The few research studies that have suggested that the decrease in crime can be attributed to increased incarceration rates have been criticized by a number of research organizations and experts (Baird 1993, 1). As Baird contends, "The evidence that the imprisonment binge has not produced the desired results is absolutely overwhelming" (1993, 7). The extensive publicity surrounding the studies supporting more imprisonment, and the fact that they are cited so often, has led some researchers to conclude that they are the product of ideology rather than science and that they have been used to facilitate a political agenda that is focused on "locking up" offenders rather than prevention and social programs (Baird 1993, 1, 3).

According to the data gathered by the Federal Bureau of Investigation and the National Crime Victimization Survey, "rates for violent crimes are at or below 1980 levels" (Mauer 1994b, 9-10). In reviewing Bureau of Justice Statistics prison admission data from 1980 to 1992, Mauer reports that only 16 percent of the increase in state court commitments to prison per year were for violent offenses while 46 percent were for drug offenses (Mauer 1994b, 10). When all of the state court commitments were reviewed between 1980 and 1992, Mauer reports that 84 percent were for nonviolent offenses (1994, 10). Clearly, changes in criminal justice sentencing policy regarding violent offenders cannot explain these reductions in violent crime.

No single reason can be given for the precipitous drop in New York City's murder rate or for the general decrease in crime across the nation. Among the reasons cited by Krauss (1995a) were fewer drug wars than occurred in the late 1980s and early 1990s that resulted in the deaths of dealers and bystanders, a decrease in crack use and an increase in heroin use, a national trend in which fewer homicides occurred in a number of major cities, and demographic changes that have resulted in fewer young people in their late teens and early twenties than in previous years. In a recent interview that appeared in *Law Enforcement News* (1995), Blumstein noted that the smallest age cohort in the United States is the group that is currently 18 years of age (the peak homicide age). If in the next few years the number of youths who are 18 or younger increases, as it is expected to do so, the number of homicides in that group will also rise (Law Enforcement News 1995, 11). Our experience with decreasing crime rates may be short-lived.

The decline in violent crime has not prompted legislators to demand that prison populations be reduced or sentencing laws revised. In October of 1995, at the urging of the United States Sentencing Commission, Congress considered the Commission's recommendation to establish equal sentences for crack and powdered cocaine. Congress quickly voted to retain the disparate sentencing structures (Isikoff 1995, 77).

Unfortunately, our desire to control offenders will cost all of us. What we will lose include a variety of services from early education programs like Head Start, to medical services for the poor, to college educations. Fiscal restraint will necessitate curtailing road construction and repair, social services, health care, and immunization programs. The costs associated with prison construction will continue to escalate, and the demand for stricter punishment will not waver. It is against this backdrop that we look at what is occurring inside the nation's prisons.

## Vocabulary

| | |
|---|---|
| determinate sentencing | returnees |
| indeterminate sentencing | sentence disparity |
| judicial discretion | sentence enhancements |
| mandatory sentencing | sentencing guidelines |
| "net widening" | three strikes laws |
| presumptive sentencing | |

## Study Questions

1. How many people are in prison today in the United States? What are the projections for the future? What are the increases attributed to?

2. Define indeterminate, partially indeterminate, and determinate sentencing.

3. What has been the effect of the various forms of determinate sentencing on prison populations? What seems to be the relationship between crime rates and incarceration rates?

4. How have drug laws and commitments of drug offenders affected prison populations?

5. What does research show regarding the effects of overcrowding on inmates?

6. What are some front-end strategies to reduce overcrowding? What are some back-end strategies?

7. What are the costs associated with the increase of prison commitments?

# Sources Cited

— Allen, Harry E., and C. Simonsen. 1995. *Corrections in America: An Introduction.* Englewood Cliffs, N.J.: Prentice-Hall.

— Austin, James. 1995. "Correctional Options: An Overview." *Corrections Today* 57(1): 48 (Special Supplement Section).

— Baird, Christopher. 1993. "The 'Prisons Pay' Studies: Research or Ideology." *Focus* (March): 1-7. National Council on Crime and Delinquency.

— Baum, Noah, and Brooke Bedrick. 1994. "Trading Books for Bars: The Lopsided Funding Battle between Prisons and Universities." *In Brief* (May): 1-9. San Francisco, Cal.: Center on Juvenile and Criminal Justice.

— Benekos, Peter J., and Alida V. Merlo. 1995. "Three Strikes and You're Out!: The Political Sentencing Game," *Federal Probation* 59 (March): 3-9.

— Bloom, Barbara, Meda Chesney-Lind, and Barbara Owen. 1994. "Women in California Prisons: Hidden Victims of the War on Drugs." *In Brief* (May): 1-11. San Francisco, Cal.: Center on Juvenile and Criminal Justice.

— Butterfield, Fox. 1996. "Study Finds a Disparity in Justice for Blacks." *New York Times* 13 February, sec. A8.

— Chesney-Lind, Meda, and Joycelyn M. Pollock. 1995. "Women's Prisons: Equality with a Vengeance." In *Women, Law, & Social Control,* ed. Alida V. Merlo and Joycelyn M. Pollock, 155-175. Needham Heights, Mass.: Allyn and Bacon.

— Clark, Charles S. 1994. "Prison Overcrowding." *The Congressional Quarterly Researcher* 4, 5 (February): 97-120.

— Clayton, Obie, Jr., and Tim Carr. 1984. "The Effects of Prison Crowding upon Infraction Rates." *Criminal Justice Review* 9: 69-77.

— Clayton, Obie, Jr., and Tim Carr. 1987. "An Empirical Assessment of the Effects of Prison Crowding upon Recidivism Utilizing Aggregate Level Data." *Journal of Criminal Justice* 15: 201-210.

— Cole, Richard B., and Jack E. Call. 1992. "When Courts Find Jail and Prison Overcrowding Unconstitutional." *Federal Probation* 56 (March): 29-39.

— *Corrections Digest.* 1994a. "Experts Doubt '3 Strikes You're Out' Laws Will Effectively Curb Crime." (February 9): 7-9.

— *Corrections Digest.* 1994b. "Senate Crime Bill Will More Than Double American Prison Population by Year 2005." (March 9): 1-4.

— *Corrections Today.* 1996. "U.S. Prison Population Grows at Record Rate." *Corrections Today* 58, 1 (February): 20.

— *Criminal Justice Newsletter.* 1994. "State Chief Justices Oppose Senate Crime Bill Provisions." (February 15): 1-3.

— Crouch, Ben, Geoffrey P. Alpert, James W. Marquart, and Kenneth C. Haas. 1995. "The American Prison Crisis: Clashing Philosophies of Punishment and Crowded Cellblocks." In *The Dilemmas of Corrections,* 3d ed., ed. Kenneth C. Haas and Geoffrey P. Alpert, 64-80. Prospect Heights, Ill.: Waveland Press.

— Dillingham, Steven D., and Lawrence A. Greenfeld. 1991. "An

Overview of National Corrections Statistics." *Federal Probation* (June): 27-34.

— Durham, Alexis M. 1994. *Crisis and Reform: Current Issues in American Punishment.* Boston: Little, Brown.

— Flores, Matt. 1995. "Cities, Counties Scramble to Find 'Paying Customers' for Lockups." *Austin American Statesman* 6 July, sec. B3.

— Furniss, Jill R. 1996. "The Population Boom." *Corrections Today* 58, 1 (February): 38-40, 42-43.

— Gaes, Gerald G. 1985. "The Effects of Overcrowding in Prison." In *Crime and Justice, vol. 6,* ed. Michael Tonry and Norval Morris, 95-146. Chicago: University of Chicago Press.

— Gest, Ted, Jennifer Seter, Dorian Friedman, and Kevin Whitelaw. 1995. "Crime and Punishment: Politicians Are Vowing to Get Tough, But Will More Prisons and Fewer Perks Really Cut Crime?" *U.S. News & World Report,* 3 July: 24-26.

— Gilliard, Darrell K., and Allen Beck. 1994. "Prisoners in 1993." Bureau of Justice Statistics Bulletin; U.S. Department of Justice. (June): 1-11. Washington, D.C.: GPO.

— Goodstein, Lynne, and John Hepburn. 1985. *Determinate Sentencing and Imprisonment.* Cincinnati: Anderson.

— Hewitt, Chet, Andrea D. Shorter, and Michael Godfrey. 1994. "Race and Incarceration in San Francisco: Two Years Later." *In Brief* (October): 1-8. San Francisco, Cal.: Center on Juvenile and Criminal Justice.

— Holten, N. Gary, and Roger Handberg. 1994. "Determinant Sentencing." In *Critical Issues in Crime and Justice,* ed. Albert R. Roberts, 217-231. Thousand Oaks, Cal.: Sage.

— Irwin, John, and James Austin. 1994. *It's About Time: America's Imprisonment Binge.* Belmont, Cal.: Wadsworth.

— Isikoff, Michael. 1995. "Crack, Coke and Race." *Newsweek* 126, 19 (6 November): 77.

— Kappeler, Victor E., Mark Blumberg, and Gary W. Potter. 1993. *The Mythology of Crime and Criminal Justice.* Prospect Heights, Ill.: Waveland.

— Kappeler, Victor E., Mark Blumberg, and Gary W. Potter. 1996. *The Mythology of Crime and Criminal Justice.* 2d ed. Prospect Heights, Ill.: Waveland.

— Kennedy, Edward M. 1985. "Prison Overcrowding: The Law's Dilemma." *The Annals of the American Academy* 478 (March): 113-122.

— Koetting, Mark, and Vincent Schiraldi. 1994. "Singapore West: The Incarceration of 200,000 Californians." *In Brief* (July): 2-12. San Francisco, Cal.: Center on Juvenile and Criminal Justice.

— Krauss, Clifford. 1995a. "Murder Rate Plunges in New York City: A 25-Year Low in First Half This Year." *New York Times,* 8 July at 1, 16.

— Krauss, Clifford. 1995b. "Crime Lab: Mystery of New York, The Suddenly Safer City." *New York Times,* 23 July, sec. 4, at 1, 4.

— Lane, Michael. 1986. "A Case for Early Release." *Crime and Delinquency* 32, 4 (Oct.): 399-403.

— Langan, Patrick A., C. A. Perkins, and J. M. Chaiken. 1994. "Felony Sentences in the United States, 1990." Bureau of Justice Statistics Bulletin; U.S. Department of Justice. (September). Washington, D.C.: GPO.

— *Law Enforcement News.* 1995. "An Interview with Professor Alfred Blumstein of Carnegie Mellon University." XXI, 422 (April 30): 10-13.

— Maguire, Kathleen, and Ann L. Pastore, eds. 1994. *Sourcebook of Criminal Justice Statistics—1993.* Bureau of Justice Statistics Bulletin; U.S. Department of Justice. Washington, D.C.: GPO.

— Maguire, Kathleen, A. Pastore, and T. J. Flanagan, eds. 1993. *Sourcebook of Criminal Justice Statistics—1992.* Bureau of Justice Statistics Bulletin; U.S. Department of Justice. Washington, D.C.: GPO.

— Marquart, James W., Steven J. Cuvelier, Velmer S. Burton Jr., Kenneth Adams, Jurg Gerber, Dennis Longmire, Timothy J. Flanagan, Kathy Bennett, and Eric Fritsch. 1994. "A Limited Capacity to Treat: Examining the Effects of Prison Population Control Strategies on Prison Education Programs." *Crime and Delinquency* 40(4): 516-531.

— Mauer, Marc. 1994a. "Americans Behind Bars: The International Use of Incarceration, 1992-1993." Report, 1-27. Washington, D.C.: The Sentencing Project.

— Mauer, Marc. 1994b. "Russia, United States World Leaders in Incarceration." *Overcrowded Times* 5(5): 1, 9-10.

— McGarrell, Edmund F. 1993. "Institutional Theory and the Stability of a Conflict Model of the Incarceration Rate." *Justice Quarterly* 10(1): 7-28.

— McDonald, Douglas E., and Kenneth E. Carlson. 1994. "Drug Policies Causing Racial and Ethnic Differences in Federal Sentencing." *Overcrowded Times* 5(6): 1, 8-10.

— Merlo, Alida V., and Joycelyn M. Pollock, eds. 1995. *Women, Law and Social Control.* Needham Heights, Mass.: Allyn and Bacon.

— Montgomery, Lori. 1995. "Prison Population Up 90,000 in U.S." *Pittsburgh Post-Gazette* 4 December, sec. A6.

— *New York Times.* 1993. "Hunt for Kidnapped Girl, 12, Is Narrowed to Small Woods." 3 December, sec. A22.

— Perkins, Craig. 1994. *National Corrections Reporting Program.* (October). Bureau of Justice Statistics Bulletin; U.S. Department of Justice, Washington, D.C.: GPO.

— Proband, Stan C. 1994. "Prison Population Exceeds One Million." *Overcrowded Times* 5(6): 4.

— Proband, Stan C. 1995. "Corrections Costs Lead State Budget Increases for 1995." *Overcrowded Times* 6(2): 1, 8-9.

— Schiraldi, Vincent. 1994. "The Undue Influence of California's Prison Guard Union: California's Correctional-Industrial Complex." *In Brief* (October): 1-4. San Francisco, Cal.: Center on Juvenile and Criminal Justice.

— Schiraldi, Vincent, and Michael Godfrey. 1994. "Racial Disparities in the Charging of Los Angeles County's Third 'Strike' Cases." *In Brief* (October): 1-4. San Francisco, Cal.: California Center on Juvenile and Criminal Justice.

— Sieh, Edward W. 1989. "Prison Overcrowding: The Case of New Jersey." *Federal Probation* 53(3): 41-51.

— Singer, Richard. 1993. "Sentencing." In *Criminal Justice: Concepts and Issues,* ed. Chris W. Eskridge, 172-174. Los Angeles: Roxbury.

— Skolnick, Jerome H. 1995. "What Not to Do About Crime — The American Society of Criminology 1994 Presidential Address." *Criminology* 33(1): 1-13.

— Tonry, Michael, and Kate Hamilton. 1995. *Intermediate Sanctions in Overcrowded Times.* Boston: Northeastern University Press.

— Travis III, Lawrence F., Martin D. Schwartz, and Todd R. Clear, eds. 1992. *Corrections: An Issues Approach.* Cincinnati: Anderson.

— Turner, Michael G., Jody L. Sundt, Brandon K. Applegate, and Francis T. Cullen. 1995. "Three-Strikes and You're Out Legislation: A National Assessment." *Federal Probation* 59(3): 16-35.

— U.S. Department of Education. 1994. *Digest of Education Statistics 1994.* National Center for Education Statistics, Office of Educational Research and Improvement. Washington, D.C.: U.S. Government Printing Office.

— U.S. Department of Justice, Bureau of Justice Statistics. 1988. *Report to the Nation on Crime and Justice—Sentencing and Corrections.* 2d ed. 90-111. Washington, D.C.: GPO.

— Vaughn, Michael S. 1993. "Listening to the Experts: A National Study of Correctional Administrators' Responses to Prison Overcrowding." *Criminal Justice Review* 18 (Spring): 12-25.

— Verhovek, Sam Howe. 1996. "Texas Caters to a Demand Around U.S. for Jail Cells." *New York Times,* 9 February, sec. A1, A10.

— Walsh, Kenneth T. 1995. "The View from Inside the Wall." *U.S. News & World Report,* 3 July: 28-29.

— Ward, Mike. 1996. "Construction Boom Leaves Texas with Ample Prison Space." *Austin American Statesman,* 8 March, sec. A1 & B1, col. 2.

— Wellisch, Jean, Michael L. Prendergast, and M. Douglas Anglin. 1994. "Drug-Abusing Women Offenders: Results of a National Survey." National Institute of Justice, Research in Brief. October. Washington, D.C.: U.S. Department of Justice, GPO.

— Wood, Frank W. 1996. "Cost-Effective Ideas in Penology — The Minnesota Approach." *Corrections Today* 58(1): 52, 54, 56.

— Zimbardo, Philip G. 1994. "Transforming California's Prisons into Expensive Old Age Homes for Felons: Enormous Hidden Costs and Consequences for California's Taxpayers." Report. November. San Francisco, Cal.: Center on Juvenile and Criminal Justice, 1-16.

— Zimring, Franklin E., and Gordon Hawkins. 1995. *Incapacitation: Penal Confinement and the Restraint of Crime.* New York: Oxford University Press.

# 4

# THE CLASSIFICATION OF INMATES

## *David Spencer*

[T]he degree to which [the absence of a working classification system] impedes the attainment of any proper objectives of a penal system cannot be overstated.

— *Pugh v. Locke,* 406 F. Supp. 318, 324
(M.D. Ala. 1980)

---

*Chapter Overview* ―――――

――― **FACTORS IN THE DEVELOPMENT OF MODERN CLASSIFICATION**
    Institutional Overcrowding
    Prisoners' Rights
        *Due Process*
        *Equal Protection*
――― **PURPOSES OF CLASSIFICATION**
    Classification for Management
    Classification for Rehabilitation
――― **METHODS OF CLASSIFICATION**
    Objective Classification Systems
        *Characteristics of an Objective System*
        *Evaluation*
    Classification by Psychological Instruments
        *MMPI-Based Classification*
        *Adult Internal Management System*
        *Interpersonal Maturity Level System*
――― **CONCLUSIONS**

In prison management, *classification* refers to the process of evaluating inmates and assigning them to appropriate categories for correctional purposes. The reasons for which inmates are classified are varied, but they may be divided into two general categories: (1) administration and management of the prison, and (2) treatment and rehabilitation of the offender. Although it has received little public attention, classification is a pressing issue in today's prisons. During the last two decades, corrections professionals have expended a great deal of effort to improve the ability of institutions to classify inmates appropriately. This effort has been driven by several factors, some of which have come into play only during this particular time period.

Classification has not always been a matter of great concern, even among those directly involved with the corrections system. Before the development of penitentiaries as the primary means of punishment, one of the main classification concerns of European jailers was to separate nobles from commoners. Beyond that, inmates were frequently housed together without regard to age or gender.

Although early American jails and penitentiaries did not have to contend with questions of nobility, it was common for the small number of females in a facility to be housed in cells adjacent to those of males. It was not until the late 1800s that American prisons began to establish separate facilities for women (Rafter 1993).

In 1870, the National Prison Association issued its Declaration of Principles, which sought to bring about changes in American corrections practices that would provide for the rehabilitation and humane treatment of inmates. The use of indeterminate sentencing as a rehabilitative tool is probably the best known of the principles. However, the declaration also proposed that inmates should be classified on the basis of their accomplishment of the goals of reformation (Rothman 1980). This method of classification remained a stated goal in American corrections from the late 1800s through the mid-1940s. Nevertheless, in practice, classification schemes were usually developed by prison administrators only as they were needed and were based largely on administrative convenience, informed by conventional wisdom and the personal experiences of the developers.

In the post-World War II period, some corrections experts and organizations attempted to professionalize the corrections process. The American Correctional Association (the successor to the National Prison Association) published the first edition of its *Manual of Correctional Standards* in 1946. The manual sought to establish standards for prisons based on the experience and research of professionals. In keeping with the medical model of corrections that prevailed at the time, the standards emphasized classification for treatment and rehabilitation purposes (American Correctional Association 1966).

The *medical model* views criminal behavior as a symptom of something that was wrong with the offender, a disease or disorder that is beyond the control of the offender, just as a physical illness is beyond the control of a medical patient. Causes of the disorder may be sociological or psychological. Regardless of the cause, the offender is seen as a sick person who should be made well rather than a bad person who should be punished. The appropriate response of the corrections system, in this model, is to diagnose the disorder and provide proper treatment. With successful treatment the offender will be rehabilitated because the disorder will have been cured, and the offender can be returned safely to the community. Although proponents of the medical model have never claimed that they have the ability to achieve complete rehabilitation of the offender population, the basic assumption underlying the model is that, given sufficient time and resources, the means to identify the causes of criminal behavior and develop effective treatments will come about. Although the medical model has fallen from favor, it still has a strong influence in the field of correctional treatment.

Despite the availability of the professional standards that were established after World War II, there was little impetus to professionalize the development of classification systems until the 1970s. At that time, two circumstances occurred that have greatly changed corrections in America during the succeeding two decades.

# FACTORS IN THE DEVELOPMENT OF MODERN CLASSIFICATION

There are two driving forces that have shaped corrections during the last 20 years: institutional overcrowding and prisoners' rights. Although their impact has not been uniform in all places, their influence has extended to every jail and prison in the country.

## INSTITUTIONAL OVERCROWDING

An examination of the full range of causes for overcrowding is covered in Chapter 3. However, some of the undesirable effects of overcrowding have particular relevance for classification. Overcrowded prisons create high stress conditions for both staff and inmates. Irritability and aggression are common results of this stress, leading to increased infractions of prison rules and to conflicts among inmates and between inmates and staff. In extreme cases, serious assaults or rioting may occur. The resulting anxiety and depression may lead to suicide attempts. High-stress conditions frequently increase demands on available health care services for inmates and cause excessive use of sick leave by staff (Clements 1979). Although these problems exist to some degree in any prison, overcrowding tends to aggravate normal institutional difficulties.

Classification is certainly no cure for overcrowding, but a good classification system can mitigate some of its effects. Because traditional classification systems are based on administrative concerns about institutional management, they tend to be conservative and to place more inmates than necessary in higher security classifications (Toch 1981). This *overclassification* phenomenon results in increased populations placed in maximum security institutions where there is less likelihood for early release. In recent years there has been some movement, born of necessity, toward the development of classification systems based on objective criteria that reduce overclassification and help to relieve some of the worst effects of overcrowding (Kane 1986).

## PRISONERS' RIGHTS

The view of the rights of prison inmates that prevailed in the American judicial system throughout most of our history came to be known as the *"hands off" doctrine*. During this so-called hands off era, prison inmates did not have any rights against the prison administration that the courts could enforce. Whatever rights they had came from the legislative branch, which wrote the laws, and the executive branch, which carried them out. Under this doctrine, the courts simply were not available as a forum to consider inmates' grievances. Some courts even went so far as to characterize felony inmates as "slaves of the state." *Ruffin v. The Commonwealth,* 62 Va. 790 (Ct. App. 1871). In the post-World War II period, however, some state and lower federal courts began to question the judicial wisdom of turning a blind eye to the way inmates were treated. The U.S. Supreme Court began to approve court intervention when some specific constitutional rights like freedom of religion were denied to inmates. *Cruz v. Beto,* 405 U.S. 319, 92 S. Ct. 1079 (1972). In the 1974 case of *Wolff v.*

*McDonnell,* 418 U.S. 539, 94 S. Ct. 2963 (1974), the U.S. Supreme Court declared that prison inmates retain some rights that may be enforced through the courts, holding that "[t]here is no iron curtain drawn between the Constitution and the prisons of this country." This announced the end of the judicial system's self-imposed hands off policy toward prisons.

*Wolff* and several subsequent cases have formed the basis for a great deal of change in America's prisons. These cases have established that conviction of a felony carries with it a restriction of the person's rights and privileges, but that even prison inmates retain a limited range of court-protected constitutional rights. Because the Supreme Court considers only those issues that are presented in the cases before it, it has never created a list of protected rights. As a result, a lot of litigation has been generated by various attempts to have the courts declare real or imagined rights to be matters of constitutional magnitude. Every issue of prison management seems to have been the subject of litigation at some time in the last 20 years. Classification is no exception. However, in the hierarchy of judicial precedence there has been little instruction from the U.S. Supreme Court itself regarding the Constitution's requirements for prison classification. Even the cases decided by the highest court have not imposed any great burdens on prison administrators, which is contrary to the common belief that the courts generally favor prisoners over prison administrators. Challenges to classification typically have involved two issues: due process of the law and equal protection of the law.

***Due Process.*** In *Meacham v. Fano,* 427 U.S. 215, 96 S. Ct. 2532 (1976), the Supreme Court held that the Due Process Clause of the Fourteenth Amendment to the U.S. Constitution does not give inmates a liberty interest in being confined in a particular prison. Neither assignment to a particular prison nor transfer between prisons is subject to any sort of constitutional requirement of due process. Such matters, the Court reasoned, are the ordinary consequences of imprisonment for conviction of a felony. Thus the Constitution itself does not prevent prison administrators from assigning inmates to any institution authorized by law, without any sort of due process procedures. Such assignments and transfers are, of course, the frequent outcomes of classification decisions.

*Hewitt v. Helms,* 459 U.S. 460, 103 S. Ct. 864 (1983), dealt more directly with classification. In that case the inmate had been transferred to administrative segregation following a riot in which he had allegedly participated. Although a prison Program Review Commit-

tee approved his continued confinement in administrative segregation, he was not given a full adversarial hearing on the matter. The
Court reaffirmed its position in *Meacham* that an inmate has no constitutionally created liberty interest in the place or type of confinement. However, it went further to hold that, while the Due Process
Clause itself does not create a protected liberty interest, the laws of
the state in question may create a liberty interest by restricting the
discretion of prison authorities. For example, a particular state law
might provide that inmates may be placed in administrative segregation only for specified reasons. In such a case, an inmate would have
a liberty interest, created by the state law, in remaining free of administrative segregation unless one of the specified reasons exists. Once
a liberty interest has been created by state law, it can be enforced in
federal court through the Due Process Clause of the U.S. Constitution. In this instance, the Court held that the applicable state law did
create such an interest, and so the inmate was entitled to due process. However, the Court went on to hold that the only process required was an informal, nonadversarial review of the facts of the case
by prison officials. The prison administrators were not required to
give an inmate a full-blown adversarial hearing before placing him or
her in administrative segregation; they were merely required to give
the inmate notice of the allegations and an opportunity to respond.
The court decided that, under the facts in the record, inmate Helms
had received all the process that was due to justify his confinement
in administrative segregation.

The Supreme Court has generally shown deference to prison administrative discretion in assigning inmates to types of custody. However, that deference is not without limits. In *Vitek v. Jones,* 445 U.S.
480, 100 S. Ct. 1254 (1980), the Court held that transfer from a
prison to a mental institution that used a mandatory behavior modification treatment program was not within the normal range of the
conditions of confinement to which a convicted felon may be subjected. Therefore, the Constitution required that the inmate be given
more due process rights than he had been afforded by state law before such a transfer could take place.

***Equal Protection.***   Claims of denial of equal protection are frequently the subjects of prison litigation. However, the Supreme Court
has said little on that topic in regard to classification. In the case of
*Washington v. Lee,* 263 F. Supp. 327 (M.D. Ala. 1966), the district court
clearly held that a classification scheme that segregated inmates by
race was unconstitutional, even in the face of claims by the prison
system that racial tensions caused security problems in the institu-

tion. The Supreme Court affirmed the decision in a per curiam opinion, under the name of *Lee v. Washington*, 390 U.S. 333, 88 S. Ct. 994 (1968). Three justices, in concurring with the majority, took care to say that, under some circumstances, prison administrators would be allowed to consider racial conflict in acting to protect the security and discipline of the institution, although they did not attempt to specify the exact conditions under which that could be done. Because it was a per curiam opinion, it did not set a binding legal precedent. However, the opinion generally has been read as a statement that any blanket policy of racial segregation that is not a good faith attempt to address a particular set of circumstances would be a clear denial of equal protection.

The Supreme Court has yet to consider a case of gender discrimination in the context of inmate classification. However, federal trial courts have dealt with that issue. For example, in *Canterino v. Wilson*, 562 F. Supp. 106 (W.D. Ky. 1983), the district court decided that it was a denial of equal protection for the state to require women inmates to participate in a behavior modification program that denied them privileges that were given to male inmates.

In general, there are two legal issues that may be raised in gender-based equal protection cases involving prison classification. One is different treatment of inmates based on their gender, which acts to the disadvantage of one or the other group. Thus, if a prison system has different classification procedures for men and women, it may be vulnerable to a legal challenge based on the disparate treatment of the sexes. *Disparate treatment* means that people of different genders are treated differently in an obvious, intentional manner. An example might be the classification of men and women for vocational training purposes into stereotypical "men's work," such as auto repair or construction, and "women's work," such as hair styling and food service.

On the other hand, if a system uses a single classification procedure that is neutral on its face, it may still be challenged on the theory that it has different effects on the genders. Thus a claim of denial of equal protection could be based on the disparate impact of an apparently neutral procedure (Nicholas and Loeb 1991). *Disparate impact* means that, although the procedures as written do not distinguish between inmates of different genders, the practical result is that the sexes are treated differently. One example of a potential challenge in this area is classification for security purposes. Some researchers in the classification of women believe that standard instruments developed for male offenders tend to show female inmates to be greater security risks than they actually are. The result, they believe, is that such classification procedures overclassify women, placing them in higher security or custody levels than are justified by the risk they truly represent (Burke and Adams 1991). If such were shown to be true in a particular case, then it might well support a successful equal protection challenge based on the different results obtained by the same classification procedures when applied to women and men.

These apparently conflicting sources of legal challenges may make prison administrators feel that they are on the horns of a dilemma; they can get sued whether they use the same classification procedure for females and males or different procedures specific to each gender. This difficulty points up the need to do frequent evaluations of the effectiveness of a classification system, which will be discussed later in this chapter.

Despite the paucity of Supreme Court cases relating to classification, federal district courts and appellate courts have considered numerous cases. This is not surprising because the Supreme Court accepts for review only a small fraction of the cases decided by lower trial and appellate courts. Some U.S. district courts have been involved in protracted prisoners' rights lawsuits that have resulted in extensive court decisions or agreed settlements. These cases have frequently brought about widespread changes in the operation of prisons, including their classification systems. Federal litigation, actual or threatened, has been a major influence in the recent movement to improve classification systems.

# PURPOSES OF CLASSIFICATION

As stated earlier, inmates are classified for many reasons, which are generally included in the categories of prison management and offender rehabilitation. There are frequently areas of overlapping concern in these two general types of classification.

## CLASSIFICATION FOR MANAGEMENT

The primary business of prisons is to incarcerate those who have been sentenced for felonies; consequently, security and custody issues are high-priority concerns for prison administrators. Management of correctional institutions involves controlling contact with the free world. Inmates must be kept on the inside, in accordance with the sentence of the court. A major part of this is to protect the public from dangerous individuals. But it is also an important part of the rule of law that those who have been required to serve a sentence of incarceration as punishment do so in accordance with the orders of the court. Therefore, even if a particular inmate does not present a threat to the public safety, it is still necessary that he be incarcerated as required by law.

Management of inmates also involves events within the institution. The actions of inmates within the facility must be controlled, and unauthorized people and things, such as weapons and drugs, must be kept out of the institution. The safety of staff members and inmates is a constant concern, as is the protection of the institution's property. For all these reasons, it is important to classify inmates according to the risks they present to institutional security and to public safety.

Classification for management purposes involves the type of facility in which the inmate will be incarcerated, which may be referred to as the security classification. *Security,* in this sense, has to do with the degree of physical separation from the outside world that the structure of the institution imposes on inmates. Management classification also includes the level of supervision with which each individual inmate will be controlled, which may be referred to as the custody classification. *Custody* means something different from the security level of the institution because inmates in the same institution may be controlled at different levels of supervision; some may be in administrative segregation, while others in the same institution may be trustees who are allowed to work outside the walls without direct supervision. These definitions of security and custody are generally accepted among corrections experts and will be so used in this chapter. However, the terms frequently are used interchangeably in practice (Levinson and Gerard 1986). Other terms, such as "confinement level" and "management level," are also used in connection with classification for institutional management.

Another reason for classification is for programmatic purposes. Inmates are involved in numerous programs, in the broad sense of that term. Programs frequently have overlapping implications for both prison administration and offender rehabilitation. A common example is the inmate's work assignment. Inmates are an important source of routine labor for most prisons. The effective use of this labor requires matching inmates with jobs that they can and will perform without requiring undue supervision from prison staff. An inmate who can be trusted to perform an assigned task without direct supervision is obviously a better choice for a work assignment that is performed with minimum supervision than is an inmate who will lay down on the job at every opportunity. However, if the hard-working inmate has a history of escape, she is a poor choice for a work assignment that is performed outside the walls. Therefore, appropriate classification for work assignment is important to both the work program and the security of the institution.

Inmate jobs are also beneficial to prison administration simply by keeping the inmates busy. Their occupation with work leaves them with less time and energy to plan and carry out an antisocial agenda. However, work assignments can also give inmates access to items that can be used as weapons or find their way into the prison economy. Assignment to or withholding of preferred jobs can be a source of conflict among inmates or between inmates and staff. These factors are additional considerations in classification.

### CLASSIFICATION FOR REHABILITATION

Work can also be a rehabilitative activity; inmates can learn job skills or work habits that can enable them to make a living in the free world without resorting to crime. Other rehabilitative programs that have implications for classification include education, mental health treatment, medical treatment, recreation, and preparation for release. Inmates are classified and reclassified for any or all of these purposes throughout their imprisonment. The next two chapters describe work and rehabilitation programs in more detail.

Although there is no evidence that prison rehabilitation programs can change the lifestyle choices of a recalcitrant inmate, the fact is that many offenders do not recidivate, that is, they do not commit new offenses after release. One function of rehabilitation programs may be seen as making it easier for offenders who are trying to change to do so, to remove as many barriers as possible from the inmate's rehabilitative efforts. Classification is one way to try to match offenders who are amenable to reformation with appropriate programs.

## METHODS OF CLASSIFICATION

The movement away from the medical model of corrections created the need for the development of classification systems based on other paradigms. Most classification systems currently in use follow one of two patterns. One type is based on objective criteria such as the inmate's criminal history and institutional behavior. These are usually referred to as *objective classification systems*. The other type is based on the psychological assessment of the offender, usually accomplished by the use of interviews or testing instruments (MacKenzie, Posey, and Rapaport 1988).

## OBJECTIVE CLASSIFICATION SYSTEMS

Classification during the 1980s and 1990s has been characterized by a trend toward systems based on objective criteria rather than the subjective judgments of prison administrators. This is particularly true of classification for management purposes.

As mentioned earlier, through the late 1960s the professional literature tended to emphasize treatment as the main focus of classification. However, doubts began to arise about the efficacy of the medical model of rehabilitation. The apparent resistance of many offenders to treatment, coupled with a general rise in the crime rate, led to disillusionment with treatment and an increasing emphasis on prisons as places of punishment. In 1974, a published report of a major study concluded that there was little or no valid evidence that any of the many treatment methods in use in prisons actually had the effect of reducing recidivism (Martinson 1974). By the late 1970s, the professional literature was including both management and treatment as goals of effective classification (Flynn 1978).

Until that time, classification systems had made extensive use of discretion on the part of those classifying the inmates. The acceptance of the medical model did not change this because treatment decisions typically involved subjective judgments on the part of professionals. Even when the trend in classification deemphasized treatment and increased emphasis on management, subjective judgments were still seen as appropriate bases for classification. For example, the U.S. Bureau of Prisons, generally considered a national trendsetter in prison management, developed a management system referred to as RAPS. This acronym stood for "rating," which meant the judgment of the evaluating staff, "age" of the offender, "prior commitments" meaning the number of prior prison commitments, and "sentence," meaning the nature of the current offense (Flynn 1978). Although the RAPS system used some objective criteria, it relied heavily on subjective staff ratings.

Toward the end of the 1970s, the use of subjective opinions for classification was increasingly seen as problematic. There was a realization that the current classification systems tended to overclassify inmates, requiring greater numbers to be incarcerated at higher security levels than necessary, thereby exacerbating the problems of overcrowding (Austin 1986). In addition, prison officials were concerned about pending or threatened prisoners' rights litigation (Buchanan and Whitlow 1987). Subjective judgments were seen as more difficult to justify when litigation involved due process and equal protection challenges. In 1979, the U.S. Bureau of Prisons adopted a classification system based on objective criteria. This event started a national trend toward the use of objective classification systems, especially for prison management purposes. An objective system has been described as including at least the following characteristics:

1. Uses test and classification instruments that have been validated for prison populations;
2. Contains the same components and scoring/classification approach for all offenders;
3. Arrives at decisions based only on application of factors shown to be related to placement decisions;
4. Assigns offenders to security classifications consistent with their background;
5. Promotes similar decisions among individual classification analysts on comparable offender cases, while minimizing overrides;
6. Involves inmates and is readily understandable by both staff and offenders; and,
7. Is capable of systematic and efficient monitoring (Buchanan, Whitlow, and Austin 1986, 273).

Two matters should be noted regarding the philosophy behind objective classification systems. First, despite the increased emphasis on management, corrections professionals have not entirely abandoned the hope of rehabilitation. Good prison management may be seen as aiding rehabilitation by placing inmates in a rational system that does not seem mysterious or arbitrary, thereby promoting positive interactions between inmates and staff (Alexander 1986). Second, although classification decisions in an objective system are based initially and primarily on objective criteria, these systems allow input of the opinions of staff members in the form of *overrides*. In most systems, a classification analyst is permitted to override, or change, the outcome of the objective evaluation. If used too frequently, these overrides can diminish the effectiveness of the system.

However, with proper staff training and appropriate criteria for over-rides they can be useful adjuncts to the objective evaluation process (Buchanan, Whitlow, and Austin 1986).

Since the early 1980s, the objective classification system has become the preferred model for the majority of prison systems. The New Jersey Department of Corrections conducted a survey of state correctional systems in January 1994. Thirty-four states responded to the survey instrument. Of those states responding, 89 percent reported that they had adopted an objective classification procedure for management purposes. A majority (53 percent) reported that their systems were computerized. Recording classification information in an automated system is important for the ongoing evaluation of a classification system, as will be discussed later. Almost all states that reported using such a system also considered it to be a benefit to the classification process (New Jersey Department of Corrections 1994). In preparing this chapter, the author requested information about classification procedures from all 50 states and the District of Columbia. Of the 28 jurisdictions responding, 26 (93 percent) had classification systems that made initial security decisions based primarily on objective criteria.

In the development of this new generation of classification systems, several models have emerged that form the bases for many of the systems. The four that were found by a national survey to be most commonly used were the National Institute of Corrections Model, the Federal Prison System Model, the Correctional Classification Profile, and the Florida Model (Buchanan and Whitlow 1987). However, prison systems generally do not adopt a model classification system without any changes. Although a model system that has already been tested serves as a convenient departure point, development of a new system usually includes adapting the model to the particular circumstances and needs of the adopting agency.

Adaptations are sometimes also made to accommodate the need to classify inmates of both genders. In a survey of 48 state correctional systems in 1991, 40 of the systems stated that they used the same classification procedures for both male and female inmates. Four of the responding states said that the same system was used for men and women, but was used differently according to gender; the remaining states reported using different classification procedures for women than for men (Burke and Adams 1991). The high number of states using one classification procedure for both men and women probably reflects concern about legal issues surrounding the equal treatment of female inmates.

*Characteristics of an Objective System.* The American Correctional Association's Standards for Adult Correctional Institutions include standards that are considered essential to an objective classification system. The standards provide that a system should have clear criteria for classifying inmates, and that the classification of each inmate and the classification plan itself should be subject to periodic reevaluation. Although the ACA standards are not binding on correctional systems, they are a good indication of the current thinking about proper prison management, and many of these characteristics will be found in all the systems in operation today. Selected standards are set out in Highlight 4-1.

The main purpose of objective classification systems is to improve management of correctional facilities and the inmates in them. Several factors are important to make objective systems function properly. The instruments used for classification should be developed and validated for prison inmates, preferably from a sample that is representative of the population on which the instruments will be used. Validation will not only make the system more accurate but also will make it more defensible in case of a legal challenge. Validation should also include periodic evaluations of the effectiveness of the system and modifications when problems show up.

The criteria for classification should be not only objective but also clear and easily understood by nonprofessionals. This is a benefit both to the staff members who will administer the system and to the inmates. For staff, the decision-making process is easier if the criteria are clear, and different classification personnel are more likely to reach consistent results for similar inmates if they have a thorough understanding of the application of the system. Clearly stated and applied criteria will serve to lessen the need for staff overrides of the classification instrument. Inmates will also benefit from understanding the bases on which they are classified; they will be less likely to consider the decision arbitrary and unfair. The system should also provide for periodic *reclassification* which takes into account the inmate's behavior since his last classification cycle.

The selection of classification criteria is one of the most important parts of an objective system. Ideally, the factors selected should be derived from an empirical study of the characteristics of a sample of the population that is to be classified. In practice, however, most correctional agencies elect to adapt a model that has already been developed by another agency (Buchanan and Whitlow 1987). Agencies choosing to use this method of development should take care to ensure that the system they are adapting is compatible with their organizational needs. Issues that should be considered include

**HIGHLIGHT 4-1**
**Standards for Objective Classification Systems**

**2-4399**   There is a written plan for inmate classification which specifies the objectives of the classification system, details the methods for achieving the objectives, and provides a monitoring and evaluation mechanism to determine whether the objectives are being met. The plan is reviewed at least annually and updated if necessary.

**2-4400**   There are classification policies with detailed procedures for implementing them; these policies are made available to all staff involved with classification, and reviewed at least annually and updated if necessary.

**2-4401**   The system for classifying inmates specifies the level of custodial control required and requires a regular review of each classification. . . .

**2-4403**   The written plan for inmate classification provides for maximum involvement of representatives of relevant institutional programs and the inmate concerned in classification reviews.

**2-4404**   The written plan for inmate classification specifies that the program status review of each inmate occurs at least every 12 months.

**2-4405**   The written plan for inmate classification specifies criteria and procedures for determining and changing the program status of an inmate; the plan includes at least one level of appeal. . . .

**2-4409**   The written plan for inmate classification specifies that, prior to a parole hearing, pre-parole material is made available to the paroling authority including a current and complete history of the inmate's activities in the institution and a proposed parole plan. (Adapted from American Correctional Association, 1981) similarity of inmate populations, availability of institutional resources, and compatibility with the agency's classification goals.

Several model systems have been developed and are in use. Highlight 4-2 is a list of classification criteria that are frequently found in current systems. None of these criteria are found in all sys-

---

**HIGHLIGHT 4-2**
**Criteria Commonly Used in Objective Classification Systems**

1. Severity of current offense
2. Degree of violence in current offense
3. Use of weapon in current offense
4. Nature of sexual offense
5. Current offense
6. Type of sentence (i.e., death, life, consecutive)
7. Length of sentence
8. Expected length of incarceration
9. Type of detainer
10. Severity of prior commitments
11. Number of prior commitments
12. Number of prior convictions
13. Number of prior felony convictions
14. Number of convictions for violence against person
15. Number of convictions for burglary/theft
16. History of violence
17. History of institutional violence
18. History of escape
19. History of prior supervision
20. Institutional adjustment
21. Behavior characteristics during incarceration
22. Demonstrated skills in escape/assault
23. Pre-commitment status (own recognizance, voluntary surrender)
24. Psychotic
25. Substance abuse
26. Age
27. Education
28. History of employment
29. Program/service needs
    (Buchanan and Whitlow 1987).

tems, and some are overlapping, but the list provides a broad view of the types of factors commonly used.

Criteria for reclassification decisions usually include the same factors as initial classification but use additional items such as time remaining until release, institutional disciplinary history, institutional work record, family and community ties, and mental stability while incarcerated. Reclassification is an important part of good institutional management because it can take into account the inmate's most recent behavior. Past behavior is generally conceded to be the best predictor of future behavior, and recent behavior is better than remote behavior. Therefore, the consideration of recent behavior is important to avoid over- or underclassifying inmates whose behavior has changed since their last evaluation.

***Evaluation.*** It is one thing to develop an objective classification system, but quite another to determine whether it is working as intended. One of the advantages of this type of system is that it readily lends itself to evaluation. Since the criteria are objective, they can be measured and reduced to a form that is suitable for statistical analysis. Subjective determinations are more difficult to operationalize, and therefore less susceptible to evaluation. Analysis is facilitated even further if the classification data is entered into a computer database. With the information in that form, periodic evaluations can be accomplished by simply running the appropriate computer program.

There are several good reasons for evaluating the operation of classification systems. One important factor is that these systems are in a period of relative infancy (Alexander and Austin 1992). Most of these systems have been in use less than ten years, and many less than five years. With such short histories, it is important to evaluate the systems to see if they are actually an improvement over the old systems. Pilot studies must be relied on in the development stage, but once a system has been implemented its actual operation should be validated to see if it is living up to expectations. Even a system that is properly developed may need some fine tuning after a period of practical experience.

Modification of the system may also be needed in response to changes in the inmate population. New laws or changing law enforcement policies may alter the characteristics of the prisoners. For example, legal changes that require violent offenders to serve a greater percentage of their sentences before release will eventually result in a higher proportion of violent offenders in the prison population. This "hardening" of the population may result in significant changes in the distribution of security and custody levels among the inmates.

In addition, evaluation is essential in defending the system from legal attack. A system that can be shown to be properly designed and to work well in practice is less vulnerable to claims that it violates inmates' constitutional rights than one that is not supported by such documentation. In some cases, courts have required ongoing evaluation as part of the resolution of prison litigation.

Evaluation is also important for staff training purposes. Examples of improper implementation by staff members might include an excessive use of overrides or improper application of the classification criteria. A well-designed evaluation will point out such problems, which then can be addressed by additional staff training that is specific to the problem.

Evaluation can be done for the entire classified population or for a selected sample of the population. One advantage of computerized systems is that they will usually allow analysis of the whole database. This is not only more accurate than using a sample, but avoids the problems of sample selection. If a sample of the population is to be used, it should be scientifically structured to achieve the specific goals of the evaluation (Alexander and Austin 1992).

An important step in an evaluation is to determine the questions that the evaluation should answer. Although the questions will vary according to specific circumstances, there are some important areas of inquiry. One is the consistency of the results of the procedures. If the system is truly objective, then different analysts should reach similar classification decisions with inmates who have similar characteristics. This area of inquiry can reveal a lack of proper staff training or staff resistance to the new system.

It is also important to know the impact of the new system on the distribution of classification decisions. States that have done these evaluations have usually found that the number of cases that are overclassified is reduced (Alexander and Austin 1992). Reductions in security and custody levels can lessen the need for new facilities.

Effects of the new system may also be seen in such matters as the frequency of disciplinary violations, participation in rehabilitative programs, and the use of medical services. In the long term, evaluation can even assess the impact of the system on percentage of sentences served by inmates before release, and on their return to prison by parole violation or new offense. With proper evaluation, the effects of the new system can be documented and appropriate adjustments can be undertaken.

## CLASSIFICATION BY PSYCHOLOGICAL INSTRUMENTS

As seen above, objective classification systems rely primarily on historical and demographic information to assign inmates to security and custody levels. However, this sort of data may not be the best method of assessment for some purposes or for some inmates. For example, some inmates will need to be assessed to determine the need for psychological treatment. While historical data can provide important clues about emotionally disturbed inmates, they are less than ideal for determining actual treatment needs. Other people, especially new inmates and young offenders, do not have an historical track record on which to base decisions. The documentation of their previous behavior may not show, for instance, that they are likely to exploit other inmates or to be subject to victimization. For these and other purposes it is useful to have other sources of information on which to base classification decisions.

While the trend toward objective systems seems to have dominated classification for security and custody purposes, another type of classification system has developed based on the use of psychological principles. These systems can be used as the sole source of classification, but more typically they are used as a supplement to objective systems; to classify for special purposes inmates who have already been assigned to security and custody levels. This means of augmenting the initial management determination may be called *internal classification* (Van Voorhis 1994).

There is certainly an overlap between the functions of these two types of systems. The determination that a prisoner is a suicide risk, for example, can be based on a history of suicide attempts or on a psychological assessment. Ideally, the two may be used together to provide prison administrators with the best information available about those whom they incarcerate.

In general, psychological classification systems base their determinations on two factors: personality traits and reasoning ability. Personality traits, such as hostility or depression, give information about how an individual will respond emotionally, which can lead to predictions of the person's behavior. They are also key indicators of the need for psychological treatment or the type of treatment that may be most efficacious. A person's reasoning ability, on the other hand, gives information about how she functions intellectually, which also allows some prediction of behavior and has implications for treatment. An inmate, for example, who thinks only in concrete terms may tend to act on impulse without thinking about the long-range consequences of his behavior.

While useful for many purposes, psychological classification systems have their drawbacks. One is that they generally require the services of a professional, such as a psychologist, psychiatrist, or social worker, to be of maximum benefit. Because these highly trained personnel are often in short supply in a prison staff, the internal classification process can easily become backlogged or can be given less attention than it should receive. In addition, the gathering of data for analysis may be a difficult process compared to the relatively straightforward information used for objective classification. For psychological classification systems to work properly inmates are usually required to undergo lengthy interviews or tests, which may create administrative difficulties. Inmates frequently are uncooperative or manipulative, either of which can affect the validity of a psychological assessment.

Several methods of psychological classification for prison inmates have been developed in the post-World War II period. In particular, the last 30 years have seen extensive research and development of these systems (Van Voorhis 1994). The following are descriptions of three of the methods that have been the subject of empirical research. All three systems are in use in various prison systems in this country. They are included as examples of the wide variety of psychological tests that may be used for internal classification, although many other psychological tests are available for that purpose.

***MMPI-Based Classification.***   The *Minnesota Multiphasic Personality Inventory (MMPI)* was developed in the 1930s as a diagnostic and research test. The original MMPI is a paper-and-pencil test, although it may be administered verbally to people who cannot read. It consists of 566 statements that the person answers "true" or "false." The answers are used to give scores on ten clinical scales, each of which describes a particular psychological characteristic. Scales of particular interest for the classification of offenders include Scale 2 — Depression (D); Scale 3 — Hysteria (Hy); Scale 4 — Psychopathic Deviate (Pd); Scale 6 — Paranoia (Pa); and Scale 0 — Social Introversion (Si). In addition, there are three scales, called L, F, and K, that are used to assess the validity of the subject's answers. Since the development of these standard scales, researchers have developed many other scales for specific research or clinical purposes.

As an example of the type of statements used, a selection of test items from the Psychopathic Deviate scale are shown in Highlight

---

**HIGHLIGHT 4-3**
**Selected Questions from Scale 4, Psychopathic Deviate (Pd)**

Some of these questions are scored on this scale if they are answered "true," others if they are answered "false."

— I am sure I get a raw deal from life.
— If people had not had it in for me I would have been much more successful.
— I do many things which I regret afterwards.
— I know who is responsible for most of my troubles.
— My way of doing things is apt to be misunderstood by others.
— My daily life is full of things that keep me interested.
— I have never been in trouble because of my sexual behavior.
— At times my thoughts have raced ahead faster than I could speak them.
— I have been quite independent and free from family rule.
— I am always disgusted with the law when a criminal is freed through the arguments of a smart lawyer.

---

4-3. The full scale is comprised of 50 test items. Some of the statements are scored on this scale if they are answered "true" and others if they are answered "false."

The subject's scores on all the scales may be plotted on a line graph so that they form a type of figure referred to as a *profile*. In the development and subsequent research of the MMPI, it has been shown that these profiles tend to fall into patterns, and that particular patterns indicate certain psychological characteristics.

The MMPI was used with offenders for diagnostic purposes from its inception. However, it was not until the late 1970s that it was used to develop a formal classification system. The Megargee MMPI-based typology was developed with prisoners at a federal correctional institution. The MMPI profiles of a sample of inmates were compared for similarity by a statistical process called *cluster analysis*. The data developed ten groups, or "clusters," with similar MMPI profiles and psychological characteristics. The psychological similarities of members of each group may be used to indicate their treatment needs and to predict their behavior. This understanding, in turn, can be used for determining appropriate treatment, as well as for management purposes such as housing and work assignments. Once the similarities of the profiles within each group were understood, a method was divised to assign new MMPI profiles to the groups. Thereafter, using the rules developed in the original research, new inmates could be classified on the basis of their MMPI scores (Megargee and Bohn 1979).

The Megargee classification method has been the subject of numerous research projects. It has been shown in a replication study that some similar groups of MMPI profiles were found in research done with a population of halfway-house residents (Mrad, Kabacoff, and Duckro 1983). Although the original subjects were males, another replication study done with female inmates found some similar groups of MMPI profiles in that population as well (Shaffer et al. 1983).

Attempts to classify various populations of offenders with this system have generally shown that about 90 percent of the MMPI profiles of individuals tested can be placed into one of the groups, with the rest forming an unclassifiable remainder. However, studies of inmates who have been classified into these groups have not shown the results to be consistent. If the groups are placed along a continuum from the least pathological to the most pathological, differences in the behaviors of the members of the different groups are generally apparent only between those that are at the extremes of the continuum. The groups in the middle of the spectrum do not show clear and consistent differences in behavior.

Since the development of the Megargee classification system, an updated version of the MMPI has been introduced. Called the MMPI-2, it maintained the same basic format but eliminated many problematic test items and introduced new items. Although the MMPI is still in use, the trend is to replace it with the MMPI-2. It has been shown that, by modifying the rules for classifying profiles, MMPI-2 profiles can be used with the Megargee system (Megargee 1994).

***Adult Internal Management System.***   The *Adult Internal Management System (AIMS)* is also known as the *Quay system* (Van Voorhis 1994). This system uses two rating instruments that are filled out by prison officials. One is the Correctional Adjective Checklist, which is completed by correctional personnel after the inmate has been through the intake or diagnostic process. It is a structured way to describe the behaviors that the inmate has displayed during his entry into the prison system. The other instrument is the Life History Checklist. This is also filled out by a classification specialist but is based on the records of the inmate's history and an interview (Levinson 1988). The use of prison personnel to complete the forms means that only minimal cooperation from the inmates is required.

The system was developed for the U.S. Bureau of Prisons. Two lists of words and short descriptions were developed to describe inmates' behaviors and life histories. These descriptions were applied to samples of inmates by correctional personnel and the results were analyzed by a statistical method known as factor analysis. The results of the analysis of the two rating instruments were used together to develop five factors, or dimensions, for the purpose of classification (Quay 1973).

The five dimensions that are rated by this system are Asocial Aggressive, Immature Dependent, Manipulative, Neurotic Anxious, and Situational (Van Voorhis 1994). These scores can be used to determine suitable housing and program assignments for inmates. AIMS, like the MMPI-based system, uses personality characteristics to predict behavior.

*Interpersonal Maturity Level System.*   A well-known internal classification system based on intellectual development is the *Interpersonal Maturity Level (I-level)* system. Initially developed as a project of the California Youth Authority, it was first applied to delinquent youths but has since been applied to adults as well (Harris 1988). The system classifies individuals according to their level of conceptual maturity, which has implications for behavior. Conceptual maturity is seen as a developmental process beginning in infancy and continuing through the course of one's life. There are several theoretical levels of maturity, but four of them are considered relevant for classifying offenders: I-levels 2, 3, 4, and 5. Subtypes have been identified within I-levels as 2, 3, and 4. The levels and subtypes are as follows:

| | |
|---|---|
| I(2) | Asocial Passive |
| | Asocial Aggressive |
| I(3) | Immature Conformist |
| | Cultural Conformist |
| | Manipulator |
| I(4) | Neurotic Acting Out |
| | Neurotic Anxious |
| | Cultural Identifier |
| | Situational-Emotional Reaction (Harris 1988) |

Both the level and subtype can be said to have behavioral consequences that can assist in making internal classification decisions.

The original I-level system is based on a clinical interview using open-ended questions. The interview is lengthy and requires the full attention of a trained interviewer. These factors make the process less desirable for the classification of large numbers of inmates. A more recent derivation is the *Jesness Inventory* (Jesness 1988). This system is based on the same levels and subtypes of development but uses a 155-item paper-and-pencil test that is easier to administer and score.

## CONCLUSIONS

Classification is currently an important topic for the corrections system. It is a valuable tool in dealing with the population pressures in modern prisons. Classification can help to relieve some of the problems caused by prison overcrowding. It has also been influenced by prisoners' rights litigation. Although the U.S. Supreme Court has handed down few decisions bearing directly on classification, lower courts have given the issue greater consideration.

Classification is used for many purposes, which may be divided into the general categories of management and rehabilitation. The recent trend has been to use objective classification systems for management purposes, such as security and custody classification. The use of objective systems has followed the decline of the medical model of corrections and the rise of the justice model, which emphasizes punishment over treatment. Objective classification systems may be augmented by psychology-based systems. These are usually used for internal classification purposes, which include some management matters such as housing and work assignment, as well as classification for treatment and rehabilitation. One important purpose of classification is job assignment. The next chapter looks at the types of work that may be done by those incarcerated in prisons.

## Vocabulary

Adult Internal Management System (AIMS)
classification
custody classification
disparate impact

disparate treatment
hands off doctrine
internal classification
Interpersonal Maturity Level (I-level)

medical model overclassification
Minnesota Multiphasic Personality
  Inventory (MMPI)
objective classification
override

reclassification
security classification

## Study Questions

1. Discuss how the movement away from the medical model of corrections has influenced the development of classification.

2. What sort of classification system would best be suited to dealing with problems of institutional overcrowding?

3. Why has there been a movement toward the development of objective classification systems for prison management?

4. What are the underlying principles of an objective classification system?

5. Why is evaluation of a classification system important?

6. What are the underlying assumptions of a classification system based on psychology?

7. What is the proper relationship between classification for management and for rehabilitation? Do the two overlap?

## Sources Cited

— Alexander, J. 1986. "Classification Objectives and Practices." *Crime and Delinquency* 32(3): 323-338.

— Alexander, J., and J. Austin. 1992. *Handbook for Evaluating Objective Prison Classification Systems.* Boulder, Colo.: National Institute of Corrections.

— American Correctional Association. 1966. *Manual of Correctional Standards.* College Park, Md: American Correctional Association.

— American Correctional Association. 1975. *Correctional Classification and Treatment*. Cincinnati: Anderson.

— American Correctional Association. 1981. *Standards for Adult Correctional Institutions*. Rockville, Md: American Correctional Association.

— Apao, W. K., L. D. Haugh, and E. Meyer. n.d. *Improving Prison Classification Procedures: Application of an Interaction Model*. National Institute of Justice. Washington, D.C.: GPO.

— Ashford, J. B., and C. W. LeCroy. 1988. "Predicting Recidivism: An Evaluation of the Wisconsin Juvenile Probation and Aftercare Risk Instrument." *Criminal Justice and Behavior* 15(2): 141-151.

— Austin, J. 1986. "Evaluating How Well Your Classification System Is Operating: A Practical Approach." *Crime and Delinquency* 32(3): 302-322.

— Austin, R. L. 1975. "Construct Validity of I-level Classification." *Criminal Justice and Behavior* 2(2): 113-129.

— Ben-Porath, Y. S., D. D. Shondrick, and K. P. Stafford. 1995. "MMPI-2 and Race in a Forensic Diagnostic Sample." *Criminal Justice and Behavior* 22(1): 19-32.

— Buchanan, R. A., K. L. Whitlow, and J. Austin. 1986. "National Evaluation of Objective Prison Classification Systems: The Current State of the Art." *Crime and Delinquency* 32(3): 272-290.

— Buchanan, R. A., and K. L. Whitlow. 1987. *Guidelines for Developing, Implementing, and Revising an Objective Prison Classification System*. National Institute of Justice. Washington, D.C.: GPO.

— Burke, P., and L. Adams. 1991. *Classification of Women Offenders in State Correctional Facilities: A Handbook for Practitioners*. National Institute of Corrections. Washington, D.C.: GPO.

— Carbonell, J. L. 1983. "Inmate Classification Systems: A Cross-Tabulation of Two Methods." *Criminal Justice and Behavior* 10(3): 285-292.

— Carey, R. J., J. P. Garske, and J. Ginsberg. 1986. "The Prediction of Adjustment to Prison by Means of an MMPI-Based Classification System." *Criminal Justice and Behavior* 13(4): 347-365.

— Clements, C. B. 1979. "Crowded Prisons: A Review of Psychological and Environmental Effects." *Law and Human Behavior* 3(3): 217-225.

— Clements, C. B. 1981. "The Future of Offender Classification: Some Cautions and Prospects." *Criminal Justice and Behavior* 8(1): 15-38.

— Clements, C. B. 1982. "The Relationship of Offender Classification to the Problems of Prison Overcrowding." *Crime and Delinquency* 28(1): 72-81.

— Dahlstrom, W. G., J. H. Panton, K. P. Bain, and L. E. Dahlstrom. 1986. "Utility of the Megargee-Bohn MMPI Typological Assignments: Study of a Sample of Death Row Inmates." *Criminal Justice and Behavior* 13(1): 5-17.

— Durham, A. M., III. 1994. *Crisis and Reform: Current Issues in American Punishment.* Boston: Little, Brown.

— Ennis, B. J., and T. R. Litwack. 1974. "Psychiatry and the Presumption of Expertise: Flipping Coins in the Courtroom." *California Law Review* 62: 693-725.

— Fauteck, P. K. 1995. "Detecting the Malingering of Psychosis in Offenders: No Easy Solutions." *Criminal Justice and Behavior* 22(1): 3-18.

— Flynn, E. E. 1978. *Handbook on Correctional Classification.* Laural, Md.: American Correctional Association.

— Forcier, M. W. 1992. *Development of an Objective Classification System.* Boulder, Colo.: National Institute of Corrections.

— Friedt, L. R., and W. D. Gouvier. 1989. "Bender Gestalt Screening for Brain Dysfunction in a Forensic Population." *Criminal Justice and Behavior* 16(4): 455-464.

— Gibbons, D. C. 1988. "Some Critical Observations on Criminal Types and Criminal Careers." *Criminal Justice and Behavior* 15(1): 8-23.

— Hanson, R. W., C. S. Moss, R. E. Hosford, and M. E. Johnson. 1983. "Predicting Inmate Penitentiary Adjustment: An Assessment of Four Classificatory Methods." *Criminal Justice and Behavior* 10(3): 293-309.

— Harris, P. W. 1988. "The Interpersonal Maturity Level Classification System: I-level." *Criminal Justice and Behavior* 15(1): 58-77.

— Hiscock, C. K., L. B. Layman, and M. Hiscock. 1994. "Cross-validation of Two Measures for Assessing Feigned Mental Incompetence in Male Prison Inmates." *Criminal Justice and Behavior* 21(4): 443-453.

— Jesness, C. F. 1988. "The Jesness Inventory Classification System." *Criminal Justice and Behavior* 15(1): 78-91.

— Kane, T. R. 1986. "The Validity of Prison Classification: An Introduction to Practical Considerations and Research Issues." *Crime and Delinquency* 32(3): 367-390.

— Kennedy, T. D. 1986. "Trends in Inmate Classification: A Status Report of Two Computerized Psychometric Approaches." *Criminal Justice and Behavior* 13(2): 165-184.

— Lerner, K., G. Arling, and S. C. Baird. 1986. "Client Management Classification Strategies for Case Supervision." *Crime and Delinquency* 32(3): 254-271.

— Levinson, R. B. 1988. "Developments in the Classification Process: Quay's AIMS Approach." *Criminal Justice and Behavior* 15(1): 24-38.

— Levinson, R. B., and R. E. Gerard. 1986. "Classifying Institutions." *Crime and Delinquency* 32(3): 291-301.

— Levitt, A., and D. Lester. 1984. "The Levitt Conscious Preference-Rejection Test." *Research Communications in Psychology, Psychiatry and Behavior* 9(4): 435-438.

— LIS, Inc. 1992. *Jail Classification System Development: A Review of the Literature*. National Institute of Corrections. Washington, D.C.: GPO.

— Louscher, P. K., R. E. Hosford, and C. S. Moss. 1983. "Predicting Dangerous Behavior in a Penitentiary Using the Megargee Typology." *Criminal Justice and Behavior* 10(3): 269-284.

— Loza, W., and D. J. Simourd. 1994. "Psychometric Evaluation of the Level of Supervision Inventory (LSI) among Male Canadian Federal Offenders." *Criminal Justice and Behavior* 21(4): 468-480.

— MacKenzie, D. L., C. D. Posey, and K. R. Rapaport. 1988. "A Theoretical Revolution in Corrections: Varied Purposes for Classification." *Criminal Justice and Behavior* 15(1): 125-136.

— Martinson, R. 1974. "What Works? — Questions and Answers about Prison Reform." *Public Interest* 35: 22-54.

— Megargee, E. I. 1994. "Using the Megargee MMPI-Based Classification System with MMPI-2s of Male Prison Inmates." *Psychological Assessment* 6(4): 337-344.

— Megargee, E. I., and M. J. Bohn. 1979. *Classifying Criminal Offenders: A New System Based on the MMPI*. Beverly Hills, Cal.: Sage.

— Megargee, E. I., and J. L. Carbonell. 1986. "Predicting Prison Adjustment with the MMPI: A Summary of Three Studies." *The Differential View* 14 (August): 8-15.

— Meloy, J. R. 1986. "Rapid Classification of the Functionally Psychotic Individual in Custody." *Criminal Justice and Behavior* 13(2): 185-195.

— Monahan, J. 1984. "The Prediction of Violent Behavior: Toward a Second Generation of Theory and Policy." *American Journal of Psychiatry* 141(1): 10-15.

— Moss, C. S., M. E. Johnson, and R. E. Hosford. 1984. "An Assessment of the Megargee Typology in Lifelong Criminal Violence." *Criminal Justice and Behavior* 11(2): 225-234.

— Motiuk, L. L., J. Bonta, and D. A. Andrews. 1986. "Classification in Correctional Halfway Houses: The Relative and Incremental Predictive Criterion Validities of the Megargee-MMPI and LSI Systems." *Criminal Justice and Behavior* 13(1): 33-46.

— Motiuk, M. S., L. L. Motiuk, and J. Bonta. 1992. "A Comparison between Self-Report and Interview-Based Inventories in Offender Classification." *Criminal Justice and Behavior* 19(2): 143-159.

— Mrad, D. F., R. Kabacoff, and P. Duckro. 1983. "Validation of the Megargee Typology in a Halfway House Setting." *Criminal Justice and Behavior* 10(3): 252-262.

— New Jersey Department of Corrections. 1994. *National Survey of Classification Operations and Procedures.* Office of Policy and Planning, New Jersey Department of Corrections.

— Nicholas, S. C., and A. Loeb. 1991. "Legal Analysis." In *Classification of Women Offenders in State Correctional Facilities: A Handbook for Practitioners,* ed. P. Burke and L. Adams. Boulder, Colo.: National Institute of Corrections.

— Oldroyd, R. J. 1975. "A Principal Components Analysis of the BPI and MMPI." *Criminal Justice and Behavior* 2(1): 85-90.

— Quay, H. C. 1973. Classification. Paper presented at the Annual Meeting of the American Society of Criminology, New York City, November 1973.

— Rafter, N. H. 1993. "Equality or Difference?" In *Female Offenders: Meeting the Needs of a Neglected Population,* ed. ACA. Baltimore, Md.: United Book Press.

— Reitsma-Street, M., and A. W. Leschied. 1988. "The Conceptual Level Matching Model in Corrections." *Criminal Justice and Behavior* 15(1): 92-108.

— Rothman, D. J. 1980. *Conscience and Convenience.* Boston: Little, Brown.

— Shaffer, C. E., C. G. Pettigrew, D. Blouin, and D. W. Edwards. 1983. "Multivariate Classification of Female Offender MMPI Profiles." *Journal of Crime and Justice* 6: 57-66.

— Sharp, J. 1994. Behind the Walls: The Price and Performance of the Texas Department of Criminal Justice. Report from the Texas Performance Review of the Comptroller of Public Accounts.

— Smith, R. L. 1985. "The Assessment of Risk: A Survey of the Current Art and Practice of the United States and Canada Procedures for Security and Custody Categorization of Prisoners Prepared for the British Home Office Research and Planning Unit." Berkeley, Cal.: Executive Management and Consultation.

— Snell, T. L., and D. C. Morton. 1994. *Women in Prison: Survey of Prison Inmates, 1991.* Bureau of Justice Statistics Special Report. Washington, D.C.: GPO.

— Toch, H. 1981. "Inmate Classification as a Transaction." *Criminal Justice and Behavior* 8(1): 3-14.

— Tzeng, O. C. S., W. A. Maxey, R. Fortier, and D. Landis. 1985. "Construct Evaluation of the Tennessee Self Concept Scale." *Educational and Psychological Measurement* 45: 64-78.

— Van Voorhis, P. 1988. "A Cross Classification of Five Offender Typologies: Issues of Construct and Predictive Validity." *Criminal Justice and Behavior* 15(1): 109-124.

— Van Voorhis, P. 1994. *Psychological Classification of the Adult Male Prison Inmate.* Albany: State University of New York Press.

— Walters, G. D. 1986. "Correlates of the Megargee Criminal Classification System: A Military Correctional Setting." *Criminal Justice and Behavior* 13(1): 19-32.

— Wright, K. N. 1988. "The Relationship of Risk, Needs, and Personality Classification Systems and Prison Adjustment." *Criminal Justice and Behavior* 15(4): 454-471.

— Zager, L. D. 1988. "The MMPI-Based Classification System: A Review, Current Status, and Future Directions." *Criminal Justice and Behavior* 15(1): 39-57.

# 5

# INDUSTRY, AGRICULTURE, AND EDUCATION

## *William Stone*

When our country is embarking upon a multibillion dollar prison construction program, it is fair to ask: "Are we going to build more expensive human 'warehouses,' or should we change our thinking and move toward factories with fences around them, where inmates can acquire education and vocational training and then produce marketable goods?" (Burger 1985, 754)

---------------- *Chapter Overview* ----------------

—— **HISTORY OF INMATE LABOR**
        England
        Early America
            *Private Sector Interest in Prison Labor*
            *Civil War and the Rise of Prison Agriculture*
—— **THE TWENTIETH CENTURY AND PRISON LABOR**
—— **PRISON LABOR TODAY**
        Agricultural Programs
        Manufacturing Programs
        Public Works and Prison Construction
        Prison Maintenance
—— **CURRENT ISSUES IN PRISON LABOR**
        Displacement of Civilian Jobs
        Inmate Wages and Compensation
        Inmate Safety and Security
        Cost Effectiveness of Prison Industry
—— **INMATE EDUCATION**
—— **CONTEMPORARY VOCATIONAL EDUCATION PROGRAMS**
        Female Inmates and Vocational Education
        External Contracting of Vocational Education
        Vocational Training and Recidivism
—— **CONTEMPORARY ACADEMIC EDUCATION PROGRAMS**
        Adult Basic Education Programs
        General Education Development Programs

Prison College Programs
Educational Release Programs
—— CONCLUSIONS

Traditionally, we are conditioned to think of forced prison labor as an integral by-product of incarceration; however, it is probably true that imprisonment is actually the by-product of the need for forced labor. In recent years the issue of inmate idleness has caused us to reexamine how inmates spend their time while in state custody. Is the role of prison simply to educate and reform prisoners? Or is there a broader obligation to make restitution to the society as well as to improve the inmate?

# HISTORY OF INMATE LABOR

Early systems of punishment generally were based on the principles of corporal punishment, capital punishment, or banishment. These punishments were logical and efficient in that they required few government resources to carry out sentences. There is some evidence of other considerations in early systems of punishment; for example, both the Sumerian Codes and the Hammurabic Code contain references to the use of forced labor as punishment (Allen and Simonsen 1992). It is very difficult to determine how frequently these early societies used forced labor because so very few records from this time period exist.

As governments became more complex and started providing more public services like road and sewer construction, the need for public labor obviously increased. With this increased need for labor came a corresponding need for containing the forced laborers while the public projects were completed. The Mamertine Prison built under the sewers of Rome in 64 B.C. was an example of an early prison built to hold inmates condemned under the Roman penal servitude concept (Johnston 1973). It is also well known that Roman roads, aqueducts, and sewers were built throughout the empire with the assistance of forced labor. Western civilization was not alone in its desire to capitalize on the use of convict labor. Much of the labor used to construct the Great Wall of China was provided by offenders sentenced under the Chinese laws of the time. While most of these early convict laborers were maintained in camps, cages, and natural sites like mines, the need for mass labor obviously contributed to the need for mass confinement.

## ENGLAND

The link between imprisonment and labor can be traced throughout history from the earliest forms of prisons to very recent penal philosophy. The English House of Corrections built at Bridewell in 1557 was based on a strict work ethic. As noted in a previous chapter, we in America generally credit the Walnut Street Jail with being the forerunner of the modern penitentiary while the English give this credit to the Bridewell Institution (Carney 1979). The forced work ethic of the Bridewell would be reflected in most of the houses of corrections of the time. The famous Hospice of San Michael, established in 1704, was also based on an ethic of hard labor and silence. Generally, the labor in these early institutions was intended to be productive in nature, such as gardening, food preparation, and tailoring. It was thought that harsh productive labor would help support the institution, teach a trade, and instill moral discipline. Traditionally men and women would be assigned work suitable to their social roles of the time. For example, women would be assigned food preparation and "domestic" labor, and men would be assigned traditional farm and manufacturing jobs.

This same work-oriented philosophy was proposed for more formal penal institutions as well. In 1696, John Bellers, a Quaker businessman, proposed his College of Industry. Bellers's plan involved creating a communitarian industrial colony within the walls of the prison at Bristol. In the same year, John Locke proposed the creation of formal industries within penal workhouses as a means of reducing the public cost of imprisonment (Ignatieff 1978). The intent of these early reformers was to devise a system that would benefit the inmates by training them in a usable trade and benefit the public by reducing the cost of confinement. There were times, however, when the "productive-work" philosophy would be subverted and result in such correctional extremes as the treadmill and shot drill, two classic forms of nonproductive inmate labor. *Treadmills* (or treadwheels) were originally designed as a source of industrial power but were later converted to provide forced unproductive labor. They consisted of a wheel, equipped with treads, that a person would step on to make the wheel move. Resistance was provided by weights or paddles in water. The *shot drill* consisted of repetitively picking up and setting down large cannon balls, or "shot." (These two means of forced labor might be considered the historical version of modern-day stair-steppers and free weights!) In general, productive labor such as the road work done by the Irish penal system was more typical of inmate labor (Carney 1979).

## EARLY AMERICA

The philosophy of sentencing inmates to hard labor was also common practice here in the United States. With the adoption of William Penn's "Great Law" in 1682, the concept of substituting hard labor for corporal punishment was clearly established (Clare and Kramer 1976). When the first state prisons were being established in the late eighteenth and early nineteenth centuries, provisions for inmate labor were incorporated into all the prison systems. The Pennsylvania prison system, with its philosophy of isolation, would adopt a system of laboring in individual cells at spinning wheels, small textile looms, and shoemaking (Wines and Dwight 1867). The Auburn penitentiary, with its congregate philosophy, would apply a more mechanized approach and operate traditional textile mills and other industries within its walls. With the ultimate dominance of the Auburn type of correctional institution and its ability to utilize industrialized production systems, it was not surprising that the "factory prison" evolved in the United States.

The early prison industries focused on several labor intensive types of industries. The choice of industries was heavily influenced by the fact that inmates generally represented an unskilled labor force. Probably the most common type of early industry was the textile mill. Textile mills could be operated by relatively unskilled labor and were a high-profit industry of the time. State legislators of this time period could see the obvious advantage of industrializing their prisons. Industrialization would reach from Maine to the frontier areas like Texas. The focus of these early industrial efforts were clearly for the benefit of the state, not to teach inmates a trade or improve the conditions of their confinement. The industrialization of American prisons was simply a state-based version of the evolving industrial systems in the United States that were exploiting the immigrant classes during this same period. In 1850, the director of the Texas prison was denied his request for $10,000 to finish the outer walls of the prison and provide living quarters for the inmate population. However, in 1854 the same legislators would appropriate $40,000 for the construction of the prison's first textile mill (Stone, McAdams, and Kollert 1974).

***Private Sector Interest in Prison Labor.***   The rise of prison industries would bring about the first efforts at privatization of prisons, a subject that Chapter 11 explores in greater detail. The earliest form of privatization was the *lease labor system*. An individual would bid for the temporary ownership of a state prison. The winning bidder would then become the leaseholder and gain almost total control of the prison and its labor. The leaseholder was responsible for providing the inmates with food, clothing, and other essentials as well as being in charge of the industrial operations of the prison. A leaseholder could maximize his profits by working the inmates as hard as possible and spending as little as possible on their care. The leases were frequently very profitable. In 1855, Zebulon Ward leased the Kentucky prison for an annual rent of $6,000. At the end of his four-year lease, he had amassed a personal fortune close to $75,000 (Wines and Dwight 1867, 260).

In Texas, the legislature passed a law in 1866 permitting the prison to lease out inmates in groups no smaller than 20 inmates per lease. These leases allowed the inmates to leave the prison to work on plantations and railroad construction, with the security being provided by the lessee. While the leasing of complete prison systems was subject to some problems, these remote site leases, like the ones in Texas, produced the worst abuses. The escapes and deaths under the Texas lease system jumped from a total of 104 in 1873 to 376 by 1875, one of the worst years for the lease system. During the calendar year of 1875 a total of 26 percent of all the inmates in Texas either escaped or died (Stone, McAdams, and Kollert 1974).

It had become clear by the 1850s that prison industries could be run at a profit. Inmates generally represented unskilled and unmotivated workers, but it was still possible to make a profit because they could be obtained so cheaply. Inmate laborers generally were worked from "bell to bell," this representing the amount of daylight hours available. During the winter months, the workday was about eight hours, however, with the coming of summer the workday might extend to twelve hours. The profitability was best described by Moses C. Pilsbury, a prominent penologist in 1866:

> The case stands thus: The labor of twelve convicts will cost no more per day than that of four citizens; yet the convicts will do nine days work while the citizens will do four. Thus every dollar paid for convict labor will produce as much as two dollars and a quarter expended on citizen labor. (Wines and Dwight 1867, 256-257)

It was obvious that inmate labor was not the equal of free-world labor, yet it was possible with effort and corporal punishment to make inmate labor a good investment.

It is important to recognize that these early prison industries were not all run in a corrupt or exploitative fashion; neither were the legislators of the time evil men. Most states established boards of labor or prison inspectors to make sure that inmates were not treated in an inhumane manner. Some of the early leases included clauses that required the contractor to rotate the job assignments to ensure that the inmates learned all the different parts of the trade they were practicing (Wines and Dwight 1867). Prison industries suffered many scandals and problems, yet they existed in almost every prison and prospered into the first part of the twentieth century.

*Civil War and the Rise of Prison Agriculture.*   While the latter part of the nineteenth century was prosperous for prison industries located in the northern states, the same could not be said for the prison industries of the South. The primary problem for the prison industries in the South was the economic depression in the post-Civil War period. In the post-Civil War depression, southern prison industries could not find suitable markets for their goods, and the supply of many of the raw materials necessary for production was very erratic.

In an attempt to support the southern prisons during this period, many southern states largely abandoned traditional industries and started to focus on agriculture as a way to generate money from the available prison labor force. During the post-Civil War depression, land was very cheap, and southern states started purchasing land in sufficient quantities to create state-run plantations. In Wines's descriptions of northern state prisons in 1867, the premises (including the surrounding grounds) ran from one-half acre in New Hampshire to 20 acres in Wisconsin. In contrast, Texas purchased the Harlem Farm in 1885, which contained 5,011 acres of farmland. Agricultural production seemed a logical choice for many southern prisons because it was low investment, used unskilled labor, and promised a reasonable profit. By the early twentieth century, immense farm labor programs evolved in Texas and Oklahoma (Clare and Kramer 1976).

Women generally were exempt from farm labor assignments because they were not perceived as suitable, except for perhaps working in "kitchen gardens." Women during this time period normally were confined separately and used for support activities like garment manufacturing and repair (Pollock 1990).

# THE TWENTIETH CENTURY AND PRISON LABOR

At the start of the twentieth century, both industrial-based and agricultural-based prison labor encountered significant problems. The development of efficient farming equipment changed the labor intensive nature of the agricultural industry. Prison farms, even with relatively cheap labor, could not compete with mechanized private farming. By the 1930s, prison farming was largely reduced to growing food crops and raising livestock for consumption by the inmate population. One of the few exceptions to this was the Texas prison system, where cotton crops, processed in the prison textile mill, continue as a viable enterprise to this date. Prison agriculture for internal consumption still represents a major function in many prisons today. In 1991, prison agricultural production exceeded $45 million in value (American Correctional Association 1992).

Traditional manufacturing industries fared little better than agriculture in the first half of the twentieth century. With the growing power of the American labor movement and the initial effects of the Depression, opposition to prison manufacturing increased. In almost every state, labor groups and manufacturers raised complaints that prison manufacturing represented unfair competition from the state. By the early part of the century, more than half of the states had adopted *state-use laws* (Clare and Krammer 1976). The state-use laws provided that goods manufactured with prison labor could not be sold on the open market. Under these laws, prison products could be used only by the prison itself or other state agencies.

With the growing power of labor in the late 1920s came federal intervention in prison-produced goods. In 1929, the Hawes-Cooper Act was passed, which required that prison-produced goods shipped interstate were subject to the laws of the receiving state. This blocked those states that did not have state-use laws from shipping their goods to any state that did have such a law. The situation became worse for prison industries in 1935 with the passage of the Ashurst-Sumner Act. It required that all prison-made goods be clearly labeled with the name of the prison and prohibited interstate shipment of almost all products to those states with laws restricting their sales. The final blow came with the 1940 amendment to the Ashurst-Sumner Act, which completely prohibited the interstate shipment of prison products except for some tractor parts and agricultural produce.

Prison industries remained stagnant from the 1940s through the early 1970s. The state-use concept continued, and some states developed a surprising array of products, all consumed by the prison and other state agencies. In 1972, over 360 prison industries were operating in the United States (Grisson and Conan 1981). The Federal prison system also adopted the state-use system. An act of Congress in 1934 established UNICOR, a wholly owned government corporation responsible for the operation of the industries within the Federal prisons. UNICOR's operations include such activities as:

1. Providing products to federal agencies at fair market prices;
2. Developing products that minimize competition with private sector industry and labor;
3. Providing inmates the opportunity to earn funds;
4. Providing inmates with job training opportunities; and,
5. Reducing inmate idle time (Snarr 1992, 172).

UNICOR became heavily involved in the production of military equipment during World War II. Several prison industries operated more than one shift per day and seven days a week during the war (Allen and Simonsen 1986). The production of equipment in support of the war effort provided both economic and political support for the Federal Bureau of Prisons. UNICOR is still in operation, currently employs about 27 percent of all federal inmates, and produces about $200 million in goods annually.

In 1979 Congress removed some of the barriers to interstate shipment of prison-made goods. The passage of the Private Sector Prison Industry Enhancement Certification Program, often called the *PIE program,* permitted certified states to sell goods on the open market. States wishing to be certified had to meet all the requirements of the PIE program, which included:

1. Paying the inmates wages comparable with similar jobs in the community;
2. Consulting with representatives of private industry and organized labor;
3. Certifying that the PIE industry does not displace employed workers in the community;
4. Collecting funds for a victim assistance program;
5. Providing inmates with benefits in the event of injury in the course of employment;
6. Ensuring that inmate participation was voluntary;
7. Providing a substantial role for the private sector (National Institute of Justice 1990, 22).

In 1984 the PIE program was revised. The original form of the PIE program only provided for the certification of 7 states to ship goods interstate. The 1984 revision of the original program provided for the certification of up to 20 states. The Bureau of Justice Assistance ultimately interpreted the act broadly enough to permit local jails in certified states to operate open market industries. The local jails had to meet all of the requirements of the PIE program but did not have to seek individual certification (National Institute of Justice 1990a).

The future of prison industries was significantly brightened in 1985 with the strong advocacy of Chief Justice Warren E. Burger. In numerous speeches and in his famous article "Prison Industries: Turning Warehouses into Factories with Fences," Burger strongly advocated the expansion of prison industries in the United States. Burger's article called for the repeal of all laws restricting the transportation or sale of prison industrial production (Burger 1985). The Chief Justice's opinion had been heavily influenced by his experiences with international industrial prisons, such as those of the Scandinavian countries and of China. While Burger's call to action had little effect on legislation, it helped promote public acceptance of prison industries.

In the 1980s prison industries expanded, both in the private-public partnership areas like the PIE program and in the state-use industries. A survey conducted in 1989 found 69 prison-based industries selling goods on the open market under the PIE program. This represents a 150 percent increase over the number of similar industries operating in 1984 (National Institute of Justice 1990b). While the expansion observed between 1984 and 1989 was impressive, it did not meet the expectations that some had for the private-public partnership concept. The private-public partnership market had made further increases by 1995, but it still employed only about 5,000 inmates. When compared to the total inmate population of U.S. prisons, this represents only about 1 percent of all inmates. The most likely stumbling block for the PIE program was its requirement to pay inmates a wage competitive with the local community. While the requirement for competitive wages was a stumbling block in one sense, it was a blessing in another. The PIE program has a provision for withholding parts of an inmate's salary to pay victim restitution, taxes, room and board, and support for the inmate's family. Between the start of the PIE program in 1979 and June 1995, over $23 million in wage withholding was attributable to the PIE program. See Figure 5-1.

Currently 36 states have active PIE programs (Bureau of Justice

Assistance 1995). The slow development of the PIE programs is also partly attributable to the quality of inmate labor. The observation made by Mr. Pilsbury in 1866, that a prisoner will produce about three-fourths as much as a free world employee, is probably as true today as it was in 1866. When the extra costs of supervision are included, it is very difficult for private-public partnerships industries in prisons to compete with traditional free world industries.

## PRISON LABOR TODAY

As we approach the twenty-first century there is every reason to believe that productive prison labor programs will gain even greater importance. In the past decade prison populations have grown at a

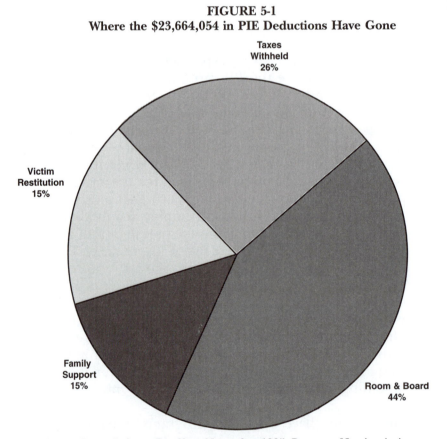

**FIGURE 5-1**
**Where the $23,664,054 in PIE Deductions Have Gone**

*Source: Prison Industry Fact Sheet, November 1995, Bureau of Justice Assistance.*

fantastic rate. The data for the early 1990s is showing an annual increase rate of about 9.5 percent per year (National Institute of Justice 1993). If we project forward at that same rate of increase the prison population of the United States will reach two million in the year 2001.

At the same time that prison populations are increasing, the politicians find themselves under increasing pressure to hold the line on taxes and spending. With the average cost of a new prison at more than $52,000 per bed, and an annual operation cost that already exceeds $20,000 per inmate, it is not difficult to see that state and federal legislators are caught in a bind. To sum up the situation, the American public wants to lock up a lot of people, but we don't want to pay a lot of money for it. The public demands that criminals be confined, and the courts demand that we feed and care for them in a specified minimal fashion. Since we cannot reduce the overhead costs of imprisonment significantly and it appears that lowering the prison population significantly is not going to happen either, the only answer seems to be using the inmates to defray the cost of their confinement.

In addition to the financial argument for productive prison labor, there are other rationales as well. The United States is based on a "work ethic" that can be traced back to our earliest history. Work is a central component of most Americans' lives, and the public generally believes that prisoners should work as well. It is also a fact of life that almost all prisoners will eventually be released, and on release, they will need jobs to support themselves. Productive prison industries, if properly operated, can reduce inmate idleness, build job skills, increase prisoner morale, and reduce the cost of confinement. Because of these advantages all states make some productive use of inmate labor. In the last ten years, the number of inmates employed in productive labor programs has more than doubled (American Correctional Association 1992). The most common labor programs are agricultural programs, manufacturing programs, public works and prison construction programs, and prison maintenance programs like food services and housekeeping.

## AGRICULTURAL PROGRAMS

In the most recent survey, 29 states report that they still have agricultural programs in operation (American Correctional Association 1992). The largest of the agricultural programs are in Texas and California. Annual production in Texas exceeds $33 million in value with an outside sales figure of over $7 million. California's total annual production is lower than that of Texas, but its outside sales exceeds $10 million in value (American Correctional Association 1992). The primary products in Texas and California are beef, eggs, poultry, swine, milk, and prunes. California, and other large agricultural states like Texas, permit the surplus agricultural products to be sold on the open markets. Agricultural commodities like eggs, milk, and fruits were exempted from the Ashurst-Sumner act and can even be sold across state lines. While some states like California, Louisiana, and Texas employ thousands of inmates in their agricultural programs, most states serve their agricultural needs with less than 200 inmates. In 1993 there were about 21,000 inmates employed in prison agriculture programs, with Texas being the largest single employer at 6,700 inmate jobs (Texas Department of Criminal Justice 1993).

Most experts do not see a bright future for prison agriculture programs. While the interstate shipment of agricultural products is possible, there is little evidence that it is occurring to any significant degree. The capital intensive, relatively low labor needs of modern agriculture make it less than ideal as a choice for a prison industry. It is also difficult to justify agricultural programs from the standpoint of job training benefits for inmates. Currently, the job market for people trained in agricultural skills is very small. The primary function of prison agriculture programs will most likely be limited to supplying the needs of the inmate population instead of as a source of cash income.

## MANUFACTURING PROGRAMS

In the most recent survey of prison industries mentioned earlier, all but one state reported operating some form of manufacturing industry within their prisons. The product lines range from modular desks in Massachusetts to stainless commodes in Texas. Production includes items as small as eyeglasses to as large as dump truck beds. Some of these products are sold on the open market through PIE programs, but most of them are restricted to state-use only markets. Currently, prison manufacturing employs about 64,000 inmates in the United States (American Correctional Association 1992). This represents about three times the number employed in prison agriculture programs. The jurisdiction with the most inmates employed in manufacturing programs is the Federal Bureau of Prisons with about 15,000 inmates employed in their program. The federal prison industries (UNICOR) produce office furniture, dormitory furniture, metal storage cabinets, and general office supplies that are purchased by a wide range of federal agencies including the Department of Defense. The total value of manufactured goods produced with prison labor in 1991 was estimated at $991 million, up $550 million from a similar survey in 1987 (American Correctional Association 1992).

Manufacturing programs utilizing prison labor offer probably the best opportunity for future development. If manufacturing industries are selected carefully, they offer the potential for reasonable profit and can provide good job training and experience. The age-old joke "How many jobs are there for license plate makers outside of prison?" is little more than an old joke. First, prisons never used any significant number of inmates to manufacture license plates. Second, license plate manufacturing is nothing but sheet metal stamping, which has an excellent free world job market. If barriers to the sale of prison made goods were lifted, the potential for these industries is excellent.

## PUBLIC WORKS AND PRISON CONSTRUCTION

Prison labor started out with public works projects, and we still use inmate labor in the construction of public projects today. A survey conducted in 1990 found that 14 states are still using inmate labor to build new prisons (Davis 1990). Prisons in the United States employ inmates in a broad range of construction jobs. Inmates are currently employed in carpentry, plumbing, electrical, bricklaying, cement work, welding, painting, surveying, and a host of other construction activities. Some of the inmates are admitted to prison with the required job skills and others are taught their skills while imprisoned.

More common than the construction of new prisons is the use of inmate labor in building additions to existing prisons and remodeling prisons and other public offices. Thirty-four states report using inmate labor in some form of construction even if they don't use it to build new prisons. Florida reported saving over $14 million on the construction of a new prison in 1990 by using inmate labor (Davis 1990). Florida does not pay its inmate construction crews, but it does award good time credit against the maximum sentence. This means that inmates in Florida can earn an early release through their construction labor. There are currently no accurate figures on the number of inmates employed in the construction industries. Because the number employed can change significantly with the start or completion of major projects, national figures probably would not be reliable even if they were available. One indicator of the relative importance of inmate labor in the construction and renovation of prison facilities is that in Texas the Construction Division has a staff of over 400 employees responsible for supervising and coordinating inmate labor in the construction process.

The construction industries represent an employment area for inmates that is clearly larger than agricultural employment, but also smaller than traditional manufacturing employment. While it is reasonable to assume that there will be some expansion in the construction industries, most experts do not expect a dramatic expansion in these areas. The strongest argument for using inmate labor in the construction industries is that it can provide training and work experience that inmates can translate into well-paying jobs after release.

## PRISON MAINTENANCE

Prisons have historically used inmate labor for their internal maintenance functions. The largest of these functions are normally food services, laundry services, and janitorial services. The use of inmate labor to provide these basic services can be tracked back to the early bridewells. Inmates have cooked, cleaned, and laundered within our institutions for over 400 years.

While there are no current surveys showing the number of inmates employed in food services, a reasonable estimate is about 7 percent of the adult prison population. This means that nationally about 70,000 inmates are employed in the food service industries within the prisons. There has been some movement into externally contracted food services in recent years, but this is generally occurring in jails and smaller special-purpose prison units. In some states, the food services functions are large enough that they run their own culinary arts schools to train inmates in the food preparation areas. Experienced wardens have always recognized the importance of providing quality food services. Food is one of the few pleasures available to inmates, and poor quality food very likely will create problems with the inmate population.

Historically, few have criticized the use of inmates in the food services areas. There is little unionization of food service at the national level, and clearly there is some market in the free world for released inmates with food services skills. However, food service jobs are not highly desirable. The food service industry generally represents the lower paying end of the service industry with many of the jobs at the minimum wage level. There is also some question as to the type of food service skills being taught in prisons. Inmates are being trained in a cafeteria or institutional style of food service, while today the food service industry is dominated by "fast food" businesses. Institutions such as public schools are the primary locations of traditional cafeteria style food services. While the employment of ex-inmates in school cafeterias is not impossible, it is reasonable to expect some resistance from community groups to this employment.

Laundry and janitorial service jobs occupy about another 7 percent of the inmate population. While these services involve some training, they are considered unskilled labor. As important as these functions are to institutional operation, it is difficult to justify them as training in anything except the work ethic. In the United States, laundry and janitorial functions represent a large segment of the unskilled service labor market. The number of public buildings, offices, and businesses that use these types of services is staggering. This market, however, is dominated by minimum wage positions that do not represent very desirable employment. The institutional support areas such as food services, laundry services, and janitorial services represent an inmate labor market that will probably remain unchanged into the future. Institutions will continue to provide these services internally, but there will be little opportunity for the expansion of these areas, except as inmate populations expand.

One exception to this forecast of a limited future is the innovative program being operated by the Federal Bureau of Prisons in Philadelphia (Byerly and Ford 1992). The Philadelphia Urban Work Cadre program allows low-security federal inmates working out of a community corrections center to provide maintenance services for the Department of Defense. The Urban Work Cadre Program was implemented in the spring of 1990 at the Defense Personnel Support Center in Philadelphia. Inmates under this program mow lawns, paint, and perform general custodial duties on the Defense Department site. The transportation to and from the job site is provided by the community corrections center. To date, the program has been in operation for over four years with only minimal problems. This model of providing off-site custodial services could be copied in many areas where public buildings are near community correctional centers or low-security prisons.

# CURRENT ISSUES IN PRISON LABOR

There are several issues that dominate the current discussions of inmate labor to reduce the cost of institutionalization. The most significant issues are:

1. Displacement of civilian jobs;
2. Inmate compensation and wages;
3. Inmate safety and security; and,
4. Cost effectiveness of prison industries.

These issues were at the center of discussions about inmate labor 100 years ago, and they still remain as the central points of debate today. Can we run humane prison industries and prison labor programs that effectively reduce the cost of confining the rapidly increasing inmate populations?

## DISPLACEMENT OF CIVILIAN JOBS

The perception that prison industries compete unfairly with private industries is pervasive among the American public. The common belief is that "slave labor" is being used to put honest hard-working people out of work. The evidence shows that this belief is a misconception. First and foremost is the fact that current legislation has largely blocked prison-made goods from the open market. In addition to the legislation from the first half of the century, there have been continuing efforts to restrict the open sale of prison-made goods. In 1987 federal legislation dealing with the purchase of highway signs restricted the future purchase of prison-made highway signs to no more than the purchase level of 1986 (Grieser 1989). This effectively prevented any further expansion of the prison industries involved in highway sign manufacturing.

In those areas of state-use where there is some possible conflict between prison labor and free world labor, the real level of conflict is minimal. Prison industries generally deal in areas like textiles and other labor intensive manufacturing where the job market has been exported wholesale to foreign countries (Sigler and Stough 1991). Most prison industries compete with Third World labor markets, not United States manufacturing jobs. Any attempt to return a significant portion of these jobs to the United States could only benefit the economy and public in general.

The total involvement of prison industries even in the state-use market is surprisingly small. UNICOR, the Federal Prison Industries, is the largest of all the prison industries groups, but it currently captures only .16 percent of the total federal market for goods and services (Grieser 1989). A similar study conducted in New York indicated that Corcraft Correctional Industries, the New York state correctional industries, was capturing only between 1 and 2 percent of the state-use market in that state (Grieser 1988). Other large prison manufacturing states like California, Florida, and Texas are also expected to provide less that 2 percent of their respective state markets.

In a model recently proposed by Sigler and Stough (1991), a prison industry would be permitted to compete in the open market when the industry could be declared an "endangered species." The criteria proposed by Sigler and Stough is that prisons could enter a production field if the United States provided less than 5 percent of the product to the world market and if the percentage of the product produced in the United States has declined for a three- to five-year period. Following this criteria, prison industrial production would represent little threat to existing industries and products, even if the laws restricting open market sales were repealed.

## INMATE WAGES AND COMPENSATION

The second major concern involving inmate labor is the issue of wages and compensation for inmates. The conservative elements of the population are strongly opposed to paying wages to offenders. Conservatives see inmate wages as a reward for criminal activity. Under this school of thought, inmates should be made to work for the state to repay the damage they inflicted during their criminal career. To a more liberal audience, the involuntary labor of any person represents a violation of human rights. Labor unions also are opposed to paying any "subscale" wages, fearing that doing so will influence the competitiveness of free world labor in negotiating contracts in the general labor markets (Sigler and Stough 1991). Successfully negotiating these various interest groups and still operating prison industries at a profit represent obvious challenges.

Prisons generally do not have a legal obligation to pay inmates required to work in prison or jail industries. Courts in most cases have held that inmates do not have any constitutional right to be paid for their work. Courts also have dismissed claims that inmates are entitled to wages under federal wage laws. The laws of some states do require the payment of inmate wages, and in those states, correctional administrators must meet the restrictions that are set by their states. See Table 5-1.

Prison industries have developed a number of methods for dealing with the problem of inmate compensation. Inmates generally need an incentive to participate in prison industries. While the opportunity to keep busy is valued by many inmates, continued motivation to work everyday is not typically the pattern of their lives. Thus

**TABLE 5-1**
**Selected Court Cases on Inmate Employment and Compensation**

| Cases (convicted offenders) | Findings |
| --- | --- |
| Holt v. Sarver (1970) | Forced uncompensated labor of state convicts does not violate the Thirteenth Amendment. |
| Hamilton v. Landrieu (1972) | Inmates may not be assigned to jobs where they have access to other inmates' records or other sensitive information. |
| Altizer v. Paderick (1978) | Inmates have no due process rights to any particular job in an institution. No procedural due process is required to transfer an inmate from one job to another. |
| Turner v. Nevada State Prison Board (1985) | Nevada officials may deduct from inmate's wages to pay for room and board and victim compensation payments. |
| Hrbek v. Farrier (1986) | State prison officials may withhold deductions from an inmate's wages to cover unpaid court costs. |
| Sahagian v. Dickey (1986) | State officials may withhold 15 percent of an inmate's wages in a "release" account that the inmate may access only on discharge. |

| Cases (unconvicted offenders) | Findings |
| --- | --- |
| Tyler v. Harris (1964) | Unconvicted offenders in federal facilities may not be subject to involuntary servitude. |
| Main Road v. Atych (1974) | Unsentenced state prisoners cannot be required to perform uncompensated labor. |

nonmonetary incentives have been used since the earliest days of prison labor. The classic nonmonetary incentives were pain (through the use of corporal punishment) and hunger (through denying food to inmates who refused to work). The withholding of food and the use of corporal punishment might sound like incentives from the dark ages, but they were used into the second half of the twentieth century. In 1951, O. B. Ellis, the director of the Texas prisons, issued a "no work-no eat" proclamation to every inmate that was found to be malingering in the Texas prisons. There is also evidence of corporal punishment being used as late as the 1960s by the order of George Beto, the then-director of the Texas prisons (Stone et al. 1974).

Today nonmonetary incentives are not based on the use of the lash. Modern correctional administrators have recognized that there is a broad range of benefits other than salary that can be used to reward inmates. Some of the benefits that are commonly used are

1.  Extra good time
2.  Extended visiting privileges
3.  Extended recreation and gym time
4.  Extended hours of TV viewing
5.  Short furloughs
6.  Extended telephone privileges
7.  Outside meals and treats

These benefits can be powerful motivators for inmates as long as they are used properly. All incentives should be based on individual performance of inmates and not on group behavior (National Institute of Justice 1990b).

## INMATE SAFETY AND SECURITY

Any prison industry program must consider security. Correctional industries create security hazards that the correctional administrator must address. One obvious security problem is that of tool control. When selecting a correctional industry the administrator must carefully select the product and the manufacturing technique to fit the security needs of the institution. Heavy metal manufacturing that involves metal cutting and welding tools is obviously not a good choice for most maximum security institutions. Tool control is important from the standpoints of preventing escapes and inmate safety. Because inmates may use tools as weapons against other inmates, tools must be tightly inventoried and counted on a regular basis. These security procedures represent an obvious impediment to running an efficient manufacturing industry.

Correctional industries require additional correctional officers to maintain control over the inmate population that is involved in the manufacturing process. These security officers represent staffing requirements that are above and beyond the manufacturing supervisors that are necessary to keep the industrial production operating. The additional security costs must be considered when comparing the cost effectiveness of any prison industry. Industries that require limited numbers of tools and limited inmate movement are ideal. One example of a minimal security prison industry is a telephone

**TABLE 5-2**
**Females Employed in Correctional Industries**

| Jurisdiction | No. of females | No. of males | Percent female |
|---|---|---|---|
| Alabama | 150 | 1850 | 8.11 |
| Alaska | 0 | 170 | 0.00 |
| Arizona | N/A | N/A | N/A |
| Arkansas | 71 | 299 | 23.75 |
| California | 200* | 7962 | 2.58 |
| Colorado | 48 | 999 | 4.80 |
| Connecticut | 50 | 500 | 10.00 |
| Delaware | 0 | 175 | 0.00 |
| District of Columbia | 29 | 482 | 6.02 |
| Florida | 167 | 2559 | 6.53 |
| Georgia | 65 | 1012 | 6.42 |
| Hawaii | 0 | 56 | 0.00 |
| Idaho | 36 | 193 | 18.65 |
| Illinois | 93 | 1217 | 7.64 |
| Indiana | 36 | 1124 | 3.20 |
| Iowa | 9 | 249 | 3.61 |
| Kansas | 10 | 540 | 1.85 |
| Kentucky | 52 | 421 | 12.35 |
| Louisiana | 90 | 1810 | 4.97 |
| Maine | 9 | 127 | 7.09 |
| Maryland | 97 | 896 | 10.83 |
| Massachusetts | 23 | 490 | 4.69 |
| Michigan | 83 | 1133 | 7.33 |
| Minnesota | 69 | 540 | 12.78 |
| Mississippi | 15 | 180 | 8.33 |
| Missouri | 103 | 964 | 10.68 |
| Montana | 5 | 185 | 2.70 |
| Nebraska | 44 | 346 | 12.72 |
| Nevada | 16 | 275 | 5.82 |
| New Hampshire | 10 | 270 | 3.70 |
| New Jersey | 162 | 827 | 19.59 |
| New Mexico | 25 | 432 | 5.79 |
| New York | 117 | 1644 | 7.12 |
| North Carolina | 115 | 1514 | 7.60 |
| North Dakota | 10 | 106 | 9.43 |
| Ohio | 94 | 1852 | 5.08 |
| Oklahoma | 93 | 687 | 13.54 |
| Oregon | 30 | 376 | 7.98 |
| Pennsylvania | 34 | 1945 | 1.75 |
| Rhode Island | 25 | 300 | 8.33 |
| South Carolina | 108 | 1056 | 10.23 |
| Tennessee | 34 | 566 | 6.01 |
| Texas | 311 | 5430 | 5.73 |
| Utah | 16 | 315 | 5.08 |
| Vermont | 0 | 130 | 0.00 |
| Virginia | 271 | 912 | 29.71 |

**Table 5-2**
(*Continued*)

| Jurisdiction | No. of females | No. of males | Percent female |
|---|---|---|---|
| Washington | 4 | 675 | 0.59 |
| West Virginia | 8 | 120 | 6.67 |
| Wisconsin | 20 | 348 | 5.75 |
| Wyoming | 0 | 124 | 0.00 |
| Federal | 1300 | 13146 | 9.89 |
| **Totals** | **4357** | **59430** | **7.33%** |

*California data represent an estimate instead of a census.

*Source:* American Correctional Association, Correctional Industries Survey Report March 1992, BJS, U.S. Department of Justice.

reservation service that is operated by one state prison. After training, the inmates are assigned to a computerized phone bank that takes reservations for a number of hotels and resorts. This industry involves no threat from dangerous tools, and it can be located in a secure isolated area with only minimal inmate movement. This allows the industry to operate with almost no additional security costs.

Prison industries must also be selected to minimize the potential for industrial accidents. Prison industries are required to meet all the same safety standards of any manufacturing industry. Prison industries receive regular inspections from the Occupational Safety and Health Administration to insure that they are in compliance with all industrial safety rules. The safety considerations are further complicated by the nature of the inmate population. Inmates often have poor work habits, which can contribute to on-the-job accidents. Inmate turnover is also high, which requires a program of constant safety training and monitoring of the compliance with safety regulations.

The prison industries in the United States employ both male and female inmates in the industrial manufacturing process. With the exception of Wyoming and Vermont, every industrial program includes women. The latest American Correctional Association survey shows that 4,357 women are currently employed in correctional industries. The largest state employer of women is Texas, followed by Virginia and California. See Table 5-2. In 1992 women represented about 6 percent of the total inmate population and about 7 percent of the inmates involved in the prison industries. Women are used in garment manufacturing, reupholstering, data entry, microfilming, telemarketing, farming, printing, optical production, and electronic circuit board production (Duncan 1992).

## COST EFFECTIVENESS OF PRISON INDUSTRY

Many people still question the cost effectiveness of prison industries. Most prison industries must rely on only six to seven hours of productive labor out of every eight-hour shift due to security checks and other inmate management problems (Grieser 1989). High inmate turnover results in higher than normal training costs. Most correctional industries also suffer from constraints in how they procure their raw materials. Almost all correctional industries have purchasing systems that must follow governmental procurement procedures. Some states such as Florida have turned their correctional industries over to a private corporation to help reduce these administrative problems.

The same governmental regulations that make purchasing difficult also make it difficult to remove inefficient employees that are involved in the industrial process. Because of these and other similar problems, the average value of production per inmate is estimated at only $20,000 per year. This is only about 25 percent of the anticipated production value of a free world employee (Grieser 1989). The net impact of these constraints is that correctional industries are hard-pressed to generate a profit even when selling their products on the open market at their fair value. In spite of these concerns most experts believe that prison industries are a valuable asset. They normally allow inmates to earn at least a token wage. They provide a structured activity that reduces inmate idleness. And industries can provide valuable job experiences for inmates prior to their release.

# INMATE EDUCATION

The use of productive prison labor occurred much earlier than programs designed to provide either vocational or academic education to inmates. This is easy to understand when you consider the functions of early prisons. Historically, there was little intent that the individuals sent to prison would ever rejoin society. Prior to the sixteenth century prison inmates were considered to be little more than draft animals, and any efforts beyond feeding and watering were considered unnecessary. The first evidence that there might be a shift in this philosophy was the development of workhouses and bridewells in Europe and England.

As mentioned in an earlier chapter, *bridewells* were somewhat like a cross between a workhouse and a prison. The first Bridewell was built outside London in 1577. It was originally designed to provide vocational and moral reformation for the serfs that were migrating from the countryside to the metropolitan areas seeking employment. The economic transition from a feudal state in the fourteenth and fifteenth centuries had created large numbers of unemployed individuals who frequently were referred to as vagrants. These individuals had no marketable skills they could employ in the metropolitan centers. Without skills, many of these individuals committed minor crimes to purchase food and necessities.

The first Bridewell was an attempt to take these minor offenders, debtors, homeless children, and other public charges and make them fit for city life. This attempt to improve the lot of the vagrants and other public wards represents the seeds of the first custodial-based vocational and academic education. Much of this early education was delivered by religious authorities, and it included a liberal dose of religious and moral instruction including the dominant "work ethic" of the time.

The bridewells ceased to be a historical influence on the evolution of prisons and prison education after less than 100 years. By 1640, the evolution of the British penal system had taken a new turn. Transportation to the colonies was the preferred solution for criminal offenders from this time period up until the American revolution. There was little incentive to improve the lot of offenders when they could be simply shipped to the New World, never to be heard from again. The British made some abortive attempts to create total institutions with both vocational and secular education, but they were short-lived. These attempts were heavily influenced by Quakers like John Bellers, who proposed a vocational-industrial prison model in 1690 (Ignatieff 1978). The Quakers were very influential in the entire history of prison reform. The first women involved in prison reform were Quakers. In December 1816, Elizabeth Fry led a group of Quaker wives into Newgate prison to reform the women's and children's section of the prison (Ignatieff 1978).

With the American revolution, the British were forced to rethink their criminal sentencing philosophy. Without the ability to transport its prisoners to the colonies, the British started to develop major penitentiaries like the Glouchester and Pentonville facilities. In these large institutions educational programs for inmates developed slowly. By 1860, the British provided reading, writing, and "cyphering" instruction to every inmate sentenced for three months or longer (Wines and Dwight 1867).

Educational programs also evolved in the United States during the first half of the nineteenth century. The first documented educational program in the United States was started in May 1826 (Wines and Dwight 1867). This program, at the Auburn Prison in New York, provided instruction in reading, writing, and arithmetic every Sunday after church. In 1829, Kentucky passed a legislative act requiring that the Kentucky state prison teach all "unlearned" inmates for at least four hours every Sunday. This first statewide prison inmate educational requirement was discontinued after only five years. In 1847, the New York legislature passed a comprehensive prison act. This act provided for the appointment of full-time teachers to each of the prisons in New York. These teachers operated the first full-time weekday school program designed to serve U.S. prisoners.

From the mid-1800s, prison officials increasingly saw inmate education as a logical and expected part of their function with inmates. While education had started out as a method of religious instruction, by allowing inmates to read the bible, it ultimately evolved into a broader rehabilitative concept. It was increasingly recognized that to prosper in the world all people needed a minimal level of education. In 1876, the state of New York opened the Elmira Reformatory. This institution, which contained young adults ages 16 to 30, was the direct by-product of the 1870 Prison Congress. The Principles developed at the 1870 Prison Congress included a strong commitment to inmate education, which was embodied in the educational program at Elmira (Allen and Simonsen 1986). Elmira would set the vocational and academic educational standard that other institutions would try to meet for the remainder of the century.

After the survey conducted in preparation for the 1870 Prison Congress, the next major survey of inmate education programs occurred in the late 1920s. In 1927, Austin MacCormick surveyed 60 prisons in the United States and discovered that 13 of the institutions reported not having any academic programs for inmates. MacCormick also concluded that the programs that did exist rarely were adequate to meet the inmates' needs. Probably the most surprising discovery in the survey was the total absence of vocational educational programs for inmates. As has happened so many times in the past, the progress of one generation had been lost due to the disinterest of the next. The progress that had been made in the last part of the nineteenth century was sacrificed during the shifting priorities and economic hardships of the early twentieth century. Many of the states would not redevelop their academic and vocational programs until after World War II (Fox 1983).

In 1945 the Correctional Education Association was formed as a result of the actions of a subcommittee of the American Prison

Association. Four years later, the *Journal of Correctional Education* was founded. This journal has provided correctional educators with a forum for the exchange of ideas and educational procedures throughout the nation. With these two important events, we entered the modern age of correctional education.

# CONTEMPORARY VOCATIONAL EDUCATION PROGRAMS

The development of systems designed to teach inmates a trade or vocation had made very significant progress by the 1960s. Vocational education had become available, at least theoretically, to almost all inmates imprisoned in the United States. The concept of teaching every inmate that was capable of learning a marketable trade was accepted as a goal of corrections in almost every state. In 1965, the Manpower Development and Training Act provided federal funding to supplement the existing efforts of the states to provide vocational education. The Comprehensive Employment Training Act replaced the Manpower Development Act in 1973, thereby securing the funding of vocational programming for the remainder of the decade.

## FEMALE INMATES AND VOCATIONAL EDUCATION

While the funding of vocational education was temporarily secure, there were still several problems to be faced. One of the problems to be faced in the 1970s was the changing view regarding vocational education for women. Because of the relatively small female inmate population and outdated cultural belief that "a woman's place is in the home," most states were operating either no vocational educational programs for women or inappropriate vocational programs. When the state of Texas opened a new facility specifically for vocational and academic education of female inmates at the Goree Prison in 1973 it was one of the first facilities of its kind in the United States (Stone et al. 1974). Unfortunately, this new facility, like most of the programs that preceded it, did not effectively address the needs of women in the changing society of the time. Those states that had vocational programs for women were typically providing programs on culinary arts (cooking), home economics (cleaning and sewing), floriculture (flower arranging), cosmetology (makeup and hair), and secretarial science. These vocational programs were suitable for some women, but they were typically preparing women to be housewives or for low-paying jobs in the "pink collar ghetto" of the marketplace. Women who were supporting families were simply not getting vocational training in skill areas that could be relied on to provide significant salaries (Allen and Simonsen 1986; Pollock-Byrne 1990).

There were two possible solutions to the shortage of meaningful vocational training programs for women. One solution was to begin new programs in women's institutions. A potential disadvantage of this solution was that it might move resources from institutions for men to those for women — in effect, requiring a correctional administrator to deny services to 100 male inmates to provide a vocational program to 20 female inmates. The second solution was to simply move the women to the male institution where the programs already existed. While co-correctional facilities presented opportunities for shared resources, they also posed potential problems, such as sexual assault, pregnancy, and emotional attachments between inmates.

A survey conducted in June of 1978 showed that there were 20 co-correctional institutions in operation in the United States (Smykla 1980). The first of these co-correctional institutions was opened by the Federal Bureau of Prisons at Fort Worth Texas in 1971 (Clear and Cole 1986). These co-correctional institutions solved some of the problems concerning female access to vocational programs, but they were not readily accepted in many regions of the country. Other problems existed, security concerns either dramatically increased the cost of vocational programs or were cited as the reason why men and women could not participate in the same program. Women also showed little interest in traditional male vocations unless they were recruited into them. Once involved in such programs women tended to show less enthusiasm and interest when participating along with males. By the early 1980s, the number of co-correctional institutions had dropped by almost 50 percent (Allen and Simonsen 1986). From this low in 1980, the number of co-correctional institutions (not counting detention, psychiatric, and other specialized facilities) rebounded to about 30, where it remains today (American Correctional Association 1994).

The 1980s were a period of fiscal hardship for most state correctional systems. During this time, vocational programs for women was one of the first areas to suffer. Even the Federal Bureau of Prisons had trouble providing adequate vocational programs for women. The Female Offender Task Force of the Federal Bureau of Prisons reviewed the programs available to women in 1980 and concluded that the vocational programs available to women were still not adequate to meet their needs (Carlson 1981). Some states have continued to experiment with co-correctional institutions as the most effective way to deliver vocational programming to women. Illinois has tried to deal with the problem of scarce funding and women's vocational needs by opening several new co-correctional institutions in the 1990s (Howell 1992). While some states are still experimenting, a 1992 survey of 85 correctional institutions that contained female offenders showed that women still do not have access to adequate vocational programming (Howell 1992).

The fiscal shortfalls of the 1980s had significant impact on the vocational programming for men's institutions as well as the institutions for women. As most states entered the 1980s, the state treasuries were experiencing dramatic reductions in revenues. With the economic recession, available funds for prison programming became very limited. This was further complicated by the shift to a more conservative correctional philosophy. As we shall see in the next chapter, rehabilitation philosophy was given a very low priority after the mid-1970s, and available funds were directed toward custodial issues rather than vocational or rehabilitative programming. These cuts have continued into the 1990s. A survey of 44 states published in 1994 showed that at least half of the states had been forced to make cuts in vocational programs in the previous five years. These cuts have been primarily in the most expensive vocational programs like machine tooling, welding, and X-ray technology (Lillis 1994).

## *EXTERNAL CONTRACTING OF VOCATIONAL EDUCATION*

Some states have attempted to deal with the funding shortages by having the vocational programs delivered through local community colleges. For institutions located where they have easy access to community colleges, it is possible to get vocational programs delivered in a much more cost-effective manner. The community colleges maintain the necessary vocational training equipment and faculty for their normal course delivery. This means that the correctional facility does not need to maintain expensive equipment inventories or full-time vocational instructors. This represents an especially cost-effective option for smaller institutions like women's prisons. The single biggest problem with this option is the physical location of many prisons. Correctional institutions frequently are built in relatively remote rural areas where community college access is not available.

Some of the larger state correctional systems use a very effective blend of colleges and in-house vocational instruction to deliver a broad range of vocational programs. For example, the Texas correctional system uses in-house vocational teachers to deliver 35 different vocational programs. These programs include air conditioning, auto mechanics, business computer applications, construction trades, and dental laboratory aid. They also contract with six local community colleges to deliver vocational programs at 24 of their prison units. The community college vocational offerings include graphic arts, drafting, electronics, and sheet metal manufacturing. To complete their vocational offerings, Texas contracts with the Engineering Extension Service of Texas A&M University to offer advanced certification in boiler operation, electrical line maintainer, heavy equipment operation, and waste water management. In total, about twenty thousand inmates participate in their vocational education program each year (Texas Department of Criminal Justice 1993).

Both New York and California run vocational programs that are very similar in size and scope to the one operated in Texas. New York and California deliver more of their total course work through community colleges, but the total course offerings are very comparable. In these three states only between 15 to 20 percent of the inmate population may be enrolled in vocational courses each year. However, this is about twice the national average of less than 9 percent enrolled in vocational programs (National Institute of Justice 1993).

The funding for these vocational programs comes from a mixture of sources. Those states that have developed their own "in-prison" school district are able to tap directly into their state's general education budgets. There is also some additional funding in most states in the form of state vocational incentive grants and some funding that is an integral part of the correctional system's budget. Educational funding is normally included as part of the programming or treatment divisions of many state correctional systems. An additional major funding source is from the federal government. Inmates enrolled in vocational courses offered through community colleges were eligible for both Pell Grants and Veterans Administration grants until 1994. In 1994 the new federal crime bill exempted prison inmates from receiving Pell Grants (Wellford and Littlefield 1985). Many community college programs were heavily dependent on federal funds and without Pell Grants some of the programs were discontinued. Many states find that it is not politically acceptable to subsidize vocational college courses for inmates when they do not subsidize the same courses for the general population (McCollum 1994).

## VOCATIONAL TRAINING AND RECIDIVISM

The ultimate goal of vocational education has been to provide the criminal offender with the skills necessary to make a successful living without resorting to crime, which assumes that if offenders are provided solid job training, they will then choose to apply those skills instead of taking the risks involved in criminal behavior. While there appears to be a logical link between a lack of job skills and crime, many experts do not believe the relationship is that simple or straightforward. The attempts to address crime through vocational training go all the way back to the bridewells of England and obviously, we are still plagued by crime. While the studies are mixed, the best evaluations of vocational training seem to indicate that the presence of vocational skills does not reduce the chances of future criminal behavior. The work of Taylor in 1992 and McCollum in 1994 is generally supportive of the link between vocational education and a lowering of recidivism, but most of the research that they reviewed to reach their conclusions is very weak from a methodological standpoint. Probably the single best evaluation of vocational programming was conducted in the late 1980s in North Carolina. In this study, a true experimental design was used including a randomly assigned experimental group and control group. The results of this study clearly showed that the programs were successful in transmitting the vocational skills. It also showed, however, that the vocational skills transmitted had no significant effect on recidivism over a four-year follow-up period (Lattimore, Witte, and Baker 1987).

There are several explanations for the failure of vocational education programs to show a reduction in recidivism in rigorous experimental evaluations. One of the possible explanations is that while the programs can teach the skills necessary for employment they cannot teach the attitudes necessary for successful employment. Many inmates lack the basic attitudes and social skills necessary for successful employment. Successful employment is frequently affected by such issues as punctuality, cordiality to supervisors and fellow employees, accountability, and respect for authority. Attitudes and values are transmitted in early life experiences, and attempts to change these attitudes and values at anything more than a superficial level through programs either has not been addressed or has not been very successful. Inmate employment after vocational education is affected by employment discrimination and civil disabilities after release. Many employers simply do not want to hire ex-offenders, and in some cases offenders have difficulty getting an occupational license or surety bonds necessary to employ their skills. The number of civil disabilities suffered by inmates has been dramatically reduced in recent years; however, the perceived desirability of inmates as employees has changed little. Perhaps the single greatest weakness of vocational programs is the lack of transition to outside employment. Few have job placement services or a guarantee of suitable employment on release.

# CONTEMPORARY ACADEMIC EDUCATION PROGRAMS

In 1826, Judge Greshom Powers reported to the New York legislature that "fully one-eighth of the prisoners in New York's Auburn prison were either wholly unable to read, or could read only by spelling out most of the words" (Wines and Dwight 1867). While the concept of functional illiteracy is more sophisticated now and the standard higher (about eighth grade), the situation has not dramatically improved. An evaluation conducted 160 years after the observation of Judge Powers indicated that about one-third of inmates could not read, write, or do math at the eighth grade level (Moke and Holloway 1986). Because of this continuing problem most states operate an Adult Basic Education program. These programs are designed to provide education to the functionally illiterate inmates that are admitted to prisons each year.

## ADULT BASIC EDUCATION PROGRAMS

The origins of the current Adult Basic Education programs can be traced back to the compulsory inmate education laws passed by state legislators. In 1956, Texas legislators passed a law that required all inmates that had less than a third grade education to attend school. At the time of its passage, this required that 15 to 20 percent of the inmate population be placed in compulsory educational classes. This minimum level was later raised to the sixth grade in the 1960s. In 1965, the Texas Correctional System instituted its first formal Adult Basic Education Program. This program was designed to deliver the first nine grades of education in a format suitable for adult inmates (Stone et al. 1974). The Federal Bureau of Prisons established its first mandatory literacy program in 1982. In its first form, the federal program required that any inmate with less than a sixth grade education be forced to go to school. The program was changed in 1986 to a minimum of eighth grade, and in 1991, the first mandatory high school equivalency requirement was established (McCollum 1992). In a survey conducted in 1993, every state that responded was operating an Adult Basic Education Program. The five largest of these state programs are located in Ohio, Missouri, Texas, New York, and California (National Institute of Justice 1993).

## GENERAL EDUCATION DEVELOPMENT PROGRAMS

The second level of educational programming that is offered in most institutions is the General Education Development (GED) program. These programs are designed to prepare inmates to take and pass the General Education Development Test. The GED is a written test that assesses general comprehension and ability in the basic academic areas. It examines general comprehension and knowledge in reading, writing, science, and mathematics. The GED is considered to be the equivalent of a high school diploma. The GED is the minimal level of education required for entrance into many employment areas (Clear and Cole 1986).

Inmates frequently choose taking the GED over completing a traditional high school program because of time limitations. The average inmate has a ninth grade education at the time of his admission to prison. With the relatively short prison sentences (actual time served) of most inmates, the vast majority of inmates would simply not be in prison long enough to finish a high school degree. Because the GED is generally the most practical educational approach for most inmates, it is by far the most sought-after nonvocational educational program in American prisons. In some major prison systems, the number of GED certificates awarded in a year is six to ten times the number of associate degrees awarded. In the most recent survey of prison educational programs, every state except New Hampshire reported offering the GED program to its inmates. The largest GED program in any of the state prisons is located in Texas (NIJ 1993). The Texas Correctional System, according to its most recent report, issued over four thousand GED certificates during the 1993 fiscal year (Texas Department of Criminal Justice 1993).

While GED certificates are the most common academic goal of the inmate population, there is a growing question as to whether it actually serves the inmates' needs on release. Society is becoming more and more educated. As the educational needs of the society increase, the GED may not serve the needs of the inmates when they reenter society. If the GED ceases to open the door to employment opportunities for the inmates, its utility will be largely lost. Recent evaluations of the impact of the GED on recidivism have not been promising. A recent study conducted in Illinois using an experimental design that included a matched control group showed that inmates that earned their GED actually had a higher recidivism rate than those who did not earn a GED. This study followed the inmates for five years after their release and raises some serious issues about the utility of the GED (Stevenson 1992). One of the possible explanations for the correlation between earning a GED and engaging in future criminality is the unrealistic expectations of benefits from earning the GED certificate. It appears that some of the inmates expected the GED to open a number of employment opportunities that were simply not forthcoming. With disappointments in the job market the inmates may have suffered negative self-image and attitude problems that contributed to recidivism. It may well be prophetic for the future of the GED-educated inmate that the U.S. military no longer accepts the GED as meeting their educational requirements.

## PRISON COLLEGE PROGRAMS

Just as prisons have become increasingly dependent on local community colleges to deliver their vocational programs, the community colleges are also playing an important role in the delivery of the academic education program. The first recorded college classes offered to inmates were in the Federal Bureau of Prisons. In the early 1950s, a college program was started at the Fort Leavenworth, Kansas, prison by St. Mary's College in Xavier, Kansas (Carney 1979). Following their lead, several states started college programs in the early 1960s. The big growth for college programs for inmates came in the 1970s. In a survey conducted in 1993, all but 7 states reported having community college programs available to inmates. The three largest state-based community college programs are located in Ohio, Texas, and New York, respectively. In addition to these two-year college programs, 17 states offer four-year college programs, and 6 states allow inmates to pursue graduate degrees (National Institute of Justice 1993).

Evaluations of the effects of college-level education on inmate recidivism generally have produced more favorable results than evaluations of high school level and high school equivalency programs. In a study conducted in New York, inmates that completed the Community College Program were found to have a 26.4 percent recidivism rate, while a similar group of noncollege graduates were found to have a recidivism rate of 44.6 percent (Clark 1991). While the research in New York is not as methodologically sound as some of the evaluations of the GED programs, it does indicate a possible rehabilitative effect from advanced education. In a study conducted in 1993, inmates in a college program were surveyed about their attitudes toward life and the future. The inmates in the college programs exhibited significantly more positive attitudes about the future than noncollege inmates (Tootoonchi 1993). Other researchers have associated college program participation with better institutional behavior and interpersonal communication skills (Taylor 1992).

Despite the positive research on the benefits of college education for inmates, the college programs in most states have several problems to overcome. Probably the most significant of these problems is the general lack of support from the public. Since the vast majority of citizens do not have access to free college courses, many people disagree with the idea of state-supported college programs for offenders. Expecting taxpayers to support the education of offenders when they are having difficulty supporting the education of their own children is a difficult political hurdle. If the country becomes more politically conservative over the remainder of this decade, even the Federal Bureau of Prisons may find their college programs coming under attack. The second major stumbling block for college programs in prison is that many inmates simply cannot perform academically at the college level. Inmates frequently have learning deficiencies that make the educational processes difficult even at the lower grades. In addition, many inmates simply do not see the need for and do not want a college degree. It is possible to force inmates into educational classes, but the benefits of forced education are questionable at best.

## EDUCATIONAL RELEASE PROGRAMS

An additional educational option for inmates is educational furlough or educational release. In these programs inmates are allowed to leave the facility to take advantage of educational programs. In the case of educational furloughs, inmates may be released for significant periods of time to become traditional academic residents of colleges that may not be near their correctional facility. Educational release normally involves leaving the facility for only a few hours to attend classes and returning to the institution at the close of classes. The use of educational furloughs was very widespread during the 1970s, but some highly visible program failures and increasing costs caused many of these programs to be cut back in the early 1980s (Allen and Simonsen 1992). Currently, 33 states are operating educational release programs. A number of other states have statutes that authorize the releases, but no inmates currently are out in the community. The largest of the educational release programs is operated in Ohio. Ohio normally has about 250 inmates out on educational release (Davis 1989). Ohio is one of the leaders in correctional education programs in the United States. Ohio has the largest basic adult education, the largest community college program, and the largest educational release program of any state. The leadership role in inmate education that was once held by the Federal Bureau of Prisons is now to a great extent in the hands of Ohio.

The role of educational release is obvious. It allows inmates access to programs that are geographically remote from the correctional institution and programs that are too specialized to be of interest to a significant group of inmates. Even when resources are available in a local college, it is not practical to bring instructors in to teach two or three inmates a class in anthropology. It is obviously more practical to allow the inmates to attend classes with the regular students at the local college. The drawbacks to educational release are also obvious, it involves putting the local community at some degree of risk. A single violent incident by an inmate on an educational release program can cause a very significant political problem for correctional administrators. There has been little effective evaluation of educational release programs because of their relatively small size and the very intense selection process that occurs before the inmates are allowed out into the community. Those evaluations that have been done show that it is very rare for an inmate to fail to return from an educational release and that the inmates are generally successful in their educational programs. These results do not surprise most correctional experts because educational release inmates generally represent the best 1 percent or less of the inmate population.

The range of educational opportunities available to prison inmates today is quite extensive. Inmates in many prisons are free to enroll in whatever type of education they choose. This does not mean that the problems of under-educated inmates and ultimately prison releasees are solved. Education programs, both academic and vocational, still have some major obstacles to overcome. In some states sudden growth in prison populations have created a waiting list for the most desirable programs. Additionally, the poor educational background of many inmates require that significant basic education has to be completed before more meaningful programs can be started.

## CONCLUSIONS

As prison populations continue to grow, it is critical that prisons find some productive activities for increasing inmate populations. Hundreds of thousands of inmates in a state of forced idleness is a very dangerous combination for inmates and correctional employees. Increases in correctional industries and increases in correctional education programs are two of the areas of inmate programming that are most likely to receive political support in the future. In this country education and work are traditional American values that no one argues should not be reflected in our prisons.

Educational and industrial programs occupy a good portion of inmates' time. It is important, however, that treatment programs that address problems like substance abuse or low social skills operate in conjunction with these programs. These programs will be discussed in the following chapter.

## Vocabulary

bridewells                 state-use laws
lease labor system         treadmill
PIE program                UNICOR
shot drill

## Study Questions

1. What is meant by "It is probably true that imprisonment is actually a by-product of the need for forced labor"?

2. What was the most common use of inmate labor in the South?

3. What laws impeded the growth of prison industry?

4. Why is prison agriculture declining in importance?

5. What are the four issues that dominate discussions of inmate labor? Discuss.

6. What has research shown regarding the effect of vocational training on recidivism? Of basic education? Of college education?

7. What educational programs are offered in prison?

# Sources Cited

—Allen, Harry E., and Clifford Simonsen. 1986. *Corrections in America: An Introduction*. 4th ed. New York: Macmillan.

—Allen, Harry E., and Clifford Simonsen. 1992. *Corrections in America: An Introduction*. 6th ed. New York: Macmillan.

—American Correctional Association. 1981. *Standards for Correctional Industries, from Standards for Adult and Local Detention Facilities*. Laural, Md.: American Correctional Association.

—American Correctional Association. 1991. *Correctional Industries Information Jail Industries Survey Final Report*. Laural, Md.: American Correctional Association.

—American Correctional Association. 1992. *Correctional Industries Information Correctional Industries Survey Final Report*. Laural, Md.: American Correctional Association.

—American Correctional Association. 1994. *Juvenile and Adult Correctional Departments, Institutions and Paroling Authorities Directory*. Laural, Md.: American Correctional Association.

—Bureau of Justice Assistance. 1995. *Prison Industries Fact Sheet*. Rockville, Md.: Bureau of Justice Assistance Clearinghouse.

—Burger, Warren E. 1985. "Prison Industries: Turning Warehouses into Factories with Fences." *Public Administration Review* 45: 754-757.

— Byerly, Karen, and Lynda Ford. 1992. "The Philadephia Story: An Innovative Work Program in the Real World." *Federal Prisons Journal* (Fall): 25-29.

— Carlson, Norman A. 1981. *Female Offender, 1979-1980.* Rockville, Md.: National Institute of Justice Microfiche Program.

— Carney, Louis P. 1979. *Introduction to Correctional Science.* 2d ed. New York: McGraw-Hill.

— Clare, Paul K., and John H. Kramer. 1976. *Introduction to American Corrections.* Boston: Holbrook.

— Clark, David D. 1991. *Analysis of Return Rates of the Inmate College Program Participants.* Albany: New York State Department of Correctional Services.

— Clear, Todd R., and George F. Cole. 1986. *American Corrections.* Monterey, Cal.: Brooks/Cole.

— Davis, Su P. 1989. "Thirty-Three U.S. Systems Have Educational Release." *Corrections Compendium* 14(8): 9-16.

— Davis, Su P. 1990. "Survey: Some States Save Millions Using Inmate Labor to Build Prisons." *Corrections Compendium* 15(7): 8-17.

— Duncan, Donna. 1992. "ACA Survey Examines Prison Industries for Women Offenders." *Corrections Today* 54: 114.

— Farkas, Gerald M. 1984. "Managing Prison Industries: The Warden's Role." *Corrections Today* 46: 71-72.

— Farkas, Gerald M. 1985. "Prison Industries: Working with the Private Sector." *Corrections Today* 47: 102-103.

— Farkas, Gerald M. 1987. "New Partnership: Industries and Education/Training Benefits Institutions and Inmates." *Corrections Today* 49: 52-54.

— Farrier, Hal. 1989. "Secure Prison Industries: Getting the Benefits without the Risk." *Corrections Today* 51: 110-112.

— Flanagan, Timothy J. 1988. "Prison Labor and Industry." In *American Prison Issues in Research and Policy,* ed. Lynne Goodstein and Doris MacKenzie, 136-139. New York: Plenum.

— Fox, Vernon. 1983. *Correctional Institutions.* Englewood Cliffs, N.J.: Prentice-Hall.

— Gaes, Gerald G., and William Saylor. 1992. "Federal Prisons: Work Experience Linked with Post-Release Success." *FBI Law Enforcement Bulletin* 61: 4-5.

— Grieser, Robert C. 1988. "Model Approaches Examining Prison Industries That Work." *Corrections Today* 50: 174-176.

— Grieser, Robert C. 1989. "Do Correctional Industries Adversely Impact the Private Sector?" *Federal Probation* 53: 18-24.

— Grisson, Grant R., and Louis Conan. 1981. "The Evolution of Prison Industries." *Corrections Today* 43 (November/December): 42-48.

— Herrick, Edward. 1988. "Hidden Handicap in Prison." *Correction Compendium* 13(3): 1, 6-10.

— Howell, N., and S. P. Davis. 1992. "Special Problems of Female Offenders." *Correction Compendium* 17(9): 1, 5-20.

— Ignatieff, Michael. 1978. *A Just Measure of Pain: The Penitentiary in the Industrial Revolution, 1750-1850.* New York: Pantheon.

— Johnston, Norman. 1973. *The Human Cage: A Brief History of Prison Architecture.* Washington, D.C.: American Foundation Press.

— Lattimore, P. K., A. D. Witte, and J. R. Baker. 1987. *Sandhills Vocational Delivery System Experiment: An Examination of Correctional Program Implementation and Effectiveness.* (National Institute of Justice). Washington, D.C.: GPO.

— Lillis, J. 1994. "Prison Education Programs Reduced." *Corrections Compendium* 19(3): 1-11.

— Linden, Rick, L. Perry, D. Ayersand, and T. A. Parlett. 1984. "Evaluation of a Prison Education Program." *Canadian Journal of Criminology* 26(1): 65-73.

— Linden, Rick, and L. Perry. 1982. "Effectiveness of Prison Education Programs." *Journal of Offender Counseling Services and Rehabilitation* 6(4): 43-57.

— Maguire, Kathleen E., T. Flanagan, and T. Thornberry. 1988. "Prison Labor and Recidivism." *Journal of Quantitative Criminology,* 4(1): 3-19.

— McCollum, S. G. 1992. "Mandatory Literacy: Evaluating the Bureau of Prisons Long-Standing Commitment." *Federal Prisons Journal* 3(2): 33-36.

— McCollum, S. G. 1994. "Prison College Programs." *Prison Journal* 74(1): 51-61.

— Moke, P., and J. Holloway. 1986. "Post-Secondary Correctional Education — Issues of Functional Illiteracy." *Journal of Correctional Education* 37(1): 18-22.

— National Institute of Justice. 1990a. *Developing Private Sector Prison Industries: From Concept to Start Up.* Washington, D.C.: GPO.

— National Institute of Justice. 1990b. *Operating Jail Industries: A Resource Manual.* Rockville, Md.: NCJRS Microfiche Program.

— National Institute of Justice. 1993. *Sourcebook of Criminal Justice Statistics, 1993.* Washington, D.C.: GPO.

— Pollock-Byrne, Joycelyn M. 1990. *Women, Prison, and Crime.* Pacific Grove, Cal: Brooks/Cole.

— Sigler, Robert T., and M. G. Stough. 1991. "Using Inmate Labor to Produce Products for the Open Market." *Journal of Contemporary Criminal Justice* 7(1): 29-40.

— Skolnik Howard L., and J. Slansky. 1991. "A First Step in Helping Inmates Get Good Jobs after Release." *Corrections Today* 53: 92-94.

— Smykla, John. 1980. *Co-Ed Prison.* New York: Human Sciences Press.

— Snarr, Richard. 1992. *Introduction to Corrections.* 2d ed. Dubuque, Iowa: Wm. C. Brown Publishers.

— Stevenson, D. R. 1992. "Rehabilitative Effects of Earning a General Educational Development (GED) While in Total Jail Confinement as Measured by Recidivism Activity." *Dissertation Abstracts International, Vol. 42.* Ann Arbor, Mich.: University Microfilms.

— Stone, William E., C. C. McAdams, and J. Kollert. 1974. *Texas Department of Corrections: A Brief History.* Huntsville: Texas Department of Corrections Printing.

— Taylor, J. M. 1992. "Post-Secondary Education: An Evaluation of Effectiveness and Efficiency." *Journal of Correctional Education* 43(3): 132-141.

— Texas Department of Criminal Justice. 1993. *Annual Report of 1993.* Austin: Texas Department of Criminal Justice.

— Tootoonchi, A. 1993. "College Education in Prison: The Inmates' Perspective." *Federal Probation* 57(4): 34-40.

— Wellford, B. I., and J. F. Littlefield. 1985. "Correctional Post-Secondary Education: The Expanding Role of Community Colleges." *Community/Junior College Quarterly* 9(3): 257-272.

— Wines, Enoch C., and T. W. Dwight. 1867. *Report on the Prisons and Reformatories of the United States and Canada.* Albany, N.Y.: Van Benthuysen & Sons.

# CHAPTER

# 6

# REHABILITATION REVISITED

## *Joycelyn Pollock*

My biggest fear is of relapsing because this is my sixth treatment. . . . I must say that it has taken me six months to find out who I really am, to deal with issues that I have suffered for so many years. . . . I'm not going to be able to run to that corner, to run to that crack house. To buy those rocks, to suppress the feelings that I'm going to feel. . . . But I know that I have to hold myself accountable because I am responsible for who I am and what I am. And what I've chosen to be is productive and to stay clean and sober. Because [name of program] has shown me that there is an easier way. That sometimes you need to be shown the right path to go and I'm grateful.

> — *Inmate interviewed after completing a therapeutic community drug program*

Nothing works.

> — *Paraphrase of Martinson (1974) report*

——— *Chapter Overview* ———

——— **THE RISE AND FALL OF THE REHABILITATIVE IDEAL**
        "Nothing Works" v. "Some Things Work"
        Treatment in a Custody Institution
——— **PRISON PROGRAMS**
        Inmate Activities
                *Recreation*
                *Religion*
                *Arts and Crafts*
                *Service Groups*
        Treatment Programs
                *Self-Help Groups*
                *Alcoholics Anonymous and Narcotics Anonymous*
                *Professional Treatment Groups*
——— **THE CHANGE EFFORT**
        Theory and Practice
        Psychological or Psychiatric Programs
                *Psychotherapy*
                *Rogerian or Nondirective Therapy*
                *Behavior Modification*
        Social Therapy Programs
                *Transactional Analysis*
                *Reality Therapy*
                *Group Therapy*
                *Family Therapy*
                *Therapeutic Communities*

As discussed in a previous chapter, one of the rationales for the existence of prison has always been prevention. Prevention may take the more obvious forms of deterrence or incapacitation, but another way to prevent future criminal behavior is reform or rehabilitation of the offender. Rehabilitation means different things to different people; it can be job training, psychological intervention, social integration programs, education, prison ministries, or even recreational programs. Typically rehabilitation programs attempt to induce an internal change within the individual offender. What occurs inside prison is most often described in negative terms, that is, the prisoner learns how to be a better criminal and undergoes *prisonization* (socialization to antisocial norms). The ideal of rehabilitation involves the idea that positive changes occur in prison as well.

# THE RISE AND FALL OF THE REHABILITATIVE IDEAL

The earliest concept of the penitentiary involved some idea of inducing internal change. Because we discuss some of the following historical events in Chapter 2, here we only touch on how they are related and form a long tradition of reform as one goal of imprisonment. For instance, an early institution in Amsterdam (1596), located in an abandoned convent, confined young incorrigible petty offenders. It was believed that a regime of labor, discipline, and routine would help these individuals change their lives (Durham 1994). Before prisons existed, workhouses, almshouses, and like institutions were designed not only to house but also to change the inhabitants within. Then came the rise of the penitentiary with its emphasis on discipline, order, routine, and labor. These elements were believed to counteract the lack of disciplined upbringing, greed, personal disorder, and inadequate moral training of the incarcerated offenders (Durham 1994, 141).

The Quakers' attempts to influence change through religious instruction and meditation led to the Walnut Street Jail and Philadelphia prison model. Also, in the mid-nineteenth century, Crofton began the slow process of individualized treatment by dividing periods of incarceration into stages based on behavior and performance. Then the National Prison Congress in 1870 endorsed and recommended other innovations that supported the notion of treating the prisoners as individuals. For instance, parole, stages of liberty, and the indeterminate sentence were proposed at the 1870 Congress. Other programs, applied through rudimentary classification systems, were also endorsed, including education, vocational instruction, industries, and religious training.

Zebulon Brockway implemented many of these ideals in the opening of Elmira Reformatory in 1876. In the same year Elmira opened, Cesare Lombroso published *The Criminal Man* (1876). This book presented a typology of criminals and proposed a biological basis to criminality. Lombroso is often presented as the "grandfather" of the "positivist" school of criminology and serves as an historical marker to theories that identify the cause of crime in the individual. The reformatory movement in the late 1870s through the early 1900s, with its emphasis on education and internal change, was influenced by the positivist belief that to change the rate of crime, one must change the individual criminal and the cause of criminality was to be found in the deviance or pathology of the individual.

The principles and practices championed by Brockway during the so-called reformatory era arguably emphasized external change rather than internal change. Reform and rehabilitation are often differentiated as an emphasis on external (reform) versus internal (rehabilitation) change. *Reform* (as in Brockway's concept of the reformatory) monitors external behavior; success is defined as conformance of behavior to expectations. *Rehabilitation* implies internal change, meaning a permanent change in values, attitudes, morals, or ways of looking at the world. Another definition of rehabilitation includes that it restores some previous state of normality or law-abidingness, which, of course, is questionable because many offenders have never experienced a previous state of pro-sociability.

It was probably not a coincidence that Brockway's efforts to implement these incipient ideas of rehabilitation began with women offenders. Before the 1870 Prison Congress, he had administered an institution for women in which he started to implement some ideas such as graduated liberty with a type of early parole or work release that were later used for males. The idea of paroling females may have been more palatable to the public than the same program with males. Early reformatories for women took a more positive approach to their task than did penitentiaries. The goal and expectation was that the institution could change the individual. In the case of early reformatories for women, the expectation was that the institution could change female offenders into law-abiding, chaste, feminine mothers and wives. This ideal, even for women, did not last long, and the reformatory ideal was not widespread or long-lived for male or female offenders.

Modern rehabilitation efforts grew naturally from the rise of the social sciences in the early part of the twentieth century. As psychology, sociology, and other sciences defined their boundaries of knowledge, some professionals turned their newfound expertise of human behavior to the area of deviance and criminality. Early efforts with female offenders in prisons placed more emphasis on psychological theories. In Bedford Hills during the early 1900s theories revolving around the women's biology were used to explain women's criminality. "Lactational insanity" was believed to be the cause of some infanticide, and some women were labeled and treated as neurotics by prison psychologists (Pollock-Byrne 1990).

Sociological approaches were more common for male offenders. Even though there were some interventions based on individual pathologies, for example, psychoanalytical groups, for the most part, the interventions tended to revolve around the social-psychological elements of criminality, for example, influence of peer group behavior, learning theory, and more pragmatic concerns such as education and job skills.

By the 1950s "prison sociologists" were hired to classify inmates and to conduct "guided groups." Through the 1960s, rehabilitation continued to be a viable element of this nation's corrections system. Public poll data indicated that about three-quarters of Americans thought that rehabilitation should be the emphasis of American prisons, while about half believed that rehabilitation was in fact the primary purpose of correctional institutions (Durham 1994, 143).

Throughout the 1950s and 1960s, prisons tried various programs from group therapy to behavior modification to transcendental meditation. One illustration of the most extreme elements of this belief in rehabilitation was California's indeterminate term from zero to life, regardless of crime. Because the purpose of the system was to treat the individual, the inmate, regardless of the crime committed, would stay in the system until "cured." Karl Menninger's idea of the diagnostic facility as the center of the criminal justice system became the model for some states in their initiation of classification or reception centers that received all incoming inmates for the purpose of "diagnosing" their problems.

Extensive exploration into the person's background to identify needs and problems — medical, social, and psychological — lies at the heart of the rehabilitative ideal. Yet, even at its zenith, the rehabilitative approach affected a small portion of this nation's prisons. Perhaps only 5 percent of correctional budgets were spent on such programs (Durham 1994, 145). And while some prison systems were employing psychologists and running educational programs, other prisons were operating in such a way as to become the basis of court suits, such as Arkansas's Cummins and Tucker prison farms. Rather than group therapy, prisoners in these institutions were subjected to cockroach-infested gruel, were placed in "hotboxes" and "holes" for lengths of time that affected their health and vision, and experienced an extreme of brutality that shocked the courts into abandoning the "hands-off era" (spurring court activism *vis-à-vis* prison issues). *Holt v. Sarver*, 309 F. Supp. 362 (E.D. Ark. 1970). The so-called rehabilitative era, slow in developing and never ripening fully into an integrated, pervasive approach, began its decline about the time people started putting a name to it.

## "NOTHING WORKS" V. "SOME THINGS WORK"

In the mid-1970s, Robert Martinson was one of a group hired by the New York State Department of Corrections to evaluate prison treatment programs. The project, one of the most extensive of its kind, looked at 231 program evaluation studies, eliminated those with extremely poor research designs, and evaluated the results. Martinson stated that "with few and isolated exceptions, the rehabilitative efforts which have been reported so far have had no appreciable effect on recidivism" (Martinson 1974, 25).

Other meta-analyses also reported dismal findings (Logan and Gaes 1993). A series of meta-evaluations through the mid- to late-

1970s reported that little or no positive effects could be measured from treatment programs (Wright 1995). The conclusion that "nothing worked" served well those politicians and conservatives who advocated a "get tough" approach and decried the "mollycoddling" of prisoners that treatment programs implied. When crime rates increased in the 1960s and 1970s, the public became less tolerant of rehabilitative efforts.

The demise of rehabilitative efforts may not have been as swift or as certain without the strange and unique coalition of conservatives and liberals. For conservatives, indeterminate sentences, parole, and individualized treatment were too "soft" on crime; for liberals, they were too vague with no due process standards to limit discretion. In 1971 the American Friends Service Committee published *Struggle for Justice,* which argued that the indeterminate sentence had been used as an instrument of repression, was the cause of unfair sentences, and ought to be abandoned. The indeterminate sentence in California, for instance, was repealed by political partnerships between groups as diverse as sheriffs' associations and the American Civil Liberties Union (ACLU). The indeterminate sentence law in California was repealed, and many other states followed suit. Determinate sentencing laws now exist in the majority of states, and, in some states, parole has been repealed.

Ironically, the Attica prison riot, which also took place in 1971 and which was caused, many believe, by prisoners' frustration over the delays in instituting rehabilitative programs, served to harden public opinion. The riot often is used as the marker for the decline of rehabilitative efforts. Yet, even while the Martinson report moved from academic circles to politicians' speeches to the front pages of this nation's newspapers, critics disagreed that rehabilitation was without merit. The most vocal critic of Martinson was Palmer (1975). Immediately and continuously throughout the years, Palmer has utilized his own research findings and meta-analyses to refute the notion that treatment does not work (1974, 1975, 1978, 1983, 1991, 1994). Gendreau and Ross (1983) also criticized the attempt to paint all treatment programs as useless and pointed out that such a view allows the correctional system to escape the responsibility of affecting recidivism (Gendreau and Ross 1983). There became a solid core of evidence *for* and believers *in* the view that at least some programs did work.

> By 1983-84 evidence for [Martinson's] "relatively-little-works" view and for an alternative, "several-things-sometimes-work" view had been marshaled and became increasingly known. As a result, a mixed and unsettled atmosphere emerged regarding effective-

ness. More precisely, some confusion and considerable uncertainty existed. (Palmer 1992b, 63)

Wright (1995) also reviewed those sources that advocated and supported rehabilitative efforts (although he concludes that they have little on which to base their optimism). He identifies four distinct arguments of the supporters of rehabilitation:

1. that treatment programs should be evaluated by outcome measures other than recidivism;
2. that efforts to match the needs of individual offenders with specific programs would result in more effective treatment;
3. that polls among offenders show strong support for treatment programs; and,
4. that treatment programs may not make offenders any better, but there is no evidence that they make them worse (Wright 1995, 25).

Advocates of the "nothing works" camp and advocates of the belief that some programs do show measurable success continued the debate through the 1980s and into the 1990s. However, the battle for a committed approach to treatment was lost through the intervention of a much larger issue: overcrowding. Whether or not treatment programs could be successful became an irrelevant issue to those prison administrators who had inmates sleeping in tents. Finding enough mattresses for prisoners to sleep on and food for them to eat, and having enough staff to manage the institution at basic safety levels became more important than finding programs that worked.

## TREATMENT IN A CUSTODY INSTITUTION

Tension between punishment and treatment has been present since the inception of the penitentiary. How can one treat in a punitive institution? Conversely, how can one feel they're being punished when they have opportunities and access to programs not available on the street? This is captured in the following quote:

The emphasis on treatment and rehabilitation may diminish the capacity of the criminal justice system to serve as a general deterrent to crime; to the extent that imprisonment is unpleasant, it will be less than an ideal environment in which to conduct treatment; to the extent that it becomes a therapeutic environment, its deterrent effect will diminish. (Clear and Cole 1986, 104)

Prison research through the 1970s and 1980s quite often described prisons along a treatment-custody continuum. It was recognized that prisons could be either treatment-oriented or custody-oriented. In the former, treatment took precedence: Outsiders were allowed in, there was high participation of prisoners in programs, visitation was flexible and generous, and so on. In the custody-oriented prison, custody concerns took precedence: Outsiders were restricted, prison programs had to be approved by custody and often were limited in scope and number by custody concerns, and so on. The placement of the prison on the continuum was viewed as an independent variable in analyses of such things as prison homosexuality rates, violence, and prisonization. Women's institutions were anomalies on this treatment-custody continuum because they often had fewer formal treatment programs, but other measures, such as visitation and staff-inmate interactions, tended to be consistent with treatment institutions.

There are inherent problems between treatment and custody. For instance, vocational programs provide the raw materials for weapons: educational and work release and furloughs allow for escapes and the entry of contraband; and the entry of outsiders to the prison creates a problem of hostages. It would be much easier to keep inmates in their cells 24 hours a day. Yet even those who don't endorse all treatment programs see the value of some programs, outside activities, and interactions with family. Some believe that no treatment program can be effective in prison due to custody concerns. In other words, the efficacy of any approach that values the offender as an individual and seeks to make him more responsible with greater self-worth is doomed in an environment that constantly tears down the offenders' self-esteem and reminds them daily of their unworthiness and banishment from society. Others believe that treatment programs can exist but should be purely voluntary and incidental to the only legitimate purpose of prison, which is punishment. There are still those, however, who believe that internal change can occur — even in prison — and offenders can be positively affected by interventions, such as those we will describe below.

## PRISON PROGRAMS

Programs in prison run the gamut from maintenance work groups to drug treatment. While some authors tend to describe all programs under the heading of prison rehabilitation, Senese and

Kalinich (1992) discuss the gradual disuse of the term "rehabilitative" when describing prison programs, with the term "activities" replacing it. This is a cue that rehabilitation is not an emphasized goal of prison any longer. In our discussion, programs (such as recreation) that do not directly affect behaviors or attitudes will be mentioned only briefly. Work, industry, and education have been discussed in a previous chapter. Psychological and medical services that are purely reactive — that is, they intervene only after an individual experiences mental distress, physical injury, or illness — will not be discussed here. Only those programs that attempt to directly change the inmates' behaviors and attitudes will be discussed in this chapter.

Rehabilitation has been defined as "a programmed effort to alter attitudes and behaviors of inmates which is focused on the elimination of their future criminal behaviors" (Senese and Kalinich 1992, 223). Another definition of rehabilitation programs includes the following elements:

1. they have specific goals;
2. they are based on a clear concept or theory;
3. they have a specific structure and method;
4. they are intense and require time;
5. they have a history of success;
6. they are run by trained counselors; and
7. they are offered to inmates who can benefit from the programs (Gottfredson 1979).

Perhaps not all of these elements are present in all programs, but having none of them present clearly differentiates the activities described below from the treatment programs discussed later in the chapter.

## INMATE ACTIVITIES

According to Senese and Kalinich (1992), inmates' activities help inmates serve their sentences less painfully and provide them with assistance in solving some of the short-term problems related to their incarceration. These activities are not designed for rehabilitation per se, although some proponents maintain that they may help to induce positive change (for example, by building self-esteem or providing pro-social outlets for entertainment or leisure activities).

*Recreation.* The images of inmates lifting weights or watching television contribute to many people's criticism of prisons as not being "tough enough." Recreational programs are found in all prisons and include outdoor activities like basketball and softball, running tracks, weightlifting, aerobics, ping pong, television, arts and crafts or hobby shops, movies — even rodeos! At least until fairly recently in Texas, inmates could participate in an annual rodeo organized and staffed almost entirely by inmates for the general public. The prison system ended this long tradition only recently. In women's prisons, one is less likely to find weight lifting and organized sports teams and more likely to find such things as aerobic dance and yoga.

Opinions on these activities vary. Most correctional administrators value the recreational programs because they relieve the boredom of the inmate's day-to-day life and give them something to do as an alternative to drug use or other deviant behavior, they act as a privilege that can be used to control behavior, and they often serve as a productive force in the inmate's life. For instance, organized sports provide opportunities to interact and cooperate with others and to follow rules and procedures, habits that many offenders have never developed. They also encourage the development of a healthy lifestyle. Many inmates have never developed leisure activities that did not revolve around drinking and drug use. For these individuals, learning a hobby or sport or pasttime may provide them with a more acceptable alternative to past patterns of entertainment. Other administrators take a dim view of recreation — weight lifting in particular, citing the irony of helping the inmate develop the strength that in some cases will be used against officers (both law enforcement and correctional) who may need to subdue the individual.

*Religion.*    All prisons have religious programs, and the chaplain is often very instrumental in getting other programs started. Senese and Kalinich say that the basic role of the chaplain is to provide "spiritual therapy" for the inmates, the function of which "is to enable a person to internalize the concept of oneself as a whole and spiritual person" (1992, 220). Religious leaders may provide services for Catholics, Protestants, Muslims, and Jews. Programs may include occasional gospel singers or visits from surrounding congregations. Mentor programs or sponsors may be provided from the outside through the activities of a particular congregation.

One issue that has arisen is the definition of religion. In some cases prisoners have developed their own religion in an effort to use First Amendment protections. For instance, "The Church of the New Song" in Texas was organized by prisoners who filed suit to force the prison to honor their requests to practice their religion, which supposedly included such practices as drinking Harvey's Bristol Cream Sherry and eating steak. The court was unimpressed with the sincerity of these religious converts. Other cases have dealt with more serious requests to practice religious beliefs, even though the practice in question may pose a challenge to the prison's operations. The legal issues involved in the balance between First Amendment protections to believe and practice a religion versus the prison's interest in running a safe and orderly prison are explored in Chapter 10.

Prison ministries are an established presence in the prison environment. Many churches' commitments to good works include providing services or engaging in activities with prison inmates. There is a long history between religion and prisons, even before the Quakers created and implemented the Walnut Street Jail and Eastern Penitentiary. This legacy continues today with prison ministers, priests, and nuns continuing to provide needed services to prison inmates.

*Arts and Crafts.* Many prisons have extensive arts and crafts programs. Leatherworks, candlemaking, and other arts are practiced by some inmates. Products are sold in prison stores, and some art shows have exclusively represented prisoner artists. Prison administrators look fairly benignly at these programs. They are privileges that can be taken away, and if products are sold, often a percentage of the profit goes to the inmate fund, which is used to buy recreational equipment and other "luxuries" for which state monies are unavailable. Some critics contend that prisoners should have to pay for their own supplies, and in some cases this is required — especially for more expensive products such as leather, paints, or canvas. There may be other potential problems with inmate artwork. It is not unknown for prisoner artists to draw or paint pornography for "rent" or "sale." Some equipment and supplies may be used as weapons, and some prisoners may put a higher priority on their art than other activities such as work or education. Others defend such programs, finding that hobby shops provide some inmates with a niche that keeps them out of trouble and enables them to develop their own methods of expression that can be quite powerful and productive.

*Service Groups.* Many prisons have inmate organizations that provide charitable services. For instance, some lifers' groups and other inmate associations record books onto tape for organizations for the blind. Other prisoner service groups sew teddy bears and rag dolls for police agencies to have available in patrol cars to soothe children in traumatic scenes, sew quilts for the poor from donated rags, repair toys for Christmas toy drives, and in many other ways contribute to the good of the community.

The rehabilitative effect of these service groups is indirect and incidental to the main function of the groups, which is to help others. Yet many inmates discuss how good they feel when they "give something back to the community." The self-esteem that comes from doing something good for someone else should probably not be underestimated, although no studies exist as to the effect participation in these groups might have on recidivism, or whether the individuals involved continue their charitable work once they leave the prison.

## TREATMENT PROGRAMS

*Self-Help Groups.*   There are a number of self-help groups that exist in various prisons. Some are organized around ethnic identity. Some are drug treatment groups such as Alcoholics Anonymous (AA), which we will describe separately. Some are ex-prisoner rehabilitative programs.

One example is the Seventh Step group, which was started by Bill Sands. While this group uses the philosophy of AA (reliance on a higher power, support from peers, and so on), it was designed not necessarily for addictive personalities but for all ex-inmates who are sincere about their reintegration back into society. The goals of this organization are to help the inmate with the practical considerations of release and to act as a sounding board for problems of readjustment, using the experience of other inmates who have been there and can understand and empathize.

The Fortune Society in New York City is another long-standing program that provides services to ex-inmates during their reintegration into society. They provide mentoring, housing assistance, and job placement for released offenders. They also apply some degree of political pressure through their board of directors, which includes some fairly influential people. Delancey Street in California runs several halfway houses and businesses that employ their clients in a program that uses an eclectic combination of treatment modalities to address addiction to drugs and alcohol. While many of the clients are ex-inmates, they do not restrict clientele to criminal justice populations.

These groups are typically run without much (or any) formal governmental support, financial or otherwise. Perhaps their greatest value is that they show inmates the possibilities of changing life patterns. Most staff members have long criminal careers, yet are crime-free. They provide a different voice than the professional treatment counselor or prison correctional officer.

*Alcoholics Anonymous and Narcotics Anonymous.* Alcoholics Anonymous (AA) is probably the best-known and most-often copied format in the treatment group. The twelve steps of AA cover such principles as:

- admitting powerlessness over the addiction;
- relying on a higher power;
- taking a personal moral inventory;
- admitting wrongs to God and others;
- asking for forgiveness;
- making amends to all people that one has hurt;
- praying and meditating to improve conscious contact with God;
- spiritual awakening;
- carrying the message to other addicts. (Senese and Kalinich 1992, 222)

AA and NA (Narcotics Anonymous) have as their guiding principles that addiction is a disease, recovery begins only after one "hits bottom," one can depend and believe in a "higher power" to help in recovery, recovery is contingent on self-scrutiny and confession, and part of the recovery process includes carrying the message to other alcoholics or addicts (Senese and Kalinich 1992). Almost all prisons have AA even if they have no other treatment programs. Because the groups are not strictly administered by treatment staff, they range in quality and sincerity from prison to prison. In some, prisoners admit the groups are little more than places to meet friends and lovers; in other prisons, offenders state that the group has been the instrumental element in changing their life. Problems of confidentiality sometimes exist. AA depends on self-disclosure and confidentiality. If inmates do not feel that what they talk about in the AA group will stay confidential, or if indeed what they talk about does come back to them via the prison grapevine or in some negative context, then there is little likelihood that the group will have any real effect on participants or that participants will take the group seriously.

One advantage of AA and NA is their very pervasiveness. Practically every town and community has at least one group so that no matter where offenders are released, they should be able to access at least one group that will support and encourage their sobriety. The program seems to have a better track record with alcoholics than with addicts and with white and middle class rather than extremely poor or ethnic group members.

*Professional Treatment Groups.*    Professional treatment programs are distinguished from inmate groups in several ways. The most obvious is that prison staff members design the program, administer it, and set policy. Even if the treatment approach emphasizes participation on the part of the inmates, as does many of the social therapy programs discussed below, the impetus for the program came from professional staff members rather than inmates. Professional treatment programs differ also in that they are based on accepted psychological theories of behavior and treatment. Programs may operate under one theory (such as a program based on reality therapy) or, more frequently, may be *eclectic,* meaning that many different treatment modalities are brought together in the program.

In some cases, the prison system may contract with a private company to provide a program. This private entity hires the teachers and runs the program. The staff, whether considered employees of the prison or the private provider, must work within the prison policies and procedures, although the content of the program is set by the provider. These providers may be for-profit or not-for-profit. Many drug treatment programs are administered by private providers that are usually in the for-profit business of developing and providing such treatment programs. On the other hand, some groups may be run by private not-for-profit organizations, such as Parents Anonymous, a national organization that seeks to reduce child abuse and that runs groups for parents in prison who have a record of child abuse or child homicide.

In other cases, the prison staff runs programs. These may range from self-esteem groups to parenting classes to life skills groups. Groups for incest survivors and for battered women are becoming more common in women's prisons as the recognition grows that many women in prison have been victims as well as offenders, and that there is an association between their victimization and their criminal behavior. This may be direct, as with women who are imprisoned for killing their abuser, or it may be indirect, as with women who were sexually or physically abused as children and who grow up to repeat extremely dysfunctional relationships with men, including prostitution, relationships involving drug use, or other relationships involving exploitation and victimization. In some cases, women tend to repeat patterns of victimization; in other cases, women themselves develop patterns of exploitation and victimization of men.

In the next section we will explore some of the treatment modalities one might find in prison. These are presented as if they are discrete, but more often the approaches overlap. The eclectic approach is probably the most common in prisons today.

# THE CHANGE EFFORT

The so-called medical or *treatment ethic* that underlies most treatment programs can be stated as follows: Crime is a symptom of an underlying pathology that can be treated. This underlying pathology may be a drug problem, alcoholism, low self-esteem, an antisocial personality disorder, or some other psychological problem. It could be lack of job skills, poor socialization, or blocked moral development. By treating the underlying pathology, it is assumed that the symptom of crime will go away. For instance, to give an offender a trade assumes that his criminal behavior occurred because of no or low job skills; fixing the problem by providing job skills and legitimate employment will eliminate criminal behavior. In the same way, treatment programs that target moral development, self-esteem, or drug addiction assume that successful intervention will address the problem and, in turn, eliminate criminal behavior.

## *THEORY AND PRACTICE*

All programs discussed in this section address mental attitudes or behavior. In most treatment programs, the individual's mental status is the focus. This may take the form of addressing the inmate's self-concept, moral development, life scripts, or communication patterns. Yet, all these modalities assume that there is such a thing as mental health and that the offender is further away from it than a non-offender. Few agree, however, on the concept of mental health, much less on the relationship between mental health and criminality.

Let's explore the concept of mental health by beginning with the analogy of physical health. What does it mean to be physically healthy? Some may say physical health is the absence of injury or disease. Yet this doesn't fully define the concept. One may not have observable symptoms of a disease but be a carrier. One may have viruses that lay dormant for years before developing any symptomology. One may have no observable symptoms, yet have diseased lungs through smoking, clogged arteries through bad diet, or poor muscle tone through lack of exercise. Are these people physically healthy or not? Everyone would probably agree that physical health is not a discrete categorization, but rather a continuum. Some of us are more physically healthy than others. Those in a hospital suffering from disease or injury are far to one side of this continuum, and those athletes who maintain their bodies with religious zeal by controlling diet and exercise are to the other end of the continuum. Most of us are somewhere in the middle.

So, too, is the case with mental health. While we would like to believe that "insane" or "mentally ill" people are entirely different from us, mental health also represents a continuum. Those who suffer from schizophrenic delusions, manic-depressive mood swings, or catatonic states are similar to those individuals described above who may be hospitalized for severe injury or illness. There may be others who fall at the other end of the spectrum and can be considered very mentally healthy. Most of us fall somewhere in the middle. We may have mild neurotic tendencies, low self-esteem, or suffer from depression. What is different about the mental health continuum, however, is that we are less sure what it means to be mentally healthy than we are about what it means to be physically healthy. Various personality inventory tests and other diagnostic tools have been designed to measure indices of mental health, but critics contend that these may be biased, for instance, by culture and gender.

Mental health has been described as having the following characteristics: good self-esteem, optimism, personal responsibility, empathy, and the ability to have committed and loving relationships. Many do not believe in the term "mental illness" at all (Glasser 1965; Szasz 1963). Rather than illness, which connotes a cure, some believe that what we consider mental illness is irresponsibility, which cannot be cured. It is up to the individual to decide to get on with her life and become more responsible.

Any further discussion is beyond the scope of this chapter, but the definition of mental health is important for the following reason. If we seek to intervene with the offender through one of the treatment modalities below or any others, what goal do we seek? If it is to move the inmate further along this mental health continuum, we must be clear about what characteristics or elements make up mental health. Can one be mentally healthy and like to steal from others? Does the concept of mental health also involve an element of morality? (Kohlberg 1976; Gilligan 1982).

Another important issue to contemplate relates to evaluation. A treatment program that targets, for instance, improvement of low self-esteem and the development of life skills may succeed very well in those goals yet have no measurable effect on recidivism. If this is the case, is it important to continue such a program? Do we care to provide intervention that makes criminals feel better about themselves?

In this section we will discuss some types of treatment modalities one might expect to find in prison. One last point should be touched on here. While in this chapter the use of such words as counseling, treatment, and therapy are used almost interchangeably, there are those who distinguish correctional counseling from psychotherapy. In this view, *counseling* deals with interpersonal problems, and *psychotherapy* deals with intrapersonal problems. Also, psychotherapy is practiced by experts with many years of training (psychologists and psychiatrists) in contrast to counselors, who may be certified but have less training or formal education (Walsh 1988). While this is obviously an important distinction, we may not stick strictly to it in this chapter.

Programs we will discuss are psychological or psychiatric programs, social therapy programs, and therapeutic communities.

## PSYCHOLOGICAL OR PSYCHIATRIC PROGRAMS

Psychological or psychiatric programs are based on the assumption that an individual's criminal behavior is symptomatic of a defect in the emotional makeup or psyche of the offender (Senese and Kalinich 1992). They may address specific problems or deal in a holistic way with the person without centering on one issue or behavior.

*Psychotherapy.* Individual therapy is the least common method of providing treatment to inmates. Typically psychologists do not have time to engage in ongoing therapy with individual offenders because they may be responsible for the mental well-being of several hundred (or thousands) in a single prison. In addition to administering psychology tests for classification purposes, psychologists are used for crisis management, such as intervening when an inmate has attempted suicide or "cut up" (mutilated some part of their body with a sharp instrument). Psychologists and psychiatrists employed by the prison make decisions as to who should be transferred to forensic units in the system and may monitor the retransfer of such inmates back into the institution after they have been stabilized. They may also staff and administer individual "psych" units in the prison, which house those prisoners who exhibit extreme symptomology of mental problems. These units, often placed in the prison hospital, have more custody controls — often there is round-the-clock monitoring of inmates, a much smaller ratio of officers to inmates, psychiatric nurses on duty, and isolation from the general population.

Psychoanalysis was the first "talking therapy." There is not just one version but many variants of Freudian and neo-Freudian psychotherapy. The primary goals of psychotherapy are self-enlightenment and the development of individual responsibility. By developing a relationship with a therapist and discussing issues of the past and present, the individual develops self-awareness of motivations for his behavior. Freudian analysis includes the idea that early life experiences are important and, if traumatic, are often buried in the subconscious. The buried memories create problems for the adult because of various psychological defense mechanisms developed to deal with the trauma: repression, projection, reaction formation, obsession, denial, sublimation, and so on (Masters 1994). With the therapist's help, the individual experiences "catharsis" when she "spontaneously discovers" the issues that have been festering in the subconscious and maladaptive behaviors are gradually used less as mental well-being is generated by a clear understanding of hidden motivations and better "sense of self."

One mechanism of treatment is "transference" where the therapist comes to be identified with an earlier character in the person's life, for instance, a parental figure (usually at the root of their problem). This relationship is worked through with the therapist standing in for the person. Transference can help the person realize issues from this earlier relationship when the therapist reacts in opposite ways or is dispassionate and doesn't fall into "countertransference" where the relationship begins to be used for the therapist's own needs. The elements of personality (superego, ego, id) and stages of development (oral, anal, phallic) are also important ingredients to psychotherapy (Masters 1994).

One example of an application of psychotherapy to delinquent or criminal populations is Redl and Wineman's description of the "delinquent ego" (described in Lester 1992, 102). According to these therapists a person with a delinquent ego has the following characteristics: cannot tolerate frustration or insecurity, experiences anxiety and fear-panic, is susceptible to contagion and poor control, has difficulty seeing self-responsibility in consequences, is not realistic about rules or routines, fails to predict others' responses, and reacts to disappointments with feelings of complete failure or hostility. Intervention consists of individual sessions with a therapist, which helps the individual to uncover hidden past traumas, to learn to see the world more realistically, and to strengthen the ego.

Obviously, this process works best with a willing and helpful patient. Psychoanalysis typically works well for intelligent, articulate, adult neurotics who can talk out their problems; it is difficult to apply to delinquent or offender groups because they don't trust the therapist and no relationship develops that forms the crux of the transference process. The other major problem, of course, is cost.

Psychotherapy is a time-intensive, individual therapy. It has never adapted well to prison populations.

> ***Rogerian or Nondirective Therapy.*** Another form of individual therapy has been called "client-centered," "Rogerian," or "nondirective." Carl Rogers developed this approach, which includes the following principle: The individual has the capacity to understand his problems and overcome them through a warm, accepting, and understanding therapeutic relationship (Rogers 1961).

One of the premises for this therapy is that the self-concept is derived from interactions with others. Problems arise when there is incongruency between the individual's self-concept and reality. Therapy involves the therapist and individual working through feelings to get to underlying issues. Therapists use active listening techniques, such as clarification, paraphrasing, and reflection of feelings ("I hear you saying you are scared and depressed over your wife leaving . . ."). Therapists are not experts in the relationship; they merely guide the individual through self-understanding. In this *phenomenological approach* the therapist attempts to "see the world" through the eyes of the client. The therapist avoids making a diagnosis or even coloring the perceptions of the client with the therapist's attitudes or value systems. This avoids dependency.

> The role of the criminal justice counselor is to provide a warm, permissive, non-threatening, non-judgmental, and emotional environment in which the offender feels enough trust to open up and freely discuss his or her problems. . . . If the counseling procedures are successful, the offender will be able to clarify and gain insight into thoughts, feelings, attitudes, values, and behaviors. (Masters 1994, 110)

Success occurs when the clients become more "congruent" in their feelings and behavior, or their perceptions and the world around them. The objectives are to raise self-esteem, discover more realistic ways of handling life's problems, reduce anxiety, develop a tolerance for life's frustration, reduce feelings of inadequacy, and have a more positive attitude toward the future.

This therapy operates with the underlying assumption that human nature is basically good, generous, and kind, and it is only when there are psychic disturbances that negative behavior results. The therapy focuses on the positive rather than the negative aspects of the person's life, and through "unconditional positive regard" (an unwavering warm accepting stance), the therapist creates a safe environment where the individual can feel comfortable about change. Nondirective therapy may not be very well-suited to criminal populations because the therapist must maintain positive regard throughout the therapeutic process, regardless of the feelings, attitudes, or behaviors expressed or shared with the therapist. This is fairly easy to do with a middle-class suburban professional suffering from anxiety attacks but is much more difficult when one is working with a criminal offender with a background of violence toward others.

*Behavior Modification.*    Behavior modification concentrates on behavior rather than attitudes or self-knowledge. Rewards and punishments are manipulated in such a way that desired behavior is rewarded and undesired behavior is punished. It is believed that all behavior is shaped and maintained by its consequences, specifically, that behavior that is reinforced is more likely to recur than behavior that is not. Effective reinforcement follows immediately after the behavior and can be either concrete (material) or social (praise). The behavior in question must be clearly identified and specified (Bandura 1969). For instance, behavior modification can be applied to the tendency to react violently to frustration but not to generalized anxiety. Two forms of programs illustrate two very different approaches.

*Aversive conditioning* relies on *classical conditioning*: It uses the autonomic nervous system to induce a decrease in undesired behavior. The movie "Clockwork Orange" was a fictional account of the extremes to which aversive conditioning can take. By associating a negative behavior with a painful stimulus (for example, an electrical shock), a connection is made in the person's mind between the behavior and unpleasant sensation. Soon the negative behavior, or even thoughts about the behavior, induce a feeling of unpleasantness. This association takes place at a physiological level rather than a rational one. For example, child molesters may be shown sexually suggestive pictures of children paired with an electrical shock. The connection between sexual arousal in response to the photo and pain is made, resulting in the "conditioned response" of a feeling of unpleasantness or anticipation of pain when presented with the stimulus of the photos. The pictures of children in provocative poses are the unconditioned stimulus, which induces sexual excitement (the unconditioned response). But with the pictures, the offender is subjected to an electric shock (which is the conditioned stimulus); the pain caused by the shock is the conditioned response. Eventually, the association is made between sexual excitement in reaction to young children and pain or discomfort, and the sexual excitement will be extinguished. Drugs are sometimes used as aversive controls. For example, anectine and antabuse are used with alcoholics because they cause violent nausea and vomiting if mixed with alcohol. Apomorphine also induces vomiting for a period of 15 to 60 minutes and causes temporary cardiovascular changes; it is used for more generalized forms of behavior.

Critics of behavior modification in prison point to the possibilities of misuse. Behavior modification can change behavior even with involuntary participants, and the power and control aspects of such a setting have given behavior modification the reputation of being tied to "Big Brother" activities. The movie "Clockwork Orange" and "1984" are two fictional accounts that illustrate the fear of mind control. The power of behavior modification is probably overstated by these critics. Behavior modification supporters believe aversive conditioning is fairly limited in its success, although they do point out that it can control negative behavior, even temporarily, so that the offender may become more amenable to learning more appropriate behavior patterns (Masters 1994).

Cases such as *Knecht v. Gillman,* 488 F.2d 1136 (8th Cir. 1973), helped to eliminate the use of aversive conditioning in prison. In this case, certain inmates with "behavior problems" at the Iowa Security Medical Facility were given apomorphine as "aversive stimuli." The record indicated that inmate nurses sometimes injected the offenders, and that the medical acceptability of this "treatment" was subject to some dispute. The court held that for this type of "experimental" therapy there must be knowing and intelligent written consent. This consent must indicate full knowledge of the program, must allow withdrawal of consent at any time, and must authorize only a doctor to give an injection after personal observation of the inmate's misconduct.

*Token economies* are as old as Maconochie's "mark system" in the 1840s wherein "marks" were awarded for good behavior on the part of inmates individually and through work groups; marks in turn could result in expanded liberties. Token economies, which rely on *operant conditioning,* can be found in honor blocks and prison programs that allow for expanded liberties for good behavior. These programs rely on the following principles of learning: first, that one can shape behavior through the use of rewards, and second, that rewards are most effective when they are important to the client (for example, food is a better reinforcer than books because everyone has to eat).

*Wyatt v. Stickney,* 325 F. Supp. 781 (M.D. Ala. 1971), restricted the use of what could be used for rewards in institutional settings.

The court said food, mattresses, grounds privileges, and privacy could not be used as rewards for hospital patients. The well-known principle that rewards work better if they are something the person uses or needs constantly (for example, food) was specifically and directly rejected by several court rulings. Conditions that are defined as basic rights cannot be used as rewards. *Morales v. Turman,* 364 F. Supp. 166 (E.D. Tex. 1973) (Wexler 1973).

Unfortunately, the real world is not at all like a token economy, and the transition to the outside world may be the weakest element of this approach. Most of us do not live in controlled environments where rewards are manipulated to shape behavior to the degree or consistency of a token economy. Working hard may have to be its own reward in the real world, and it's not always true that performing tasks well ensures success. It is important that the individual offender learns to "administer their own rewards"; that is, the concrete rewards of privileges must be translated to psychic rewards of feeling good about oneself or greater self-esteem derived from a feeling of accomplishment, so that the person can continue successful change after leaving the token economy.

In a prison, behavior modification may easily be subverted to control the population rather than be used for productive rehabilitative change. Making prisoners easier to handle is not necessarily the same thing as helping them become better citizens. Advocates say our behavior is being shaped all the time and that it is not a question of whether to do it, but rather how to do it in a logical, pro-social way. However, today few aversive conditioning programs can be found in prisons, and token economies, while they do exist, may be not much more than honor blocks.

## SOCIAL THERAPY PROGRAMS

While individual therapy treats the individual as a discrete entity, social therapy programs concentrate on the relationship between the individual and the people around him. The treatment modalities discussed in this section are not discrete categories. Although group therapy is described, it must be remembered that other treatment approaches may be implemented through the group process. Some groups may use overlapping approaches.

*Transactional Analysis.*   This therapy uses a theory of personality that resembles the psychoanalytic school. The personality is viewed as made up of three parts: the Parent (which corresponds roughly to the superego), the Adult (which corresponds roughly to the ego), and the Child (which corresponds roughly to the id). Although these seem similar, Berne (1962) points out that the Parent, Adult, and Child are all portions of the ego — the conscious element of the personality as postulated by Freud.

Individuals, through some malfunction of development, may have one part dominate their personality, although all parts are represented in some degree in everyone. For instance, the Child is concerned with wants and needs, emotions and nurturance. The individual who operates from her Child may constantly seek reassurance, be openly affectionate but also openly hostile, and have difficulty with delayed gratification. The Parent is the conscience and the responsible element of the personality. All the messages one has absorbed from real parents and other authority figures are stored in the Parent portion of the personality. The "shoulds," "oughts," and "must nots" we tell ourselves come from our Parent. Our Parent is also the source of judgments and condemnations of others. Our Parent is able to give nurturance and reassurance but also is able to alienate by making sweeping generalizations and verbal reprimands. The Adult is the knowledge-seeking, reality-testing, compromising portion of our personality. A well-balanced person can moderate the needs and immediate wants of the Child and the stringent requirements of the Parent to reach some balance between responsibility and fun.

Transactional analysis is primarily a social therapy program because it concentrates on communication and on the image of self that is affected by others' perceptions. A negative self-image could be represented as "I'm not OK, You're OK," which then affects behavior and decision making through "life scripts." (Harris 1969). Even a good childhood may result in this life position if an individual grows up feeling that adults are perfect and that the individual (child) can never hope to be as good, as smart, or as successful as his parents. If childhood is devoid of caring or positive affirmation, or if there is neglect or brutality, the child may grow up to the "I'm not OK, You're not OK" or the "I'm OK, You're not OK" life position.

The reason why, for instance, some women get involved repeatedly with men who are abusive and degrading is because in their life script they perceive themselves as unworthy of someone who would treat them kindly. Until they address this perception, they will continue to live out over and over again the role that they have set for themselves. Therapy involves understanding and changing these life scripts.

Recognizing communication patterns can lead to greater understanding of why some things happen in one's life. Some communications or "transactions" are complementary, that is, adult to adult. These types of communications are basically information-seeking ("Have you seen my notebook?" "I think it's over on the bookshelf"). Some are conflicted, that is, adult to parent ("Have you seen my notebook?" "If you would put things where they belong, you wouldn't lose them"). These transactions may form patterns; for instance, an offender may continually enter into conflicted transactions with all adult figures ("Can I see your identification, sir?" "Make me!") These conflicted transactions create miscommunication and dysfunctional relationships.

"Games" form another recognizable pattern of communication. Some games are common to criminal justice populations. The following were observed in a juvenile population: "You ain't shit," a challenge to a staff member physically; if the staff member does not meet the challenge, she loses legitimacy. "You're not quite yourself today," which shows that the inmate knows the staff member well enough to identify moods. Calling attention to the mood or playing on it by making problems in order to get the staff member to explode results in a payoff for the offender. "Don't expect too much from me," a self-diagnosis offered as an explanation of why the offender is the way he is or why change is impossible (Miller et al. 1974).

Other games of offenders are described by Berne (1964) as "See What You Made Me Do," "Cops and Robbers," "Alcoholic," "Addict," "Now He Tells Me," "If It Weren't for You," "Little Old Me," "Courtroom," "Now I've Got You, You Son of a Bitch," "Kick Me," "Stupid," "Uproar," "Let's You and Him Fight," and "Psychiatry." These games are recognizable patterns of inmate communication. Once again, games are described as patterned communication that results in payoffs to the players; typically these payoffs are antithetical to true communication or productive change.

One communication game often played with therapists, or others trying to help the inmate change her life, is the "Why don't you . . . ," "Yes but . . ." game. The therapist suggests options and the person finds reasons for why each option would not work. The goal of the individual being helped is really to shoot down the ideas, not to find a solution, thereby making the transaction a game instead of true communication. The underlying reason for such a game may be that the individual has unmet "child" needs. The attention derived from the game is more rewarding than solving the problems the discussion is about.

Through group or individual therapy, the individual offender learns the basic premises of transactional analysis, as summarized above, and begins the process of identifying communication patterns. In a group, one might hear the phrase, "You're coming out of your Child today," or "That's your Parent talking." Life scripts are also analyzed, and the individual learns to identify patterns of relationships in his life, with the expectation that if his self-image changes, these patterns won't be repeated.

Transactional analysis was popular in prisons during the 1970s because it could be understood and implemented fairly quickly. It is well-adapted to the group process and can be used with other treatment approaches. However, today one hears very little of transactional analysis in correctional programs; it seems, in fact, to have fallen out of favor in correctional circles. However, because interest in various treatment modalities seems to be cyclical, one might predict that transactional analysis will be "rediscovered" in the future and used again with correctional populations. Also, some of the elements of transactional analysis, such as the idea of "life scripts," are used extensively in eclectic treatment programs, although homage to the source of the concept is rarely made. Finally, the relevance of dysfunctional communication patterns among offenders seems to warrant attention to this "old" treatment program.

***Reality Therapy.*** According to William Glasser (1965), humans have two basic needs: to be loved and to feel worthwhile. When someone develops maladaptive behavior patterns they are trying to meet these two needs without understanding the reality of the world around them. The first step in intervention is to develop a close relationship or involvement with the individual, and then, through teaching, reject irresponsible behaviors. More specifically, the steps have been described as follows:

1. Achieve involvement.
2. Understand but deemphasize personal history.
3. Help the client understand attitude and behavior and the elements that contribute to it.
4. Explore alternative behaviors.
5. Get commitment to change.
6. Monitor and evaluate. Accept no excuses, enact no punishments. Rewrite the commitment to ensure success. (Walsh 1988, 142)

Responsibility is defined as the ability to fulfill one's needs in a way that does not deprive others of the ability to fulfill their needs (Glasser 1965, 13). Many offenders and delinquents may never have had to deal with reality responsibly because they have not learned that their behavior has consequences: "Parents who are willing to suffer the pain of the child's intense anger by firmly holding him to the responsible course are teaching him a lesson that will help him all his life" (Glasser 1965, 18).

The therapy concentrates on the "here and now" and emphasizes behavior rather than motivation. "What are you doing?" is asked, not "why are you doing it?" The therapist helps the person to evaluate the behavior in question and to develop a plan for future behavior. No excuses are accepted, no punishment is used, but success receives praise and approval. Many offenders have a "failure identity," thus it is vitally important to get a commitment to change that has every chance of being successful. Even small successes are powerful because they contribute to the individual's "success identity" and help build a foundation of continued responsibility.

Glasser developed these concepts working with delinquent girls at Ventura School for Girls in California. Reality therapy has been a fairly popular treatment modality in prison because it is consistent with common sense (that offenders are acting irresponsibly) and does not require in-depth training. Because behavior contracts are often used in reality therapy, it may be difficult to differentiate this type of therapy from behavior modification, yet there are important differences. First, unlike behavior modification, this therapy depends on the connection and relationship with the therapist. Second, this therapy depends much more on the individual assessing what behavior needs to be changed and what conditions could reduce the behavior. Finally, reality therapy rests on the principle that individuals must take responsibility for their actions, both their failures and their successes.

*Group Therapy.* Group therapy programs use facilitators to guide discussion in a group of people, often with similar problems. Much has been written about the group process, which involves the group going through separate and easily identifiable phases. The first stage is the security stage, which is when members initially enter. This stage is marked by anxiety, discomfort, and tentative communication efforts. Exercises to increase trust usually are used to move through this phase. The second stage is the trust stage, during which members feel comfortable enough to share life experiences. Cooperation and sharing characterize this stage. Cohesiveness grows, and people interact honestly. The next stage is the responsibility stage. The group does not progress if people just talk about their lives and their problems; they must take responsibility to change. The group must go beyond simply empathizing; it must confront resistance and problem solve. The next stage is the work stage. This stage is different for each group. Some groups may work on the same problem for all members (for example, assertiveness or child abuse); others may work on individual member's different problems. In this stage members try out new behaviors or attitudes. The final stage is the closing stage in which members debrief and give each other feedback and encouragement (Trotzer 1981, 362).

Economic constraints make group therapy programs more common than individual therapy. Many intervention modalities used in individual therapy have their counterparts in groups: Some groups use psychotherapy, some use transactional analysis, and so on. Other types of groups include process-centered groups, task-oriented groups, interpersonal discussion groups, expressive-projective groups, and analytic groups. Roles develop in each group no matter what the modality or focus is. Some recognizable roles are "the resister" (who resists change or argues against any ideas brought out in the group), "the expert" (who assumes the role of expert in all conversations), "the monopolizer" (who attempts to continually steer discussion to her problem), "the withdrawn" (a nonparticipant in the group process), and the "masochist-sadist pair" (two members who develop an abuser-victim conversational pattern) (Walsh 1988, 197).

Some examples of group therapy among inmate populations include the "guided group interaction" program used at Highfields, New Jersey and Provo, Utah. In both places, juvenile offenders were placed in a group by court order as an alternative to juvenile detention. The group process involved the juveniles meeting daily and developing rules and agendas for the group. Long, intense discussions occurred covering everything from behaviors to attitudes of group members. At Highfields the group lived together and did volunteer work. At Provo, the group lived at home but met every day. Although success rates (reduced recidivism) in these programs were impressive, dropout rates were also high, calling into question whether the group therapy made the difference or whether the group of juveniles who completed the program were highly motivated (Empey and Rabow 1961).

The advantages of group therapy for offender populations include the following:

1. It is more economical than individual treatment.
2. It can provide immediate peer pressure, feedback, and information.
3. Challenges from peers are harder for offenders to deny or rationalize.

4. It helps to relieve everyday tension from the prison environment and provides a better way to deal with conflicts.
5. It can help to address the prisoner subculture.
6. It can help communication between staff and offenders.
7. It is helpful to use for problem solving.
8. It provides reinforcement for positive values.
9. Lay group leaders do not need extensive training.
10. Many different treatment modalities can be adapted to the group process. (Masters 1994, 146)

Of course, there are problems with group therapy as well:

1. It may be the site for mere game playing with no sincere effort to deal with problems.
2. Members may discuss only superficial concerns rather than substantive issues.
3. Quiet inmates may hide in the group without dealing with their own problems.
4. Dominant inmates may exploit and control the group.
5. Prison norms explicitly reject the principles of the group process (for example, confidentiality and sharing confidences) and thus may be more powerful than the group itself (Masters 1994).

*Family Therapy.*   Underlying all social therapy programs is the understanding that the individual lives in a world where relationships are important and affect the self. Family therapy treats the family as a unit rather than treating the individuals in the family. Family dynamics are implicated in many psychological problems, such as schizophrenia, autism, suicide, alcoholism, and so on. Role playing, communication patterns, and intimacy are issues that are central to all models of family therapy. According to the principles of family therapy, each family strives for homeostasis, or balance. Changes in one individual result in changes in the family as a unit as it tries to adjust back to a balance. One classic example of this is when an alcoholic or addict changes, another family member may take on the "sick" role. Dysfunctional family units have some or all of the following characteristics:

1. secrets (incest, abuse, alcoholic member);
2. poor communication patterns (passive-aggressive, hostile, indirect);
3. boundary problems (individuals do not protect their autonomy from demands);

   4. enmeshments (members are involved in each others lives' to an extreme);
   5. stifled feelings (no honest expression of feelings);
   6. lack of freedom and power;
   7. system rules (unspoken rules, for example, ignoring or never mentioning the alcoholic's behavior);
   8. rigid roles;
   9. isolation (few contacts outside the family);
  10. an inability to be real (no expression of feelings); and
  11. unmet needs (of self-worth or love). (Masters 1994, 149)

A partial list of issues that might be dealt with in family therapy are as follows: role playing, communication patterns, issues of abandonment, anger, humiliation, life scripts, practical economic issues, child rearing, and faithfulness (Kaslow 1987). Many of these are central to problems offenders have with their families. Kaslow and others believe that there are many issues that should be dealt with through family therapy during a prerelease or immediate postrelease time period, such as

   1. anger (children or spouses left behind may be very angry at the offender);
   2. blame (offenders may blame family members for losing children or being imprisoned in the first place);
   3. resentment (offenders may resent a lack of visits, family may resent the offender not having to deal with problems of living during the prison term);
   4. the offender playing the black sheep or "naughty child" role in the family;
   5. role usurpation (when the inmate-mother is replaced by the grandmother in child rearing or the inmate-father is replaced by the mother as the breadwinner during the period of incarceration);
   6. expectations (such as how long the offender can stay with parents or expecting the offender to immediately begin making enough money to live on and take back child rearing responsibilities); and
   7. demands. (Kaslow 1987)

Family therapy involves the family members working with the therapist to discover these issues, identify dysfunctional communication patterns, and identify roles in the family that are detrimental or block individuals from truly communicating. Family therapy is not commonly used in prison settings, primarily because it is impractical.

Family members often live long distances from the prison, and visitation, if it does occur, tends to be short and unorganized. Although the lack of family therapy in prison is unfortunate for all offenders, it is especially ironic when considering female offenders. Over three-fourths of female prisoners are mothers, and most plan to live with their children on release. Research shows that women in prison typically come from family backgrounds of alcoholism, addiction, criminal behavior, incest, or abuse. These women, who despite periods of incarceration raise their own children, are largely ignored by prison programming, arguably perpetuating yet another generation of dysfunctional families (Pollock-Byrne 1990).

*Therapeutic Communities.*   The therapeutic community model originated with Maxwell Jones's efforts to create an alternative to institutionalized treatment for war combat veterans after World War II (Jones 1968). It was observed that the typical hospital environment was not very conducive to making the individuals responsible and ready to reenter society. In fact, the patient role was contrary to empowerment and personal responsibility and often led instead to the patient abandoning responsibility for his own recovery. In the therapeutic community developed by Jones, patients became partners in the therapeutic process instead of being subjects acted on. Each individual, whether client or counselor, staff or patient, took responsibility for her own actions. Doctors, for instance, were given no more power than the newest patient unless hospital regulations were at stake. Voting decided all issues concerning the running of the ward, and groups were conducted each day to deal with issues of irresponsibility and to encourage patients to take on greater and greater roles of responsibility.

These types of programs that use everything about the environment, milieu, or community in the therapeutic process were adapted for use with groups of mentally retarded, the mentally ill, and eventually prisoners. Therapeutic communities in prison have had problems similar to all programs that have attempted to give inmates power. Early programs had problems when prisoners voted to give those who violated prison rules either more or less punishment than what prison officials would have given them. Ordinarily, however, program staff found that prisoners were harsher in distributing punishment than officials or staff persons might have been (Toch 1980).

Therapeutic communities accomplish at least one thing: They tend to negate, at least partially, the overwhelming negativity of the prison environment. The programs typically are housed in special units or at least segregated from the general population. They tend to be successful in developing a general atmosphere of positivism and reciprocal self-worth. The members express very positive feelings toward the staff and fellow residents. Unfortunately, individuals leave such communities to go back to less supportive environments.

## OTHER PROGRAMS

There are a few other programs that do not fit into any of the categories above. The three programs discussed next use "cognitive approaches" that address the thinking patterns of the individual inmate.

Moral development programs address the moral development level of offenders. These programs use the work of Kohlberg and others to assess and improve the moral development level of the offender. Under Kohlberg's theory, all of us develop moral reasoning, but some develop further than others. In his theory he identifies three levels and six stages. See Highlight 6-1.

Offenders tend to cluster in Kohlberg's Stages 1 and 2, whereas most nonoffender adults with similar backgrounds to the offenders tend to cluster in Stages 3 and 4. Few people reach Stages 5 and 6. Intervention can help a person move up to a higher stage of development. Intervention has been shown to improve moral development scores (studies cited in Smith and Faubert 1990; see also Lester 1992, Pollock-Byrne 1991). Typically the treatment program engages the offenders in discussions in which they are expected to support their moral reasoning. Those with less-developed moral reasoning have more difficulty presenting logical arguments for why their rationale is superior and learn from those in the group discussion who present higher-level thinking.

One example of the use of moral development theory in corrections was Scharf, Kohlberg, and Hickey's work in Niantic prison in Connecticut. There they created the elements of a therapeutic community, but employed Kohlberg's moral reasoning findings to guide the development and implementation of the group meetings. That is, the living environment was like a therapeutic community in that it was isolated from the rest of the prison and it held daily group meetings to take care of the "business" of the community, but in addition, Scharf, Kohlberg, and Hickey instituted the ideas of morality in discussions. Moral reasoning was emphasized, and individuals, in group discussions, were asked to defend their moral decisions and were exposed to higher level moral reasoning: "Moral change is associated with active role taking and participation in the political and justice

**HIGHLIGHT 6-1**
**Kohlberg's Stages**

**Stage 1.** Obedience to authority and avoidance of punishment are the elements of moral reasoning. Associated with a young child, what is right is what Mommy or Daddy says is right. What is wrong is what is punished. There is little independent thought regarding right and wrong, and an egoistic view of the world prevails.

**Stage 2.** There is still a strong egoistic element to morality. What is right is what feels good to self. There is, however, awareness of relativism, that is, what feels good may be different for different people. There is some commitment to exchange and reciprocity.

**Stage 3.** This is the good boy-good girl orientation. Role modeling is a major mechanism for shaping values and behavior. Actions are judged by intent as well as consequence.

**Stage 4.** Morality is associated with doing one's duty and showing respect for authority. Maintaining the social order is seen as the sum result of moral rules.

**Stage 5.** There is recognition of legalistic agreement in the social order and that the social order may be an arbitrary creation at any particular point in time. "Majority rules," is a rule of morality.

**Stage 6.** This is the conscience- or principles-based orientation. Social universality and consistency are the themes that are used to determine moral decisions. (Adapted from Kohlberg 1976)

process of the setting" (Scharf, Kohlberg, and Hickey 1981, 413). They found that participation in their "just community" raised offenders' moral development scores.

Rational emotive therapy (RET), founded by Albert Ellis, also addresses the thinking patterns of clients. It is believed that faulty thinking and irrational beliefs lead to dysfunctional behavior. The therapist can help the individual by pointing out these irrational thinking patterns. RET is highly directive, didactic, and confrontational. The main body of the therapy involves analyzing the ABC of personality. A is the experience or objective fact, B is the individual's subjective perception of the fact, and C is the consequence of the perception. If the subjective interpretation is faulty, dysfunction may occur. Examples of "thinking errors" include:

- It's essential to be loved by everyone.
- One must be perfect to be loved.
- Unhappiness is caused by circumstances, therefore we can't control happiness.
- It's easier to avoid responsibility than to face it.
- One must have someone stronger to depend on.
- Past experience determines present behavior. (Walsh 1988, 140)

Other types of irrational thinking involve

- all-or-nothing thinking;
- overgeneralization (Why does this always happen to me?);
- mental filtering (filtering out positive messages and only remembering negative ones);
- magnification (hearing relatively mild criticism as extreme, assuming the worst possible outcome of an event);
- name calling; and
- jumping to conclusions. (Lester, Braswell, and Van Voorhis 1992, 119)

Yet another cognitive approach was developed by Yochelson and Samenow (1976) who identified 52 "thinking errors" practiced by criminals. With all of these faulty thinking patterns, RET helps the individual identify thinking errors as they occur and to correct them to revise and improve his cognitive approach to the world, thereby affecting behavior.

A related approach targets a broader spectrum of thinking than solely moral rationales or "thinking errors." The Ross program addresses cognition, self-evaluation, expectations, understanding, and appraisal of the world and its values (Ross, Fabiano, and Ewles 1988). All of the following elements can be found in this program:

- structured learning therapy (social skills);
- lateral thinking (creative problem-solving);

- critical thinking (to teach logical rational thinking);
- values education;
- assertiveness training (social appropriateness);
- negotiation skills training;
- interpersonal cognitive problem-solving;
- social perspective-training (to teach how to recognize and understand other people's views and feelings); and
- role-playing and modeling (demonstration and practice of socially acceptable and efficacious interpersonal behaviors). (Smith and Faubert 1990, 144)

## COUNSELING OFFENDERS

Certain specific themes are addressed in each of the therapeutic modalities described above. Some issues are common to all interventions with correctional clients, regardless of the type of therapy chosen. These issues will be discussed in this section.

*Dependency and the Counseling Relationship.* All of the techniques except behavior modification depend on the relationship between the counselor and the client. In family, group, and therapeutic milieu therapy the relationship is expanded to include many others. Many consider counseling an art rather than a science because so much depends on the personal characteristics of the counselor.

Many of the treatment modalities rely on developing a relationship of trust through empathy and nonjudgmental listening on the part of the therapist. This is more difficult with criminal offenders. First, offenders are disinclined to trust any person associated with the system, and second, offenders tend to be individuals that have no history of trusting, caring relationships. Also, it is more difficult for the counselor to maintain a nonjudgmental stance when their clients have engaged in very negative behaviors, such as violent or sex offenses.

If the counselor is successful in establishing a trusting, caring relationship with the client, another problem may be that dependency results. Various modalities deal with the potential of dependency differently. The therapist's role as dispassionate and reflective as opposed to interactional and judgmental is partially motivated by the necessity to avoid dependency relationships with clients. The goal of therapy is ultimately to enable the person to make their own judgments and control their own lives. There is a great temptation to defer to the therapist, however, and come to depend on the therapist's advice and judgment in making any decisions. Addictive personalities, especially, seem to be inclined toward dependent relationships. The therapist must take care to prevent this dynamic.

*Mixed Goals.*    Some problems exist in treating offenders that do not exist when the same treatment approaches are applied to nonoffender populations. All those who work in rehabilitation programs have mixed goals or loyalties. The typical client-counselor relationship is direct; the therapist has one loyalty — to the client. With criminal justice populations, whether that therapist is employed in a prison, a probation agency, or attached to the court and whether they are a counselor, psychologist or psychiatrist, they have some loyalty to the system and the community as well as to the client. If, for instance, the therapist obtained information during treatment that indicated a community member was in danger from the client, it would be necessary for the therapist to do something. In prison, if the therapist was informed of a future escape attempt, the ethical duties of the therapist are to prevent such an escape from occurring. One may be able to maintain confidentiality and still accomplish the goal of protection, but if there is a choice to be made, the ethical duty is to protect the community, even at the expense of the client. These issues may be less clear-cut in other cases (Pollock 1994).

*Assumption of Risk.*    All treatment efforts involve the assumption of risk. In nonoffender populations, the client bears most, if not all, of the risk: for example, a person suffering from nonassertiveness at some point in the treatment attempts to take a stand and to test new-found assertiveness skills. With offenders, the public bears some of the risk when the time comes to see if the intervention has truly affected drug use, violent behavior, or the sexual desire for children. Because prison is specifically designed to eliminate or reduce risk during incarceration, regardless of how far one has come in treatment, the opportunity to test whether the treatment has been effective comes largely upon release. Also, once the person leaves the prison, she often has no further opportunity for treatment so, unlike traditional counseling relationships, there is no debriefing or support during the undertaking of the risk.

*Institutional Setting.*    There are a number of problems inherent in trying to conduct treatment in an institutional setting. High caseloads and burnout are two fairly common ones with correctional personnel. Few incentives are offered for correctional counselors to do more than the minimum level of work required. Management often does not support treatment goals, especially today, and treatment staff may feel that they are used for little more than "window dress-ing" or control. Also, there is a very limited amount of influence they can have over individuals compared to the total institutional environ-ment.

*Clientele.*    Finally, there is the issue of the offenders themselves. Reminiscent of the humorous lament of teachers that it wouldn't be a bad job if it weren't for the students, counselors with offender pop-ulations may also express the view that treatment would work a lot better if it weren't for the offenders. Criminal populations tend to be untrusting, manipulative, resentful, and hostile. Many programs have offenders who are mandated to attend or who think that their participation will help them in the parole decision. These less-than-willing participants may cast a negative pall over an otherwise posi-tive treatment environment. It is questionable whether any treatment program can be helpful unless the participants are truly motivated. Even behavior modification, which some purport to be the only suc-cessful program with less-than-willing clients, may have transitory ef-fects unless the clients participate in their own treatment; ultimately, the offenders must be their own "rewarders." This issue of voluntari-ness is one reason why many abandoned the concept of rehabilita-tion as a factor of parole. Many believe that while programs should be available in prison, they should never be mandatory, thereby avoiding this problem of individuals who feel forced to take part in programs that require individual motivation.

Some offenders have such a multitude of problems that it is a daunting task to know where to start. Others have severe problems that may be too extreme for typical treatment approaches. Some spe-cial populations are described in the next section.

## SPECIAL POPULATIONS

### DRUG ADDICTS AND ALCOHOLICS

No one can ignore the impact of drugs on this society. "The War on Drugs" has become a rallying cry for most politicians, and the association between drugs and crime is strong and pervasive. The criminal justice system is inundated with drug offenders, legislation is constantly written and rewritten to try and cope with the "drug problem," and untold millions are spent on interdiction, prevention, and treatment. Drug addicts have a multitude of problems: They may suffer from physical symptoms or illnesses like lesions of the skin, damage to the membranes of the nose, or cirrhosis of the liver. They risk death from needle-contracted AIDS or drug overdoses by pure or contaminated batches of drugs. They may eventually lose jobs, families, and friends (Hirschel and Keny 1990, 111).

Interestingly, the statistics available on the nature and extent of the "drug problem" vary widely. For instance, Pallone (1990) cites a number of studies that report that arrestees who are under the influence or are recent drug users occur in as wide a range as 21 percent to 56 percent (for homicide), 8 percent to 53 percent (for violent crime), and 17 percent to 57 percent (for property) (1990, 99). The Drug Use Forecast (DUF) system funded by the Bureau of Justice reports that 40 percent or more arrestees show positive signs of drug use. Reported use varies widely by city, however, and reaches 87 percent in some cities (Rouse 1991). Even with these inconsistencies, it seems clear that drug use is associated with a greater degree of criminality. In one study of a group of addicts, it was reported that greater criminal activity occurred with those who used drugs daily than those who used them less often; daily users reported more arrests, more drug dealing, more felony property offenses, and a higher level of income from crime (McGlothlin 1985, 166). Another statistic indicates that $59 billion annually is lost by illegal drug use and related crime (Hirschel and Keny 1990, 112).

Drugs affect criminality in a number of ways. Obviously the act of selling and distributing drugs is a crime itself. Although not all those arrested for distribution are addicts, there is a strong overlap between those who sell and those who use. Those under the influence of drugs or alcohol may commit crimes at least partially due to the intoxication. Many, if not most, personal assaults are related to alcohol or drug intoxication. Alcohol drinking by perpetrator or victim or both precedes at least half of all violent events. Alcohol may act to reduce inhibition allowing an individual to act on impulses ordinarily controlled, which may result in crimes such as rape or assault. Finally, drugs may serve as the motivation for other crimes, for instance, burglaries and carjackings to obtain money to buy drugs or assaults and homicides related to drug deals "gone bad." Not all individuals who are in prison for drug crimes are addicts. But many are, and many who are in prison for other crimes have problems with addiction to alcohol, drugs, or both.

One of the basic problems with drug treatment is that there is no clear understanding of what addiction is or why some people become addicted. At one end are those who propose that addiction is merely a matter of "weak will"; at the other end of the spectrum of theories are those that postulate genetic predisposition to addiction to alcohol and perhaps to other drugs. Some researchers describe the "addictive personality." The characteristics that make up this personality include:

- expectation of failure,
- problems of sexual identification,
- disturbances of interpersonal relationships,
- low tolerance for anxiety and frustration,
- weak ego structure,
- weak superego functioning,
- inadequate male identification, and
- distrust of major institutions.

The addict is described as a manipulative personality who is often not in touch with internal feelings, who suppresses or denies powerful emotions of anger, depression, and anxiety, and who suffers from low self-esteem and poor self-image.

One study indicates that only one-quarter of drug abusers in prison have ever been in a drug treatment program. This is true even though the same study found that over one-third of all state prisoners had committed their crimes while under the influence of drugs, and more than one-half had taken drugs during the month prior to their crime (reported in Hirschel and Keny 1990, 114). Rouse reports that 62 percent of prisoners reported regular use of drugs, but only 11 percent were in any type of prison treatment program (1991, 32).

Drug treatment programs use a number of approaches: psychotherapy, counseling, education, vocational training, and the therapeutic community. Treatment specifically used with alcoholics may include tranquilizing drugs and vitamin B complex to help lessen withdrawal symptoms, proper diet, antidepressant medication, antabuse, hypnotherapy, dynamic or analytic therapy, family therapy, and self-help groups like AA.

Treatment programs for addicts are notoriously unsuccessful in "curing" the addiction, and many adhere to the AA belief that an alcoholic will always be an alcoholic but may become a nondrinking alcoholic. Drug programs like AA and NA have been described in a previous section. Other professional therapeutic interventions rely on many of the same elements: recognition of the problem and dealing with it through goal setting and support from others.

Rouse (1991) reports on a study of 59 prison drug programs in which the following therapeutic approaches were used:

| Therapeutic approach | % of programs using |
|---|---|
| Group counseling | 97 |
| Individual counseling | 83 |
| Addiction education | 83 |
| Confrontation group counseling | 48 |
| Work assignments | 46 |
| Vocational counseling/training | 41 |
| Therapeutic community | 27 |
| Family therapy | 17 |

He reports that all of these programs showed minor success in recidivism rates. The optimum time for a therapeutic community approach was 9 to 12 months; anything shorter had less effect on recidivism. The only other variable that seemed to make a difference in success was age; younger offenders were less likely to be successful on release. Follow-up seemed to be an important variable also. Those programs that had continuing services in the community posted better success rates than those that did not, although it was just as true that if the offender did not take advantage of aftercare services, she was likely to recidivate. Rouse (1991) concludes that drug programs can improve recidivism by about 10 percent (compared to control groups) and are low cost if run in prison.

Hirschel and Keny (1990) report on evaluation studies that find a positive correlation between legal coercion and the completion of the program and success afterwards. The strongest factor associated with program success seems to be length; the longer the program, and the longer an offender is in the program, the greater the success rate.

One example of a drug treatment program is the Cornerstone therapeutic community at the Oregon State Hospital in Salem. Durham (1994) describes the clientele of this program as recidivistic drug addicts who average 13 prior arrests and more than 7 years in prison at the time of program entry. The basic principles of the program include:

- segregation of participants from the general population,
- unambiguous rules regarding actions and consequences,
- incentives for privileges for motivation,
- inmate participation,
- intensive treatment interventions,
- a simultaneous focus on drug abuse and criminal involvement, and
- provision of transition and aftercare services to assure successful community reentry.

An evaluation followed 200 program graduates for three years after release. It was found that longer time spent in the program was associated with a lower level of rearrest: 74 percent of those who graduated avoided subsequent incarceration, only 37 percent of nongraduates who had been in the program for at least 6 months avoided rearrest, and only 15 percent of those who left within the first 60 days were not rearrested within three years (Durham 1994, 159).

## SEX OFFENDERS

Typically a sex offense is defined as a legally punishable overt act committed by a person for his or her own immediate sexual gratification. A sexual dysfunction (for instance, fetishism) is not a sex offense unless the individual commits a crime related to it (for instance, stealing women's shoes or underwear). Sex offenses include rape, incest, child molestation, exhibitionism, and voyeurism.

It has been found that rapists often start with nonaggressive sex offenses such as voyeurism and progress to sexual assault. Many types of rapist typologies exist. Groth's (1979), the most often reported, is composed of the anger rapist, power rapist, and sadistic rapist. Anger rapists use more physical force than necessary to subdue because of anger and depression; their offenses are episodic and impulsive. Language is abusive, and the rape event takes place as retribution for perceived wrongs, injustices, or put-downs the offender has experienced by women. The power rapist is usually motivated to seek control of the victim. The assault is premeditated and often preceded by rape fantasies; offenses are repetitive and may show an increase in aggression over time. Giving orders, asking personal questions, or requiring the victim to respond in certain ways are ways to exert power. The rape event makes up for deep-seated insecurities and feelings of inadequacy. The victim may be held captive for a longer period of time to satisfy the power rapist's need for control. Sadistic rapists represent the smallest percentage and are the most dangerous. With this individual, aggression and sex are intertwined. Assault is calculated and may be ritualistic, involving bondage, torture, or bizarre acts. Language is commanding and degrading. There is a symbolic destruction of some other (for example, a sexually abusive mother). The victim is most likely to be seriously injured or killed in this type of rape. Other typologies present other diagnoses of the characteristics of the rapist. For instance, some typologies include the "subcultural" rapist for whom rape is part of a larger identification with the male role. The relevance of rapist typologies is clear: Treatment may be approached very differently depending on the motivation for the rape itself.

The relationship between social mores and sexual offenses is unclear. Societal images of women support certain rationalizations excusing sexual aggression (for example, "She asked for it," "I couldn't help myself," "Maybe means yes . . ."). Violence in pornography, slasher movies, and general societal humor often supports norms of violence against women or that women are to be treated as sexual objects. Rapists in prison usually are not looked on with any degree of approbation unless they are "baby rapers." To what extent these cultural messages influence the motivation to rape is unclear.

Theories about child molesters typically point to feelings of inadequacy, immaturity, vulnerability, helplessness, and isolation. Sexual behavior is compulsive and repetitive because it does not meet underlying needs of affiliation. Other descriptions include feelings of worthlessness and low self-esteem, an underlying mood-state of anger, fear, and depression, and a tenuous masculine identity. Child molesters may have been sexually abused as children. Some theorists posit that both groups — rapists and child molesters — are threatened by adult sexuality, but rapists attack the source of their insecurity (women) while molesters retreat to safer love objects (children) (Walsh 1988).

Treatment programs for sex offenders typically offer reeducation (sex education, sex roles, and so forth), resocialization (interpersonal relationships, management of aggression, appropriate relationships), and counseling (dealing with personal victimization, issues of sexual identity). They may also work on improving psychological attitudes, problem-solving, moral judgment training, developing self-esteem, communication skills, interpersonal skill development, and empathy skills (Smith and Faubert 1990). Chemotherapy is sometimes used for compulsive sexual behavior. Use of DepoProvera (a female contraceptive hormone) curbs sex drive by suppressing production of male hormones. Treatment may be effective for only those who want to control their urges.

Behavior modification is also used in treating the sex offender and seems to offer the greatest potential for success in reducing recidivism (Knopp 1989). Aversive conditioning is used to eliminate the connection between inappropriate stimuli (for example, children) and sexual arousal. Evidently the greatest challenge is not breaking the "habit" of arousal, but rather having the new behavior continue over a long period of time. Without some training and attention to relapse, the individual offender may successfully complete a program but, over time, go back to old behaviors. Moderately successful programs are those that link electric shocks or other noxious stimuli to visual and verbal images that are sexually arousing for the offender (for example, of children). Programs also use satiation therapy (requiring masturbation using the inappropriate stimuli to such frequency that it loses its pleasurable aspects), as well as training the offender to recondition himself to appropriate masturbation fantasies. Most programs also attempt to improve the offender's social skills and self-esteem (Knopp 1989). Other programs teach the offender to recognize precursors of a deviant act, such as emotional states like anger, depression, conflict, or stress. The offender is taught to stop the sequence of events — for example, feel impulse, fantasize, plan — that leads to a deviant act (George and Marlott 1989).

Unfortunately, much research indicates that therapy does not work very well for sex offenders (Furby, Weinrott, and Blackshaw 1989). Ironically, prisons and juvenile facilities provide probably the worst environment imaginable for treating the sex offender. Psychosexual development is a problem with young men who have spent most of their life behind bars in juvenile or adult facilities. There, the hypermasculine environment and sexual activities make developing healthy adult relationships with women extremely problematic.

## THE MENTALLY ILL

As many as 10 percent of inmates may suffer from mental health problems as defined in the Diagnostic and Statistical Manual of Mental Disorders (DSM-IV) (Smith and Faubert 1990, 133). Some suggest that as the mental health profession deinstitutionalized a great portion of the mentally ill in this country during the late 1970s, many of these people ended up in the criminal justice system. There are similarities in the socioeconomic and environmental conditions that nurture criminal behavior and those that foster severe mental illness.

Prison has a significant deleterious effect on mental health. Its conditions may trigger or accelerate a psychotic breakdown in a prisoner who, on entering, loses his useful social role, faces the traumatic loss of his social ties and support, and suffers harassment and stress from officers and other inmates. Management and treatment of the mentally ill in prison presents unique challenges that go far beyond rehabilitative treatment as previously described in this chapter.

The DSM-IV is the diagnostic manual used by all those involved in the mental health field. It classifies mental illness in the following way:

— Disorders usually first diagnosed in infancy, childhood, or adolescence
— Delirium, Dementia, and Amnestic and other Cognitive Disorders
— Mental Disorders due to a General Medical Condition
— Substance-Related Disorders
— Schizophrenia and other Psychotic Disorders
— Mood Disorders
— Anxiety Disorders
— Somatoform Disorders
— Factitious Disorders
— Disassociative Disorders
— Sexual and Gender Identity Disorders
— Eating Disorders
— Sleep Disorders
— Impulse-Control Disorders
— Adjustment Disorders
— Personality Disorders

Psychotic illness causes personality disorganization, inappropriate or absent affect, distorted thinking, and breaks with reality. The psychotic individual typically experiences auditory and visual hallucinations, delusions, and extreme forms of behavior. Individuals who may suffer from anxiety, phobias, and depression do not experience the altered sense of reality that those who suffer from psychotic disorders do. Theories explaining poor mental health fall into several categories: biological (for example, hormonal or brain wave dysfunctions), environmental (for example, poor parenting or lack of bonding), or personality (some interaction of individual personality characteristics and environmental triggers).

The *sociopath* (or psychopath or antisocial personality) has a chronic personality disorder, not a mental illness, and appears often in offender populations. These individuals are egocentric, manipulative, hostile, impulsive, charming, insensitive to others, asocial, and disloyal. They often possess poor judgment, blame others for their troubles, are devoid of emotions and inner feelings, do not learn from experience and punishment, are indifferent to others and therefore incapable of deep love, and have no recognition that they have a problem (Masters 1994). Two major themes are lovelessness, or inability to feel affection, and impulsivity. These two may lead to aggression: If you lack empathy for anyone and also act impulsively, hostile behavior may result (Rabin 1979). Theories of causation include environmental (lack of mother-figure to establish bonding or lack of consistent parental discipline) and somatic (brain wave patterns appear to be different from normal groups, although it is questionable whether this is causal or correlational and whether the differences are significant). The sociopath diagnosis is a controversial one; some critics point out that the diagnosis is merely a description of an individual with little theory behind it.

Sociopaths are difficult to work with because they lie and are extremely manipulative. Often highly intelligent, they can absorb knowledge that enables them to mimic mental illness or a healthy adjustment. For instance, they can appear to change and become model clients only to commit a crime or go back to their old forms of behavior immediately on release. Treatment is also problematic. If not biological, then certainly the diagnosis of sociopath implies a resistance to treatment that may be difficult, if not impossible, to overcome. Little success has been reported in working with this offender group. This is not hard to understand when one considers that most treatment programs require a recognition of the problem and a motivation to change. Because sociopaths do not see themselves as having a problem, they cannot understand why they should change.

## EVALUATION OF REHABILITATION

As discussed earlier in this chapter, when there were attempts to evaluate correctional programs to see what works, the answer received was "nothing." Martinson's report has been heavily criticized, and he later softened his negative conclusions (1979). Also, others who have analyzed the same findings have concluded that there are "pockets" of treatment that may be effective for some people.

The first question to ask, of course, is what is success? Typically the answer to that question has been the reduction of recidivism. Measures of recidivism vary widely; recidivism may be measured as rearrest, conviction, or return to prison. If rearrest is used, figures of failure are higher because many ex-convicts are arrested even though no charges are ultimately filed. Return to prison would result in lower figures of recidivism, but some returns to prison may be for technical violations of parole rather than new crimes. Would the technical violation of not reporting to a parole officer although still sober and crime-free be considered a failure or a success? Interestingly, some prisoners are returned to prison after they have already been in treatment programs on the outside because it is then that they stay in one place long enough to get caught by police on warrants issued when they absconded from parole. Other measures of success might be employment or attitudinal change, but these measures are used very seldomly. Almost all evaluations depend on recidivism, no matter the means chosen to measure it.

Another issue is to what degree must recidivism be reduced for a program to be considered a success. Many evaluations show relatively modest reductions of 10 to 13 percent. Is it feasible to expect drops of more than 40 percent or higher? Are other programs that target human behavior held to these same standards? Success rates of smoking programs, weight reduction programs, or other attempts to change behavior are fairly modest, yet we expect much more from correctional programs.

Another factor is how the program operates. If the program was designed under a certain theory of criminality, with a structure and content that was consistent with such a theory, it is important to note whether the operation of the program — how it was implemented — was faithful to the initial plan. Many times and for many reasons, programs on paper do not resemble the programs in reality. Staff changes, poor training, or implementation problems may result in the content being different than the philosophy of the program. This is especially troublesome when one considers that certain modalities are evaluated in comparison to one another. Therefore, it would be important to know, for instance, if a reality therapy program was actually using the assumptions, premises, and programmatic elements of reality therapy or if these elements had somehow become attenuated or ignored. A related issue is the eclectic approach used by many programs, which makes replication and the ability to measure the relative efficacy of any one approach impossible.

A major problem of evaluation is high attrition. If one measures the recidivism of only those who finish the program, it may be that they also have higher motivation, which contributes to their success. What is measured may not be a treatment effect, but rather individual differences between those who drop out and those who stick with it to the end. On the other hand, one can hardly measure a program's effectiveness by monitoring the behavior of those who dropped out.

Another problem of evaluation is the difficulty of obtaining an adequate control group. A *control group* is a group similar to the treatment group in all characteristics except for the treatment effect (the exposure to the treatment one is attempting to evaluate). Ordinarily, *random assignment* is used to ensure the groups are the same. Random assignment is defined as every individual in the universe has an equal chance of being selected. For instance, if the universe you wished to project your findings to was a prison population, random assignment from that population to a treatment group and a control group would be necessary. Random number tables or other methods can be used as long as no bias is introduced. If random assignment to the treatment group is not possible, the only control group that would be appropriate would be matching characteristics. Matching is not as effective and is very difficult to do. For instance, if one was evaluating a drug treatment program, a control group would have to be matched to a treatment group on all potentially influential factors such as drug history, criminal background, age, family characteristics, and so on. Unfortunately few designs are so careful, and often you see drug treatment programs compared to general prison populations or, at best, groups committed for drug crimes. Since drug addicted offenders are more likely to recidivate, one could expect higher recidivism rates from an addict group than a general prison population group; therefore, a treatment program that shows the same recidivism after treatment as a general population control group may actually be a success since one would expect higher recidivism figures. On the other hand, with voluntary treatment programs, program effects may be partially due to the nature of the highly motivated inmate. The only way to control for that would be to get volunteers first and then randomly assign some to a treatment group and some to a control group. This is not a popular approach in program delivery.

Another important issue to address is the so-called black box of prison. Treatment programs are only one part of the prisoner's life. The prison experience is like a "black box" that the researcher cannot look inside. We can measure the outcome of the black box (higher or lower recidivism), but we can never identify which elements of the prison experience contributed to the results. It may be that treatment programs provide positive elements to a course of changing one's life, but the negative aspects of imprisonment — prisonization (the socialization to the prisoner subculture), violence, attacks on self-esteem, loss of family support — may override any treatment effects.

At this time, there are growing numbers of researchers who conclude that there are "pockets" of success or modest successes in rehabilitation that encourage continued faith in the attempts to change behavior.

[Several meta-analyses and literature reviews of experimental programs found converging evidence that most such efforts reduced recidivism when compared to their control programs; and for all programs combined the average reduction was moderate, i.e., 10-12 percent.] (Palmer 1992b, 63)

Palmer believes that three principles exist for working with serious or multiple offenders: first, that multiple modality programs are needed; second, that increased intensity of contact is important; and, third, that greater attention has to be given to offenders' needs and characteristics (1992b, 63).

No general categories of programs — only individual programs — have been proven successful. Palmer believes that continuing the modest progress seen thus far depends on replicating those successful programs or creating program variations that combine the most successful elements (Palmer 1994). Studies should describe offender subgroups within the sample, and these subgroups should be analyzed separately (Palmer 1994). Reviewing many meta-analyses and literature reviews of programs for juveniles, Palmer finds that behavioral, cognitive-oriented, lifeskills, or family intervention programs were successful (1994). Group counseling and individual counseling programs, confrontation and diversion were programs which showed the poorest success in reducing recidivism (1994, 35).

Louis and Sparger (1990, 150) review several studies and conclude that counseling procedures that depended primarily on open communication and friendship models were nondirectional, or involved self-help groups resulted in negligible effects. Behavior modification programs, on the other hand, either showed impressive successes or were dismal failures. Others report that individual and small-group counseling that is directive and focuses on sources of a subject's criminality seems to reduce recidivism in incarcerated offenders who seek it voluntarily, but not in those who are coerced to participate (Glaser 1994, 719).

Others also present elements of successful programs. Highlight 6-2 shows the structural characteristics associated with successful programs.

Two final issues will be discussed here: the importance of individual therapists and the related topic of individualization of treatment.

Martinson credited special qualifications of therapists when he found success "may well have been the therapists' special personal gifts rather than the fact of treatment itself which produced the favorable result" (Martinson 1974). Another author points to research that finds that "good" counselors — those who are open, warm, accepting, and empathetic — are more similar to each other even if they operate from very different theoretical perspectives than any of them are to poor counselors, even within the same theoretical perspective or treatment modality (Walsh 1988, 118).

Certainly there is evidence that the strength of any program may rest more in the personnel than in any power of the modality itself. This calls into question the whole attempt to evaluate programs.

**HIGHLIGHT 6-2**
**Elements of a Successful Treatment Program**

**1. It provides specific guidelines for the use of positive reinforcement.** Behavioral programs have been found to be more successful than nondirective or "talking" programs. This element implies that there should be clear and consistent procedures for awarding positive reinforcements.

**2. It draws from a variety of sources.** As mentioned before, many programs are eclectic. This may be the most effective mode of service delivery, in that some elements may work for different types of offenders.

**3. It is heavily scripted.** The value of this element is that it reduces the chance of counselor bias or diminishing program content through counselor apathy or lack of training. A heavily scripted program implies that one should be able to go to several different locations and observe the same program.

**4. It is based on evaluated results.** Obviously, it is a waste of time or money if the program has not been evaluated or results indicate no change is induced in program participants.

**5. It requires structured activity of the learner.** This principle is consistent with other learning theory that supports the notion that we learn by doing, not by listening or watching.

**6. It requires transfer of training to everyday life.** Programs that have little applicability to the offender's life will be forgotten as soon as the offender is released.

**7. It includes a method of teacher monitoring.** This is to reduce the possibility that the program is made less effective or is changed by the individual counselor.

**8. It contains an outcome evaluation.**

**9. It contains a technique and rationale for client selection.** This is consistent with several studies that indicate that certain types of programs work better for certain types of offenders.

**10. It is repetitive and integrated.**

**11. It requires active participation from the teacher.**

**12. It is constructed for a specific purpose and for a specific client.** (Coulson and Nutbrown 1992)

Maybe we should evaluate the people who work in prison programs and try to discover if their qualities of success are something that can be taught.

Many of those who continue to support treatment do so with the caveat that treatment must be individualized to the offender. Panaceas do not exist, and no treatment modality or approach will be successful with all offenders. Andrews cites three conditions under which treatment programs have been shown to be more successful: first, that rehabilitative services are delivered to high-risk offenders; second, that the criminogenic needs of offenders are identified; and, third, that treatment matched to client needs and styles of learning is provided (Durham 1994, 156).

One related idea to individualization is the "consumer perspective" important in inmate therapy. There is documented evidence that voluntariness is an essential element in therapy success. Inmates who are surveyed as to their needs or desires for programs express their desires for treatment programs. In a study of 348 inmates in three different federal institutions, inmates overwhelmingly wanted programs, most said to "improve themselves." Only a third felt they needed help for a psychological or medical problem; most felt they were owed programs because of their incarceration, because they needed it, or because it would help them stay away from criminal options. The programs cited most by inmates as being needed were job-related, vocational, or educational to help prepare them to get work on the outside (Erez 1987). Perhaps one of the greatest failings of therapy in the "rehabilitative era" of the 1970s was the failure to individualize treatment. Except for a few programs, there was a one-size-fits-all approach to treatment programs such as TA, group therapy, or reality therapy. No treatment approach is appropriate for all offenders. The goal is to successfully match the type of program to the type of offender.

## CONCLUSIONS

We still spend only about 10 percent of prison correctional budgets for inmate programs, which includes all recreational, service, and educational programs as well as those we have described above as more purely rehabilitative (Senese and Kalinich 1992). With this less than generous support for intervention, it is hard to see how one can conclude that the concept has been tried and has failed. The philosophical position that it is not the function of prison to rehabilitate (even if we could) is more supportable. Clearly, one can see the logic of the argument that the only function of prison is to punish (Logan and Gaes 1993). Yet, we haven't yet given up the idea that we expect some positive change to come about through that prison experience.

There is still some support for the rehabilitative ideal. A 1982 Harris poll found that 44 percent of the public supported rehabilitation as the main purpose of prison. While this is down from 73 percent in 1967, it still indicates a considerable degree of support (Durham 1994, 153). Other studies have also found support for rehabilitation. Even correctional officers have supportive attitudes toward rehabilitation. Seventy percent of surveyed officers in Illinois agreed with the statement that "rehabilitating a criminal is just as important as making a criminal pay for his or her crime" (Durham 1994, 153).

Clearly, what we are doing is not working. In a recent Bureau of Justice study, it was found that within three years of their release, 63 percent of prison releasees had been rearrested for a new felony or serious misdemeanor charges; 47 percent had been reconvicted; and 41 percent had been returned to prison or jail. Age was the factor most strongly related to recidivism rates, as well as number of prior arrests. Nearly 1 in 3 released violent offenders and 1 in 5 property offenders were rearrested within three years for a violent crime (Dillingham and Greenfeld 1991, 32).

Burgeoning prison populations, newly constructed prisons, and other methods of correctional supervision are taking larger and larger portions of state and federal budgets. Texas recently curtailed its ambitious treatment program, citing financial problems. Under a previous governor, a plan to have 12,000 treatment beds was scaled back by the legislature to 4,500 beds. Treatment programs for released offenders were also cut back (Ward 1995). This occurred after Texas announced that it would meet the goal of having over 150,000 prison beds by 1996, even though some of these beds remain empty because of lack of prisoners to fill them. One suspects this situation won't last long.

It is not just a cliché that money spent on prisons is money taken away from schools and health care — it is reality. If this future is not acceptable, perhaps it is time to revisit some of the ideas of the rehabilitative era.

## Vocabulary

aversive conditioning            psychotherapy
classical conditioning           random assignment
control group                    recidivism
counseling                       reform
eclectic                         rehabilitation
operant conditioning             sociopath
phenomenological approach        treatment ethic

## Study Questions

1. Who was Robert Martinson, and what impact did his research have on corrections?

2. What are the problems of measuring the effect of treatment programs on recidivism?

3. What is the treatment ethic?

4. What are the differences between social therapy programs and individual programs?

5. Discuss the issue of dependency in treatment.

## Sources Cited

— Allen, F. A. 1981. *The Decline of the Rehabilitative Ideal: Penal Policy and Social Purpose.* New Haven: Yale University Press.

— Andrews, D. A., I. Zinger, R. D. Hoge, J. Bonta, P. Gendreau, and F. T. Cullen. 1990. "Does Correctional Treatment Work? A

Clinically Relevant and Psychologically Informed Meta-Analysis." *Criminology* 28: 369-404.

— Astone, N. 1982. "What Helps Rehabilitation? A Survey of Research Findings." *International Journal of Offender Therapy and Comparative Criminology* 26(2): 109-120.

— Bailey, W. C. 1966. "Correctional Outcome: An Evaluation of 100 Reports." *Journal of Criminal Law, Criminology and Police Science* 57: 153-160.

— Bandura, A. 1969. *Principles of Behavior Modification.* New York: Rinehart and Winston.

— Berne, E. 1962. *Transactional Analysis in Psychotherapy.* New York: Grove.

— Berne, E. 1964. *Games People Play.* New York: Grove.

— Clear, T., and G. Cole. 1986. *American Corrections.* Monterey, Cal.: Brooks/Cole.

— Coulson, G., and V. Nutbrown. 1992. "Properties of an Ideal Rehabilitative Program for High-Need Offenders." *International Journal of Offender Therapy and Comparative Criminology* 36(3): 203-208.

— Cullen, F., J. Cullen, and J. Wozniak. 1988. "Is Rehabilitation Dead? The Myth of the Punitive Public." *Journal of Criminal Justice* 16: 33-58.

— Cullen, F. T., and K. Gilbert. 1982. *Reaffirming Rehabilitation.* Cincinnati: Anderson.

— Cullen, F. T., S. E. Skovron, J. Scott, and V. Burton. 1990. "Public Support for Correctional Treatment: The Tenacity of Rehabilitative Ideology," *Criminal Justice and Behavior* 17: 1-16.

— Dillingham, S., and L. Greenfeld. 1991. "An Overview of National Corrections Statistics." *Federal Probation* 55(2): 27-34.

— Doob, A., and Brodeur, J. 1989. "Rehabilitating the Debate on Rehabilitation." *Canadian Journal of Criminology* 31(2): 186-194.

— Durham, A. 1994. *Crisis and Reform: Current Issues in American Punishment.* Boston: Little, Brown.

— Empey, L. T., and J. Rabow. 1961. "The Provo Experiment in Delinquency Rehabilitation." *American Sociological Review* 26 (October): 679-695.

— Erez, E. 1987. "Rehabilitation in Justice: The Prisoner's Perspective." *Journal of Offender Counseling, Services and Rehabilitation* 11(2): 5-19.

— Furby, L., M. R. Weinrott, and L. Blackshaw. 1989. "Sex Offender Recidivism: A Review." *Psychological Bulletin* 105: 3-30.

— Galliher, J. 1989. *Criminology: Human Rights, Criminal Law, and Crime.* Englewood Cliffs, N.J.: Prentice-Hall.

— Gendreau, P., and R. R. Ross. 1987. "Revivification of Rehabilitation: Evidence for the 1980s." *Justice Quarterly* 4: 349-407.

— George, W. H., and G. A. Marlott. 1989. *Relapse Prevention with Sex Offenders.* New York: Guilford.

— Gilligan, C. 1982. *In a Different Voice.* Cambridge: Harvard University Press.

— Glaser, D. 1994. "What Works, and Why It Is Important: A Response to Logan and Gaes." *Justice Quarterly* 11(4): 711-723.

— Glasser, W. 1965. *Reality Therapy: A New Approach to Psychiatry.* New York: Harper and Row.

— Gottfredson, M. 1979. "Treatment Destruction Techniques." *Journal of Research in Crime and Delinquency.* 16: 39-54.

— Groth, N. 1979. *Men Who Rape: The Psychology of the Offender.* New York: Plenum.

— Hamm, M. S., and J. L. Schrink. 1989. "The Conditions of Effective Implementation — A Guide to Accomplishing Rehabilitative Objectives in Corrections." *Criminal Justice and Behavior* 16: 2-20.

— Harper, R. 1975. *The New Psychotherapies.* Englewood Cliffs, N.J.: Prentice-Hall.

— Harris, T. 1969. *I'm OK — You're OK.* New York: Avon.

— Hirschel, J. D., and J. Keny. 1990. "Outpatient Treatment for Substance-Abusing Offenders." In *The Clinical Treatment of the Criminal Offender in Outpatient Mental Health Settings,* ed. N. Pallone and S. Chaneles, 111-129. New York: Haworth.

— Jones, M. 1968. *Beyond the Therapeutic Community.* New Haven: Yale University Press.

— Kaslow, F. 1987. "Couples of Family Therapy for Prisoners and Their Significant Others." *American Journal of Family Therapy* 15(4): 352-360.

— Knopp, Fay H. 1989. *Retraining Adult Sex Offenders: Methods and Models.* Orwell, Vt.: Safer Society Press.

— Kohlberg, L. 1976. "Moral Stages and Moralization: The Cognitive Developmental Approach." In *Moral Development and Behavior: Theory, Research and Social Issues,* ed. T. Lickona, 31-53. New York: Holt, Rinehart and Winston.

— Kratcoski, P. 1981. *Correctional Counseling and Treatment.* Monterey, Cal.: Duxbury.

— Lab, S. P., and J. T. Whitehead. 1990. "From 'Nothing Works' to 'The Appropriate Works': The Latest Stop on the Search for the Secular Grail." *Criminology* 28: 405-417.

— Lester, D., M. Braswell, and P. Van Voorhis. 1992. *Correctional Counseling.* Cincinnati: Anderson.

— Lipton, D., R. Martinson, and J. Wilks. 1975. *The Effectiveness of Correctional Treatment: A Survey of Treatment Evaluation Studies.* New York: Praeger.

— Logan, C. H., and G. G. Gaes. 1993. "Meta-Analysis and the Rehabilitation of Punishment." *Justice Quarterly* 10: 245-263.

— Louis, T. P., and J. Sparger. 1990. "Treatment Modalities within

Prison." In *Are Prisons Any Better? Twenty Years of Correctional Reform,* ed. J. Murphy and J. Dison, 147-161. Newbury Park, Cal.: Sage.

— Marshall, W. L., and M. M. Christie. 1981. "Pedophilia and Aggression." *Criminal Justice and Behavior* 8: 145-158.

— Martinson, R. 1974. "What Works? Questions and Answers about Prison Reform." *Public Interest* (Spring): 22-54.

— Martinson, R. 1979. "New Findings, New Views: A Note of Caution Regarding Sentencing Reform." *Hofstra Law Review* 7(2): 244-266.

— Masters, R. 1994. *Counseling Criminal Justice Offenders.* Thousand Oaks, Cal.: Sage.

— McGlothlin, W. H. 1985. "Distinguishing Effects from Concomitants of Drug Use: The Case of Crime." In *Studying Drug Abuse: Series in Psychosocial Epidemiology, VI,* ed. L. N. Robins, 153-172. New Brunswick, N.J.: Rutgers University Press.

— Miller, S., C. Bartollas, D. Jennifer, E. Redd, and S. Dinitz. 1974. "Games Inmates Play: Notes on Staff Victimization." In *Victimology: A New Focus Volume V Exploiters and Exploited: The Dynamics of Victimization,* ed. I. Drapkin and E. Viano, 143-155. Lexington, Mass.: Lexington Books.

— Okun, B. 1976. *Effective Helping and Interview Techniques.* Monterey, Cal.: Duxbury.

— Orsagh, T., and M. E. Marsden. 1985. "What Works When: Rational Choice Theory and Offender Rehabilitation." *Journal of Criminal Justice* 13: 270-271.

— Pallone, N. 1990. "Drug Use and Felony Crime: Biochemical Credibility and Unsettled Questions." In *The Clinical Treatment of the Criminal Offender in Outpatient Mental Health Settings,* ed. N. Pallone and S. Chaneles, 85-111. New York: Haworth.

— Palmer, T. 1974. "The Youth Authority's Community Treatment Project." *Federal Probation* 38(1): 3-14.

— Palmer, T. 1975. "Martinson Revisited." *Journal of Research in Crime and Delinquency* 12: 133-152.

— Palmer, T. 1978. *Correctional Intervention and Research: Current Issues and Future Prospects.* Lexington, Mass.: Lexington Books.

— Palmer, T. 1983. "The Effectiveness Issue Today: An Overview." *Federal Probation* 47(2): 3-10.

— Palmer, T. 1991a. "The Effectiveness of Intervention: Recent Trends and Current Issues." *Crime and Delinquency* 37: 330-346.

— Palmer, T. 1991b. "The Habilitation/Developmental Perspective: A Missing Link in Corrections." *Federal Probation* 55(1): 16-33.

— Palmer, T. 1992a. *The Re-Emergence of Correctional Intervention.* Newbury Park, Cal.: Sage.

— Palmer, T. 1992b. "Growth Centered Intervention: An Overview of Changes in Recent Decades." *Federal Probation* 56(1): 62-67.

— Palmer, T. 1994. *A Profile of Correctional Effectiveness and New Directions for Research.* Albany, N.Y.: SUNY Press.

— Petersilia, J. 1991. "The Value of Correctional Research: Learning What Works." *Federal Probation* 55(2): 24-32.

— Pollock, J. 1994. *Ethics in Crime and Justice: Dilemmas and Decisions. 2d ed.* Belmont, Cal.: Wadsworth.

— Pollock-Byrne, J. 1990. *Women, Prison and Crime.* Pacific Grove, Cal.: Brooks/Cole.

— Pollock-Byrne, J. 1991. "Moral Development and Corrections." In *Justice, Crime and Ethics,* ed. M. Braswell, B. McCarthy, and B. McCarthy, 221-237. Cincinnati: Anderson.

— Rabin, A. 1979. "The Anti-Social Personality, Psychopathy and Sociopathy." In *Psychology of Crime and Criminal Justice,* ed. H. Toch, 322-347. Prospect Heights, Ill.: Waveland.

— Redl, F., and H. Toch. 1979. "The Psychoanalytic Perspective." In

*Psychology of Crime and Criminal Justice,* ed. H. Toch, 183-198. Prospect Heights, Ill.: Waveland.

— Rogers, C. 1961. *Client-Centered Therapy.* Boston: Houghton-Mifflin.

— Ross, R. R., E. A. Fabiano, and C. D. Ewles. 1988. "Reasoning and Rehabilitation." *International Journal of Offender Therapy and Comparative Criminology* 32: 29-35.

— Roth, J. 1994. "Psychoactive Substances and Violence," NIJ Research in Brief. Washington, D.C.: GPO.

— Rothman, D. J. 1971. *The Discovery of the Asylum: Social Order and Disorder in the New Republic.* Boston: Little, Brown.

— Rouse, J. J. 1991. "Evaluation Research on Prison-Based Drug Treatment Programs and Some Policy Implications." *International Journal of the Addictions* 26(1): 29-44.

— Scharf, P., L. Kohlberg, and J. Hickey. 1981. "Ideology and Correctional Intervention: The Creation of a Just Prison Community." In *Correctional Counseling and Treatment,* ed. P. Kratcoski, 409-422. Monterey, Cal.: Duxbury.

— Senese, J., and D. B. Kalinich. 1992. "Activities and Rehabilitation Programs for Offenders." In *Corrections: An Introduction,* ed. S. Stojkovic and R. Lovell, 213-244. Cincinnati: Anderson.

— Smith, J., and M. Faubert. 1990. "Programming and Process in Prisoner Rehabilitation: A Prison Mental Health Center." *Journal of Offender Counseling, Services and Rehabilitation* 15(2): 131-153.

— Szasz, T. 1963. *Law, Liberty and Psychiatry.* New York: Macmillan.

— Szasz, T. 1979. "Insanity and Irresponsibility: Psychiatric Diversion in the Criminal Justice System." In *Psychology of Crime and Criminal Justice,* ed. H. Toch, 133-145. Prospect Heights, Ill.: Waveland.

— Toch, H. 1979. *Psychology of Crime and Criminal Justice.* Prospect Heights, Ill.: Waveland.

— Toch, H. 1980. *Therapeutic Communities in Corrections.* New York: Praeger.

— Trotzer, J. 1981. "The Process of Group Counseling." In *Correctional Counseling and Treatment,* ed. P. Kratcoski, 361-387. Monterey, Cal.: Duxbury.

— Walsh, A. 1988. *Understanding, Assessing and Counseling the Criminal Justice Client.* Pacific Grove, Cal.: Brooks/Cole.

— Ward, M. 1995. "Convict Treatment Programs Trimmed." *Austin American Statesman,* 27 June, pp. A1, A7.

— Wexler, D. B. 1973. "Token and Taboo: Behavior Modification, Token Economies, and the Law." *California Law Review* 61: 81-109.

— Whitehead, J. T., and S. B. Lab. 1989. "A Meta-Analysis of Juvenile Correctional Treatment." *Journal of Research in Crime and Delinquency* 26: 276-295.

— Wilson, J. Q. 1991. "What Works? Revisited — New Findings on Criminal Rehabilitation." In *The Dilemmas of Corrections,* 2nd ed., ed. P. Haas and G. Alpert, 343-356. Prospect Heights, Ill.: Waveland.

— Wright, R. A. 1994. *In Defense of Prisons.* Westport, Conn.: Greenwood.

— Wright, R. A. 1995. "Rehabilitation Affirmed, Rejected, and Reaffirmed: Assessments of the Effectiveness of Offender Treatment Programs in Criminology Textbooks, 1956 to 1965 and 1983 to 1992." *Journal of Criminal Justice Education* 6(1): 21-41.

— Yochelson, S., and S. E. Samenow. 1976. *The Criminal Personality.* Vol. 1. New York: Jason Aronson.

— Zamble, E. 1990. "Behavioral and Psychological Considerations in the Success of Prison Reform." In *Are Prisons Any Better? Twenty Years of Correctional Reform,* ed. J. Murphy and J. Dison, 129-145. Newbury Park, Cal.: Sage.

# 7

# THE SOCIAL WORLD OF THE PRISONER

*Joycelyn Pollock*

*Everyone* is afraid. It is not an emotional, psychological fear. It is a practical matter. If you do not threaten someone at the very least someone will threaten you. When you walk across the yard or down the tier to your cell, you stand out like a sore thumb if you do not appear either callously unconcerned or cold and ready to kill. Many times you have to "prey" on someone, or you will be "preyed" on yourself. After so many years, *you are not bluffing*. No one is. (Abbott 1981, 144)

What sort of world exists behind prison walls? The complex interchanges and power systems that characterize all human aggregates develop special characteristics within an institutional setting. Some propose that prisons are microcosms of society. If this is true, then society is a strange place, for the world that prisoners inhabit turns the values most of us live by upside down. Some inmates escape the most alienating aspects of the subculture by finding either niches or places to hide. These individuals lead a fairly comfortable, if very circumscribed, existence. They rarely enter the yard or the mess halls where the risks of running into trouble are higher. They make themselves invisible — to the staff as well as to other prisoners. Some enter the prison world actively and aggressively, those who are strong enough become the hunters, the powerbrokers, and the leaders of the yard; those who are weak or without allies become prey.

## THE PRISONERS

Before we begin to explore the social world of the prison, it is important to describe its inhabitants. Increasingly, prisoners are poor, black or Hispanic, and in prison for drug-related crimes. We can also no longer ignore the fact that the prisoner may be a woman. She is also likely to be poor, black or Hispanic, and even more likely than male prisoners to be incarcerated for drug-related crimes.

African Americans have always represented a disproportionate number in our nation's prisons, meaning that their numbers far exceeded the roughly 11 percent that represents their numbers in the general population. Now, however, they are not just disproportionately represented, they form the majority of the prison population, comprising 50.8 percent (Bureau of Justice Statistics 1995). In 1993, the incarceration rate of blacks was seven times higher than the rate for whites. At the end of 1993, there were 1,471 black inmates per 100,000 black residents compared to 207 white inmates per 100,000 white residents (Bureau of Justice Statistics 1995).

The increase in total prisoner population is well known. What may not be as well reported is how widely this increase varies by race. Between 1980 and 1993, the number of white males grew 163 percent, but the number of black males grew by 217 percent; black females showed the single largest increase in imprisonment at 343 percent compared to the white females' increase of 327 percent (Bureau of Justice Statistics 1995). The growth in the number of Hispanics in prison is also large. Between 1980 and 1993, the incarceration rate for Hispanics tripled, from 163 sentenced prisoners per 100,000 Hispanic residents in 1980 to 529 per 100,000 Hispanic residents in 1993. The number of Hispanics in prison may be even larger than official figures since some states do not keep accurate records of those with Hispanic origins. At the end of 1993, nearly two-thirds of all sentenced prison inmates were black, Asian, Native American, or Hispanic (Bureau of Justice Statistics 1995).

The number of female inmates has increased at a faster rate (an average of 12 percent per year) than that for males (an average of 8.5 percent per year). Still, at year-end in 1994, women comprised only 6 percent of the total prison population, and the rate of incarceration for males at 746 per 100,000 was more than 16 times that for females at 45 per 100,000 (Bureau of Justice Statistics 1995).

The crimes of convicted prisoners have also changed in the last 13 years. Violent offenders fell from 57 percent of the prison population in 1980 to 45 percent in 1993. Property offenders fell from 30 percent to 22 percent. These decreases are no doubt caused by the dramatic rise in drug convictions (from 8 percent in 1980 to 26 percent in 1993). Nearly ten times as many inmates were serving time in

**TABLE 7-1**
**Prisoners in 1993, by Race**

| Race/Hispanic origin | State and federal inmates | |
| --- | --- | --- |
| | Number | Percent |
| White, Non-Hispanic | 333,100 | 35.8 |
| Black, Non-Hispanic | 410,800 | 44.1 |
| Hispanics | 163,500 | 17.6 |
| Other | 24,000 | 2.6 |

*Source:* Adapted from Bureau of Justice Statistics (1995, 8). Notes omitted.

TABLE 7-2
**Sentenced Prisoners in State and Federal Prisons by Sex and Race**

| Year | Total | Male | | | Female | | |
|---|---|---|---|---|---|---|---|
| | | All | White | Black | All | White | Black |
| 1980 | 315,974 | 303,643 | 159,500 | 140,600 | 12,331 | 5,900 | 6,300 |
| 1985 | 480,568 | 459,223 | 242,700 | 210,500 | 21,345 | 10,800 | 10,200 |
| 1990 | 739,980 | 699,416 | 346,700 | 344,300 | 40,564 | 20,000 | 20,100 |
| 1993 | 932,266 | 878,298 | 416,900 | 446,400 | 53,968 | 25,200 | 27,900 |
| % change | 220 % | 214 % | | | 386 % | | |

*Source:* Adapted from Bureau of Justice Statistics (1995, 8). Notes omitted.

state prisons for drug offfenses in 1993 (186,000) as in 1980 (19,000). Public order offenses also rose, from 5 percent to 7 percent (Bureau of Justice Statistics 1995). Even though their percentage of total prisoners fell, violent offenders accounted for the largest numerical increase and for 42 percent of the growth in prisoners between 1980 and 1993 (with drug offenders adding another 31 percent of the growth).

Prisoners are likely to be fairly young. Most prisoners are under the age of 30; the largest age group (for all admissions to prison) is from 18 to 24. This young population is likely to have less than a high school education. Only 38 percent are high school graduates (GEDs are probably included in this group, although it is not clear). There

TABLE 7-3
**State Prison Admissions and Sentences**

| New court commitments | 1985 | 1990 | 1991 | 1992 |
|---|---|---|---|---|
| Most serious offense (% of prison population) | | | | |
| violent | 35.1 % | 27.2 % | 29.1 % | 28.6 % |
| drug | 13.2 % | 32  % | 30.3 % | 30.4 % |
| Maximum sentence (months) | | | | |
| mean | 78 | 70 | 69 | 67 |
| median | 48 | 48 | 48 | 48 |
| 10 years or more (% of prison population) | 19.7 % | 17.9 % | 18.0 % | 17.7 % |

*Source:* Adapted from Bureau of Justice Statistics (1995, 11). Notes omitted.

**TABLE 7-4**
**State Prison Admissions by Age and Education, 1992**

| Demographics | All admissions (%) |
| --- | --- |
| **Sex** | |
| Male | 92.1 |
| Female | 7.9 |
| | |
| **Race** | |
| White | 44.9 |
| Black | 54.3 |
| Other | .9 |
| | |
| **Age at admission** | |
| Under 18 | 1.3 |
| 18-24 | 29.7 |
| 25-29 | 23.1 |
| 30-34 | 20.0 |
| 35-44 | 20.1 |
| 45-54 | 4.5 |
| Over 54 | 1.3 |
| Median age (years) | 29 |
| **Education** | |
| 8th grade or less | 16.4 |
| 9th-11th grade | 46.0 |
| High school graduate | 29.6 |
| Some college | 7.6 |
| Other | .4 |
| Median education (grade) | 11 |

*Source:* Adapted from Perkins, C. (1994). *National Corrections Reporting Program, 1992.* U.S. Dept. of Justice. Washington, D.C.: GPO.

seems to be no substantial difference in age among different types of offenders: The mean age for violent offenses is 29 years, the mean age for property offenses is 29 years, and the mean age for drug offenses is 30 years. The mean age ranges from 26 for robbery and motor vehicle theft to 36 for driving while intoxicated (Perkins 1994, 14).

Most prisoners are in prison for drug trafficking. The single largest group of prison admissions in 1992 was for drug trafficking (17.6 percent), with the next largest admission group for robbery (10.7 percent). Parole violators returned to prison are most likely drug traffickers (14.8 percent) or burglars (10 percent). The offense categories with the lowest parole revocation rates are nonnegligent manslaughter (0.3 percent), negligent manslaughter (0.5 percent), and arson (0.4 percent) (Perkins 1994, 13). Property offenders are still the largest group of prison admissions (at 34.1 percent), but drug offenses are catching up (at 29.2 percent). Violent crimes of conviction comprised 27.1 percent of prison admissions in 1992, and public order crimes only comprised 8.1 percent of admissions (Perkins 1994, 13).

In sum, prisoners are likely to be male, black or Hispanic, in prison for drug trafficking or robbery, and under 30 years of age. They are likely to have less than a high school education.

# THE SUBCULTURE

Sociologists and others have been interested in prison life for decades. The social world inside prison is called a *subculture*. If one defines "culture" as "the customary beliefs, social forms, and material traits of a racial, religious or social group" (Merriam Webster's 1994), then a subculture could be defined as a subterraneous or sub rosa system of power and interchange, including norms, values, and behavior patterns.

Very early the studies of prison became focused on the *inmate code*, the Magna Carta, so to speak, of prisoner subculture. Then interest turned to such things as the various types of individuals (identified by values, behaviors, and prior criminal history) one might find in a prison society. Also, the factors that could be correlated with prisoner socialization to the subculture were explored. Some inmates adhered more strongly to the inmate code, and some changed their pattern of acceptance during different times of their prison sentence. The type of prison seemed to affect the level of prisoner subculture as well. It became increasingly clear that not all inmates fitted nicely into subcultural types or participated in subcultural activities. Although early research on subculture ignored minorities, research during the last 20 years has focused almost exclusively on the role of racial gangs. Women prisoners and their unique subculture were also ignored in the early literature.

In this chapter we will first discuss the early literature on prisoner subcultures, that is, those studies that were describing the prisons of the 1940s through the early 1960s. Then we will turn to more current information to describe the prison of today. When describing the social world of today's prisons, one cannot ignore the impact of gangs and drugs, and these two areas will be focused on in our discussion.

## RESEARCHING THE PRISON SUBCULTURE

Various methods have been used to study the prison subculture, including participant observation, questionnaires, and interview methods. Each of these methods has advantages and disadvantages.

*Participant Observation.* This method involves the researcher living or being with the subject population for a length of time, participating to some degree in daily activities, and recording observations and impressions to be analyzed at some later date. Participant observation was one of the earliest methods to be used in prison research: In 1913 Thomas Mott Osborne, a prison reformer, spent a week in Auburn; and in 1936, Hans Reimer spent three months in the Kansas State Penitentiary (Bowker 1977). Often those who did research this way had positions as prison psychologists, counselors, or classification sociologists. Polansky (1942) was a psychologist at the prison where he carried out research exploring the effects of different kinds of prisons on the atmosphere of the prison community. Ash served as an intern at the Monroe Reformatory in Washington, and data gathered there was compared with data gathered from several other correctional institutions in Washington by Norman Hayner, Ash's teacher (Hayner 1943; Hayner and Ash 1939; Hayner and Ash 1940). Another student on the project, Clarence Schrag, was a classification counselor at the penitentiary (Schrag 1944, 1954).

Often, the researcher supplements his observations by structured or semistructured interviews, questionnaires, and prison records. Sykes, in the course of his three years at Trenton State Prison, used files, regulations, questionnaires, and interviews in addition to his personal observations (Sykes 1958). The use of this method has continued. Giallombardo employed it in a women's prison (Giallombardo 1966a), while Carroll (1974) and Jacobs (1977) have published studies of prisons for men using this technique. The most recent example is Fleisher's (1989) study of a federal facility, undertaken while he was a correctional officer at the facility.

*Questionnaires and Interviews.* Other studies have used questionnaires and interviews. The quality of this method ranges widely. On one end, there are the very simple questionnaires of the earliest studies such as Corsini's, which found that 50 percent of the inmate population he studied were "happy" (1946, 133). At the other end of the spectrum are those studies that attempt to measure complex correlations and to explore points of issue, such as the importation or deprivation theories, commitment to inmate code, and other questions. Questionnaires used alone have been used to measure alienation, opposition to formal organization, and other indexes of prison socialization. Questionnaires and interviews together have been used to compare institutions and to explore attitudes about parole (Rasmussen 1940).

Interviews allow for more detailed information gathering, but they are also time-consuming and expensive. Greater care must be taken in the analysis to ensure that interviewer bias doesn't affect the interpretation of the data. There are several studies that have used in-depth interviews to explore the individual's life in prison (Toch 1975, 1977). These are unique and different from other interview studies, in that they are looking at the individual's ability to cope in their social world, while other methods merely describe that world.

Grusky (1968) mixed methods to study leadership in a prison setting. First he identified leaders by questionnaires administered to a large sample, then interviewed the leaders that were identified. Another study that employed several methods was a cross-cultural comparison of prisons. This study looked at characteristics of architecture, used on-site observations, measured the custodial-treatment continuum, used backgrounds of inmates, measured roles, explored the importation-deprivation question, and studied homosexuality and drug use (Akers, Hayner, and Gruninger 1975).

The main problem facing the researcher who uses interviews and questionnaires is convincing inmates that their responses will remain confidential or anonymous. There is also the problem of nonrespondents, which seemingly is worse in prisons than in other settings. In addition, one might question the truthfulness of the responses. Interviewer bias, misunderstandings, and the educational levels of the respondents affect comprehension.

There are usually several methods for measuring any given research issue. For instance, "role" has been measured by attitudes (Garabedian 1963), background characteristics, and short descriptions given by the inmates of their own or other role types (Akers, Hayner, and Gruninger 1975). The advantages of questionnaires are that greater numbers of inmates can be represented and the results can be subject to statistical analysis.

*Other Methods.*    Several other methods have been used to study prison life, either alone or in conjunction with the methods described above. Some authors have used prison autobiographies to get a first-hand perspective (Irwin 1970). Others have used interviews but have dealt with the material in a less analytical and more journalistic manner (Burkhart 1976; Mittford 1974).

## THEORIES OF ORIGIN: IMPORTATION AND DEPRIVATION

The earliest descriptions of the prisoner subculture explained that the subculture developed and existed in response to the deprivations of prison life. Later researchers questioned this hypothesis, and in the tumultuous times of the 1960s and 1970s, the question of origin became somewhat moot.

Clemmer (1938), Sykes (1956), and other researchers postulated a deprivation model: specifically, that the subculture compensated for the deprivations of prison life. Gresham Sykes (1956) described these deprivations first. The deprivation of *liberty* not only restricted inmates' movements but also banished them from society. The deprivation of one's former life and everything associated with it was part of this banishment. The deprivation of *goods and services* reduced prisoners to an almost infantile dependence on institutional staff to provide everything from toilet paper to shampoo. Although necessities were available, they had to be requested, and there were no luxuries like favorite shampoo or cigarettes. *Normal sexual contact* was another deprivation, as was *denial of autonomy*. The latter involved the fact that rules guided and restricted every aspect of life; the individual was not free to make any decision at all regarding how to live, what to do, or even when to sleep. Finally, Sykes noted the deprivation of *security*; most inmates feared for their personal safety. When Sykes was writing, inmates probably more feared brutality from officers, whereas today the reverse is true. Inmates now have less reason to fear correctional officers, but the danger from other prisoners is greater. Deprivations are less extreme today. In fact, prisons in the 1940s and 1950s were much drearier than prisons of today, though the essential elements of the deprivations remain the same. Inmates still cannot move very freely; they are still banished; they still fear for their safety, perhaps now more so than ever.

Much later came the so-called importation theory which held that, in reality, the subculture was brought into the prison from the outside (Irwin and Cressey 1962, Jacobs 1977). Irwin and Cressey

(1962) described the following prison types that originated from street culture.

1. The Thief: This prisoner valued the notion that criminals should neither trust nor cooperate with police, should not betray other thieves, should be reliable, cool-headed, and "solid" in eyes of other inmates. This would be the equivalent of the "right guy" (a social type describing a prisoner who upholds the values of the prisoner subculture).
2. The Convict: This individual had spent many years in institutions and was very comfortable in a prison setting. Utilitarianism, manipulation of the prison system for personal advantage and gain, and working toward positions of power characterized his value system.
3. The Square: This individual was without a criminal background and therefore was very uncomfortable in the prison environment. He would be involved in counseling programs and have minimal involvement in the inmate social system.

Some support can be found for both theories. It may be, for instance, that the type of prison influenced the prevalence and power of the subculture. Berk (1966) found that whether the management style of an institution was described as "benign," "partial," or "lock" affected the subculture. "Lock" resulted in the most negative views, and "benign" resulted in the most positive attitudes. Others have studied the treatment-custody continuum and have found substantially similar findings (Wilson 1968; Wilson and Snodgrass 1969; Grusky 1968). In other words, the management style of the prison had a great deal to do with the intensity of the subculture. Institutions having treatment-oriented philosophies create less antisocial subcultures, and the more traditional custody-based facilities have stronger antisocial prisoner subcultures (as measured by adherence to antisocial norms and values). These types of findings support the view that deprivation is a causal factor in the development and strength of the subculture. Only Alpert (1978) found no relationship between type of prison and prisonization; he believed that it was the nonrandom assigning of people to institutions that resulted in the findings other researchers claimed to have discovered.

Other research supports the importation theory. For instance, some evidence suggested that criminal background pre-dicted adoption of social roles (Akers, Hayner, and Gruninger 1975). This evidence would support the importation theory since the pre-prison experience influenced the adherence or presence of subcultural values. Related findings indicate pre-prison background is important in prison life, for instance, the strongest correlate of prison drug use was pre-prison drug use (Thomas 1977; Akers, Hayner, and Gruninger 1975). The same has been found true of homosexual behavior (Akers, Hayner, and Gruninger 1975).

Applying these models to the female prisoner subculture was complicated. The deprivations for women in prison might be more severe or less severe, depending on how one evaluates the prison world. Arguably, separation from family is harder for women, women are less likely to have lived in an institutional setting, and they are less likely to have been imprisoned. Under deprivation theory, this should mean the subculture would be stronger for them because they are more deprived. On the other hand, the prisons for women in this country are notably less rigid and less punitive than those for men, arguing toward a less solid subcultural adaptation. There is some support for this: Early research indicated that in women's prisons, the commitment to the convict code was not as strong, sanctions against snitches were not as severe, homosexuality was more typical of the free world, and so on. These facts support the deprivation theory if one assumes that the deprivations for women are less severe.

There is also only mixed support for the importation model from what we know of the female subculture. Sex roles, expectations, and needs from the outside obviously affect behavior in prison. Giallombardo (1966) was a proponent of the theory that women develop pseudofamily systems because a woman has only a few roles to form her identity. These roles are all relevant to a family system (for example, wife, mother, daughter), and because she does not have outside roles available (for example, breadwinner, professional thief), she must necessarily create a substitute family system to meet her needs. This, of course, may have changed since Giallombardo did her research in the 1960s. Thirty years later, many women are not as dependent on family roles for their self-identity.

Another piece of evidence that supports the importation thesis is that evidence which indicates that homosexual relationships are prevalent, arguably because society more easily accepts women expressing affection and therefore their greater tendency to express their affection physically. Also, an association was found between pre-prison sexual orientation and prison sexual behavior (Nelson 1974). Zingraff (1980) and Hartnagel and Gillan (1980) concluded that deprivation factors seemed relevant to the male subculture, but importation was the only theory that seemed to explain female subcultural adaptations.

It is probably safe to say that both theories contribute to the genesis of the prison subculture and can be seen as complementary. The deprivation model includes factors such as the organization of the prison and conditions, while the importation model supplements these factors with pre-prison experiences and socialization of the inmates. Together, they combine to influence the nature of the subculture and the degree of socialization to the subculture by prisoners (Thomas 1977).

# THE INMATE CODE: PRISONS 1940-1960

The "inmate code" was a major tenet of all early studies of prison subcultures. The features of this code are:

Don't interfere with inmate interests.
Never rat on a con.
Don't be nosy.
Don't have a loose lip.
Keep off a man's back.
Don't put a guy on the spot.
Be loyal to your class.
Be cool.
Do your own time.
Don't bring heat.
Don't exploit inmates.
Don't cop out.
Be tough.
Be a man.
Never talk to a screw.
Have a connection.
Be sharp. (Sykes and Messinger 1960)

The prescriptions for behavior in this code of behavior are different from official values. The "code," if accurate, described a world where convicts left each other alone, shunned guards, and never lost their "cool" even in the face of great provocation. The prisoner who followed the code valued loyalty, autonomy, and strength.

The inmate code was perceived to be part of every prisoner subculture, except that few researchers thought to look at females in prison to see whether they endorsed the code too. Certainly some of the elements of the code — "be a man" — didn't apply. Giallombardo (1966) was one of the few researchers who made any attempt to describe the female prisoner subculture, and she started her work decades after Clemmer (1938) and Sykes (1956) first described prison subcultures. In her study at Alderson, a federal prison for women, she found that different themes were emphasized in the female prisoners' world.

> You can't trust other women.
> To live with other women is to live in a jungle.
> Every woman is a sneaking, lying bitch.
> If I don't get there first, someone else will. (Giallombardo 1966, 100)

Some elements of the male code, such as "do your own time," were specifically rejected as inapplicable to the women's culture. Giallombardo found that more women were involved in relationships that encouraged interaction rather than isolation. Pollock-Byrne (1990) reviewed the literature on female prisoners' culture and concluded that it was not extremely efficacious to study the women's subculture *in comparison* to men's. This approach did not readily absorb the reality of women's world but only how it was similar or different from that of men's. There is still a need for original studies in women's prisons, although several researchers are currently making updated and interesting findings available (Owens 1996).

## ARGOT

An early study by Hargan (1934) devoted itself entirely to the language, or *argot,* of the prison subculture. He stated that the prison argot had a purpose: It was a secret code against outsiders and prison officials and, therefore, acted to reinforce solidarity. Sykes also referred to the power of argot in stereotyping guards (Sykes 1958, 84). Knowledge of argot has since been used as a measure of integration into the subculture (Garabedian 1964).

One might characterize prison argot as a variation of street jargon. Many of the terms are quite likely found in any street culture. The drug culture has generated many new terms. One can identify the important elements of a culture from the number of terms used to identify it. For instance, there are dozens of argot terms for various drugs: "shit," "horse," "shag," "stuff," "boy," "Mexican Mud," and "China White" are only a few of the argot terms used for heroin (Bentley and Corbett 1992). Informers (or "snitches," "rats," "grasses" in England) and guards (or "hacks," "screws") have a number of terms ascribed to them. Things like prison programs that have few or no terms assigned to them are less relevant to the culture. The prison subculture's focal points can be studied by the terms ascribed to it.

As is any language, prison argot is a dynamic, constantly evolving entity. Only some of the terms described by the early studies are still current. As the language filters through to officers and the prison staff, it changes. Also some terms are specific to the institution or group involved. For instance, the term "dropping her belt (or pants)" refers to a female inmate who discards the male role in favor of a more feminine identity. "She's down" in a certain federal institution not only means a state of mind, it also refers to an inmate's sitting on her floor, which is the only way to achieve privacy in a dormitory room with chest-high partitions. In this subculture, when someone is (literally) "down," her need or wish to be left alone is respected.

## ARGOT ROLES

*Argot (or social) roles* are distinguishable discrete types in the subculture, each with attached values and behavior systems. As stated earlier, the social roles in prison have been measured in several ways. One could differentiate *roles* (which incorporate the personal values of the individual) and *types* (which are descriptive labels attached to individuals); however, no differentiation will be made here.

There are actually many different typologies that have been developed, some more well known than others. Sykes identified rats (informers), centermen (those aligned with correctional officers), gorillas (aggressive predators), merchants (involved in the black market), wolves (a sexual aggressor), ball busters (often engaged in violent confrontations), real men (old style convicts), toughs (affiliated with violent crime), and hipsters (newer drug-involved criminals) (1956b). Hayner and Ash confirmed the real men type (although they called them right guys); merchants were referred to as racketeers or rangatangs; wolves were called smoothies. In addition, Hayner and Ash identified the politician (an inmate who was articulate, political, and acted as an intermediary with authorities) and the "ding" (an inmate who was — or at least acted as if he was — mentally ill) (1939, 1940).

Schrag's (1944) roles probably have become the most well known. Identified by both the prison term and a more descriptive term, he listed square john (prosocial), right guy (antisocial), con politician (pseudosocial), and outlaw (asocial). The square john was the individual who did not have an extensive criminal history, nor did he associate with or hold criminal views or values. Prison was extremely uncomfortable for him because he was not affiliated in any way with the prisoner subculture. In effect, he identified more with the officers than his cellmates. He was not trusted by those in the subculture. At best, he was left alone. At worst, he was victimized. The *right guy* was the old style con. This Jimmy Cagney-type character was respected for his criminal professionalism; he was a thief, or a bank robber, or an organized crime figure. He would have been a leader in the yard and not afraid of violence (although he would not have used it indiscriminately, as did the outlaw). The outlaw was an individual who did not follow any code of behavior, even a criminal code. Anybody could be his victim, unless the person was stronger or had allies. Power and violence were the stock in trade of the outlaw. Even inmates feared him. The con politician role included those inmates who held most of the formal leadership roles in the prison or who were very visible interactors with prison administration. They were articulate, intelligent, and manipulative. Although superficially they looked as if they were performing services for the convict body for altruistic motives, actually their motives were much more egoistic. For instance, a prisoner representative to the inmate council might use his pass that allowed free movement between tiers to further his black market or drug trade.

Finally, Hayner (1961) gives us another typology, relating more or less to Schrag's by type of offense, including the heavy (right guy), graduate (outlaw), con forger (con politician), alcoholic forger (square john), and rapo (ding). The way Hayner chose these types is explained by the following quote.

> Con forger. An inmate was selected as a "politician" if his case record showed four earmarks out of the following five: IQ above average as determined by a standard test, educational achievement tenth grade or above as measured by achievement tests, holds job either as an inmate clerk in some office or as a runner, one minor rule infraction per year or less, smooth verbalizations and willing cooperation but a recidivist. Socio-economic status was determined by the occupation and source of income of the father. . . . (1961, 99)

Roles have been related to pre-prison background by others besides Hayner. Thomas and Foster found associations between first arrest, first conviction, and role type (1973, 231). Irwin and Cressey's typology (thief, hustler, dope fiend, and so on) is organized around the prisoner's background offenses (1962).

Social role identity has been correlated with participation in prison programs, adjustment to prison, alienation, and a host of other personal and behavioral indices. Findings show, not surprisingly, that square johns participated most frequently in prison programs (Garabedian 1964). It was found that square johns and outlaws did "harder time" than other inmates, meaning that prison adjustment was more difficult and involved more stress for these two groups (Garabedian 1964).

The validity of role types is by no means unquestioned. Garabedian's method of identifying roles by values expressed in responses to hypothetical situations has been especially criticized (1964). One study was only able to classify 34 percent of their sample using Garabedian's method (Akers, Hayner, and Gruninger 1975). Leger (1976) also criticized Garabedian, stating that there was little correlation between behavioral components and the attitudinal component that Garabedian tapped.

Increasing criticism of the validity of the "right guy" role developed when it became clear that the role type was more an illusion than reality. Very few inmates could be described as right guys or even knew any other prisoners who might be described as such (Johnson 1996, 137). From most accounts it seemed that "honor among thieves" existed only in the minds of those writing fictional accounts of prison life. In the real world, male inmates were much more likely to be snitches than right guys.

Argot roles in women's prisons did not match those described above for men, at least according to some researchers. Giallombardo (1966) wrote that there was no corresponding "real woman" to the "real man" role because the positive qualities associated with the role had no place in the female world. Giallombardo described a prison world where women prisoners were spiteful, deceitful, and untrustworthy. Of course, in retrospect, we might hypothesize that men were no less spiteful, deceitful, and untrustworthy, but that researchers accepted the concept or ideal of the "right guy." Heffernan (1972), in her study of a women's prison, did describe a "real woman" type that came fairly close to the male role with the same characteristics of responsibility, loyalty, and standing up to authority.

The social roles described by Giallombardo included the snitchers (informers), inmate cops (affiliated with the correctional officers), squares (square john equivalents), jive bitches (those who stirred up trouble), rap buddies or homies (friends), boosters (shoplifters), pinners (a trusted inmate who serves as a "lookout" when illicit activities are undertaken), and the cluster of roles associated with homosexuality — penitentiary turnouts, butches, lesbians, femmes, stud broads, tricks, commissary hustlers, chippies, kick partners, cherries, punks, and turnabouts (1966, 105-123). Only the snitches, homies, and squares overlap with the male role types of Schrag or other researchers. Simmons (1975), another researcher studying female role types, did identify the politician role and the outlaw role among women, although since her purpose was to look for Schrag's role types in a prison for women, it is probably not surprising that she found them (1975). Another writer who made clear parallels to a system set up for male prisoners is Heffernan (1972). Her "square," "cool," and "the life" correspond almost identically to Irwin and Cressey's "square," "thief," and "con" roles.

## VALUES

The values of the prisoner subculture can be deduced from the behaviors prescribed by the inmate code. Group loyalty, violence, strength, and sexual proclivity were the major values of the inmate subculture as studied by researchers through the 1970s (Wilder 1965).

Violence is a predominant theme in all prisons except for perhaps some minimum security or treatment facilities. The threat of violence may be muted in women's facilities, but even there, inmates are fearful and the weak are often intimidated by aggressors. In maximum security institutions for men, the violence is palpable, ever present, and, at times, lethal.

> In jail you blow up more. You're not scared to blow up. If you bump into someone in jail, you can turn around and say, "'Watch out, goof, or I'll tear your face off." But if you say that to someone on the street, you've got a good chance of the guy callin' the cops. (Liaison 1984, 8, cited in Johnson 1996, 106)

> The first day I was in prison, two dudes busted in on this guy in the cell next to mine and stuck him twenty-six times with shanks. (Earley 1992, 50, cited in Johnson 1996, 106)

The values connected with group loyalty and the proscription against snitching point up the importance of the rat in prison society. Virtually every writer has at least mentioned this theme of prison life. One could almost describe its importance as a paranoid response to the institutional setting. As mentioned before, there is an overproportionate number of names attached to informers (Weinberg 1942); the names are even differentiated by actions (Johnson 1961, Johnson 1996).

The person identified as a snitch is often scorned by officials and inmates alike, yet his role is a complex one. Officials indicate they could not run the prison without informers. Despite the social and sometimes lethal sanctions against rats and the clear opposition they pose to the inmate code, they seem to exist in abundance (Wilder 1965; Johnson 1996).

Snitching was present in both female and male subcultures, but sanctions against this behavior were more heavily enforced in male prisons. Social isolation was (and is) used by both male and female prisoners, but gossip was also used in women's prisons, and only infrequently did the sanctions for women snitches include violence. Serious violence is rare among women prisoners; it is more common with men, such as what occurred during the 1980 New Mexico prison riot in which informers were subjected to extreme forms of torture, including burning of genitals, and then execution (Colvin 1992).

It may be that the degree of sanctions differs according to what is at stake. Because contraband and black market trade, including drug trafficking, are not as prevalent in institutions for women, there may be less need for extreme sanctions. With the subcultural changes occurring today, it will bear watching whether snitches become more severely sanctioned among women as well.

Prisoners' cynical attitudes towards the "working stiff" and society in general have been well documented. Rasmussen characterized the prevailing view as "everyone has a racket" (1940, 593). It is true that for at least a portion of the inmate body, the working world holds no attraction or interest (Johnson 1996). This is important because this value is left unaddressed in most vocational or rehabilitative programs. Giving someone a skill who has a value system that discards regular work in favor of "the fast life" will not change that person's behavior. Earning quick money and living a flashy life is a goal and value that bears little resemblance to the straight life the inmate is expected to lead on the outside, performing typically low-paying, low-skilled work.

There has always been a system of trade within the prison that has been an integral part of the male subculture (although not as prevalent in prisons for women). The value of reciprocity — a sharing of resources — is emphasized to some degree (Strange and McCrory 1974), but more often "conniving" — "getting over" on someone by taking advantage of them is accepted and respected (Hayner and Ash 1939). The prison's illicit trade system has been described as a coping mechanism that achieves two purposes: First, it is a means of obtaining contraband items that make prison life easier; second, it is a vehicle that provides excitement and risk to an otherwise dull existence (Hayner and Ash 1939). *Contraband* is any item that is possessed in violation of prison rules. Contraband obviously includes drugs or weapons, but it also can be money, cigarettes, or even some types of clothing. The importance of contraband in the subculture has been researched in detail by several authors who describe its importance in secondary adjustment (Guenther 1975; Kalinich 1980).

> The contraband system can also contribute to the psychological well being of the inmates. . . . Being active in the contraband system gives an inmate an opportunity to use his mental skills, keeps him busy rather than being idle, gives him something to look forward to that otherwise would not exist, and may keep his mind off his status as a prisoner, helping to break up the monotony of daily prison life. (Kalinich 1980, 33)

Selke (1993) provides a more recent account of the powerholders in the inmate economy, including the drug dealers, the kitchen staff (who can steal food), the hospital orderlies (who steal medicine or can cut through red tape to get a prisoner to the doctor faster), the barber (who has access to weapons), and the administrative clerk (who has access to records).

An inmate can get almost anything he wants in a maximum security prison if he has the resources to buy it. He can get coffee in the morning, sandwiches (from stolen bread and meat) delivered to his cell door, pornography drawn or smuggled in if contraband (some prisons have no rules against soft porn), any type of drug he wants, and even sex, from a "boy" or "punk," penitentiary "queen," or heterosexual sex through more complicated means with the cooptation of officers. He can have his clothes starched, pressed and returned to him, have others do his correspondence courses in order to acquire college credit, and get anyone he wants assigned to his cell, or get a single cell if he so desires. He can find out the "jacket" (file information) of those coming into prison and perhaps get someone transferred out. He can have someone killed. All he needs is money or the equivalent barter.

## MYTHOLOGY

Another way to explore the subculture is through its mythology or stories. These are present in all groupings of people and are enlightening to the individual attempting to detail the subculture. Prisoners' stories include those that tell of successful escapes, "putting one over" on guards or administration, and stories of famous exploits (one of the most circulated stories in one prison was a former inmate who robbed a bank and walked across the street into a waiting helicopter to get away). Obviously these stories, while often based in fact, do not necessarily need to be truthful. Other stories dramatize the brutality of the guards and others talk about prison conditions ("it was so bad at X prison that . . .") (Haynes 1948). Many researchers have observed how prison talk tends to revolve around sexual exploits. Bragging about one's prowess or one's desirability to women evidently serves to pass the time and assuage the inability to prove manliness through relations with women.

Drugs also have become part of the prison folklore. Mythology becomes the best "high" or the entertaining experiences (true or not) associated with drug use. "Crimes of the century" are stories of the best "score," the most exciting robbery, or the most violent episode with police. These stories, again, may or may not have elements of truth. Their purpose is not to impart information, but to pass the time and to build up one's reputation as a man.

> We try to live through words and self dramatization. . . . We try to live by pretending to live in tall stories based on how we'd like to live, or we long to live. . . . (Cited in Johnson 1996, 73)

Women's mythology develops differently. Women may have similar drug stories (the best drug, the worst high, and so forth), but, in other areas, their stories tend to be less braggadocio. Their conversations revolve around their crimes and their partying, but also their children and their relationships with men (which tend to have a theme of how rotten the men were rather than how many they slept with). It may be that the need to prove oneself as a woman involves creating the identity as a mother, in the same way that creating an identity as a man involves sexual proclivity with women. In both cases, the mythology serves the same purpose, but the definitions are different.

## HOMOSEXUALITY

Homosexuality is another element of prison life. It is notable that homosexuality was largely ignored in the research of male prisoner subcultures, yet studied to the virtual exclusion of all other aspects of the subculture in prisons for women. It is interesting to speculate why early subculture research on women focused almost exclusively on their sexual behavior. The most obvious reason is that women were seen primarily as sexual beings. As the early criminological theories of females focused on biological or psychological theories of criminality, long after theories for men had evolved to sociological and multicausal theories, so too the tendency in prison research was to view women in a single light — through their sexual identity. Another reason is that homosexuality in women's prisons seemed so much more open than in men's prisons. It also seemed different, more pervasive and more consensual.

Homosexuality in men's prisons was characterized by violent assaults or coercion; older inmates (wolves) offered protection to young men (punks) for sexual favors and commissary articles (Bowker 1980; Lockwood 1980). In women's prisons, homosexuality was (and is) more often consensual and those females (femmes) who are interested in a relationship compete for the few women who have assumed the male role (butches) (Gagnon and Simon 1968; Ward and Kassebaum 1964; Van Wormer 1978; Halleck 1962; Hammer 1965).

Even with all the research that has explored prison homosexuality, it is still unclear how prevalent it was (or is). Vagueness in defining the term may account for some of this confusion. Homosexuality has been defined as genital sexual relations; participation in relationships (in women's prisons) that only involve notewriting, kissing, or hugging; a committed sexual orientation; or "being in the game" (in women's prisons), which ordinarily meant that the woman would return to heterosexual relationships after release. Many studies have used unreliable estimates of homosexual activity, such as reports from officers or other inmates. Even self-reports may not have accurately represented participation rates because some inmates would not identify themselves as homosexual or their activities as homosexual, instead opting for other definitions of their behavior. It seems that there are varying amounts of homosexuality in prisons, but the variables that contribute to the level of activity are hard to identify.

One seemingly unique feature of women's prisons is the *pseudofamilies* that, by all accounts, have no parallel in prisons for men. Pseudofamilies are make-believe family systems that include all the familial roles including grandparents, parents, daughters, sons, cousins, aunts, and so on. Some studies seem to support the thesis that participation in these "families" is negatively associated with participation in homosexual relationships; in juvenile institutions, one is more likely to find family systems, while in adult prisons, more homosexual activity will occur (Propper 1976). The advent of relaxed visiting rules, weekend visitation, more programs, and interaction with community groups may have reduced the strength of this social pattern in prisons. Fox (1982) pointed out that fewer women seemed to be involved in these social groupings in the 1980s than he observed was the case in the 1970s.

One interesting observation about homosexuality as it occurs in male prisons is that only the punk or queen and not the wolf was identified as homosexual, and the relationship was one of power and submission rather than affection (Strange and McCrory 1974; Gagnon and Simon 1968; Hayner and Ash 1939). Later research indicates that, at least in today's prisons, homosexuality among imprisoned men may not be as violent or coercive as earlier described. Johnson (1996) reviews descriptions of homosexual marriages in prisons for men, open flaunting of homosexual availability, and other indications that consensual relationships between men do exist.

One explanation of the pattern of homosexuality in women's and men's prisons can be termed the "cost-benefit" theory. One might look at the advantages and disadvantages of each role. In the prison for men, the wolf role has the advantage of sexual gratification, commissary articles, and power from controlling the boy or punk for either trade or sale; the disadvantages are that he might have to physically prove himself either to the boy or punk or someone anxious to usurp him. It is a role that is fairly consistent with the traditional male role. The punk, on the other hand, has few advantages other than protection. Besides being the virtual slave of the wolf, the role completely destroys his male identity; he becomes, to all purposes, a "wife."

In the women's prison, the femme role has the advantage of the status acquired by being attached to a male (butch), some affection, and some sexual gratification; but the femme is also required to wait on her partner and to share commissary articles with her. Also, there is a good chance that she is expected to share her partner with other women. The butch role has advantages similar to the wolf in the male prison: She is the taker in the relationship by virtue of the male sex role she has adopted. She is obeyed and gains the right to the material possessions of her femme. In fact, she may get away with having several female partners, either with her partner's knowledge or not. The disadvantage is that she has to give up her female identity and may have trouble reconciling her prison identity with her free-world identity, a problem that especially arises if she has visitors. She is also subject to discipline by prison staff for too obviously adopting the male role.

It is clear from even this superficial analysis that the butch role for women has many more advantages than the punk role for men.

Thus, it is not surprising that women take on the butch role voluntarily while men most often are beaten or coerced into the punk role. Of course there is a difference between punks and queens. Queens — those who openly adopt a feminine manner and dress in a prison for men — are very much in demand. If they have the protection of a stronger inmate, they may operate in a semi-autonomous manner and pick and choose partners at will, for monetary or other reasons. In many respects, queens may be more comparable to butch roles in women's prisons, while there is no true comparison to the role of punks or boys.

Most prisoners, male or female, whose pre-prison sexual orientation is toward the same sex may not openly advertise that fact in prison or may not involve themselves at all in prison sexuality. In fact, they may look with some disdain upon the sexual activities of "jailhouse turnouts." Other relationships are not advertised as romantic relationships and are camouflaged as friendships or hidden from view to avoid the attention and envy of others.

## LEADERSHIP

The process of identifying leaders is not as simple as it would seem. Leaders may be defined in a variety of ways: as the best known, the most feared, the most respected, or those who possess power to command others. Utilizing some of these factors, early researchers found that leaders appeared to be somewhat younger and more criminalistic than the general population (Clemmer 1938).

> Leaders, as a group, do not differ from the other inmates with respect to age, occupation, educational attainment, ethnic status, marital status, or scores on an intelligence test. However, leaders have served more years in prison, have longer sentences remaining to be served, are more frequently charged with crimes of violence, and are more likely to be repeated offenders. Significantly more leaders than other inmates are officially diagnosed as homosexual, psychoneurotic, or psychopathic. Finally, the institutional adjustments of leaders are marked by a significantly greater number of serious rule infractions, including escape, attempted escape, fighting, and assault. (Schrag 1954, 40)

However, there are many types of leaders. Even in small groups instrumental and expressive leaders have been differentiated. The method for identifying leaders in prison typically involved simply asking inmates to list "leaders," and those inmates who were mentioned most often were assumed to be the leaders in that prison body. It might be the case, therefore, that what was measured was merely those who were better known (which would explain them being more violent). Additionally, the existence of leaders presupposes a somewhat solid subculture but is less relevant in a context where social relations are tenuous. Again, those who would emerge in any quantitative method would be those of the most cohesive group, however small.

Leadership can involve respect and admiration with the leader possessing *status*; or it can involve coercion and submission, the leader possessing not status but *power*. This relationship becomes even more complicated in the prison society, which values power and strength, so that one might be measuring some combination of fear and respect.

Along these lines, it is interesting to find that right guys, who elicit the most respect from the population, are not overly represented when leaders are identified. Sykes hypothesized about this fact.

> [I]t is a role in the inmate social system which is filled by relatively few prisoners, partly, we suspect, because of the ambivalence of the prestige system, partly because prestige and material rewards do not coincide, and partly because criminals in prison are peculiarly unfitted both by previous experience and inclination to adapt themselves to the needs of the collectivity. (1956b, 136)

Leadership research then moved to questions of how leadership was affected by changes in prison management styles or, conversely, how treatment plans were affected by existing leaders (Garabedian 1970). It is interesting that Berk (1966) found that informal leadership was more structured in a custodial institution, while those leaders who emerged in a treatment facility tended to be more flexible and instrumental, exercising far less control over the prisoner population.

Giallombardo (1966) believed that leaders within the female system were to be found only within the kinship system; the male or father figure was the unquestioned leader for that family and to some extent gained status in the eyes of those outside the family by virtue of her position. This has clear implications for what qualities are valued in a leader — namely, those values associated with masculinity. In one women's prison during the early 1980s, two of the three formal leadership roles for inmates were held by a female who was in the process of surgically becoming a man. She had facial hair, a deep voice, no breasts, and only lacked a penis (which was why the state declared her legally a female and incarcerated her in a prison for women). Thus, the one "male" in a prison of 500 women held two of the three leadership roles (Pollock-Byrne 1990).

Other studies of leadership in women's prisons found that leadership (as observed in a classroom situation) had no relation to age or race. Education was a more influential factor than male or female roles (Van Wormer 1978). Another study found that leaders tended to be young, black, high interactors, and homosexually active (Simmons 1975). These findings are similar to those for male prisoners, which could be due to the same methodological problem: In a loosely held together, atomized subculture with few ties, those who emerge as leaders in any quantitative study are those who belong to a cohesive group, however small. Because these individuals emerge from a survey method does not necessarily mean that they are status leaders for the total inmate population. With females, the homosexually active leaders might be represented because their group was the only cohesive group in the prison.

## ALIENATION AND SOCIALIZATION

Theoretically a prison subculture is a secondary adjustment to institutional life, a mechanism that gives the individual a cohesive base to depend on. It is a family, so to speak, in an otherwise alienating environment. The subculture was supposed to give inmates a sense of solidarity, but did it? Even the earliest writers, while describing the subculture, could not ignore the presence of a certain amount of alienation. In fact, Clemmer states that 40 percent of inmates played a solitary role.

> The concept that prisoners are geographically near but socially distant would seem to be substantiated by the following data obtained from the followers who were given a schedule on social affiliations. (1) 70% of these men state that friendships in prison result from the mutual help that man can give man. (2) 77% of the subjects stated that familiarity in prison breeds contempt. (3) 72% report that friendships in prison are of short duration. (4) 95% conclude that most prisoners are more interested in hemselves than in any other prisoners. (1938, 870)

Roebuck (1963), paraphrasing Clemmer, stated that the prison was an "atomized world lacking a uniform value system where exploitation, trickery, and dishonesty overshadowed cooperation" (197). Sykes stated:

> Far from being a prison community, men in prison tend to react as individuals and refuse to suspend their intra-mural conflict when confronting the enemy, the prison officials. Those who dominate others are viewed with a mingled fear, hatred, and envy; and the few who manage to retreat into solitarity may well be penalized in the struggle to evade the poverty-stricken existence. . . . (1956b, 134)

A picture emerged in which the so-called subculture described in the prison literature of the 1940s through the 1960s was one that did not offer much social support for the individual and was probably more of a coercive force strengthened by the most antisocial, aggressive inmates. Further, "the individual who becomes most deeply enmeshed in criminal modes of behavior is the individual who is alienated from both fellow-prisoners and prison officials" (Sykes 1956, 134).

Other data indicating the existence of a good deal of alienation came from Polansky, who found that in an autocratic institution, liking for inmates went down (1942, 20). Thomas and Poole confirmed this; they found that the more coercive the formal organization, the greater the degree of alienation in the inmate population (1975, 32). Although Thomas and Poole used powerlessness as a measure rather than alienation, it might be assumed that the two have sufficiently close ties to be comparable. There was also an association found between powerlessness and adopting prison values and between adopting such values and criminal identification.

It might be said that the only ones buying into the idea of the prisoner subculture as a supportive force were some of the researchers and journalists writing about prison life. Later researchers who studied women then mistakenly believed that women were different, in that they did not exhibit the same degree of solidarity. In fact, more support seemed to exist for the proposition that neither males nor females in prison showed much liking or trust for each other. How can we explain this seemingly contradictory situation: The subculture, which supposedly decreases alienation, actually is positively associated with it? To explore this question, researchers have looked at what factors are associated with socialization to the subculture.

## FACTORS ASSOCIATED WITH PRISONIZATION

Socialization is the process whereby one adopts the values, behaviors, and norms of the subculture. In the particular case of the prisoner

subculture, socialization is called *prisonization*. The term prisonization means that the individual has become so acclimated to prison
life and so institutionalized that the free world becomes strange and
the prison world becomes normal. " 'To many,' states one penitentiary inmate, 'there is no place so natural and so much like home as
a prison' " (Johnson 1996, 115).

Some variables affecting socialization include the prisoner's personality, the kind and extent of relationships the prisoner had on
the outside, affiliation with prison groups, chance placement in work
gangs, cellhouse or roommate, acceptance of the dogmas and codes
of the prison culture, and other factors such as race, criminality, regional origin, and conditioning (Haynes 1948, 440).

Clemmer cited the following as factors affecting prisonization:
long sentences, a somewhat unstable personality, the dearth of positive relations with persons outside the walls, a readiness and capacity
for integration into a prison primary group, a blind or almost blind
acceptance of the dogmas and mores of the primary group and general prison population, chance placement with other persons of a
similar orientation, and a readiness to participate in gambling and
"abnormal" sex behavior (Clemmer, 1938b). Basically, Clemmer
(1938b) saw socialization into the prison subculture as increasing
proportionally with the amount of time spent in prison (*The Prison
Community*). Wheeler (1961), on the other hand, characterized socialization as relating to expectation of release, so that prosocial
norms were high on entry and decreased during the prison sentence;
then, as release approached, commitment to inmate norms decreased and prosocial norms were reestablished. Thus a U-shaped
curve was observed in prison subculture commitment. Finally, Garabedian (1963) further refined "Wheeler's U" by correlating it with
social roles. He found that outlaws showed a steady decline in prosocial norms, square johns showed the most exaggerated U-shape
(dropping most precipitously and rising again in prosocial commitment before release), and politicians and right guys had a less exaggerated U-shaped commitment pattern. Dings actually showed a
rising commitment to prosocial norms throughout the prison term.
Other studies have found significant correlations between social
types, socialization, and phases of institutional career (Wellford
1967). Others have found a U-shaped curve, but it does not necessarily relate to role types (Atchley and McCabe 1968).

It has been found that the type of facility affects the level of prisoner subculture and the extent to which most are socialized to the
subculture (Wilson and Snodgrass 1969; Street, Vinter, and Perrow
1966; Berk 1966). An alternative hypothesis, of course, is that institu-

tional assignment is not random: Treatment-oriented institutions house those with prosocial norms, and maximum security prisons with little treatment philosophy house less amenable inmates.

An integration of these theories seems to make the most sense. Thomas and Foster (1972) provide us with a path analysis that includes post-prison expectations and social role adaptations in the factors affecting socialization. More recent analyses point out that methodology has been less than perfect and many definitions of prisonization, powerlessness, and alienation were used in these early studies. More current studies approach these issues as a question of "prisoner adjustment" rather than socialization to a subculture (Goodstein and Wright 1989).

Stripped of heroic imagery and drama, the prisoner subculture was exposed as more of a coercive than supportive system. It seemed most prevalent when conditions were oppressive, increasing along with alienation. Its leadership consisted of those most involved in the subculture. These men seem to possess the same characteristics that Irwin described as state-raised youth, namely, they had a highly criminal background, were more violent, and were quite at home in the prison (1970). The right guys seemed, at best, to be an infrequent ideal. The values attributed to such a role were seldom lived up to. Although the main tenet of the so-called inmate code was inmate loyalty, and "snitches" were scorned, a great deal of informing went on. In summary, one must put aside the view of a cohesive subculture when presented with evidence that the prison described by early research consisted of individuals, isolated from most others, where the strong preyed on the weak and invoked the notion of the inmate code to suit their interests.

## A TIME OF CHANGE: PRISONS IN THE 1960s TO THE 1990s

Between the 1940s and 1960s prison researchers were concerned with the definition of, and socialization to, the prisoner subculture. However, even as researchers were utilizing various research modalities to study the prison world, it was changing rapidly and inevitably in response to events both outside and inside the prison walls. These changes, which will be described in this section, have led to the prison of today. It is a world arguably more violent than the one Clemmer or Sykes studied, where prisoners have more legal rights but perhaps less ability to protect themselves from the most danger-ous elements of the subculture. Gangs, of course, dominate the social world of the prison today. Interestingly, the genesis of gangs might be found in the prisoner rights movement of the 1960s.

## POLITICIZATION IN THE 1960s AND 1970s

During a short period of time in the 1960s and 1970s, some prisoners became more politically aware and defined themselves as "political prisoners" (Fairchild 1977; Huff 1975). The role of the political pris-oner was one that held more rewards to the individual than the iden-tity as a criminal. One author compared the psychic benefits of the political prisoner model over the sick role or the bad role (Brody 1974). Defining oneself as a political prisoner made it easier to ratio-nalize past crimes. This definition even received some support from celebrities and prisoner rights groups on the outside. Men such as George Jackson were seen as heroes and martyrs fighting a corrupt system.

The origins of this identification were found in the general un-rest and protest-ridden Sixties during which students, civil libertari-ans, and other assorted groups were sometimes sent to prison. Once there, they sensitized prisoners to this new form of power (Reasons 1973). The prison inmates proved to be good students, and soon the advantages of employing such strategies began to be apparent.

> When these "kids" came in they started making the decisions and soon the older prisoners were following them. They turned us off from beating on each other to beating on the "bulls" and sud-denly we started to get things done. (Cited in Brody 1974, 104)

The trend, however, was short-lived. After a spate of prisoner riots around the time of the Attica rebellion in 1971, most of the politicalism among prisoners ended. No clear reasons for the demise of this stance are evident. Perhaps the grievance mechanisms and legal aid opportunities that were created by prisoner rights cases dif-fused some of the anger, or perhaps the movement went the way of the larger social protest movement, which faded away after the Viet-nam War wound down.

Other writers postulated that the sincere radical role was one that held little reward for any individual (Johnson and Dorian 1975). The relative powerlessness of prisoners meant that in any confronta-tion, the individual was sure to lose. The more rewarding response to the monolithic character of the prison was the "cool" role, which, at least for blacks, supplanted a more militant and hence personally dangerous stance (Johnson and Dorian 1975). The cool role demands that the individual maintain a detachment that, although not submission, allows him to avoid hostile confrontations with authorities in no-win situations.

There is no question that the black awareness movement of the 1960s changed the prison atmosphere considerably. Many prisons had black solidarity clubs such as the Black Forum Unlimited in the Washington State Penitentiary. In fact, some authors go so far as to say that the black power and militancy movement was synonymous with the "prisoner movement" of the time (Johnson 1996, 142). Black solidarity translated into real problems for correctional staff who found that when confronting a black inmate, they were instead faced with twenty or so hostile "brothers" (Carroll 1976). Whether it was membership in an identity group as described above or, later, a street-based gang, racial identity became an important part of prisoners' lives (Jacobs 1977). Racial identity also changed the nature of prison violence. With racial gangs, blacks became the powerholders and whites the victims.

> Increasingly, violence among inmates took on racial connotations, with formerly repressed black inmates rising to positions of dominance within the prison culture. (Johnson 1996, 144)

## THE PRISON WORLD TODAY

At least for minority groups, the political groupings that occurred in the 1960s and 1970s have given way to less idealistic and more criminalistic gangs. Racial gangs, in those prisons that have them, have eclipsed any of the role types described in early research. Gangs have replaced all the older powerholders, such as the building tenders and inmate cops of the southern prison systems. Carroll (1982) writes that race determines almost every aspect of a prisoner's life — where he cells, who his friends are, what his job assignments are. He writes that prisons are "balkanized" with racial gangs holding territories such as portions of the yard, certain television rooms, and recreation room areas (Carroll 1982).

"What was once a repressive but comparatively safe 'Big House' is now often an unstable and violent social jungle" (Johnson 1996, 133). So reads one recent description of today's prison. The upheaval and furor created in the 1960s by the prisoners' rights movement, legal mandates, and changes in management philosophies, combined with the flood of drug offenders and the rise of gangs, have wrought tremendous changes in the prison, all of which have led to more violence. Even the title of Johnson's book chapter describing prison life connotes the problem: "Prowling the Yard" chronicles the predatory convicts who roam much more freely now than ever before and who often combine together to form groups of thugs who are unrestrained by staff and largely invincible to challenge (1996). Other changes have contributed to greater freedoms and opportunities for inmates. Johnson and Toch (1988) mention greater privileges, staffed law libraries, reduced censorship, expanded visiting, grievance procedures, and less regimentation in day-to-day rules. However, there has also been a reduction in classification, extreme overcrowding, and greater violence.

## DRUGS IN PRISON

As early as the 1960s and through the 1970s, many writers have identified the drug culture as substantially changing the character of prison life.

> Officials and knowledgeable older prisoners interviewed by this author were unanimous in emphasizing the strong drug orientation of prisoners incarcerated within the last decade. These prisoners were generally younger than prisoners had been in the past and were characterized as having no loyalty to anyone or anything. (Bowker 1977, 110)

Irwin (1970) also placed a great deal of emphasis on the drug culture, allocating two new social roles to it (the addict and the head). While it is true that drugs have always been available in prison — certainly alcohol — the availability of some drugs in the 1970s and through the 1980s dramatically changed the black market of the prison as well as the structure of power. Drugs are easier to hide than alcohol, they are easier to smuggle in, and they are more powerful in their effect.

One impact of drug use is an increase in violent assaults. Drugs in prison produce violence in several ways: First, drug deals that do not work out may result in assaults; second, incentives increase for "rip offs," robberies, or thefts of drug caches; and, finally, inmates may react violently while under the influence of some drugs, such as PCP. Drugs have increased the power of those who market them, and marketing is controlled to a large extent by gangs if they exist or by organized crime figures. Drugs have also undermined officer authority because smuggling is extremely tempting due to the high monetary rewards that result. Once an officer has succumbed to the temptation to bring in drugs, his authority is basically destroyed, and inmates who threaten exposure can control him.

We have previously discussed the impact of drugs and drug laws on sentencing and prison overcrowding. The result of this nation's War on Drugs has been the incarceration of large numbers of low-level, young offenders who may cycle in and out of prison many times before they even reach the age of 30. In their world, it is inconceivable to live the life of a nine-to-five job at minimum wage when they can make thousands of dollars a day selling drugs. They also may use drugs themselves or enjoy the lifestyle that goes with them.

Women are also increasingly incarcerated for drugs. Drugs generally are available in women's institutions with a weaker or nonexistent black market, but drugs are still an important part of the female inmates' lives and the topic of conversation among them. For some, prison serves as a brief respite from the life they lead on the outside; they stay only long enough to dry out and achieve some semblance of health before they are out again, sometimes getting their first "hit" in the car after being picked up at the prison gate.

Drug use may be so pervasive in prison that officers overlook the smoking of marijuana or the drinking of prison "hootch." Interestingly, as prisons and jails ban cigarette smoking inside prison, cigarettes become contraband and, for some, are more important than any other type of drug.

## PRISON GANGS

The presence of racial gangs in Illinois was described by Jacobs (1976, 1977); those in California were described by Davidson (1974). Jacobs described how the major Chicago gangs had very active branches in Statesville Prison. All four of the largest gangs were represented in Statesville: the three black groups — the Disciples, Rangers, and Vicelords, and the one Chicano group — the Latin Kings. The gangs maintained strong communication ties to the community, and the power hierarchy was a reflection of outside lines. Davidson also found gangs operating in California prisons. In fact, two rival Chicano gangs waged such a bloody feud that prison officials were obliged to allocate a separate prison to each gang (1974).

Probably no one would have predicted at the time how completely gangs would come to dominate the prison social world. In some states — California, New York, Illinois, Texas, and several others — the prisoner subculture can be more accurately described as the gang subculture. The rise of prison gangs has been ascribed to "rising ethnic identification, the importation of extant street gangs, a backdrop of political rhetoric evoking racial struggle comparisons, and the segregation activities of correctional authorities (which actually helped gang recruitment)" (Hawkins and Alpert 1989).

Ralph and Marquart (1992) described gang development during the 1980s in the Texas prison system. In their study, they explain that 1984-1985 were the "war years," so called because of events that occurred from, ironically, a prisoner rights case. The court basically dismantled the old *building tender* system that involved officers choosing some of the most violent and physically intimidating inmates to be "building tenders" who then controlled the tier or work group through fear and coercion. It was an effective system in that little violence occurred except for the sanctions imposed on some who challenged the authority of the building tenders, and they were dealt with quickly and severely. After the building tender system had been dismantled in response to court mandates, gangs fought each other for power. Prison officials recorded the highest number of murders (52) in the prison's history. "They killed more people in a two year span than had been killed in the twenty years prior" (Ralph and Marquart 1992, 47). After these two years, some control was re-established, and murders decreased dramatically — between 1985 and 1992, only 9 murders were recorded (Ralph and Marquart 1992, 47).

The Federal Bureau of Prisons has identified and classified several prison gangs found in the federal prison system. They include the Aryan Brotherhood; the Mexican Mafia, perhaps the most active of the gangs; the Texas Syndicate; the La Nuestra Familia; and the Black Guerrilla Family (Trout 1992). "Super gangs" have been defined as an organized group of inmates who are racially homogeneous and have members in more than one prison in a state, or even across several states (Hawkins and Alpert 1989). They have strong communication ties to the outside and control most of the illegal activities inside. Prison gangs are involved in the black market, drug smuggling and selling, extortion, and other forms of prison corruption. Some researchers find that they are also involved in gambling, drug trafficking, prostitution, and contract murder on the street (Fong and Buentello 1991).

Recent accounts have found that prison gangs and street gangs have a complicated relationship (Pelz 1988; Pelz and Pelz 1996; Ralph and Marquart 1992). Pelz and Pelz (1996) find that the prison gangs are equivalent to their street gang affiliates but separate in leadership; thus, individuals do not necessarily transfer their leadership roles from their street gang to the parallel prison gang. Other observers note that prison gangs seem to be more organized than street gangs, with more control over members.

Race-based gangs fulfill the same functions that the old subculture was supposed to provide for the inmate. They give the inmate a feeling of solidarity, they provide services and protection, and they help to maintain a level of self-esteem. The gang becomes the individual's family in a way that perhaps his real family never did.

The development of racial gangs has also led to the rise of neo-Nazi and white supremacist groups in prison. These groups apparently develop as a way for some white inmates to protect themselves against victimization from black and Hispanic gangs (Pelz and Pelz 1996). Whites are still less likely to belong to a gang than minority prisoners, and only a fraction belong to neo-Nazi or other groups.

*Membership and Initiation.* "Blood In, Blood Out," which is also a title of a popular movie chronicling the life and death of a gang member, refers to the initiation and membership of a gang member. It means that to join, blood must be spilled. Those who seek initiation may be instructed to kill an enemy of the gang to prove their loyalty. Once a member, the only exit is death. While this may dramatize the degree to which initiation and membership is tied to violent death, there is no doubt that gangs exert such control over their members that an instruction to kill must be carried out or the individual would face fatal consequences himself.

Recruitment is made easier by the violent world of the prison. Gang members may join largely for protection from other gangs. Unattached individuals are likely to be victimized, and membership in a gang brings with it the protection of all the members. Membership comes at a price, of course, and the individual must obey the commands of the gang leaders.

*Activities.* As stated previously, gangs are involved in running the black market in prison. The only enterprises that escape their attention are those too small to bother with. Where gangs have a presence, one can be fairly sure that the contraband and drugs are controlled by one gang or another. Turf wars or power conflicts ensue when gangs try to take over each other's businesses.

Fong (1990) has shown how coded messages are used by Texas prison gangs to order "hits" on fellow inmates and correctional staff. The gang members use a system in which the first letters of sentences or paragraphs are put together to form the true purpose of the letter. Another technique is to assign certain numbers to corresponding letters in the alphabet. These numbers are systematically revealed through what seems to be a normal letter describing dates, money, and so forth, when, in reality, they are instructions. The reach of prison gangs exceeds the perimeters of prison walls. They can intimidate family members of other prisoners and coerce them through fear to smuggle in drugs by threatening the life of the prisoner or some other family member. They can order hits on released prisoners to be carried out by members on the outside.

***Women.*** Although it is by no means clear, women do not seem to form gangs in the same manner that men do (Pollock-Byrne 1990). Some research does seem to indicate that gang membership (in "posses") among teenage females is increasing (Taylor 1993). Other researchers have found that gangs in women's prisons are beginning to become a measurable force (Mahan 1984), although others have found little or no evidence (Pollock 1996). It may be that the pseudofamily groupings discussed earlier serve the same purpose for women that gangs serve for men. Both social organizations provide companionship and identity. Fox (1982) found that there was less participation within kinship networks in 1978 than in 1973, when he conducted his study in a New York prison for women. He speculated that the increased number of prison programs took up women's time in the way that families did before. Families that did exist were smaller. Owens's (1995) California study finds that, ten years later, family groups are still present but not to the same degree as in the past.

Safety is less of a concern for women in prison, thus there is less need to have gang protection. Also, because there is less marketing in drugs and other contraband, there is less incentive to group together for protection and power. However, if some researchers are accurate in finding that women are increasing their participation with drug rackets on the street, we may soon see that the female presence in drug dealing and organized gang activity on the outside will change the social structure of the prison.

> Just as male gangs are in the business of narcotics, these females view themselves as capitalists. They refer to themselves as business women and to selling drugs as just business. (Taylor 1993, 199)

## *VIOLENCE*

The interrelated problems of increased drug trafficking and the increasing power of prison gangs has led to more violent prisons than ever before. However, violence has always been present in this nation's prisons. There are many types of violence in prison. One way to categorize violence is through the following typology:

1. Intrapersonal violence: self-mutilation, suicide attempts, expressive behavior that leads to being injured by others, and self-destructive behavior (for example, destroying one's own cell or swallowing toxic substances)
2. Interpersonal violence: sexual, physical, or psychological attacks between inmates
3. Group violence: gang activity; either formal gangs or more loosely organized groups banding together for one assault or for other reasons
4. Organized violence: riots or organized attacks on officers or the prison structure
5. Institutional violence: beatings or other physical or emotional harm inflicted by officers (Braswell 1994)

*Intrapersonal Violence.*   Prison life is stressful, and those who enter prison in a vulnerable state may not be able to withstand the stress of a prison term (Toch 1975a). Such inmates react, oftentimes, by attempts at self-destruction. Suicide attempts and self-mutilation may be calls for help, or they may be attempts to regain some sense of personal power. The depersonalizing nature of imprisonment make the individual feel that they have lost their sense of self. One female inmate, describing why she "cut up" (mutilated her arms with sharp objects) explained that doing so was the only way she could "feel something." Sometimes it is hard to distinguish between intrapersonal and interpersonal violence. Attacks on a powerful inmate or a correctional officer may simply be masked suicide attempts. Suicide attempts or other forms of self-injury may be attempts to protect oneself against others by ensuring a more protected living situation.

*Interpersonal Violence.*   Violence in prison may be expressive or instrumental (Bowker 1980; Lockwood 1980). Individuals use violence to take what they want from weaker inmates: sexual services, commissary goods, personal possessions, "action" in the black market, and anything else of value, including reputations. Thus, "dissing" somebody would be reason enough to be killed. Violence is also used to protect oneself. In fact, the possibility that inmates "act crazy" by committing seemingly senseless violent assaults on other inmates or correctional officers to make others believe that they are not vulnerable targets is recognized by both correctional officers and other inmates.

Bowker (1980) described four types of victimization in prison: physical, psychological, economic, and social. Physical victimization can include assault, rape, and death. Psychological victimization can include harassment, intimidation, and, for women, ostracism. Economic victimization may include extortion or outright theft. Social victimization, which may be more prevalent with women than with men, includes ostracism, gossip, and games. The reasons to victimize are simple — one can gain goods, services, and status through abusing another. Bowker hypothesized that some victimizers assuage the powerlessness they feel by controlling someone else. Some violence is in self-defense, either directly or to establish a "rep" that will forestall attacks.

In Toch's (1975a) study of prisoner breakdowns, fear of attack played a large role in some individuals' problems. In general, whites had greater safety concerns than minority members, which supports the notion that they feel less secure because of the lack of a gang to protect them. Fear may lead to an inmate seeking protective custody, obtaining the protection of a more powerful inmate through sexual service, or becoming proactively violent (to make it clear that they will not accept victimization.)

*Group Violence.* The presence and activities of gangs has already been discussed in detail above. Other groups, while perhaps not meeting the definition of gangs, are also active in violence. Biker's clubs fight with ethnic gangs for control of the black market in prison and may engage in racial violence. Ironically, the prevalence of gang violence creates a need for the individual to join a gang for protection, thus continuing the pattern of victimization and violence.

*Organized Violence.* The two most violent riots in this nation's history also serve as bookmarks to the different eras in which they occurred. The Attica Prison riot in 1971 lasted from September 9-13. Prisoners took over large portions of the prison after overcoming officers and breaking down a gate that gave them access to other tiers in the building. Once in control, some groups, particularly the Black Muslims, shepherded all hostages into a central location for safety and presented the administration with a set of demands, largely for things such as more due process, better food, and better programs. Negotiations took place over several days and included "observers" chosen by the inmates who were outside the prison structure — for example, journalists and civil rights attorneys. After several days of fruitless negotiating, the decision was made to storm the prison, at whatever cost to the hostages. State police were used but were supplemented by some correctional officers. Of the 43 individuals killed, 39 of them were killed by state officers in the retaking of the prison. The violence did not end there. Prisoners were stripped and beaten by correctional officers and state police after obtaining control. Eyewitness accounts testified to the fact that officers beat inmates who were lying on stretchers; inmates were forced to run naked through a gauntlet of officers wielding sticks, clubs, and guns. Injured and dying inmates were denied basic medical care for many hours. The riot served as an end to the growing political consciousness of prisoners. It also closed the last chapter in official misuse of power and physical abuse of prisoners. Although physical abuse still occurs, of course, there has never been a time since Attica where officials so blatantly, openly, and seemingly with little fear or compunction engaged in such extreme and observable abuse of prisoners.

Nine years later (1980) in Santa Fe, New Mexico, the second "bookmark" riot occurred. In this riot, there was no clear agenda, no political consciousness, and no demands for the administration. Instead, inmates engaged in a melee of torture and killing for personal revenge or profit, killing 33 fellow inmates. Inmate snitches and those who owed money were the primary targets and were subjected to sodomy, beatings, and more extreme forms of brutality — such as using blowtorches to burn genitals or decapitation — before being killed (Colvin 1992).

> There were many such groups . . . ferociously slashing open stomachs, cutting off genitalia, beating on corpses that were strewn over the catwalks. The floors were covered with clotted pools of blood, the cells with bloody drag marks, the air with cries of men being tortured. (From Useem and Kimball 1983, 11-12, cited in Hawkins and Alpert 1989, 260)

Thus, the riot symbolized the new prison where prisoners may have little to fear from officials and everything to fear from other inmates, and where there is little solidarity, except within warring factions, and prisoners show little interest in anything but themselves.

Riots are said to occur when there is a build-up of tension in the prison unrelieved by any means to divert or reduce the feeling of grievance. Attica occurred, arguably, because the rhetoric of rehabilitation failed to live up to the reality of lack of prison programs. Other riots during the early 1970s also involved an identification of grievances and demands to improve conditions. Other violent disturbances may not be as planned or purposeful. Expressive riots may be purely destructive, with no observable purpose or agenda. Typically, a precipitating event that may be happenstance — a gate breaking down, an officer being careless with keys — will spark a riot, but for a riot to ensue, the conditions have to be present: tension, grievances, and a feeling of hopelessness on the part of numbers of inmates.

In many riots, the number of inmates who would like to remain uninvolved may be greater than the number of inmates actually involved. For those inmates who are inside during the riot, however, there is little they can do to escape or to clearly disassociate themselves from the rioters. While attempts have been made to predict and prevent the occurrence of riots and disturbances, one might predict only when an institution has a probability of experiencing a disturbance since prediction of a precipitating chance event would be impossible. Prevention efforts include grievance procedures, legal aid to resolve complaints, and identifying and isolating inmate leaders. Riots will continue to occur, and some believe they may become more frequent in today's overcrowded, violent prisons.

## NICHES AND SANCTUARIES

One way to avoid victimization is to organize one's life to avoid notice. Johnson (1996) provides an excellent description of the way many inmates avoid the more negative aspects of today's prisons. Many inmates, according to Johnson, find *niches* — jobs or positions that are fairly safe, away from the mainstream, and relatively comfortable for the individual. Johnson describes an inmate whose job in a clothing issue office provided him with a comfortable existence: The officers were congenial, the inmates were friendly, they could cook food there for their lunch and avoid the mess hall, and the work was not difficult. After the work shift ended, this inmate spent most of his time in his cell.

Women, too, find niches. Jean Harris, the so-called Scarsdale diet doctor murderess, was a former headmistress and the epitome of a square jane. She has provided astute accounts of prison life in the form of books (1986, 1988). Harris's adaptation to prison was to find a safe niche, specifically, a program for children of women inmates. Like the inmate that Johnson described, she spent the rest of her time in her cell. Harris wrote that she never went to eat in the mess hall, preferring to eat cereal and other food purchased in the commissary, rather than interact with the other inmates.

Prison treatment programs can become niches and sanctuaries, especially those modeled after a therapeutic community. These environments provide a positive alternative to the general negativism of the prison environment. Typically, one senses the difference immediately on entering these living units. Bulletin boards are filled with inspirational messages, there is typically a closer relationship between staff and inmates, and inmates seem to like each other (and themselves) more than those in the general population.

Johnson points out that prison officials should make niches and sanctuaries available to those who want to avoid the negative influences of prison life. These adaptations serve to keep these individuals relatively safe. They are, at worst, neutral environments to spend the term in, and, at best, positive influences on the individual's life.

# CONCLUSIONS

In the last 20 years, demographic changes turned prisons into repositories for younger and more violent offenders. Racial identity has became a powerful force in the prisoner power structure. It should be apparent by now that there is no one prisoner subculture. Rather there is a subculture present in every prison, shaped by many variables, including the demographic characteristics of the prisoners, the level of custody, population size, physical layout, regional location, characteristics of the cities from which the prisoners are drawn, the average length of sentences, and a whole range of other elements that contribute to shape the unique prisoner subculture of that prison.

The prisoner subculture has different effects on individual prisoners. Some enter the fray willingly and successfully; those who are strong and ruthless may survive very well in the predatory world of the yard, "prowling" for goods and services and, in general, finding a comfortable home in prison. Many others try to escape the prison world by finding places to hide, work positions that keep them fairly anonymous and safe. Women's prisons are a different world — less violent, with little presence of gangs, and more family groupings. Although the women's prison may be less violent, it is still unpleasant. Women fight over jealousies and relationships, they ostracize and gossip, and try to intimidate through verbal threats. In some cases, violence does occur, and women can and do injure and maim those who are perceived to be snitches or inmate-cops or because of love triangles.

We know that there are elements in the subcultures of prisons today that are different from past decades. Inmates are more likely to be in gangs, they are more likely to be abusing drugs, and they are more likely to engage in violence, either to gain some benefit or simply to protect themselves. Thus, the prisons of today may have more programs, more legal assistance, and better trained staff, but they also have more violence, fewer controls on movement, and overcrowding. Even prison officials and correctional officers are probably not fully aware of the subculture of prisoners. Prison staff, however, do share the prison world with the inmates. Their social world will be the subject of the following two chapters.

## Vocabulary

| | |
|---|---|
| argot | niches |
| argot roles | prisonization |
| building tenders | pseudo-families |
| contraband | right guy |
| inmate code | subculture |

## Study Questions

1. Discuss the elements of the prison subculture. Mention specifically the inmate code, argot, mythology, values, and argot roles of the subculture.

2. What are the "deprivations" of prison life? Are they the same for men and women?

3. Differentiate between women prisoners' subculture and that found in prisons for men.

4. Discuss leadership in prison. How are leaders identified? Are there different types of leaders?

5. Discuss the importation and deprivation theories of the origin of prisoner subcultures.

6. Describe the types of violence one finds in prison.

7. Discuss how the prison subculture is different today than in the 1950s.

# Sources Cited

— Abbott, Jack. 1981. *In the Belly of the Beast.* New York: Vintage.

— Akers, Ronald L., Norman S. Hayner, and Werner Gruninger. 1975. "Homosexual and Drug Behavior in Prison: A Test of the Functional and Importation Models of the Inmates System." *Social Problems* 21 (Winter): 410-422.

— Alpert, Geoffrey. 1978. "Prisons as Formal Organizations: Compliance Theory in Action." Paper presented at the Pacific Sociological Association, Spokane, Washington.

— Atchley, Robert C., and M. Patrick McCabe. 1968. "Socialization in Correctional Communities: A Replication." *American Sociological Review* 33 (October): 774-785.

— Bentley, William, and James Corbett. 1992. *Prison Slang: Words and Expressions Depicting Life Behind Bars.* Jefferson, N.C.: McFarland.

— Berk, Bernard. 1966. "Organizational Goals and Inmate Organization." *American Journal of Sociology* 71 (March): 522-531.

— Bowker, Lee H. 1977. *Prisoner Subcultures.* Lexington, Mass.: Lexington.

— Bowker, Lee H. 1980. *Prison Victimization.* New York: Elsevier.

— Braswell, Michael, Reid Montgomery, and Lucien Lombardo. 1994. *Prison Violence in America.* New York: Anderson.

— Brody, Stuart A. 1974. "The Political Prisoner Syndrome." *Crime and Delinquency* 20 (April): 94-110.

— Bureau of Justice Statistics Bulletin. 1995. "Prisoners in 1994." U.S. Department of Justice. Washington, D.C.: GPO.

— Burkhart, Kathryn W. 1976. *Women in Prison*. New York: Popular Library.

— Carroll, Leo. 1974. *Hacks, Blacks and Cons: Race Relations in a Maximum Security Prison*. Lexington, Mass: Lexington.

— Carroll, Leo. 1976. "Race and Three Forms of Prisoner Power: Confrontation, Censoriousness and the Corruption of Authority." Paper presented at the ASC meeting, Tucson, Arizona.

— Carroll, Leo. 1982. "Race, Ethnicity and the Social Order of the Prison." In *The Pains of Imprisonment*, ed. R. Johnson and H. Toch, 181-201. Beverly Hills, Cal.: Sage.

— Clemmer, Donald. 1938a. "Leadership Phenomena in a Prison Community." *Journal of Criminal Law, Criminology and Police Science* 28 (March): 861-876.

— Clemmer, Donald. 1938b. *The Prison Community*. Boston: Christopher.

— Colvin, Mark. 1992. *The Penitentiary in Crisis: From Accommodation to Riot in New Mexico*. Albany, N.Y.: SUNY Press.

— Corsini, Raymond. 1946. "A Study of Certain Attitudes of Prison Inmates." *Journal of Criminal Law and Criminology* 37 (July): 132-140.

— Davidson, Theodore R. 1974. *Chicano Prisoners, The Key to San Quentin*. New York: Rinehart and Winston.

— Denfeld, D., and Andrew Hopkins. 1975. "Racial-Ethnic Identification in Prisons: 'Right On from the Inside.'" *International Journal of Criminology and Penology* 3: 355-375.

— Fairchild, E. S. 1977. "Politicalization of the Criminal Offender: Prisoner Perceptions of Crime and Politics." *Criminology* 15(2): 287-295.

— Fleisher, Mark. 1989. *Warehousing Violence*. Beverly Hills, Cal.: Sage.

— Fong, R. S. 1990. "The Organizational Structure of Prison Gangs: A Texas Case Study." *Federal Probation* (March): 36-43.

— Fong, R. S., and S. Buentello. 1991. "Detection of Prison Gang Development: An Empirical Assessment." *Federal Probation* (March): 66-69.

— Foster, Thomas. 1975. "Make Believe Families: A Response of Women and Girls to the Deprivations of Imprisonment." *International Journal of Criminology and Penology* 3: 71-78.

— Fox, James. 1982. "Women in Prison: A Case Study in the Social Reality of Stress." In *The Pains of Imprisonment*, ed. R. Johnson and H. Toch, 205-220. Beverly Hills, Cal.: Sage.

— Gagnon, John H., and William Simon. 1968. "The Social Meaning of Prison Homosexuality." *Federal Probation* 32 (March): 23-39.

— Garabedian, Peter G. 1963. "Social Roles and Processes of Socialization in the Prison Community." *Social Problems* 11 (Fall): 137-152.

— Garabedian, Peter G. 1964. "Social Roles in a Correctional Community." *Journal of Criminal Law and Criminology* 55 (September): 338-350.

— Garabedian, Peter G. 1970. "The Natural History of an Inmate Community in a Maximum Security Prison." *Journal of Criminal Law and Criminology* 61 (March): 78-89.

— Giallombardo, Rose. 1966a. *Society of Women: A Study of a Women's Prison.* New York: John Wiley & Sons.

— Giallombardo, Rose. 1966b. "Social Roles in a Prison for Women." *Social Problems* 13: 268-288.

— Goffman, Irving. 1961. *Asylums.* Garden City, N.Y.: Doubleday.

— Goodstein, Lynn, and Keven Wright. 1989. "Inmate Adjustment to Prison." In *The American Prison: Issues in Research and Policy*, ed. L. Goodstein and D. L. MacKenzie, 229-251. New York: Plenum.

— Grusky, Oscar. 1968. "Organizational Goals and the Behavior of Informal Leaders." *American Journal of Sociology* 65 (March): 452-472.

— Guenther, Anthony. 1975. "Compensations in a Total Institution: The Forms and Functions of Contraband." *Crime and Delinquency* 21 (July): 242-255.

— Halleck, Seymour, and Marvin Herski. 1962. "Homosexual Behavior in a Correctional Institution for Adolescent Girls." *American Journal of Orthopsychiatry* 32: 911-917.

— Hammer, M. 1965. "Homosexuality in a Women's Reformatory." *Corrective Psychiatry and Journal of Social Therapy* 11(3): 168-169.

— Hargan, James. 1934. "The Psychology of Prison Language." *Journal of Abnormal and Social Psychology* 30 (October-December): 359-361.

— Harris, Anthony R. 1976. "Race, Commitment to Deviance and Spoiled Identity." *American Sociological Review* 41: 432-450.

— Harris, Jean. 1986. *Stranger in Two Worlds*. New York: Macmillan.

— Harris, Jean. 1988. *They Always Call Us Ladies*. New York: Scribner's.

— Hartnagel, J., and M. E. Gillan. 1980. "Female Prisoners and the Inmate Code." *Pacific Sociological Review* 23(1): 85-104.

— Hawkins, Richard, and Geoffrey Alpert. 1989. *American Prison Systems: Punishment and Justice*. Englewood Cliffs, N.J.: Prentice-Hall.

— Hayner, Norman. 1943. "Washington State Correctional Institutions as Communities." *Social Forces* 21 (March): 317-327.

— Hayner, Norman. 1961. "Characteristics of Five Offender Types." *American Sociological Review* 26 (February): 96-128.

— Hayner, Norman S., and Ellis Ash. 1939. "The Prisoner Community as a Social Group." *American Sociological Review* 4 (June): 362-370.

— Hayner, Norman, and Ellis Ash. 1940. "The Prison as a Community." *American Sociological Review* 5 (August): 577-585.

— Haynes, F. E. 1948. "The Sociological Study of the Prison Community." *Journal of Criminal Law and Criminology* 39 (November): 432-450.

— Heffernan, Ruth. 1972. *The Square, the Cool and the Life*. New York: John Wiley.

— Hepburn, John R., and John R. Stratton. 1977. "Total Institutions and Inmate Self Esteem." *British Journal of Criminology* 17(3): 237-245.

— Huff, Ronald. 1975. "The Development and Diffusion of Prisoners' Movements." *Prison Journal* 55(2): 4-25.

— Irwin, John. 1970. *The Felon*. Englewood Cliffs, N.J.: Prentice-Hall.

— Irwin, John. 1980. *Prisons in Turmoil*. Boston: Little, Brown.

— Irwin, John, and Donald R. Cressey. 1962. "Thieves, Convicts and the Inmate Culture." *Social Problems* 10 (Fall): 142-155.

— Jacobs, James. 1974. "Street Gangs Behind Bars." *Social Problems* 21 (Winter): 395-414.

— Jacobs, James. 1976. "Stratification and Conflict among Prison Inmates." *Journal of Criminal Law and Criminology* 66 (Dec): 478-482.

— Jacobs, James. 1977. *Stateville: The Penitentiary in Mass Society*. Chicago: University of Chicago Press.

— Johnson, Elmer. 1961. "Sociology of Confinement, Assimilation and the Prison 'Rat.' " *Journal of Criminal Law and Criminology* 51 (January): 528-540.

— Johnson, Robert. 1996. *Hard Time: Understanding and Reforming the Prison*. Belmont, Cal.: Wadsworth.

— Johnson, Robert, and Dennis Dorin. 1975. "Dysfunctional Ideology: The Black Revolutionary in Prison." Presented at Workshop on Inmates and Institutions, Annual Meeting of ASC, Toronto, Canada.

— Johnson, Robert, and Hans Toch. 1988. *The Pains of Imprisonment.* Prospect Heights, Ill.: Waveland.

— Kalinich, David. 1980. *The Inmate Economy.* Lexington, Mass.: D. C. Heath.

— Leger, Robert. 1976. "Socialization Patterns in the Correctional Community: A Replication and Critique." Paper presented at the Annual Meeting of the American Sociological Association, New York.

— Lockwood, Daniel. 1980. *Prison Sexual Violence.* New York: Elsevier.

— Lombardo, Lucien. 1981. *Guards Imprisoned: Correctional Officers at Work.* New York: Elsevier.

— Mahan, Sue. 1984. "Imposition of Despair: An Ethnography of Women in Prison." *Justice Quarterly* 1(3): 357-385.

— Mitchell, Arlene Edith. 1975. *Informal Inmate Social Structure in Prisons for Women: A Comparative Study.* San Francisco: R & E Research Assoc.

— Mittford, Jessica. 1974. *Kind and Usual Punishment.* New York: Vintage.

— Nelson, Catherine. 1974. "A Study of Homosexuality among Women Inmates at Two State Prisons." Ph.D. dissertation. Temple University.

— Otis, Margaret. 1913. "A Perversion Not Commonly Noted." *Journal of Abnormal Psychology* 8: 113-115.

— Owen, Barbara, and Barbara Bloom. 1995. "Profiling Women Prisoners: Findings from National Surveys and a California Sample." *The Prison Journal* 75(2): 165-185.

— Pelz, M. E. 1988. "The Aryan Brotherhood of Texas: An Analysis of Right Wing Extremism in the Texas Prison." Unpublished doctoral dissertation. Sam Houston State University.

— Pelz, M. E., J. Marquart, and C. Terry Pelz. 1991. "Right Wing Extremism in Texas Prisons: The Rise and Fall of the Aryan Brotherhood of Texas." *Prison Journal* 71(2): 38-49.

— Pelz, M. E., and T. Pelz. 1996. Work in progress.

— Perkins, Craig. 1994. *National Corrections Reporting Program, 1992.* U.S. Department of Justice. Washington, D.C.: GPO.

— Polansky, Norman. 1942. "The Prison as Autocracy." *Journal of Criminal Law and Criminology* 33 (May-June): 16-25.

— Pollock, J. 1986. *Sex and Supervision: Guarding Male and Female Prisoners.* New York: Greenwood.

— Pollock, J. 1996. Unpublished study of Texas women prisoners.

— Pollock-Byrne, J. 1990. *Women, Prison and Crime.* Belmont, Cal.: Wadsworth.

— Propper, Alice. 1976. "Importation and Deprivation Perspectives on Homosexuality in Correctional Institutions: An Efficacy." Ph.D. dissertation. University of Michigan.

— Ralph, P. H., and J. Marquart. 1992. "Gang Violence in Texas Prisons." *Prison Journal* 71(2): 38-49.

— Rasmussen, Donald. 1940. "Prisoner Opinions about Parole." *American Sociological Review* 5 (August): 584.

— Reasons, Charles. 1973. "The Politicizing of Crime, the Criminal and the Criminologist." *Journal of Criminal Law and Criminology* 64 (March): 471-485.

— Reimer, Hans. 1937. "Socialization in the Prison Community." Proceedings of the American Prison Association.

— Roebuck, Julian. 1963. "A Critique of Thieves, Convicts, and the Inmate Culture." *Social Problems* 11 (Fall): 193-201.

— Schrag, Clarence. 1944. "Social Role Types in a Prison Community." Unpublished Master's Thesis. University of Washington.

— Schrag, Clarence. 1954. "Leadership among Prison Inmates." *American Sociological Review* 19 (February): 37-45.

— Selke, William. 1993. *Prisons in Crisis.* Bloomington: Indiana University Press.

— Selling, Lowell. 1931. "The Pseudo-Family." *American Journal of Sociology* 37(2): 247-253.

— Simmons (Moyer), Imogene. 1975. "Interaction and Leadership among Female Prisoners." Ph.D. dissertation. University of Missouri.

— Strange, Heather, and J. McCrory. 1974. "Bulls and Bears on the Cell Block." *Society* 11 (July-August): 51-67.

— Street, D., R. Vinter, and G. Perrow. 1966. *Organization for Treatment: A Comparative Study of Institutions for Delinquents.* New York: Free Press.

— Sykes, Gresham. 1956a. "The Corruption of Authority and Rehabilitation." *Social Forces* 34 (March): 257-265.

— Sykes, Gresham. 1956b. "Men, Merchants and Toughs: A Study of Reactions to Imprisonment." *Social Problems* 4 (October): 130-145.

— Sykes, Gresham. 1958. *The Society of Captives.* Princeton: Princeton University Press.

— Sykes, Gresham, and Sheldon Messinger. 1960. "The Inmate Social System." In *Theoretical Studies in the Social Organization of the Prison*, ed. R. Cloward et al., 6-10. New York: Social Science Research Council.

— Taylor, Carl. 1993. *Girls, Gangs and Drugs.* East Lansing: Michigan State University Press.

— Thomas, Charles W. 1977. "Theoretical Perspectives on Prisonization: A Comparison of the Importation and Deprivation Models." *Journal of Criminal Law and Criminology* 68(1): 135-150.

— Thomas, Charles W., and Samuel Cay Foster. 1972. "The Importation Model Perspective on Inmates' Social Roles: An Empirical Test." *The Sociological Quarterly* 14 (Spring): 226-240.

— Thomas, Charles W., and Samuel Cay Foster. 1973. "On the Measurement of Social Role Adaptations in the Prison Community." *Criminal Justice Review* 1 (Spring): 16-30.

— Thomas, Charles W., and David M. Petersen. 1977. *Prison Organization and Inmate Subcultures.* Indianapolis: Bobbs-Merrill.

— Thomas, Charles W., and Eric C. Poole. 1975. "The Consequences of Incompatible Goal Structures in Correctional Settings." *International Journal of Criminology and Penology* 3: 3-18.

— Tittle, Charles, and Drollene Tittle. 1964. "Social Organization of Prisoners: An Empirical Test." *Social Forces* 43: 216-221.

— Toch, Hans. 1975a. *Men in Crisis.* Chicago: Aldine.

— Toch, Hans. 1975b. *Living in Prison.* New York: Free Press.

— Trout, C. H. 1992. "Taking a New Look at an Old Problem." *Corrections Today* (July): 62, 64, 66.

— Van Wormer, Katherine. 1978. *Sex Role Behavior in a Women's Prison.* San Francisco: R & E Research Associates.

— Ward, David, and Gene Kassebaum. 1964. "Homosexuality: A Mode of Adaptation in a Prison for Women." *Social Problems* 12: 159-177.

— Merriam Webster's Tenth New Collegiate Dictionary. 1994. Springfield, Mass.: Merriam-Webster.

— Weinberg, S. Kirson. 1942. "Aspects of the Prison Social Structure." *American Journal of Sociology* 47 (March): 709-722.

— Wellford, Charles. 1967. "Factors Associated with Adoption of the Inmate Code: A Study of Normative Socialization." *Journal of Criminal Law and Criminology* (June): 197-203.

— Wheeler, Stanton. 1961. "Role Conflict in Correctional Communities." In *The Prison: Studies in Institutional Organization and*

*Change,* ed. D. Cressey, 229-260. New York: Holt, Rinehart and Winston.

— Wheeler, Stanton. 1968. "Socialization in Correctional Communities." *American Sociological Review* 26: 697-712.

— Wilder, Harry A. 1965. "The Role of the 'Rat' in the Prison." *Federal Probation* 29 (March): 44-60.

— Wilson, Thomas P. 1968. "Patterns of Management and Adaptations to Organizational Roles: A Study of Prison Inmates." *American Journal of Sociology* 74 (September): 146-160.

— Wilson John M., and Jon D. Snodgrass. 1969. "The Prison Code in a Therapeutic Community." *Journal of Criminal Law and Criminology* 60 (December): 472-486.

— Wooden, W. S., and J. Parker. 1982. *Men Behind Bars: Sexual Exploitation in Prison.* New York: Plenum Press.

— Zingraff, Matthew. 1980. "Inmate Assimilation: A Comparison of Male and Female Delinquents." *Criminal Justice and Behavior* 7(3): 275-292.

# 8

# MANAGEMENT AND ADMINISTRATIVE ISSUES

## *Robert Freeman*

I look for the best and the brightest. I look for people who don't just talk golden rule but those who practice it, people who are loyal, and people who will be responsible to both the real and imagined concerns of inmates and staff. I look for staff who have commitment and are dedicated and able to convince other people that our profession is important and noble and that we can make a difference.

*Interview with Warden Frank Wood, qtd. in Bartollas and Conrad 1992, 370*

--- *Chapter Overview* ---

--- **A SYSTEMS APPROACH TO CORRECTIONAL MANAGEMENT**
--- **AUTOCRATIC AND BUREAUCRATIC WARDENS**
     The Era of the Autocratic Warden
     The Era of the Bureaucratic Warden
     The Transition from Autocratic to Bureaucratic
     Beyond the Bureaucratic Warden
--- **CHALLENGES FOR THE CORRECTIONAL MANAGER**
     The Rehabilitation Model
     Increasing Accountability
     Civil Service
     Unions
     Judicial Intervention
     Legislative Action and Prison Overcrowding
     Legislative Action and Workforce Diversity
     The Media
     Special Needs Inmates
     Upgrading Correctional Personnel
--- **MANAGING THE WOMEN'S PRISON**
--- **CONCLUSIONS**

Management is the process of planning, organizing, controlling, budgeting, influencing, and supervising staff and staff development for the purpose of achieving organizational goals. The individuals responsible for carrying out the management process are the managers. Modern correctional systems have numerous layers of management, each layer differing in their degree of authority. The individuals responsible for overall policy formulation and decision making are often referred to as administrators. In this chapter, manager and administrator will be considered synonymous terms because "there are no significant differences between the terms management and administration" (Robbins 1984, 10). The chief administrator of a correctional institution is referred to as the warden or superintendent. The chief executive officer of a correctional system is referred to as a director, commissioner, or secretary.

Correctional managers are charged with the responsibility of managing a unique environment: a self-contained world with a population of convicted offenders, many of whom are violent, angry, and unpredictable. Inmates must have all of their needs met by their keepers. They must be fed, housed, clothed, provided with medical treatment, work and treatment opportunities, and be allowed communication and personal contact with friends and relatives. All of these activities are carried out with an overriding concern for security. Issues as seemingly simple as the length of inmate visits or whether inmates may wear shoes similar to those worn by the correctional officers may require long planning sessions, union discussion, and periodic review by managers struggling with dozens of other issues.

Above all else, the correctional manager is expected to maintain the stability of the prison environment. If stability is not maintained, the results can be expensive in terms of both money and lives. In a study of prison riots that occurred between 1971 and 1986, Useem and Kimball (1989) concluded that disorganization stemming from a breakdown in managerial control is always a factor in a riot. Breakdowns can be the result of scandals, escapes, inconsistent and incoherent rules for staff and inmates, fragmentation, instability in the chain of command, weak administration, conflict among staff, public dissent, disruption of the daily routine, or a combination of any of these factors, usually in conjunction with severe overcrowding.

## HIGHLIGHT 8-1
### A Day in the Life

**7:15-9:00 A.M.:** The Warden of the State Correctional Institution enters her office. There have been no calls during the night, an indication that there have been no unusual events within the 52-acre facility housing nearly 3,000 adult male inmates. She begins to read through the in-house mail. Two notes from the Deputy Warden for Operations are of particular interest: Nation of Islam activity has increased and the Aryan Brotherhood is once again recruiting on the yard.

**9:00 A.M.-12:00 P.M.:** The weekly department-head meeting goes well. Medical reports an additional 7 HIV-positive inmates, bringing the total to 97. Business reports a projected $350,000 budget shortfall unless additional cuts in Security overtime are made. Food Services reports 27 cases of inmate food poisoning resulting in the disposal of 2,000 pounds of improperly cooked chicken. Personnel provides a list of the 40 new recruits who had just completed the 4-week basic training course at the academy and are now certified for post assignment. Correctional Industries advises that the new line of conference tables and chairs is ready for unveiling.

**12:30-1:30 P.M.:** The Warden participates in a conference call with the Commissioner, Chief Counsel, and 22 other wardens concerning inmate lawsuits, coordinated at seven institutions, challenging the agency policy on prohibiting books and magazines featuring child pornography.

**1:30-2:15 P.M.:** Review of all disciplinary decisions made by the Hearing examiner during Inmate Court is conducted. The Warden sighs. Two hours of returning phone calls and reading the morning mail before she can conduct her daily walking inspection. The private line rings. It's the Deputy Warden For Treatment. An 18-year-old inmate in C-Block has attempted suicide by slashing his wrists. Medical is working to stabilize him. An ambulance had been called; the Public Information Officer is ready for the media; the family is being notified.

**4:00-6:00 P.M.:** The daily inspection goes well. The usual complaints about the quality of food in the dining room and the lack of variety in cigarettes in the commissary, but no unusual signs of tension or anger. Yard activity is peaceful with several inmates coming up to thank her for the new handball courts. She returns to her office to find the afternoon mail waiting.

**7:30 P.M.:** Home to the family.

**11:30 P.M.:** The phone rings. The inmate on C-Block has just died at the community hospital.

# A SYSTEMS APPROACH TO
# CORRECTIONAL MANAGEMENT

The correctional manager operates within both an *internal environment* and an *external environment*. The internal environment is small and consists of:

1. The inmate social culture with rigid antiauthoritarian value systems that dominate the social reality of the inmate and create a hostile atmosphere with a high potential for violence.
2. A physical environment of walls, fences, cells, bars, locked doors, and communal bathing and eating facilities referred to as the "total institution" (Goffman 1961) that breaks down the barriers that ordinarily separate sleep, play, and work while erecting barriers between the inmate and the outside world.
3. A prison staff culture that can be just as negative and problematic to the correctional manager as the inmate culture.

A review of current research yields the distinct impression that COs are alienated, cynical, burned out, stressed but unable to admit it, suffering from role conflict of every kind, and frustrated beyond imagining. No one plans careers as prison guards for their children, job turnover is high, salaries are low, and COs often fear for their lives. (Philliber 1987, 9)

The external environment consists of a variety of outside forces that may interact with and have a dramatic impact on the internal environment. There are two types of systems: closed and open (von Bertalanffy 1950). Closed systems consist only of the internal environment. The influence of any outside force on the operation of a closed system is minimal or nonexistent. Closed systems tend to stagnate. Open systems consist of internal environments that interact with outside forces, are strongly influenced by them, and tend to change over relatively short periods of time. Today's prison is an open system. Its operation is influenced by a wide range of outside forces. For example, mandatory sentencing laws passed by a legislature increase the inmate population. This increase negatively affects the quality of life for staff and inmates. If a federal court rules that conditions of confinement are now cruel and unusual because of this decreased quality of life, administrators may have to modify the physical plant, rewrite policy, change procedures, and reorient staff and inmates.

# AUTOCRATIC AND BUREAUCRATIC WARDENS

The study of correctional management is the study of a 180-year evolutionary process that can be divided into the era of the autocratic warden and the era of the bureaucratic warden (Bartollas and Conrad 1992).

## THE ERA OF THE AUTOCRATIC WARDEN

The era of the autocratic warden came into existence with the first penitentiaries in the 1820s and lasted until the early 1950s. The autocratic warden was an absolute ruler who held and exercised power unilaterally within a closed system dominated by a primitive custody-oriented paramilitary management structure that relied on military uniforms, protocol, rigid rules and regimentation, impersonal relationships, and a downward flow of communication, power, and control (Houston 1995, 10).

The mission of both the autocratic warden and the prison staff was the punitive control of the inmate population. Punitive control was accomplished through the following methods:

1. The maintenance of order by keeping down internal disruption and violence and preventing escapes through: (a) the enforcement of very strict inmate count, movement, and monitoring procedures, a control process so intense that officers of that era are

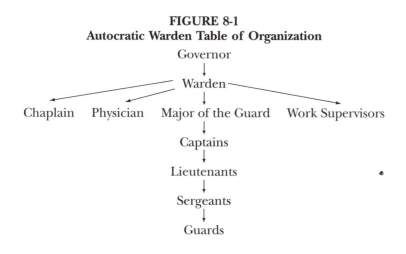

**FIGURE 8-1**
**Autocratic Warden Table of Organization**

sometimes referred to as suffering from "lock psychosis"; and (b) disciplinary procedures that were brutal and degrading by any standard. Correctional officers were called guards because that was their only function. Inmates had few rights and could be severely disciplined simply on the unsupported word of a guard.

2. Supplying the inmates with only minimal life necessities by providing the most basic medical care, food, clothing, and shelter. Because so few standards governed inmate care, inmates were at the mercy of the warden. Uncontested control of food, water, clothing, shelter, and medical care allowed the warden to exert maximum influence over the inmate population.

3. Management of any prison industries in the prison or on the institutional property, especially those that could reduce the cost of housing the inmate. Working conditions, as typified by the southern chain gang, were a brutally effective method of punitive control.

The lack of interaction with the external environment gave the autocratic warden an enormous amount of discretion. Decisions were made on the basis of personal philosophy, beliefs, and individual evaluation of any given situation without reference to any constraints that might be imposed by the external environment. Typical of the autocratic warden were Elam Lynds, warden of Auburn and Sing Sing (1821-1830) and Joseph Ragen, warden of Stateville and Joliet Penitentiaries in Illinois (1936-1961). Lynds was described as a strict disciplinarian who believed that all convicts were cowards who could not be reformed until their spirit had been broken through a system of brutal punishments and degrading practices: flogging with a whip, the imposition of total silence during daily activities (the Silent System), the lockstep formation, the wearing of striped uniforms, no mail or visiting privileges, and identification by number, not name (Beaumont and Tocqueville 1833).

Ragen personally made every decision that had to be made during his tenure of 25 years. He was an absolute ruler who allowed no challenge to his authority. Inmates who defied him were brutally disciplined. Staff who questioned his orders were summarily dismissed without a hearing. Outsiders were not permitted into the institution. Ragen recruited guards who were totally dependent on him for their livelihoods. The hallmark of his management style was the daily inspection of the prison, accompanied only by his two dogs. He personally dominated every aspect of prison life. So total was Ragen's power that there were no riots or escapes during his tenure and only two guards and three inmates were killed in 25 years (Jacobs 1977).

The only person the autocratic warden answered to was the

state's governor who had hired him. Most governors allowed their wardens to run the prisons as they saw fit as long as there were no problems that could be politically embarrassing. Illustrative of this relationship is a 1935 conversation between Joseph Ragen of Stateville and Governor Henry Horner:

> Once the warden made up his mind that this was the place to start, he picked up the phone and called the governor. "I'm going to start reorganizing the guard force, Governor," he said. "I'm going to fire the incompetents and look around for men who can do this job right." "That's fine, Joe," the governor said. "If I can be of any help, just say so." (Erickson 1957, 51)

The era of the autocratic warden was characterized by a homogeneous work force. The warden, or a closely supervised ranking officer trusted by the warden, personally hired the guards. The criteria for hiring was highly subjective and, in the absence of legal or standardized hiring standards, often represented personal opinion. Once hired, the new guard was given a set of keys and directed to his post where he learned the job by trial and error. Guards were traditionally white males from the rural areas where the majority of prisons were located. They had relatively little education (Smith, Milan, and McKee 1976); tended to be politically conservative; and had mixed job histories, often coming to corrections after failure in other careers or discharge from the military (Davidson 1974).

Women generally were excluded from prison work, often kept out of the male institutions because they could not meet minimum height, weight, and strength hiring requirements. In most state and federal institutions for males, the only women employees were clerks and secretaries. The idea of a woman guarding male convicts was not even considered worthy of consideration. The majority of women who were employed in supervisory positions worked in adult and juvenile female institutions. The few women who held administrative positions were the wardens of the female institutions.

Minorities were overrepresented in the inmate population and underrepresented in the correctional staff ranks. To a large extent, racial imbalance was the result of the practice of building prisons in rural white areas where urban minorities were reluctant to move (Nagel 1974). Racial imbalance between inmates and guards has had serious consequences for corrections. Prior to the 1971 Attica Prison riot, there was not a single minority guard in that institution even though 55 percent of the 2,000 inmates were members of a minority (Sheehan 1977).

In 1969, the Joint Commission on Correctional Manpower and Training reported that of the 110,000 correctional employees in the United States, only 12 percent were female (with women making up 40 percent of the general workforce), 8 percent were black, 4 percent were Chicano, and less than 1 percent were American Indian, Puerto Rican, or "Oriental." The Joint Commission concluded that the hiring requirements of many institutions eliminated minority and women applicants.

Because corrections historically has promoted on the basis of correctional work experience, the practical result of low numbers of females and minorities at the officer level has been significant underrepresentation of women and minorities in the managerial ranks. In 1969, all prison administrators in the adult correctional system were white, virtually all of them male. Very few minority group members were managers, supervisors, or rehabilitation specialists (Joint Commission 1969).

Neither the autocratic warden nor his guards were required to possess a formal education or skills beyond those required for maintaining rigid physical control of the inmate population. Skills and activities were limited to those that allowed the warden to maintain control of the inmate population and prevent any situation that might embarrass the governor. The prison was a self-contained world run in accordance with the personal philosophy of the warden. The ability to appropriately respond to external forces was not required because the external world was generally indifferent to prison conditions. This indifference was not to last. In the years following World War II, American society underwent a process of enormous change that inevitably engulfed corrections, shattered the power of the autocratic warden, and created the need for the bureaucratic warden.

## THE ERA OF THE BUREAUCRATIC WARDEN

As corrections entered the late 1950s, prison inmates and guards witnessed the gradual emergence of the bureaucratic warden. Bureaucratic managers understand and accept that they cannot run a prison by themselves:

> [T]hey need the support, commitment, and contributions of their staff to sustain the vitality of the organization. . . . Effective prison leaders view their staff as mutually interdependent, and they constantly work to ensure a sense of community among them. (Houston 1995, 10-11)

The era of the bureaucratic warden encompasses the period of the late 1950s to the present. The bureaucratic warden has the complex responsibility of developing and maintaining a safe, secure, and humane prison environment in accordance with the external demands of the U.S. Constitution, sound management theory, applicable court decisions, and collective bargaining provisions. In the world of the bureaucratic warden, correctional management involves specific activities:

1. development of the mission statement for the organization,
2. coordination of the budget process,
3. strategic evaluation and emergency planning,
4. management of daily activities,
5. management of labor relations,
6. the formulation of policy, and
7. the supervision and professional development of staff.

All of these activities are influenced by both the internal and the external environments. They require well-developed communications and analytical skills such as:

(1) the capacity for two-way verbal communication with staff, inmates, union leadership, headquarters staff, and a wide range of outside groups, including legislative bodies, the media, and inmate and victim advocacy groups;

(2) the ability to develop written policy and procedure manuals that clearly define the roles of staff in everything from how to run a routine meal line to how to manage a riot; and

(3) the ability to formulate and communicate short-term and long-term goals, organize resources, influence and control staff and inmate activities, make difficult decisions under stressful conditions, and provide leadership, all within the framework of desired organizational goals (Houston 1995).

The bureaucratic manager must be able to direct the operations of a complex bureaucracy. Communications and analytical skills must be grounded in a general working knowledge of

1. prison security, communications, and surveillance systems,
2. people management principles,
3. food service procedures and requirements,
4. physical plant and grounds maintenance,
5. public relations,

6. fiscal management,
7. educational programming at all levels, both academic and vocational,
8. occupational health and safety and environmental regulations,
9. the basic rules of law,
10. personnel policy, and
11. principles of sound planning (Wright 1994, 176-177).

**FIGURE 8-2**
**The Bureaucratic Warden Table of Organization**

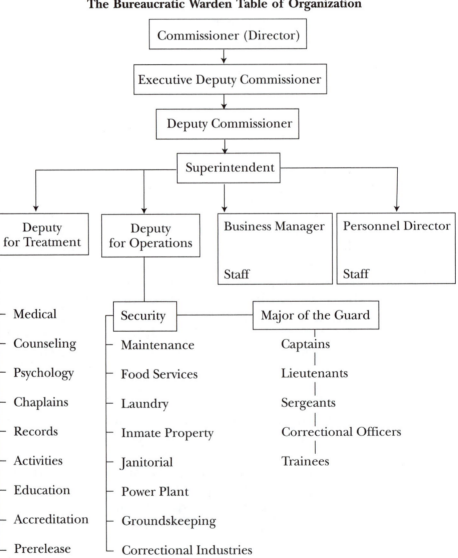

The workforce of the bureaucratic warden is heterogeneous, not homogeneous, although this transition was not without conflict. In his foreword to Lynn Zimmer's *Women Guarding Men,* James B. Jacobs states:

> In the 1970s I often encountered top corrections officials who dismissed out of hand the possibility that they would ever be required to assign women to the toughest tiers of their prisons. Despite pressures from their affirmative action officers and sometimes from their unions, they frequently remained steadfast, allowing the issue to go to litigation. (Zimmer 1986, ix)

Although many correctional managers did challenge the right of women to work in the male prison, court decisions, the civil rights and feminist movements, and the embracing of affirmative action by civil service divisions and unions combined to increase the number of women and minorities in corrections. In 1992, 186,510 line-level custody staff worked in state and federal correctional facilities. About 16.7 percent were women and 30.5 percent were minority (Camp and Camp 1995). The advent of a diverse workforce undermined the authority of autocratic wardens by challenging the assumption that the warden always knows best.

Despite the differences in their workforces, the autocratic warden and the bureaucratic warden are similar in one area. Most bureaucratic managers are promoted from within the system and have no formal training in management, the criteria for promotion being satisfactory job performance. A national survey found that on average correctional managers have eight and a half years of institutional experience; 70 percent have less than six years of experience as chief executive officers; and few have corrections-related college training (Duffee 1980).

However, because of the complexity of the bureaucratic manager's job, education has become a particularly valued asset. Although it is true that even today there are superintendents who have no more than a high school education, the number of minimally educated correctional managers is rapidly dwindling. A 1989 survey of the wardens of 512 state and federal prisons found that wardens had a mean of 16.6 years of education (Cullen et al. 1993). Unfortunately, the majority of college degrees held by correctional administrators are in the social sciences, with 10 out of 65 holding law degrees or doctorates. Very few correctional administrators have degrees in management (Shannon 1990), so that

> [w]ithout formal training, managers often make decisions without benefit of staff input, implement policy through the writing

of memoranda, and motivate employees through the threat of disciplinary action. (Houston 1995, 5)

## THE TRANSITION FROM AUTOCRATIC TO BUREAUCRATIC

Change does not occur at the same rate across correctional systems. Change is often threatening and resisted by individuals with a significant investment of time and energy in the old way of doing business. Some states moved more easily into the era of the bureaucratic warden than did others. DiIulio (1987) provides an example of the difficulties a correctional system can experience when the external environment changes, but autocratic managers cling to the old ways. DiIulio's basic premise is that "prison management may be the single most important determinant of the quality of prison life and that prisons are best viewed as mini-governments" (DiIulio 1987, 215).

DiIulio views management as a process of governing based on a specific correctional philosophy, specifically the degree of emphasis placed on strict staff control and surveillance of the inmate population. In developing this premise, DiIulio examined the correctional systems in Texas, Michigan, and California (DiIulio 1987).

Prior to 1974, the Texas prisons were governed in accordance with a *control model* that emphasized the internal environment of inmate obedience, work and education and largely ignored the external environment. The founder of the Texas control model was Dr. George Beto, a close friend of Stateville's Joseph Ragen. Beto's goal during his tenure as director of the Texas Department of Corrections from 1962 to 1972 was to run a very tight ship. He earned the nickname "Walking George" because of his habit of showing up at prisons every day, unannounced so he could observe firsthand the actual operation of the institution. The Texas wardens were autocratic and strongly resistant to change.

In contrast, the Michigan prison system was governed in accordance with a *responsibility model* that deemphasized paramilitary structure and stressed inmate classification and elaborate grievance procedures. The California correctional system was a mixed model, a *consensus model,* that inserted inmate grievance procedures into a paramilitary structure. The wardens in Michigan and California were bureaucratic.

DiIulio (1987) concluded that the Texas control model created a high level of stability and a low level of inmate violence until the external environment demanded a shift from the autocratic to the bureaucratic style of management. In the 1970s, Texas managers fought to retain their control model of inmate management. The old style of management collided with the external environment in *Ruiz v. Estelle,* 688 F.2d 266 (5th Cir. 1982). This massive class-action suit, filed in 1974, challenged the conditions of confinement and management of the Texas prison system. Before it was over, changes in correctional leadership were made, with directors being brought into the system with a complete change of management philosophy. During this process, however, the Texas system experienced an increased level of violence and inmate unrest, plummeting staff morale, and organizational chaos as the traditional strict system of inmate control was involuntarily dismantled

## *BEYOND THE BUREAUCRATIC WARDEN*

The autocratic and bureaucratic warden have been discussed within a management framework, but the effective correctional administrator is both a good manager and a good leader (Houston 1995). The administrative issue of leadership is critical to understanding the role of the bureaucratic manager. Leadership can be defined as the ability of an individual to actively influence people to work willingly and enthusiastically toward the achievement of established group goals (Koontz, O'Donnell, and Weihrich 1986).

Douglas McGregor (1984) postulates two theories of human behavior, Theory X and Theory Y, each of which can provide the foundation for leadership style. *Theory X* assumes that

1. the average person has an inherent dislike of work and will avoid it whenever possible;
2. people must be coerced, controlled, directed, and threatened with punishment if they are to be motivated to achieve organizational objectives; and
3. the average person prefers to be directed, avoids responsibility, has little ambition, and prizes security.

Management based on Theory X assumptions emphasizes the need for strict supervision constantly exercised by the ever vigilant and suspicious manager who dares not trust subordinates to do the right thing. The autocratic warden who focuses on results and performance through a rigid process of "management by walking around" and expounds the belief that strict supervision is the answer to the problems of correctional management (DiIulio 1991), is the epitome of the Theory X manager. As Toch notes in his review of DiIulio's discussion of correctional leadership:

> He envisages a mix of pre-bureaucratic organization at the top and bureaucratic organization at the bottom. His conception of an ideal-type head of a correctional agency is a well-connected leader who promiscuously attends to quotidian details and freely intervenes everywhere. DiIulio's rank and file, by contrast, are a tightly controlled arm that follows minute prescriptions to the letter. (1989, 86-88)

Many bureaucratic wardens view leadership in Theory X terms because it provides them with a ready explanation for inadequate managerial performance. Theory X managers confronted with a correctional failure can find the cause of that failure in their subordinates. They do not have to examine their role in the event. The Theory X manager is unlikely to be a leader. Staff working under a Theory X manager rarely work willingly and enthusiastically toward the achievement of group goals. The rise of unions in corrections can be viewed as evidence of the inability of Theory X managers to provide leadership.

Correctional management has become too complex and the cost of failure too high for managers to continue to be governed by Theory X. What corrections needs in the next century are managers who are also leaders. The manager who is a leader has a vision of corrections as a profession rather than just a job and welcomes change instead of stubbornly resisting it in the name of "If it ain't broke, don't fix it."

The correctional manager of the next century must be a Theory Y leader. *Theory Y* postulates that people represent a potential that can and must be realized by administrators. The Theory Y leader will assume that people

1. are motivated by an inherent need to work;
2. will voluntarily commit to working toward objectives without being subjected to external control and the threat of punishment;
3. will exercise self-direction and self-control if the work environment is supportive of these qualities;
4. will accept and seek responsibility;
5. have the ability to exercise a high degree of imagination, ingenuity, and creativity in the solution of organizational problems; and

6. have intellectual potentials that are only minimally utilized by Theory X managers.

The Theory Y leader views change as positive and seeks out opportunities to challenge subordinates to use their potential to address and solve the critical issues confronting corrections as it moves into the next century.

The difficulty of the challenge for the Theory Y leader cannot be understated. Correctional institutions are designed for Theory X management styles. To be successful, the Theory Y leader will have to be resourceful and capable of surmounting the challenge presented by subordinates conditioned to the paternalistic attitude of the Theory X managers who have dominated correctional management.

## CHALLENGES FOR THE CORRECTIONAL MANAGER

The bureaucratic manager functions within an open system influenced by external forces that sharply limit personal power and the ability to exercise discretion.

### THE REHABILITATION MODEL

In 1870, the National Prison Association (predecessor of the American Correctional Association) met in Cincinnati, Ohio, and developed a Declaration of Principles that advocated that the goal of the prison should be the treatment of criminals through a process of moral regeneration: reform through change. Rehabilitative philosophy held that the critical element in reforming the offender was education, and the responsibility of the warden was to facilitate the process of criminal reform through innovative educational programming emphasizing classification and the development of courses in academic, vocational, and moral subjects.

In the 1960s, the rehabilitation model became extremely influential, and guards were joined by cadres of college-educated treatment staff: counselors, psychologists, social workers, psychiatrists, activity specialists, and casework managers responsible for evaluating and diagnosing inmates for the purpose of developing treatment programs designed to correct the personal deficiencies underlying their criminality. These newcomers challenged the autocratic warden's reliance on strict discipline and created the need for wardens with an understanding and acceptance of basic sociological, psychological, and counseling approaches to changing human behavior. The effectiveness of this challenge can be seen in a 1968 Harris poll of correctional administrators that found strong support for rehabilitation.

The rehabilitation movement made visible the need for a professional correctional staff possessing an educational level far above that of the typical autocratic warden. It also significantly changed the role of the correctional officer and created a host of management and personal issues, which will be discussed in Chapter 9.

## INCREASING ACCOUNTABILITY

After World War II, governors and legislators began to demand the creation of management systems that would ensure their control of prisons through chains of accountability. State after state organized independently managed correctional institutions into "departments of correction" run by a commissioner, director, or secretary of correction.

Wardens no longer had absolute control of their prisons or direct access to the governor. Bureaucratic wardens and managers must now operate within a complex bureaucracy that inserts layer upon layer of decision makers and resource people between the warden and the chief executive officer of the agency. Each layer of bureaucracy represents different personality styles, specialized knowledge, and different goals and agendas. Policy decisions at the institution level are no longer automatic and are made at the discretion of the warden.

## CIVIL SERVICE

Traditionally, the appointment of correctional staff was a matter of political patronage, with the basis of appointment more often party or family loyalty than merit. Patronage systems are disruptive because staff can change as often as the political power changes. Recognizing the need for employee stability and professionalism in corrections, governments began converting the old patronage systems into civil service divisions designed to severely limit the ability to arbitrarily hire, promote, and fire. Hiring is now a process of adhering to proce-

**FIGURE 8-3**
**Table of Organization for a Correctional System**

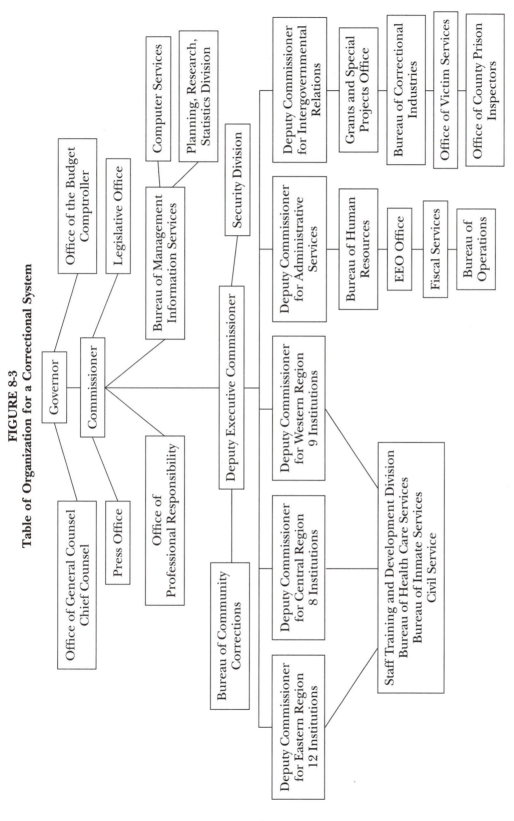

dures of legal standardization set by civil service divisions charged with

1. determining objective, standardized minimum education and experience qualifications for positions;
2. advertising vacancies;
3. administering objective examinations;
4. developing requirements for hiring based on examination performance;
5. setting rules for the promotion and dismissal of staff; and
6. implementing and managing affirmative action programs.

Employment practices must be in compliance with volumes of policy, regulations, and rules.

## UNIONS

Collective bargaining for prison staff is a fairly recent phenomenon. The first unions for prison employees with collective bargaining rights were established in 1956 in Washington, D.C., and New York City. In the 1970s, many states passed laws allowing correctional staff to unionize and guaranteed their right to engage in collective bargaining. Unionization is a process that often creates conflict between staff and manager, sometimes in the form of organized strikes, although most states now prohibit correctional officers from striking. Many managers resent unions because they view the union leadership as making the manager's job even more difficult. Unions challenge the authority of correctional managers. No longer can the warden arbitrarily determine pay, benefits, promotional standards, disciplinary procedures, policy, and working conditions. The demand for better pay and benefits confronts the warden with loss of control over the budgetary process, with money going to current staff instead of being used to hire new staff or make modifications to the prison environment. The demand for a say in policy strikes at the heart of the warden's belief in his right to control the destiny of the institution.

## JUDICIAL INTERVENTION

Prior to the 1960s, state and federal courts employed a hands-off doctrine of noninterference in the operation of correctional institutions

based on the principle that correctional managers were more qualified to decide prison policy than were judges. As we shall explore in
Chapter 10, in the 1960s the courts began to take an interest in the
issues raised by inmate litigants. This interest resulted in legal rulings
that have significantly reduced the authority and discretion of correctional managers. In 1974, for example, the disciplinary process in
American prisons changed dramatically. In *Wolff v. McDonnell*, 418
U.S. 539, 94 S. Ct. 2963 (1974), the Supreme Court established a set
of minimum requirements for discipline that closely parallel some of
the basic rights the accused has in a court of law. Inmates can no
longer lose good time credits or in-house privileges without due process.

The inmate lawsuit is a particular source of anxiety for correctional managers because inmates are legally entitled to include the
name of top administrators in every lawsuit they file, even though
those individuals may have played no role in the issue being litigated.
The result for managers, especially those in institutions with a cadre
of active jailhouse lawyers, is a steady stream of litigation, much of it
frivolous.

During a typical year in Pennsylvania, for example, the Attorney
General's office must defend correctional administrators against
1,000 or more lawsuits, at an annual cost of $2 million a year. Inmates
have sought judicial relief because state-issued underwear was too
tight; officials are sending transmissions to a microchip implanted in
the plaintiff inmate's head; the inmate is owed $700 trillion because
his family owns all oil and mineral rights in Texas and Pennsylvania;
an inmate contracted "cancer incubus" from a cheeseburger; First
Amendment rights were violated when an inmate was refused permission to buy books featuring themes of rape, bestiality, and incest; and,
two inmates sued to force the taxpayers to pay for sex-change surgery
(The Evening News 1995).

Managerial response to litigation takes time, costs money, and
creates stress as managers must explain in open court practices and
procedures never before challenged. But the challenge to the power
of the correctional manager goes beyond ruling on specific issues. As
of June 30, 1992, the entire adult department or one or more institutions were under court order in 34 states. Twelve states had one or
more juvenile institutions under court order (American Correctional
Association 1993).

## LEGISLATIVE ACTION AND PRISON OVERCROWDING

Because prison construction has not been able to keep pace with overcrowding, correctional managers have no choice except to try and create additional bed space within the existing physical plant, even if that means turning classrooms, exercise areas, storage rooms, and hallways into dormitories. The warden must manage the inmates, but has no control over the number of new commitments the institution will receive on any given day. When notified that another group of inmates is at the main gate, all the warden can do is determine how and where those inmates will be housed. The result is that in most prisons the number of inmates housed greatly exceeds the design capacity of the prison. These issues were covered in detail in Chapter 3; we revisit them here only to illustrate the role of correctional administrators in responding to the overcrowding crisis.

The result for the warden is budgetary strain, an increase in physical plant problems (as plumbing, electrical, ventilation, sewage, water, food service, and laundry systems are used for periods of time far exceeding their design specifications), an eroding of the quality of life for inmates and staff alike, increases in violence, and an extremely high level of personal stress. A warden in North Carolina reports:

> There is no question that the prison has taken its toll on me. I had ulcers at twenty-eight, heart problems at thirty-nine, and have hypertension now. A warden in Illinois confirms: It is a hard struggle, and you just have to be prepared for it. Any decision you make takes a toll on you. If you make a mistake, you may not have a job tomorrow. If you make a mistake, the [prison] population won't let you forget it. (Bartollas and Conrad 1992, 360)

## LEGISLATIVE ACTION AND WORKFORCE DIVERSITY

The legal right of a woman to apply for the job of correctional officer in a male prison is guaranteed by the 1964 Civil Rights Act, as amended in 1972. *Title VII* of the act proscribes employment discrimination on the basis of race, religion, sex, and national origin. The amendment also increased the enforcement powers of the Equal Employment Opportunity Commission, the federal agency established in 1964 to oversee implementation of Title VII's mandates.

The legislation that benefited women also precluded discrimination in the hiring of minorities. This legislation, a growing civil rights movement, and the increasing number of minority inmates combined to prompt many correctional agencies in the 1960s to begin actively recruiting minority staff, and minority members are increasingly moving into management. As of 1989, 13.1 percent of the 375 wardens responding to a national survey were minority members (Cullen et al. 1993, 77).

The American Correctional Association, in its "National Policies on Corrections" statement, specifically states that corrections is to actively recruit women and minority applicants. The challenge to the correctional manager is to develop innovative personnel policies that will continue to promote diversity at all levels of correctional staffing. The question of whether or not there is a racial effect on management style requires research. There is evidence that members of minorities are more favorable to both treatment and custody than are white staff.

> This raises the prospect that minority members might bring a distinctive style to prison management, perhaps a "tough love" approach that emphasizes social support within the context of discipline — or what Braithwaite (1989) has called "reintegrative shaming." (Cullen et al. 1993, 86)

## THE MEDIA

The media plays such an influential role in shaping public opinion about corrections that *Corrections Today,* the official publication of the American Correctional Association, titled the February 1989 issue "Corrections and the Media: A Pressing Problem?". The articles in that publication revealed a strong consensus among correctional professionals that there is indeed a problem with the media. Specifically, the media does a disservice to corrections by only publicizing the negatives: escapes, killings, riots, and staff incompetence and corruption:

> Nothing can be more frustrating than working diligently on a day-to-day basis to manage correctional institutions; cope with the stress of crowding; deliver services in an acceptable fashion; and maintain a humane and effective system, only to read in the morning newspaper that your efforts and hard work have been crystallized into one newspaper story about a female inmate injured on her way to court, or the inmate who was erroneously discharged from one of your institutions. (Koehler 1989, 16)

Negative media attention undermines the authority of correctional managers and may make them reluctant to make changes, take a position on a controversial issue, or use discretion. The challenge to managers is to learn how the media works and develop a relationship encouraging factual, nonsensational coverage of the issues most concerning corrections.

## SPECIAL NEEDS INMATES

There are growing numbers of inmates who require a disproportionate share of limited resources. These groups can be called *special needs* inmates and include the elderly, mentally ill, retarded, handicapped, and HIV-positive inmates. The HIV-positive inmate represents a particularly difficult challenge for the correctional manager because of the ignorance and fear surrounding HIV and AIDS. Various studies have estimated the number of HIV-positive inmates to be between 1 and 18 percent (Moiri and Hammett 1990, 16; Smith 1991, 35).

In the late 1980s, the superintendent of an institution that had a large number of HIV cases was met by a demand from the correctional officers' union for the names of every HIV-positive inmate, a request that violated the inmates' rights to medical confidentiality (Freeman 1995). Noninfected inmates threatened to sue or take assaultive action if HIV-positive inmates were allowed to remain in population. Even some of the medical staff expressed fears far out of proportion to the actual threat represented by fewer than 20 inmates. Staff in general became tense, a situation aggravated by the threats of two of the HIV-positive inmates to spit on officers. The media became interested and wanted to interview staff and inmates about their fear of becoming infected (Freeman 1995).

A decision was made to segregate all HIV-positive inmates into a special isolation unit above the prison infirmary, a move intended to concentrate medical treatment and diminish inmate and staff fears. As soon as the move was accomplished, the union demanded hazardous duty pay for officers assigned to supervise the inmates in the HIV unit. The HIV-positive inmates sued in federal court on the grounds that isolation deprived them of the programming opportunities available to general population inmates. Prior to trial, the U.S. Department of Justice intervened on behalf of the inmates. Prison administrators were warned that they were violating inmate rights by isolating them solely on the basis of their status as HIV-positive.

The commissioner of corrections, after appropriate discussion with legal staff, agreed that the HIV-positive inmates should be returned to population. After an intensive two-month program of staff and inmate education about AIDS, HIV-positive inmates were quietly returned to population (Freeman 1995).

Special needs inmates such as the elderly may require special housing, special medical services, or protection from the general population. As the age of the nation gradually increases, so too is the age in some prison populations. "Geriatric wards" are growing in prison, and purchases such as walkers, wheelchairs, and other equipment designed for the elderly are increasingly making their way into prison budgets. Elderly inmates may be the most difficult group to parole; if they have been in prison for a long time, they may have no family to return to. Often they are paroled directly to a government nursing home on the outside. While their numbers are small at this point, projections indicate that aging inmates will be a growing problem for correctional management.

It is estimated that about 10 percent of a prison population is either mentally ill or is suffering some form of mental handicap. These individuals also require special handling. General population inmates often victimize and harass the mentally ill or mentally retarded. If they are housed in general population, they may pose special problems of discipline. If they are housed in medical or protective settings, there are cost factors associated with increased security and services. With the deinstitutionalization of mental health patients in the 1970s, many individuals who had been hospitalized found themselves on the street, arguably being served by "community mental health centers." Where they often ended up, however, was in jail or prison. Today, many institutionalized felons also have had hospital stays and make repeated trips to forensic units or mental hospitals, only to be returned to the prison after being stabilized.

## UPGRADING CORRECTIONAL PERSONNEL

The correctional manager can succeed in discharging increasingly complex and legalistic responsibilities only if the prison has employees who are physically, emotionally, educationally, and motivationally able to work as a team in meeting group objectives. Historically, this has not been the case:

> Never mind what the rule book says . . . the fact is you've got to work it out for yourself. . . . One day this is O.K. and the next day it's not O.K. And the next day . . . well maybe it's O.K. There are no rules, no regulations for the correctional officer himself. . . . There is no direction and he more or less fends for himself. (May 1981, 25-26)

Salaries tend to be low. As of 1993, the national average entry-level annual salary was $18,000 (around $19,500 after probation), and entry-level annual salaries range from $27,778 in New Jersey to $12,200 in Arkansas (Camp and Camp 1993). The current minimum qualifications for correctional officer applicants in many states are a high school diploma or equivalent (GED) and no criminal record. Military backgrounds continue to be valued because of a perception that applicants who have served in the military are comfortable with a rigid chain of command, are not squeamish about the use of violence, and are less inclined to challenge the orders or management style of their superiors (Freeman 1995). Despite the low hiring qualifications, current correctional turnover rates in many states are high. High turnover denies managers a stable professional workforce.

Low salaries, unpleasant working conditions, and a negative media-generated public perception of correctional staff creates a general lack of interest in prison employment by the very people whose skills and talents are most needed. As a result, the correctional manager is forced to develop policies and procedures that the weakest links in the *chain of command* can carry out. The result is management to the lowest common denominator, and too many managers assume nothing further can be done. The challenge to correctional managers is to select individuals who have the desire to achieve professionalism and develop training programs that will continually upgrade the quality of staff.

In recognition of the complexity of their duties, guards are now called correctional officers, and training academies routinely provide new hires with weeks of orientation and sophisticated training covering skill areas ranging from use of physical force to report writing to sensitivity to cultural diversity. Many managers have moved beyond the training academy and developed systems of ongoing professional training for employees that include in-service activities and membership in organizations such as the American Correctional Association.

## MANAGING THE WOMEN'S PRISON

The external environment did not significantly influence men's prisons until after World War II; however, outside forces did influence women's prisons in the nineteenth century. Although very few women were incarcerated during the nineteenth century, incarceration did occur. Until 1870 most women inmates were housed in the same massive, fortress-like prisons as men and were treated essentially the same as men (Rafter 1992). Separate quarters for women were eventually established within men's prisons, but female inmates received no more consideration than did male inmates. In some cases, their living conditions were actually worse (Freedman 1981, 15).

Prison reformers, predominately middle-class women, became a powerful outside force when they demanded that prison conditions for female offenders be changed. Key to this change was the belief that there should be separate institutions for women. This idea was most strongly expressed by Elizabeth Fry, an English Quaker who became involved in prison reform because of an 1813 visit to Newgate Prison in London.

Female offenders were viewed by reformers as misguided women who needed help and protection within a female environment rather than as dangerous criminals like the male offenders, who had to be isolated from society. They were "fallen women" rather than hardened criminals. Most female offenders were working-class women guilty of such crimes as "promiscuity, vagrancy, and saloon-visiting." The goal of proper correctional management was to "retrain them to become chaste, proper, and domestic" (Rafter 1983b, 288-289). However, becoming "chaste" was a goal that applied only to white inmates. The treatment of white women and black women differed significantly. White women were placed in reformatories where they were taught feminine skills, manners, and attitudes. Black women, although they were often placed in reformatories, were generally segregated from white inmates and considered less likely to benefit from reformatory programming. White administrators also seemed to be extremely concerned about white inmates becoming sexually attracted to black inmates. This concern was frequently used to justify the racial segregation in housing and programming opportunities (Rafter 1985, 152-154).

A critical element in achieving the goal of reforming the woman offender was architectural change. The reformers

> soon decided that traditional prison architecture was unsuitable for the care and treatment of women, whose milder, more passive nature required a gentler environment. (Rafter 1985, xxi)

Women reformers were concerned with more than the living conditions being experienced by female inmates. Fry joined with American reformers in fighting for the idea that women's prisons should be run by women superintendents, called warders, for three specific reasons:

1. they would prevent sexual abuse by male guards, a not uncommon practice;
2. they would set a proper moral example of true womanhood for women who had fallen from grace; and
3. they would provide a sympathetic ear for female inmates. (Pollock-Byrne 1990, 41)

Female superintendents were expected to be capable of exerting a maternal, nurturing influence. The nineteenth-century female superintendent typically brought a background in volunteer work and a strong sense of religious obligation to the prison. However, the twentieth-century female superintendents considered themselves to be professional administrators. Many of them had received the benefits of a college education and professional training in women's prisons before becoming superintendents (Rafter 1985). However, the position of superintendent of a women's prison was often a terminal position. Employment discrimination usually prevented advancement to agency-wide administrative positions.

Typical of the twentieth-century female superintendent was Mary Belle Harris. Born in Pennsylvania in 1874, Harris was an archeologist, a teacher, and a social worker until 1914 when she was offered a job by Katherine Bennett Davis, New York Commissioner of Corrections. The job was superintendent of the Women's Workhouse on Blackwell Island, at that time considered to be the worse of New York's twelve prisons. Seven hundred female inmates were crowded together in a dilapidated facility designed to hold 150 inmates. Harris created a library, developed an inmate classification system, built an exercise yard, and rescinded many of the petty rules that she blamed for staff-inmate conflict. She left her position as superintendent after reform Mayor John Mitchell was defeated in the 1917 election. In 1927, Harris opened the Federal Institution for Women in Alderson, West Virginia. She was warden at that institution until her retirement in 1941. Harris was a strong advocate of rehabilitation and believed that much of the criminality among women resulted from economic dependency on men. She worked to create educational programs that would prepare women for reentry into society by providing the skills and self-respect they needed to become economically independent of men (Clear and Cole 1994).

Not all female managers were as fortunate as Mary Belle Harris. Elizabeth Farnham, chief matron at the women's wing of Sing Sing prison from 1844 to 1847, instituted a program of education that included the reading of library books, kept rules to a minimum, modified the rule of total silence, and introduced flowers, music, and outside visitors. These moves

> shocked many of Farnham's contemporaries. Conservatives such as Sing Sing's chaplain considered novel-reading irreligious. Moreover, Farnham's relaxation of the silent rule sowed dissension at the neighboring men's prison, where the rule still prevailed. Farnham's opponents publicly attacked her and her reforms. She fought back but eventually lost the struggle, resigning in 1847. (Rafter 1985, 18)

The creation of reformatories created employment opportunities for women in corrections, and many states passed legislation prohibiting male employment in women's prisons. By 1966, many of these laws had been repealed because of a shortage of qualified women managers and male legislators' lack of faith in the managerial capabilities of women (Pollock-Byrne 1990, 109). All but ten women's prisons were administered by male wardens or superintendents (Allen and Simonsen 1980, 295). Despite the repeal of legislation, women managers are no longer assigned exclusively to the women's prison. In 1993, women were in charge of 67.3 percent of the women's prisons, 7.1 percent of the men's prisons, and 22.2 percent of the coeducational prisons (American Correctional Association 1993).

The practical impact of this change in the gender of correctional management is an area that requires additional research. Pollock (1995) suggests that males and females have different management styles. The female style of management is best characterized as emotional and nurturing, with decreased social distance between supervisor and subordinate. The male management style is characterized as authoritarian, with greater social distance and increased reliance on formal rules. In other words, women tend to adopt a more personal style of supervision, which encourages greater cooperation and reduces tension and instances of abuse.

If women do enter corrections with a different inmate management style, will they retain this style in managing subordinates? Or will the effect be lessened by the demand for legalistic procedures, upholding of union contracts, the leveling effects of academy training, and the accommodations that have to be made for promotion to the higher levels of management, which are still dominated by men?

To meet the unique needs of the women inmates and to eliminate sexual abuse by male guards, the female superintendent had to create a new category of employee: the *matron*. The first matron was hired in 1822, and in 1832 matrons were hired at Auburn Prison in New York. In 1873, the first prison for women, the Indiana State Reformatory for Women, was constructed. It was staffed largely by matrons who were hired on the basis of two criteria: they had a good reputation and they possessed feminine skills. In addition to providing security, the matrons were to be role models for the inmates:

> [F]emale officers should be distinguished for modesty of demeanor, and the exercise of domestic virtues, and . . . they should possess that intimate knowledge of household employment, which will enable them to teach the ignorant and neglected female prisoner how to economize her means, so as to guard her from the temptations caused by waste and extravagance. (Wines and Dwight 1867, 107)

Matrons were often older women who were widows and who were forced to work by economic hardship, although they were paid less than male guards. Sometimes the wardens' wives became matrons. Matrons often had very little authority and, like their male counterparts, were subject to arbitrary discipline and dismissal (Rafter 1985). Formal education was not required, training was minimal, and working conditions were poor. The matrons were required to live in prison, had little time off, and were not allowed visitors.

> Some women working in corrections married and had children, even though until the 1960s women who married or became pregnant were often fired from their jobs. For those who did not marry, the correctional facility became their home and the staff and inmates their family. (Morton 1995, 78)

The primary challenge for the female superintendent and her matrons was to take a lower-class unmarried female offender and somehow change them into a middle-class wife and homemaker. In attempting to accomplish this, the women's prison perpetuated a double standard. Traditionally the programming was inferior to male programming, sex-stereotyped, and left female inmates unprepared to cope with a return to a society where they would have to be the sole provider for their children, even though they lacked saleable skills (Rafter 1989). This situation represents an irony because the wardens of women's prisons and coeducational prisons were more protreatment than the wardens of men's prisons, suggesting that women offenders were viewed as most suitable for rehabilitation (Cullen et al. 1993, 86).

Unfortunately, the women's prison has remained the stepchild of the correctional system. The fact that only 6 percent of the prison population is female has long been used to justify the minimal allocation of resources to women's prisons. Fewer programs are offered in women's prisons than in men's prisons, and those offered lack the variety found in the men's prisons (Glick and Neto 1977). In the 1960s, women inmates began to file litigation protesting the inferiority of their programming. In an attempt to equalize programming opportunities, the concept of the coeducational institution was developed. The first coeducational prison was a federal institution opened in Morgantown, West Virginia, in 1971. By 1992, 71 state and federal prisons exclusively housed female offenders and 77 prisons contained housing for both sexes (Greenfield 1992).

The challenge for the manager responsible for female inmates is to acknowledge the unique needs of the female offender by

1. making educational and vocational training programs more realistic for the female offender;
2. establishing counseling programs to address psychological issues such as the challenge of pregnancy when incarcerated and the trauma many women experience when denied the role of mother by physical separation from the child;
3. ensuring proper medical care; and
4. developing appropriate parole programs for women. (Clear and Cole 1994)

## CONCLUSIONS

Correctional management has evolved from the autocratic warden focused on punitive control of the inmate to the bureaucratic warden charged with simultaneously meeting a number of complex goals in a setting influenced by a dramatically changing environment. The nature of the job and the diversity of the workforce has changed over time. As corrections enters the next century, the nature of correctional management must change from a model of strict supervision of subordinates to a model of working with, and developing the potential of, subordinates. The responsibilities of the manager will increase in complexity. To meet the challenges of the future, correctional managers must embrace standards of leadership, change, higher education, professionalism, and racial and gender diversity.

---
## Vocabulary
---

| | |
|---|---|
| chain of command | responsibility model |
| consensus model | special needs inmates |
| control model | Theory X |
| external environment | Theory Y |
| internal environment | Title VII of the 1964 Civil Rights Act |
| matron | |

---
## Study Questions
---

1. What are the general responsibilities of a correctional manager? Why is effective management important?

2. What constitutes the internal and external environment of a correctional institution? What effects do these environments have on the management of a prison?

3. Define closed system and open system. A prison in 1850 is an example of which system? A prison in 1995 is an example of which system? Explain your answers.

4. What elements in the external environment have most significantly affected the evolution of correctional management from autocratic to bureaucratic?

5. Compare and contrast the autocratic and the bureaucratic warden in terms of goals, methods, chain of command, accountability, and nature of the workforce.

6. Why were women's reformatories developed? How did they differ from men's prisons? What was the role of the matron in the women's prison?

7. Compare and contrast male and female management styles. Do

you think different styles produce different results? Why or why not?

8. What are the current challenges facing the managers of women's prisons? Do they differ from the challenges facing managers of men's prisons?

9. What are the managerial challenges presented by judicial intervention, legislative action, the media, special needs inmates, and inmate litigation?

10. Discuss the issue of workforce racial and gender diversity. Why must a correctional manager be concerned with workforce diversity?

11. What are the assumptions of Theory X management? How does a Theory X manager direct the workforce? What are the assumptions of Theory Y management? How does a Theory Y leader direct the workforce?

# Sources Cited

— Allen, Harry, and Clifford Simonsen. 1980. *Corrections in America*. New York: Macmillan.

— American Correctional Association. 1993. *Directory: Juvenile and Adult Correctional Departments, Institutions, Agencies, and Paroling Authorities*. Laurel, Md.: American Correctional Association.

— Bartollas, Clemens, and John P. Conrad. 1992. *Introduction to Corrections*. New York: Harper Collins.

— Beaumont, G. D., and A. de Tocqueville. 1833. *The Penitentiary System in the United States and its Application in France*. Carbondale: Southern Illinois University Press (1964).

— Bertalanffy, Ludwig Von. 1950. "The Theory of Open Systems in Physics and Biology." *Science* 13 (January): 23-29.

— Camp, George M., and Camille G. Camp. 1995. *Corrections Yearbook*

*1993: Adult Corrections.* South Salem, N.Y.: Criminal Justice Institute.

— Clear, Todd R., and George F. Cole. 1994. *American Corrections.* Belmont, Cal.: Wadsworth.

— Corrections Today. 1989. "Corrections and the Media: A Pressing Problem." *Corrections Today* 1(51): 16-43, 58-66, 94-98.

— Cullen, Francis T., Edward J. Latessa, Velmer S. Burton, and Lucien X. Lombardo. 1993. "The Correctional Orientation of Prison Wardens: Is the Rehabilitative Ideal Supported?" *Criminology* 31(1): 69-92.

— Davidson, R. T. 1974. *Chicano Prisoners: The Key to San Quentin.* New York: Holt, Rinehart and Winston.

— DiIulio, John J., Jr. 1987. *Governing Prisons.* New York: Free Press.

— DiIulio, John J., Jr. 1991. *No Escape: The Future of American Corrections.* Scranton, Pa.: Harper Collins.

— Duffee, David. 1980. *Correctional Management.* Englewood Cliffs, N.J.: Prentice-Hall.

— Erickson, Gladys A. 1957. *Warden Ragen of Joliet.* New York: E. P. Dutton.

— The Evening News. 1995. "Prisoner Suits: They Want Their MTV." Harrisburg, Pa. (August 2): A2.

— Freedman, Estelle B. 1981. *Their Sisters' Keepers.* Ann Arbor: University of Michigan Press.

— Freeman, Robert M. 1995. Personal experience.

— Glick, Ruth M., and Virginia V. Neto. 1977. *National Study of Women's Correctional Programs.* Department of Justice, National Institute of Law Enforcement and Criminal Justice. Washington, D.C.: GPO.

— Goffman, Irving. 1961. "On the Characteristics of Total Institution: The Inmate World." In *The Prison: Studies in Institutional*

*Organization and Change,* ed. Donald Cressey, 15-67. New York: Holt, Rinehart and Winston.

— Greenfield, Lawrence A. 1992. *Prisons and Prisoners in the United States.* U.S. Department of Justice. Washington, D.C.: GPO.

— Houston, James. 1995. *Correctional Management: Functions, Skills and Systems.* Chicago.: Nelson-Hall.

— Jacobs, James B. 1977. *Stateville.* Chicago: University of Chicago Press.

— Joint Commission on Correctional Manpower and Training. 1969. *A Time to Act.* Washington: JCCMT.

— Koehler, Ricard J. 1989. "Like It or Not: We Are News." *Corrections Today* 51(1): 16-17.

— Koontz, Harold, Cyril O'Donnell, and Heinz Weihrich. 1986. *Essentials of Management.* 4th ed. New York: McGraw-Hill.

— May, E. 1981. "Prison Guards in America — The Inside Story." In *Prison Guard/Correctional Officer,* ed. R. R. Ross, 19-40. Toronto: Butterworth. (Originally published in *Corrections Magazine* 1976.)

— McGregor, Douglas. 1984. "Theory X and Theory Y." In *Organization Theory,* 2d ed., ed. D. S. Pugh, 317-327. New York: Penguin.

— Moiri, Saira, and Theodore M. Hammett. 1990. *1989 Update: AIDS in Correctional Facilities.* Washington, D.C.: National Institute of Justice.

— Morton, Joann B. 1995. "The Agency of Women — Women in ACA." *Corrections Today* 57(5): 74-84.

— Nagel, William G. 1974. *The New Red Barn.* New York: Walker.

— National Advisory Commission on CJ Standards and Goals. 1973. *Report on Corrections.* Washington, D.C.: GPO.

— Philliber, Susan. 1987. "Thy Brother's Keeper: A Review of the Literature on Correctional Officers." *Justice Quarterly* 4(1): 9-33.

— Pollock, Joycelyn M. 1995. "Women in Corrections: Custody and the 'Caring Ethic.'" In *Women, Law, and Social Control,* ed. Alido V. Merlo and Joycelyn M. Pollock, 97-116. Needham Heights, Mass.: Allyn and Bacon.

— Pollock-Byrne, J. 1990. *Women, Prison, and Crime.* Monterey, Cal.: Brooks/Cole.

— Rafter, Nichole Hahn. 1983a. "Prisons for Women, 1790-1980." In *Crime and Justice,* 5th ed., ed. M. Tonry and N. Morris, 129-191. Chicago: University of Chicago Press.

— Rafter, Nichole Hahn. 1983b. "Chastising the Unchaste: Social Control Functions of a Women's Reformatory, 1894-1931." In *Social Control and the State,* ed. Stanley Cohen and Andrew Scull, 288-311. New York: St. Martin's Press.

— Rafter, Nichole Hahn. 1985. *Partial Justice: Women in State Prisons, 1800-1935.* Boston: Northeastern University Press.

— Rafter, Nichole Hahn. 1989. *Gender and Justice: The Equal Protection Issue.* In *The American Prison: Issues in Research and Policy,* ed. Lynne Goldstein and Doris Layton MacKenzie, 89-101. New York: Plenum.

— Rafter, Nichole Hahn. 1992. "Equality or Difference?" *Federal Prison Journal* 3: 16-19.

— Robbins, S. P. 1984. *Management: Concepts and Practices.* Englewood Cliffs, N.J.: Prentice-Hall.

— Shannon, Douglas. 1990. "Correctional Executives: Who's Leading the Way?" *Corrections Today* 491: 48, 94.

— Sheehan, Susan. 1977. "Annals of Crime: A Prison and a Prisoner." *New Yorker* 53(36): 48-142.

— Smith, Perry F. 1991. "HIV Infection among Women Entering the New York State Correctional System." *The American Journal of Public Health* 81: 12-38.

— Smith, R. R., M. Wood Milan, and J. McKee. 1976. "The Correctional Officer as a Behavioral Technician." *Criminal Justice and Behavior* 3(4): 345-360.

— Sykes, Gresham, and Sheldon L. Messinger. 1960. "The Inmate So-
    cial System." In *Theoretical Studies in Social Organization of the
    Prison,* ed. R. Cloward et al., 130-144. New York: Social Sci-
    ence Research Council.

— Toch, Hans. 1989. "No Escape: The Future of American Correc-
    tions (A Review of John J. DiIulio, Jr.)." *Society* 26 (Mar.-Apr.):
    86-88.

— Useem, Bert, and Peter Kimball. 1989. *States of Siege: U.S. Prison
    Riots; 1971-1986.* New York: Oxford University Press.

— Wines, E. C., and Theodore W. Dwight. 1967. *Report on the Prisons
    and Reformatories of the United States and Canada.* Albany, N.Y.:
    Van Benthuysen and Sons.

— Wright, Kevin N. 1994. *Effective Prison Leadership.* Binghamton,
    N.Y.: William Neil.

— Zimmer, Lynn E. 1986. *Women Guarding Men.* Chicago: The Uni-
    versity of Chicago Press.

# 9

# CORRECTIONAL OFFICERS: UNDERSTUDIED AND MISUNDERSTOOD

## *Robert Freeman*

Prison guards are truly imprisoned: They are not physically confined but are locked into movie caricatures, into pejorative prophecies (sometimes self-fulfilling), into anachronistic supervision patterns, into unfair civil service definitions, into undeserved hostilities and prejudgments of their actions. Officers are imprisoned by our ignorance of who they are and what they do, which is the price they pay for working behind walls. (Toch 1981, xiv)

---

*Chapter Overview*

---

—— **THE WORLD OF THE CORRECTIONAL OFFICER**
      The Officer-Inmate Relationship
      The Organizational Structure
      Supervision of the Inmates
      Enforcement of the Rules
—— **THE CUSTODY-ORIENTED CORRECTIONAL OFFICER**
—— **THE PROFESSIONAL CORRECTIONAL OFFICER**
—— **THE FEMALE CORRECTIONAL OFFICER**
—— **THE MINORITY CORRECTIONAL OFFICER**
—— **CORRECTIONAL OFFICER STRESS**
      Alienation
      The Subculture of Violence
         *Corruption*
         *The Human Service Worker Response*
—— **STAFF TRAINING**
      The Preservice Phase
      On-the-Job Training Phase
—— **CONCLUSIONS**

Central to the operation of any correctional institution is the correctional officer. Although prisons have been in existence in America since the early 1800s, scholars have only recently focused their attention on the men and women engaged in the direct supervision of prison inmates. Prior to the 1960s, the public perception of the correctional officer was shaped by two powerful forces: social science literature and Hollywood.

In focusing on the inmate by portraying the horrors of confinement, the social science literature traditionally presented correctional officers as low in intelligence, sadistic, alienated, cynical, burned out, stressed, and repressors of the poor (Philliber 1987). This image was reinforced by Hollywood, which traditionally has presented the inmate as either a fun-loving victim of circumstances or, at worse, a basically good person in a bad situation (*Caged* 1950; *I*

---

**HIGHLIGHT 9-1**
**Reflections of Two Officers**

**Officer 1.** This job is stupid. All the brass does is sit on their dead butts and give me the blues over my report writing. I'm fed up with it, but I can't quit. I have too many years in. I feel a Mental Health Day coming on, then I'm going to file a grievance when I return to work. Meanwhile, guess it's time for my rounds. Sure hope Swanson is asleep. All that punk does is bitch and moan about how tough life is. He should have my job!

**Officer 2.** I better check on Swanson first thing tonight. He's been working real hard to hold it together since the divorce papers came. I wish his wife could have held off until he made parole. It'd be a shame to see him throw away four years of progress. Talked to his counselor today and she says the reality therapy is working, thanked me for supporting her recommendation that he be placed on an outside work detail. Then I better check on Bradley. He's fresh out of reception and I saw Wolf Johnson eyeing him up at yard this evening. I better clue him in on inmates like Wolf. Then I'll read the new directives on pre-parole planning. My comments on the next group up for parole are due in a week.

*Want to Live* 1958; *Cool Hand Luke* 1967; *The Longest Yard* 1974; *Escape from Alcatraz* 1979). The protagonists in these movies are thrown into an uncaring bureaucracy of filthy prisons staffed by corrupt, indifferent wardens and sadistic guards who wear reflecting sunglasses and delight in finding new ways of torturing and humiliating their captives. Or the inmate is portrayed as a criminal who has repented and found in prison a humanity that surpasses that of his keepers (*Birdman of Alcatraz* 1962; *Weeds* 1987; and *The Shawshank Redemption* 1994). Even worse are movies like the Penitentiary series (1972-1988), where the image of prison life is so distorted that it bears no resemblance to even the most badly managed American prison (Freeman 1995a).

The sadistic guard has been a reality in the history of America's prisons, especially during the era of the autocratic warden, and undoubtedly still exists today. However, the role of the correctional officer and the expectations administrators and society have for those officers have changed dramatically in the past 30 years. The purpose of this chapter is to explore the nature of that change and develop a more accurate description of the role of the correctional officer.

# THE WORLD OF THE CORRECTIONAL OFFICER

## THE OFFICER-INMATE RELATIONSHIP

The relationship between the correctional officer and inmate is one of "structured conflict" (Jacobs and Kraft 1978). Inmates do not want to be incarcerated and naturally resent the staff assigned to control them. This conflict situation demands that staff place an emphasis on the anticipation and prevention of threats to the safe and orderly operation of the institution. Prisons have a great potential for violence, and correctional officers in direct contact with inmates are unarmed and greatly outnumbered.

> The danger may be in the form of a direct attack on the guard by one emotionally disturbed or hostile prisoner, in the risks involved in breaking up a fight between prisoners, or in being taken hostage in an escape or in a riot. The threat of harm to guards has become even more salient in recent years as the prisoner pop-

ulations in most prisons have swelled dramatically and become increasingly comprised of younger and more violent persons. (Hepburn 1985, 192)

The officer must be constantly alert and ready to respond to potential and actual dangerous, even life-threatening, situations. However, the threat is not just physical, nor is it confined solely to the work environment. The threat can be psychological and extend beyond the prison.

> The last officer bringing drugs into the institution was married and had a family. The whole thing was set up by inmates finding out that he went to a certain bar one night a week. All of a sudden this officer found himself in a motel room with a prisoner's girlfriend. Then two days later she said, "There'll be a package mailed to you that you'll take into the prison." When he resisted, she said, "Well, do you want your wife to know that you slept with me night before last?" The prisoner had him in the jaws of a vice. (Bartollas and Conrad 1992, 408)

This constant threat of both physical and psychological danger often produces a defensive posture toward inmates, who are perceived with a mixture of suspicion, fear, contempt, and hostility (Jacobs and Kraft 1978).

## THE ORGANIZATIONAL STRUCTURE

The prison work environment requires that the correctional officer function as a social control agent who has the primary responsibilities of custody, security, and control. The correctional officer staff is organized along rigid paramilitary lines consisting of a *chain of command* structure composed of the ranks of officer trainee, officer, sergeant, lieutenant, captain, major, deputy for custody, and the superintendent or warden.

The trainee is a newly hired officer in a probationary status designed to teach the skills necessary to become a good correctional officer. Once promoted to officer, the trainee is expected to be able to do any officer job in the institution. Officers are line staff responsible for the direct supervision of inmates and the daily enforcement of all policy and procedures set forth by the managerial staff. Sergeants are first-level supervisors responsible for a complement of officers assigned to a specific location. The restricted housing unit sergeant, for example, would be responsible for the supervision of all officers assigned to the disciplinary block. Lieutenants function as second-level supervisors and are responsible for the sergeants, officers, and trainees assigned to a specific section of the prison. A block lieutenant, for example, may be assigned responsibility for several cell blocks, each of which is under the control of a sergeant. Captains are shift supervisors responsible for all subordinate officers. During the period of 5 P.M. to 7 A.M. on weekdays and during the weekends and holidays, the shift captain may be the highest ranking management person in the institution. The major (often referred to as the major of the guard) is an administrator with the responsibility of overseeing the captains and ensuring that overall institutional custody and control are being maintained. The deputy for custody is the administrator providing the link between the officers and the superintendent or warden and all other managers.

The correctional officer is both a manager and a worker: a low-status worker in relationship to superior officers, but a manager of inmates. As the lowest level in the correctional hierarchy, the officer is under the constant scrutiny of supervisors in the same way the inmate is under the surveillance of the officer. Because of the fear of contraband, officers are frequently searched as they enter the institution. They face inspections, write-ups, and disciplinary action for their rule violations, just as the inmate faces disciplinary action for rule violations. Officers often experience a sense of emotional isolation. They work alone, or as part of a small team, but always with the expectation that they are capable of performing the functions of the job independently, calling for help only when it is absolutely necessary, as in the case of physical assault. Interaction with other officers as a group is usually minimal, limited to brief periods of contact at roll call, in the dining room, and at the end of the shift.

## SUPERVISION OF THE INMATES

Lombardo (1981) uses the term "people worker" to analyze the role of the correctional officer, noting that the officer must work with inmates on a personal level, in an environment of physical closeness over long periods of time, while functioning as a member of a complex bureaucratic organization. The primary responsibility of all correctional officers is the control of the inmate population through a process of direct supervision. There are seven basic types of correctional officer job assignments based on location within the institution, the duties required, and the nature of the contact with the inmate population.

1. block officers,
2. work detail supervisors,
3. industrial shop and school officers,
4. yard officers,
5. administration building assignment officers,
6. wall post officers, and
7. relief officers (Lombardo 1981).

Each type of assignment requires a specific set of skills and abilities that are not uniformly distributed throughout the population of officers. A good wall officer, for instance, may be a very poor block officer and, in fact, may be assigned to a perimeter tower instead of a cell block for exactly that reason. The job of the supervisor is to assess officers and determine the best match between officer and assignment.

The block officer is responsible for the supervision of the inmates when they are in the housing unit. The housing unit may be a traditional cell block housing 400 or 500 general population inmates, a dormitory housing no more than 50 or 60 inmates approved for parole, a specialized modular unit designed to serve as a therapeutic drug community, a restricted housing unit housing violent predators, a weight room converted to temporary housing to ease overcrowding, or a trailer located in a forestry camp. Regardless of the nature of the housing unit, the block officer is responsible for ensuring both the safety of every inmate in the unit and the security of the housing unit. Management of this responsibility involves direct observation of inmates, periodic cell searches, inmate searches, and visual inspection of every part of the unit for signs of attempts to breach the physical integrity of the structure. The block officer coordinates movement of the inmate to meals, recreation, showers, school, work, the infirmary, the visiting room, the records office, religious services, and meetings with counselors and the parole board. The block officer must also handle the personal problems and questions of inmates. Management of a housing unit is often dangerous because the officers are unarmed, outnumbered, and can easily be physically overwhelmed by the inmates at any given time. Because of the complexity of the job, a block officer must possess critical organizational and people skills.

Work detail supervisors are responsible for inmates who have been assigned to perform the work necessary to keep the prison running. Inmates cook the food, do the laundry, mow the lawns, tend the flower beds, work on the farms, and perform a wide range of maintenance jobs, some of which (plumbing and electrical work, for example) require a high degree of skill and experience. Inmate work details tend to be small and the relationship between officer and inmate one of informality, especially where there are clear-cut production goals (Crouch 1980). Although work detail supervisors must be concerned with physical safety and the possibility of escape, especially if the assignment takes the work detail outside of the institution, they generally face a much lower degree of physical threat than does the block officer.

Industrial shop and school officers work with civilian teachers, instructors, and administrators and most often serve a traffic control function. They are responsible for seeing that inmates arrive on time, stay in class, and leave only when scheduled to do so. They handle inmate complaints and maintain the security of the building by searching inmates to prevent theft and the possession of contraband. There often is very little personal officer-inmate contact.

Yard officers are responsible for the supervision of inmates when they are engaged in recreational activities, meals, or moving from location to location within the institution. These officers are concerned with security and the maintenance of order. There may be no contact at all with the vast majority of inmates. These officers require good observation skills, but the job is much less structured than the job of the block officer.

Administration building assignment officers often are responsible for the administration building, the visitor's entrance, the visiting room, and the institutional perimeter gates or mobile patrols. Because these are the officers the general public is most likely to come into contact with, managers usually try to select officers who have good public relations skills. An officer who treats visitors or civilian guests of the staff like inmates can be a significant embarrassment to the administration. At an institution touted to be in the forefront of correctional reform in the early 1970s, the superintendent was frequently embarrassed by a main control officer (in possession of this coveted post because of union seniority) who liked to greet visitors with "And which piece of pond scum are you here to see today?" (Freeman 1995b).

The wall post officer is assigned to a tower or a perimeter patrol vehicle. These officers are almost completely removed from contact with inmates. This assignment is boring and lonely, but safe. Officers assigned to the tower are often those who cannot get along with inmates, who are tired of the frustration and stress of working a block, or who are close to retirement and simply too burned out to work with inmates.

Relief officers are experienced officers who can temporarily handle any assignment within the institution. They often have a superior knowledge of the institution and the inmates.

## ENFORCEMENT OF THE RULES

Central to the correctional officer's role as social control agent is rule enforcement. Prison rules provide formal guidelines for the regulation of inmate conduct, orderly operation of the institution, and the protection of inmates, staff, and visitors. Because prisons focus on security, and every problem encountered produces a new set of rules and regulations intended to prevent a reoccurrence of the problem, prisons typically have numerous rules and regulations defining inappropriate inmate behavior (President's Commission 1967).

To enforce the rules, the correctional officer must maintain control over an inmate population that views the officer as an agent of repression and oppression and that expresses open contempt and defiance of the officer's authority with hostile, dangerous, and unpredictable behavior (Poole and Regoli 1981). In any correctional institution, there are five possible bases of control:

1. legitimate power,
2. coercive power,
3. reward power,
4. expert power,
5. and referent power (Hepburn 1985).

*Legitimate power* is rooted in the legal authority given the officer to exercise control over inmates because of their structural relationship within the prison. The position of the officer in this relationship confers the right to have orders obeyed and authority respected. The position of the inmate in the relationship conveys the duty to obey orders.

*Coercive power* is based in the inmate perception that officers have the ability to punish rule violators, either formally (through the use of written misconduct reports) or informally (beatings and other forms of physical or psychological abuse). Although the use of this power is limited by the possibility of legal or administrative action against the officer who relies too heavily on coercion, periodic cell searches, assignments to disciplinary units, random strip searches, and the ready availability of lethal force remind the inmate that coercion is a basis of power within the prison.

*Reward power* entails the ability to issue rewards and privileges to inmates. But this basis of power depends on inmate perception. Reward power exists only when inmates believe that the correctional officers actually have the ability to issue rewards. The role of treatment staff in recommending assignment to housing and work sites, participation in programs, especially community-based programs, accumulation of good time credits, and eligibility for parole can be viewed by inmates as evidence that the real reward power is found in the treatment staff. However, an informal reward system in the form of reciprocity is possible.

> Prison leaders were expected to maintain control over other prisoners, in exchange for which minor violations would be tolerated, petty pilferage would be permitted, and special favors would be granted. (Hepburn 1985, 148)

*Expert power* is based on an inmate's perception of some special skill, ability, or expertise on the part of the officer. Cressey (1965) has suggested that power based on technical competence and judgment is more likely in treatment-oriented prisons, where correctional officers are expected to use professional judgment in the assessment of inmate needs, than in a prison where the orientation is custody. Thus, a correctional officer working in a therapeutic drug community within a prison is more likely to be seen as having expert power than an officer working in a super-max institution where coercive control rules.

*Referent power* is personal authority: the ability of officers to deal with inmates fairly and with respect. An officer holds power to the extent that the inmates respect and admire the officer.

> Guards who are fair and evenhanded in their relations with prisoners, who display a degree of respect to the prisoners, who fulfill their promises to prisoners, and who exercise their coercive power with impartiality and without malice gain respect from prisoners. (Hepburn 1985, 149)

Legitimate power provides the primary base for the formal control system within the prison. Inmate disciplinary practices differ from state to state, but a common practice is for inmates being received at an institution to be provided with a written list of prohibited activities, ranked by severity, and accompanied by a schedule of punishments. Inmates are informed that they are expected to follow all the rules or suffer the consequences. If an inmate violates the rules, the officer witnessing the violation has the authority to file a misconduct report that is then reviewed by a disciplinary committee composed of either supervisory staff (treatment as well as custody) or an independent hearing examiner. If a finding of guilty is rendered, the committee may impose such sanctions as loss of privileges, solitary confinement, transfer to another institution, or denial of parole.

Prison rule violations are usually defined in terms of two categories. The first category, major misconduct, is primarily based on the criminal code and includes such behaviors as murder, assault, rape, rioting, extortion, and possession of contraband drugs. The second category, minor misconduct, is based on institutional rules and procedures and includes such behaviors as horseplay, failure to follow sanitary regulations, and disrespect to a staff member. In 1986, 53 percent of the 450,000 inmates in state prisons were charged with at least one rule violation during their incarceration (Stephen 1989).

There is evidence that the reported rule violations in 1986 do not represent all of the rule violations committed by inmates or observed by correctional officers. Rule enforcement in the prison by the correctional officer is analogous to enforcement of the law in the community by the police officer. Just as the police officer does not arrest every observed violator, the correctional officer does not write a misconduct report for every inmate observed violating the rules. Hewitt, Poole, and Regoli (1984) found that inmates are much more extensively involved in rule violations than official reports record, and correctional officers claim to observe nearly the same number of violations admitted to by inmates. It appears that very few rule violations are responded to with a misconduct report. Rule enforcement within a particular facility can vary from officer to officer and shift to shift. Correctional officers appear to exercise a considerable amount of discretion in rule enforcement.

The basis of this discretion in rule enforcement has been a matter of concern. Held et al. (1979) found that black inmates received a disproportionate number of misconduct reports because white officers rated black inmates as being more aggressive and dangerous than white inmates. They concluded that the number of misconducts received was the result of white officers' perceptions of dangerousness rather than inmate behavior. Freeman (1994) found that officer attitudes toward social distance influenced the filing of written misconduct reports in a prison for women. Correctional officers who favored a low degree of social distance between officer and inmate filed fewer misconduct reports for minor rule violations than did officers who favored a high degree of social distance.

# THE CUSTODY-ORIENTED
# CORRECTIONAL OFFICER

The organizational goals of American prisons directly proscribe or indirectly influence the role of the correctional officer (Hepburn and Albonetti 1980). Historically, prisons have emphasized the custody functions of control and security and have been classified in terms of three security levels: maximum, medium, and minimum. Prior to the 1960s, the role of the correctional officer was clear and unambiguous: It was rigidly custodial. The *custody-oriented officer* maintained security and control by enforcing the rules, and he possessed the legitimate, coercive, and reward power to do so without fear of contradiction (Poole and Regoli 1981).

As noted in Chapter 8, the traditional custody-oriented officer was a rural, white male who possessed limited education, was politically conservative, was slow to accept change, and who often came to corrections at a relatively late age after mixed success in civilian life or retirement from the military. The traditional public perception of the custody-oriented correctional officer is best summed up by the following quote:

> A correctional officer assigned to tower duty is a residue of the dark ages. He requires 20/20 vision, the IQ of an imbecile, a high threshold for boredom and a basement position in Maslow's hierarchy. For officers — who are better than this — a tower assignment is palatable as an undiluted sinecure. The tower guard "does his time" because we offer him a paycheck for his presence. He is paid not only to be non-professional, but to be flagrantly non-contributing. (Toch 1978, 20)

What kind of person is motivated to become a custody-oriented correctional officer? A 1968 Harris survey of teenagers found that only 1 percent had ever considered a career as a correctional officer (Joint Commission 1968). One of the primary incentives for custody-oriented correctional officers has been the security that civil service employment provides. Since most prisons are located in rural areas, prison work may be more appealing and lucrative than farm work or low-paying service or industry jobs threatened by automation. Correctional officers are also pushed into prison work by unfortunate circumstances, such as the unavailability of other jobs (Jacobs and Retsky 1975), or because of layoffs, injuries, or failure in their initial occupations.

I flunked out of college and was in the dumps. I just played around for three years, worked in a factory, and got married. I hated the factory: not much money, hot and rotten. They were hiring guards in 1972-73, and the pay was good: $12,000 per year and overtime. I took the test, sat around for a year, and got called. (Lombardo 1981, 21)

This viewpoint of officer motivation is best summarized by a statement from an ex-inmate: "Many of the officers simply answered all the want-ads and Corrections gave them a job" (Schroeder 1976, 153).

# THE PROFESSIONAL CORRECTIONAL OFFICER

Beginning in the 1960s, mere confinement in prison was no longer viewed as sufficient to correct deviant behavior. Rehabilitation programs (vocational training, education, counseling and psychotherapy, work release, furloughs, and self-improvement activities) were introduced into prisons that had previously viewed custody as the sole organizational goal (Farmer 1977). Fundamental to this emphasis on rehabilitation was an expectation that correctional officers should move beyond the comfortable, clearly defined security role and function in the more ambiguous role of the highly qualified human service-oriented professional capable of assisting in the rehabilitation of the offender. This role, which included helping prisoners to cope with prison life, moved beyond the limitations of their custodial role (Jurik 1985; Johnson 1987).

However, the introduction of rehabilitation as a new correctional goal created an ambiguous social organization (Cressey 1959). When rehabilitation was introduced into the traditional structure of custody, security, and control, a set of contradictory goals was created. The goal of custody demands that the principal rule of interaction between officers and inmates is to maintain maximum social distance. To maintain the authority necessary for the exercise of coercive control, the correctional officer must avoid informal relationships, affective ties, and discretionary rule enforcement (Cressey 1965; Hepburn and Albonetti 1980). However, the goal of treatment requires nonpunitive control of inmates, relaxed discipline, a willingness to form affective ties, informal relationships, minimized social distance with inmates, and the exercise of discretion based on individual inmate characteristics and situations. Controls are to be subordinated to the expectation that officers will be human-oriented and flexible (Cressey 1965).

In addition, correctional officers had to share their environment with a new set of players. In the 1970s, correctional administrators became concerned about high staff turnover, a lack of treatment-oriented officers, and minority inmate demands that the correctional workforce be diversified (Philliber 1987). The administrative solution to these problems was the development of recruitment and staff policies that emphasized higher standards of education, selection, training, and performance. A new goal emerged: to produce a diverse group of correctional officers with a more professional orientation.

This change in demographics carried with it a conflict of stereotypes that still exists today. Treatment staff often regard themselves as highly skilled professionals who are uniquely qualified to assist the inmate and have chosen to enter prison work even though other employment opportunities are available. All too often they regard correctional officers as ignorant Neanderthals capable only of physical violence. Correctional officers, on the other hand, often view themselves as doing the real work of the institution and regard treatment staff as rich college bleeding hearts who put the entire staff at risk. Yet each group is expected to respect and work with the other group in a team effort to meet organizational goals.

Most correctional facilities today combine the dual roles of custody and treatment. Administrators formally and informally create an expectation that correctional officers should define themselves as agents of inmate change who will use discretion as they engage in the daily process of helping the treatment staff to rehabilitate inmates, while at the same time maintaining security and enforcing the rules (President's Commission 1967; Cressey 1965; Poole and Regoli 1981). In addition to providing custody, the correctional officer is to be a provider of mental health services who

> resonates to adjustment problems of humans-in-crisis, and seeks to respond to inmate suffering. Such activity falls into the human services realm and it is intrinsically non-custodial, though it may be clothed in a rationale of violence-prevention. (Toch 1978, 21)

The dual roles of custody and treatment create a role conflict for the correctional officer. Although the central goal of an officer's custody role is well defined (maintaining order and security), the central goal of the treatment role (assisting in the rehabilitation of the inmate) entails flexibility, the use of discretionary justice, and the ability to secure inmate compliance through informal exchange relationships that deviate from the written rules. Knowing which rules can be bent, how far they may be bent, and under which circumstances they may be bent is not always apparent or understood by the officer. The process of acquiring this knowledge introduces uncertainty and danger because correctional officers, expected to exercise professional judgment and flexibility in performing their job, are subject to disciplinary action if they violate, or permit inmates to violate, the numerous official rules and procedures of the prison (Hepburn 1985).

Officers motivated primarily by their own financial security may find the uncertainty of the rehabilitation process to be overwhelming. But financial security is not the sole motivation for all correctional officers. Many officers are drawn to the job to help other human beings and to engage in activities that are intrinsically worthwhile:

> They hunger for opportunities to improve the quality of life in the prison community and grasp them when they can. Like most of us, they want to be people who matter. In the prison, the skills that matter are human relations and human service skills. These are the skills that can be used to develop relationships and hence to reduce tension, defuse crises, and conduct daily business in a civilized (and potentially civilizing) manner. (Johnson 1996, 224)

These officers readily grasp the importance of the human service role. Yet, even when correctional officers are open to the expectation of being a human service worker, years of experience as a custody-oriented officer and the lack of formal education may prove detrimental. In the early 1970s at a correctional facility in the forefront of implementing the new goal of rehabilitation, a counselor supervisor was given the task of training the captain of the guard as a cotherapist in a new group therapy program. The captain was a highly respected ex-Marine and 20-year veteran of a maximum security institution who had become a legend for refusing to open the gate for rioting inmates even though they were stabbing him through the bars. The superintendent anticipated that when the correctional officers saw their captain functioning as a cotherapist, they would stop their resistance to working with the new treatment staff. The counselor supervisor approached the captain, found he was interested in working in a structured therapy setting, and gave him a selection of books and journal articles to study. A month later, having been assured by the captain that he now understood the dynamics of group therapy, the counselor supervisor held the initial orientation session with a group of ten inmates. After half an hour of talking about confidentiality, the value of open expression and constructive criticism, the need to explore childhood experiences and gain insight into their relationship to criminal behavior, and the reality that therapy can be a painful though rewarding process, the counselor supervisor asked if the captain had anything to share. The captain nodded and said enthusiastically, "I have some really great Dempsey-Lewis fight films I can bring in for us to watch. I know that'll help you guys get your minds off being in prison" (Freeman 1995b).

Introducing such rehabilitation-related practices as due process rights in disciplinary actions, limited use of solitary confinement, and formal inmate grievance mechanisms has undermined the ability of the correctional officer to use coercive power, with a corresponding loss of officer control, and provided inmates with a countervailing power (Poole and Regoli 1981). Officers may believe that inmates now actually possess more power than officers (Fox 1982; Hepburn 1985).

Having to compromise security and control functions daily to comply with the new requirements of rehabilitation, and having to substitute referent and expert power for coercive power, places the officer in the stressful position of having to serve two masters while interacting on a daily basis with inmates who may be threatening and negative. The result is a strained and unhealthy atmosphere (Duffee 1974). Many officers express the opinion that administrators and treatment staff have more respect and more affinity for inmates than for officers, suggesting that the social distance between correctional officers and administrators may even be greater than that between officers and inmates. Officers often share the perception that they are actually treated more unfairly and have less say in institutional policy decisions than inmates. Positive feelings arise from their manager-of-inmates role, but feelings of frustration, anger, and lack of appreciation are created by the relationship with superiors (Jacobs and Retsky 1975).

## THE FEMALE CORRECTIONAL OFFICER

The employment of women as correctional officers in men's prisons in the early 1970s resulted from the convergence of two factors. The first factor was the dissatisfaction of women working as matrons in the women's prison or as clerical or support staff in the men's prisons. Because promotional criteria favored staff with direct supervision of male inmates, the women who supervised female inmates or worked in support positions had little hope of professional advancement (Chapman et al. 1983).

The second factor was the passage of amendments to *Title VII* of the 1964 Civil Rights Act in 1972, which extended the prohibition of employment discrimination to public employers at the state, county, and local levels. Women used this amendment to file civil suits against correctional administrators who refused to hire them as correctional officers in men's prisons. Many male officers and administrators fought the hiring of women as equal-status correctional officers on the grounds that (1) women are not fit for the job because they lack physical strength, are too easily corrupted by inmates, cannot provide the backup that safety demands, and are vulnerable to assault, which jeopardizes officer safety and facility security; and (2) are a disruptive influence because inmates will not follow their orders, will fight for their attention, and will react negatively to the violation of their privacy (Hawkins and Alpert 1989).

Despite the widespread perception that women are more vulnerable to assault, there is little empirical evidence to support this concern. Shawver and Dickover (1986) found little to confirm the safety fears of male officers. According to this study, female officers were assaulted significantly less than male officers, and when they were assaulted they were about as likely to be injured or to suffer a major injury. The study also found no relationship between the percentage of women officers and the number of assaults against male staff. However, male opposition was based on factors other than security and safety. Zimmer (1986, 155) has noted that a majority of male correctional officers are unhappy with the introduction of women into their ranks because they resent the elimination of their all-male world. More specifically, the presence of female officers in the men's prison denies males their macho role:

> [B]ecause they have this little 5′2″ 115 lb. woman standing beside them, putting a guy that is 6′4″, 230 lbs. in cuffs . . . saying, "Come on now, act right," and not having any problem doing it. Whereas he might have to go in there with 2 or 3 other guys and tackle him down to cuff him. It also forces them to recognize that they can't go home and talk about how bad and mean they are . . . because some little chickie can do the same thing that he is doing. (Owen 1985, 158)

Male officer hostility to the female officer was often direct, such as openly disparaging comments made in the presence of both the women officers and inmates, or more subtle, such as the burden of tokenism. Although there has been progress made in recruiting and hiring women, they are still a numerical minority in most men's prisons. This makes them highly visible, and their appearance, demeanor, behavior, performance, and mistakes receive a disproportionate amount of attention. Their mistakes are quickly communicated throughout the prison and discussed for weeks. Many of the women soon become self-conscious and are afraid to take risks that might make them stand out (Zimmer 1986). The mistakes of one female correctional officer are often overgeneralized to all female officers. Unsatisfactory performance by one officer is assumed to indicate that all female officers will perform in an unsatisfactory manner. An outstanding female officer is viewed as an exception (Zupan 1992).

A particularly vicious example of indirect opposition by male officers is found in the practice of making allegations about the on-duty sexual behavior of female officers. Male officers frequently spread rumors that female officers are actively engaged in sexual conduct with both inmates and male officers. These rumors not only caused a high degree of personal discomfort, they had a direct impact on employment and career stability. Female correctional officers report being fired for sex-related reasons or being driven to resign.

> A third woman, on leave . . . was uncertain about whether she would return to work because of the rumors about her unborn child's heritage. Another woman, under an investigation for (allegedly) having sexual intercourse in the institution kitchen with a male colleague, was removed temporarily from her shift, while the male officer remained untouched. . . . [A]nother woman was . . . deciding whether to file civil charges of slander against two male colleagues who had made unfounded sexual allegations about her. (Petersen 1982, 453)

In addition to opposition from colleagues, there is the issue of differential treatment by supervisors. Male supervisors often assign female correctional officers to low-risk assignments such as visiting rooms, control rooms, and clerical areas that involve little direct inmate contact. This practice limits the officer's chance for promotion, denies them the opportunity to build confidence in their skills, and further antagonizes male officers who feel they are forced to work the more dangerous jobs while the women get the easy jobs (Zimmer

1986; Jurik 1985). Evaluations performed by antagonistic male superiors also limit the ability of the female officer to advance.

Male inmate reaction to the presence of female correctional officers has been mixed. Some thought that the presence of women on the block was positive because women were more willing to listen to problems, more helpful, more compassionate, and more understanding than male officers. This observation is also shared by many female correctional officers:

> Women are a little more soft. . . . [W]e feel that we like to be treated decent and so we try to treat other people decent. . . . With the men, they are more . . . short and curt with their answers. (Pollock 1986, 89)

Other inmates expressed the fear that female officers could not protect weaker inmates from the attacks of predatory inmates. Some inmates shared the male officer view that a woman's place was in the home or in the secretarial pool, but certainly not in the prison (Zimmer 1986). However, in a survey of 120 male inmates in four Wisconsin men's prisons, Petersen (1982, 452) found the following:

> In summary, it is clear that the women officers are not disliked by the male inmates. In fact, quite the contrary, the women seem to be received quite positively by the inmates. One of the primary reasons the women are so greatly liked is that they fulfill a role as sex objects to the inmates. Another reason they are liked . . . by the inmates is because of their different styles of intervention.

The presence of women correctional officers in the men's prison has been defended on the grounds that a personal style of supervision, as practiced by women, can bring a "normalizing" influence into prison:

> Women officers tend to ask inmates to do things rather than tell them. Female correctional officers foster personal interest in the inmate and use the relationships they develop as a technique of control. This relieves some of the tension found in prisons for men and encourages male prisoners to interact with correctional officers rather than cultivating isolation and separate subcultures. (Pollock 1995, 111)

Supervision requires enforcement of the rules. Zimmer (1986) has raised the question of whether female correctional officers actually possess the authority to enforce the rules against male inmates. In a study of a medium-security state prison in the Midwest, it was found that female officers wrote approximately the same number of misconduct reports for the same types of violations as male officers did. There was no difference in the likelihood of those reports being upheld by the hearing officers or in the sanction that would be imposed. The authors concluded that the authority of female correctional officers is as legitimate as that of the male officers (Simon and Simon 1988).

It is often assumed that because female correctional officers are different they will have a different response to the job than do male officers. The data does not support this assumption. Jurik and Halemba (1984) found only two differences between male and female officer perceptions of the job. The men wanted more discretion; the women wanted more structure. And the women were more likely to express negative attitudes toward male coworkers and to indicate that many of their problems were caused by male coworkers. Both men and women officers tended to have negative attitudes toward their superiors and to believe that the majority of their work-related problems were caused by superiors. There was little difference in levels of job satisfaction, and women's negative attitudes toward male coworkers had little impact on those levels. Fry and Glaser (1987) found that the only difference between male and female officers was that the female officers were more negative in their evaluation of inmate services. However, women officers have been found to experience a significantly higher level of stress than male officers (Stinchcomb 1986; Zupan 1992). There is also little difference in attitudes towards inmates. Research has found no significant difference between male and female officers on the factors of punitive attitude or insensitivity to identification of inmate needs (Jurik and Halemba 1984; Zupan 1992).

To cope with the demands of the job, women appear to adopt one of three work styles: the institutional role, the modified role, and the inventive role. In the institutional role, the woman adheres closely to the rules and tries to maintain a highly professional stance. Their preoccupation with obedience makes these women inflexible and rigid. In the modified role, the women believe they cannot perform the role as well as men and come to sympathize with the men who oppose women in corrections. These women come to fear inmates and avoid contact with them. They rely heavily on male workers for backup. In the inventive role, women rely heavily on the inmates for support, express little fear of them, and prefer working in direct contact with them (Zimmer 1986). It should be noted that

Zupan (1992) argues that Zimmer has failed to make the case that these work styles are different from the styles adopted by male correctional officers. Jacobs and Retsky (1975) have noted similar work styles among male officers.

In 1970, the U.S. Supreme Court ruled in the case of *Dothard v. Rawlinson,* 97 S. Ct. 2720 (1970), that under certain circumstances women could be prohibited from employment as correctional officers in men's prisons. The court accepted the assumption that the presence of women would threaten the security of any maximum security prison housing only male inmates, but no department of corrections was subsequently able to use it to exclude women from correctional employment (Potts 1983). Women are no longer confined to work with women inmates. As of January 1, 1995, 45 correctional systems reported that 25,623 female correctional officers were working in male institutions. Of 213,370 supervisory and nonsupervisory correctional officers in 52 correctional systems, 18 percent were female (Camp and Camp 1995, 70-73).

## THE MINORITY CORRECTIONAL OFFICER

In the late 1960s, the civil rights movement coincided with a growing need for correctional manpower. Many prison administrators found it necessary to look beyond the local, white manpower pools from which correctional officers had traditionally been drawn. Pressure from inmate groups demanding diversity in the workforce also pressured administrators to hire more minorities, with the argument that it was necessary to have a more sympathetic workforce with which minority inmates could identify (Jacobs and Kraft 1978). Veteran white officers often responded with an attitude that the "new breed" of nonwhite, urban guard was more pro-inmate and less trustworthy (Irwin 1977). Racism was prevalent among the white officer staff.

> There were no black officers on the yard, I was the only one. I talked to the inmates and they trained me. They taught me how to watch my back, what to do if the alarm goes off in South Block. They even told me to stay on the yard with them if something happened inside. The white officers never talked to me. I had to be alone on the yard for 8 hours because they ignored me. They said I didn't do my job because I was talking to the inmates all the time. (Owen 1985, 153)

The result was racism on both a personal and institutional level that hindered the recruitment and promotion of minorities. However, changes have been significant, and as of January 1, 1995, 52 correctional systems reported that 30.8 percent of their correctional officers were nonwhite (Camp and Camp 1995, 70).

Racism, however, still exists. In her review of the literature, Philliber (1987) notes that studies have documented the tendency of black correctional officers to quit their jobs more often than whites, primarily because of conflicts with superior officers. Blacks also are more likely to experience job dissatisfaction than are whites. Whether or not minority status makes officers more favorable toward inmates remains an open question. Jacobs and Kraft (1978) found that black correctional officers were more punitive than whites toward inmates. Klofas and Toch (1982) found that minority officers expressed the need for high social distance between officer and inmate and suggested that minorities be hired for reasons other than their assumed ability to relate better to inmates. Johnson (1996) also discusses the idea that racism permeates the prison system, affecting both guards and inmates.

# CORRECTIONAL OFFICER STRESS

## *ALIENATION*

The role conflict created by organizational goals and shifting officer demographics has created an *alienation* for correctional officers. Poole and Regoli (1981) note the existence of five types of alienation: powerlessness, normlessness, meaninglessness, social isolation, and self-estrangement.

Powerlessness and normlessness are the result of conflict in organizational goals. Powerlessness is experienced because rehabilitation policies have eliminated many rules, regulations, and practices previously used to regulate inmate behavior, thus undermining officer authority and leaving officers to the mercy of administrators who do not support them. Normlessness is experienced because introducing treatment goals into a traditionally coercive institution results in contradictory and ambiguous role definitions that leave officers with a sense of not knowing the new rules and a fear of breaking them. Social isolation is a function of the officer having to work in a highly individualized manner, which creates a perception of being alone in a hostile environment. Prior to the rehabilitation era, the effect of social isolation could be lessened by the knowledge that prison staffing was homogeneous: white, conservative, rural males sharing a common custody orientation. However, affirmative action policies transformed this homogeneous workforce into a heterogeneous one by introducing minority and female staff, many from urban areas, into the institution. Many of these newcomers were college-educated people entering corrections because they wished to help people disadvantaged by society. They readily accepted rehabilitation as an organizational goal. This new staff introduced a set of treatment-oriented attitudes that conflicted with the traditional custody orientation of the white rural male (Owen 1985).

Klofas and Toch (1982) have suggested that the degree of professional orientation accepted by correctional officers places them in one of three categories of role definition: Subcultural Custodians (the traditional custody-oriented officer) who are strongly pro-custody, anti-inmate, and uncomfortable with a lack of social distance between officer and inmate; Lonely Braves who are prorehabilitation but believe they are surrounded by hostile conservatives; and the Supported Majority who are in favor of rehabilitation, are treatment-oriented, are comfortable with a limited social distance between officer and inmate, and support the use of discretion. The Lonely Braves and Supported Majority are considered to possess a professional orientation instead of a custody orientation. Traditional custody-oriented officers have often viewed the officer with a treatment orientation, particularly the female officer, as unqualified, lacking in basic work skills, unable to meet minimum work performance standards, easily manipulated or corrupted by inmates because of a tendency to compromise the rules by exempting certain inmates from restrictions and obligations. There are doubts that this type of officer can be trusted to do the job properly.

Antagonistic relations frequently develop between old and new staff as they attempt to meet conflicting goals in an atmosphere described as reverse racism or sexism, where females and black officers have the inside track on choice work assignments and promotions. The result in many institutions is formation of an alliance between female and minority member officers that is based on a shared perception that white male officers oppose and harass both women and minorities (Zimmer 1986). Conflict between officers of different race, gender, and professional orientation make work solidarity difficult, and division between cliques of staff are frequently found in a prison environment (Owen 1985).

As a consequence of powerlessness, normlessness, and social isolation many officers experience meaninglessness: a perception that officers, abused by inmates, unappreciated by superiors or the public, and unsupported by their colleagues, are fighting a lost cause. The result is self-estrangement: a lack of pride in work performance and little incentive to put self into the job. Alienation is a powerful form of stress that may lead to high rates of divorce and serious health problems such as hypertension, ulcers, and heart disease at higher levels than those found among police officers (Cheek and Miller 1983, 116).

Unfortunately, alienation can create problems above and beyond personal health problems. It can create a subculture of officer violence and lead to a wide range of corrupt activities.

## THE SUBCULTURE OF VIOLENCE

Violence for the sake of violence is prohibited in today's prisons. Officers are repeatedly told during training that force is to be used only for self-defense, the protection of others, or to prevent escape, and only the minimum amount of force necessary is to be used: "Today, violence has become a tool of alienated officers, who feel abandoned or betrayed by the institution and come to feel authorized to make their own rules" (Johnson 1996, 208).

Some alienated officers work alone, but others form small groups called goon squads. These groups operate in accordance with an "us against them" model of conflict that requires physical abuse to be the primary method of inmate control. Violence as a solution to alienation is doomed to failure because it automatically precludes more constructive ways of working with inmates and other officers who are not in favor of the goon squad. Violence, in fact, increases alienation because for the officers employing it there is no connection with a larger environment that deplores the unnecessary use of force.

*Corruption.* Corruption is a broad term. It can include trafficking in contraband, theft (major or minor), warehouse sabotage, sexual relations with inmates, bartering with inmates, assisting in an escape, and theft of weapons, especially firearms (Florida 1981). Officers engage in corrupt activities when they ask for money or sexual favors as an incentive to do their job or to overlook illegal inmate activities such as prostitution and drug trafficking. Officers can also mismanage the finances of a particular area of operation in order to skim off money. Fortunately, the responses to alienation are not always negative and self-destructive.

*The Human Service Worker Response.*   Many correctional officers, if not the vast majority, shun the use of unnecessary violence and avoid the temptation to engage in corrupt activities. Instead, they try to expand their roles and make them more fulfilling.

> These officers discover that in the process of helping inmates and thereby giving them more autonomy, security, and emotional support, they gain the same benefits: more control over their environment, more security in their daily interactions with prisoners, and a sense of community, however inchoate or ill-defined, with at least some of the men under their care. In solving inmate adjustment problems, in other words, staff solve their own problems as well. (Johnson 1996, 242)

Administrators have a moral, ethical, and professional obligation to assist staff in developing effective, constructive methods of coping with alienation. One of the most effective methods is training.

# STAFF TRAINING

Training prior to the 1960s was often limited to issuing a uniform and a "stick."

> "Tread softly and carry a big stick," was my first lesson in penology, on my arrival at Clinton Prison on March 1, 1905. It was to be followed literally. When I reported for duty that night, I was handed a pair of sneakers and a club. The sneakers, to enable the guard to make his rounds noiselessly, so as not to disturb the sleeping forms within the dark cells, and the club to be used in emergencies should any of those forms become unduly active. (Lawes 1932, 12)

Correctional officers today require a far more sophisticated training program that is often divided into two phases: The preservice phase and the on-the-job training phase.

## THE PRESERVICE PHASE

At the academy level, new hires will be exposed to courses organized in four basic categories:

1. Personal: maintaining a professional image, cultural sensitivity, interpersonal communications, stress management, first aid techniques, techniques of observation, and report writing.
2. Organizational: prison subcultures, classification of inmates, legal aspects of corrections, inmate disciplinary procedures, fire prevention, basic security procedures, and emergency preparedness.
3. Special needs inmates: HIV-positive inmates, suicidal inmates, emotionally disturbed inmates, and special management problems.
4. Control and security skills: nonphysical management of aggressive inmates; assertive communication techniques as a control mechanism; count, key, and tool control procedures; the use of force; principles of physical control; basic and advanced defensive tactics; use of the 26″ baton; detection of drug use and trafficking; contraband and chain of evidence procedures; searches of property, physical plant, and body; weaponry (shotgun, revolver, and rifle); use of restraints; and transportation of inmates by car, van, and bus.

A hands-on approach to skills learning is typically employed. Pre-service training hours for correctional officers can be as high as 400 (Alabama) or as low as 120 (Wyoming), with the Federal Bureau of Prisons requiring 160 hours. The average number of hours is 224 (Camp and Camp 1995, 85).

## ON-THE-JOB TRAINING PHASE

Once the trainee has completed the course work at the training academy, skills learning in the work environment may be structured as follows:

1. Assignment to multiple posts (14 weeks) where more seasoned officers can provide support and assistance as the trainee learns the daily routine of the institution.
2. Assignment to a single post (17 weeks) where the trainee works independently.
3. Assignment to restricted posts (13 weeks) such as disciplinary units, transportation vehicles, and community hospital or court assignments.

After the end of the first year of employment, if training evalua-tions have been satisfactory, the trainee becomes a permanent mem-ber of the workforce. But training does not end. On average, correctional officers undergo 43 hours of training every year of their employment (Camp and Camp 1995, 85).

## CONCLUSIONS

The correctional officers in any given correctional institution can no longer be considered a monolithic group. The introduction of rehabilitation as an organizational goal and the shift in officer demographics have created a work environment where the tradi-tional role definition of "hacks," "screws," and "bulls" (traditional derogatory terms for guards indicating limited intelligence) no longer applies to all correctional officers.

Affirmative action has significantly changed both the racial and gender makeup of the modern correctional staff and has created problems of perception, which must be addressed. The task of the correctional officer now is to reconcile the contradictory goals of cus-tody and treatment in an environment that is constantly becoming more complicated and more diverse.

## Vocabulary

alienation
chain of command
coercive power
custody-oriented officer
expert power

legitimate power
referent power
reward power
Title VII of the 1964 Civil Rights Act
    in 1972

## Study Questions

1. What has been the influence of the social science literature and Hollywood on the public perception of the correctional officer?

2. Discuss the term "structured conflict" as it relates to the role of the correctional officer.

3. In what ways does the prison organizational structure treat correctional officers like inmates? How do officers respond to this treatment?

4. What purposes do institutional rules serve? Define and discuss discretion in the correctional officer enforcement of the rules.

5. There are five bases of control. Name and discuss each base. Which base underlies the enforcement of the rules?

6. What is meant by the term custody-oriented officer? How does this officer differ from the professional correctional officer?

7. What effect has the introduction of rehabilitation as an organizational goal had on the role definition of the correctional officer?

8. What role has affirmative action played in the development of the professional officer?

9. What two factors were most responsible for bringing women into the ranks of the correctional officers in men's prisons?

10. What has been the male officer response to female correctional officers? Male inmate response?

11. What are the research findings concerning the difference, if any, between male and female correctional officers?

12. Name and discuss the five types of alienation. How can officers respond to alienation?

## Sources Cited

— Bartollas, Clemens, and John P. Conrad. 1992. *Introduction to Corrections.* New York: Harper Collins.

— Camp, Camille, and George Camp. 1995. *Corrections Yearbook.* South Salem, N.Y.: Criminal Justice Institute.

— Chapman, Jane R., E. K. Minor, P. Rieker, T. L. Mills, and M. Bottum. 1983. *Women Employed in Corrections.* Washington, D.C.: GPO.

— Cheek, F. E., and M. D. S. Miller. 1983. "The Experience of Stress for Correction Officers: A Double-Bind Theory of Correctional Stress." *Journal of Criminal Justice* 11: 105-120.

— Cressey, Donald R. 1959. "Contradictory Directives in Complex Organizations." *Administrative Science Quarterly* 4: 1-19.

— Cressey, Donald R. 1965. "Prison Organization." In *Handbook of Organizations,* ed. J. March, 1023-1070. Chicago: Rand McNally.

— Crouch, Ben M. 1980. "The Book vs. the Boot: Two Styles of Guarding in a Southern Prison." In *The Keepers,* ed. Ben Crouch, 207-224. Springfield, Ill.: Charles C. Thomas.

— Duffee, David E. 1974. "The Correctional Officer Subculture and Organizational Change." *Journal of Research in Crime and Delinquency* 11: 155-172.

— Farmer, Richard E. 1977. "Cynicism: A Factor in Corrections Work." *Journal of Criminal Justice* 5: 237-246.

— Florida Department of Corrections. 1981. Response to the Findings and Recommendations of the Ad Hoc Subcommittee of the House Committee on Corrections, Probation and Parole.

— Fox, James G. 1982. *Organizational and Racial Conflict in Maximum Security Prisons.* Boston: D. C. Heath.

— Freeman, Robert M. 1994. "Correctional Officer Attitudes Toward Inmates and Discretionary Rule Enforcement: A Study of Professional Orientation." Unpublished dissertation.

— Freeman, Robert M. 1995a. "The Unmet Challenge of Media Coverage of Corrections: Six Years Later No News Is Still Good News." Paper presented at the annual meeting of the Pennsylvania Association of Criminal Justice Educators in Harrisburg, Pa.

— Freeman, Robert M. 1995b. Personal observation.

— Fry, Lincoln J., and Daniel Glaser. 1987. "Gender Differences in Work Adjustment of Prison Employees." *Journal of Offender Counseling, Services and Rehabilitation* 12: 39-52.

— Hawkins, Richard, and Geoffrey P. Alpert. 1989. *American Prison Systems: Punishment and Justice.* Englewood Cliffs, N.J.: Prentice-Hall.

— Held, Barbara S., David Levine, and Virginia Swartz. 1979. "Interpersonal Aspects of Dangerousness." *Criminal Justice and Behavior* 6, 1: 49-58.

— Hepburn, John R. 1985. "The Exercise of Power in Coercive Organizations: A Study of Prison Guards." *Criminology* 23(1): 146-164.

— Hepburn, John R., and C. Albonetti. 1980. "Role Conflict in Correctional Institutions: An Empirical Examination of the Treatment-Custody Dilemma among Correctional Staff." *Criminology* 17(4): 445-459.

— Hewitt, John D., Eric D. Poole, and Robert M. Regoli. 1984. "Self-Reported and Observed Rule-Breaking in Prison: A Look at Disciplinary Response." *Justice Quarterly* 3: 437-448.

— Irwin, John. 1977. "The Changing Social Structure of the Men's Correctional Prison." In *Corrections and Punishment,* ed. D. Greenberg, 21-40. Beverly Hills, Cal.: Sage.

— Jacobs, James B., and Lawrence Kraft. 1978. "Integrating the Keepers: A Comparison of Black and White Prison Guards in Illinois." *Social Problems* 25: 304-318.

— Jacobs, James B., and Harold G. Retsky. 1975. "Prison Guard." *Urban Life* 4 (April): 5-29.

— Johnson, Robert. 1987. *Hard Time: Understanding and Reforming the Prison.* Belmont, Cal.: Wadsworth.

— Johnson, Robert. 1996. *Hard Time: Understanding and Reforming the Prison.* Belmont, Cal.: Wadsworth.

— Joint Commission on Correctional Manpower and Training, Corrections. 1968. *A Climate for Change.* Washington, D.C.: GPO.

— Jurik, Nancy C. 1985. "Individual and Organizational Determinants of Correctional Officer Attitudes Toward Inmates." *Criminology* 23(3): 523-539.

— Jurik, Nancy C., and Gregory J. Halemba. 1984. "Gender, Working Conditions and the Job Satisfaction of Women in a Non-Traditional Occupation: Female Correctional Officers in Men's Prisons." *The Sociological Quarterly* 25: 551-566.

— Klofas, John, and Hans Toch. 1982. "The Guard Subculture Myth." *Journal of Research in Crime and Delinquency* 19(2): 238-254.

— Lawes, L. L. 1932. *Twenty Thousand Years in Sing Sing.* New York: Ray Long and Richard R. Smith Publishers.

— Lombardo, Lucien X. 1981. *Guards Imprisoned.* New York: Elsevier.

— Owen, Barbara. 1985. "Race and Gender Relations Among Prison Workers." *Crime and Delinquency* 31 (January): 147-159.

— Petersen, Cheryl Bowser. 1982. "Doing Time with the Boys: An Analysis of Women Correctional Officers in All-Male Facilities." In *The Criminal Justice System and Women,* ed. Barbara R. Price and Natalie J. Sokoloff, 437-460. New York: Clark Boardman.

— Philliber, Susan. 1987. "Thy Brother's Keeper: A Review of the Literature on Correctional Officers." *Justice Quarterly* 4(1): 9-33.

— Pollock, Joycelyn. 1986. *Sex and Supervision: Guarding Male and Female Inmates.* New York: Greenwood.

— Pollock, Joycelyn M. 1995. "Women in Corrections: Custody and the 'Caring Ethic.'" In *Women, Law, and Social Control,* ed. Alida V. Merlo and Joycelyn M. Pollock, 97-116. Needham Heights, Mass.: Allyn and Bacon.

— Poole, Eric D., and Robert M. Regoli. 1981. "Alienation in Prison: An Examination of the Work Relations of Prison Guards." *Criminology* 19(2): 251-270.

— Potts, Lee W. 1983. "Employment Opportunity Issues." *Federal Probation* 47: 37-44.

— President's Commission on Law Enforcement and Administration of Justice. 1967. *Task Force Report: Corrections.* Washington, D.C.: GPO.

— Schroeder, A. 1976. *Shaking It Rough.* New York: Doubleday.

— Shawver, Louis, and R. Dickover. 1986. "Research Perspectives: Exploding a Myth." *Corrections Today* 48(5): 30-34.

— Simon, Rita J., and Judith D. Simon. 1988. "Female C.O.A.: Legitimate Authority." *Corrections Today* 50(5): 132-134.

— Stephen, James. 1989. *Prison Rule Violators.* Washington, D.C.: GPO.

— Stinchcomb, Jeanne B. 1986. "Correctional Officer Stress: Looking at the Causes, You May Be the Cure." A paper presented at the annual meeting of the Academy of Criminal Justice Sciences in Orlando, Florida.

— Toch, Hans. 1978. "Is a 'Correctional Officer,' By Any Other Name, a 'Screw?' " *Criminal Justice Review* 3(2): 19-35.

— Toch, Hans. 1981. Foreword in Lucien X. Lombardo's *Guards Imprisoned.* New York: Elsevier.

— U.S. Department of Justice. 1992. *SourceBook of Criminal Justice Statistics.* Washington, D.C.: GPO.

— Zimmer, Lynn E. 1986. *Women Guarding Men.* Chicago: University of Chicago Press.

— Zupan, Linda. 1992. "The Progress of Women Correctional Officers in All-Male Prisons." In *The Changing Roles of Women in the Criminal Justice System,* 2d ed., ed. Imogene L. Moyer, 323-343. Prospect Heights, Ill.: Waveland.

# 10

# PRISONERS' RIGHTS:
# THE PENDULUM SWINGS

## *John McLaren*

[T]he obligation ... to eliminate existing unconstitutionalities does not depend upon what the Legislature may do, or upon what the Governor may do. . . . If Arkansas is going to operate a Penitentiary System, it is going to have to be a system that is countenanced by the Constitution of the United States.

— *Holt v. Sarver,* 309 F. Supp. 362
(E.D. Ark. 1970)

*Chapter Overview*

The cyclical nature of successful litigation on behalf of prisoners is consistent with the waxing and waning of general support for liberal social reform. The prisoners' rights movement swept into popular consciousness on the coattails of the broader reforms of the civil rights movement. As public support for democratization of education, the workplace, and other institutions has receded, so too have the successes of litigation as a tool for reform of prison conditions. The prison reform movement is of great symbolic significance in defining the rights of all persons in our society, and it has served as a vehicle for public debate regarding those elusive standards.

There now exists a significant body of legal precedent defining the basic premises of institutional confinement. This body of knowledge, to be summarized in this chapter, defines the minimum acceptable framework of constitutional rights to which persons imprisoned

---

**HIGHLIGHT 10-1**
**Legal Terms**

**Cause of action.** Facts sufficient to support a valid lawsuit or the legal theory on which a lawsuit is based.

**Damages.** Money that a court orders paid to a person who has suffered a loss or injury by the person whose fault caused the injury or loss. Damages may be actual or punitive.

**Habeas corpus.** Latin for "you have the body." A judicial order to someone holding a person to bring that person to court. It is used to force a captor to bring the person being held to court for a decision on the legality of the confinement.

**Holding.** The court's opinion, which includes the specific answer to the legal issue as well as "dictum" — the rationale the court gives for its decision.

**Injunction.** A judge's order to a person to do or to refrain from doing a particular thing.

**Litigation.** A lawsuit or series of lawsuits.

**Penumbral right.** A right not specifically mentioned or guaranteed in the Constitution but implied from other guarantees.

**Per curiam.** Latin for "by the Court," meaning an opinion backed by all judges in a particular court, usually with no one judge's name as author.

in the United States are entitled. Excluded from the scope of this chapter are issues of fairness in sentencing and litigation concerning the rights of those persons under other forms of correctional supervision. The rights of parolees, probationers, those released on bail, and other persons under some form of reduced liberty will be addressed only tangentially.

## ERA OF HANDS OFF DOCTRINE

Prior to the civil rights movement of the 1960s, prisons held little interest for the courts, press, or general public. Federal courts had assumed a comfortable and convenient posture with regard to the occasional grievances prisoners brought to their attention. Although *Ruffin v. Commonwealth,* 62 Va. 790 (1871), was a case decided in state court, its holding that a prisoner had the status of a "slave of the state" with no rights was embraced by both state and federal courts well into the twentieth century. *Ruffin* offered the judiciary a convenient doctrine to justify dismissal of any claim of unlawful treatment by prisoners.

The *Ruffin* doctrine later gave way to a more liberal rule that recognized that "a prisoner retains all the rights of an ordinary citizen except those expressly, or by necessary implication, are taken from him by law." *Coffin v. Reichard,* 143 F.2d 443 (6th Cir. 1944). Although this appears to be a departure from the uncompromising perspective of the *Ruffin* case, it initially had little impact on the rights of prisoners. The *retention of rights theory* was initially applied in such a narrow manner that its advantage to prisoners challenging conditions of confinement was illusory. For in almost every case of prisoners who alleged a grievance related to the conditions of confinement, the holding was that "lawful incarceration brings about necessary withdrawal or limitation of many privileges and rights, a retraction justified by the considerations underlying our penal system." *Price v. Johnston,* 68 S. Ct. 1049 (1948). Only in circumstances where serious bodily harm or death was deliberately inflicted on an inmate by prison authorities were courts, state or federal, prepared to entertain the lawsuits of inmates. The reluctance of courts to hear the merits of cases filed by or on behalf of prisoners was not necessarily due to indifference to the conditions and dilemmas of incarceration. The *hands off doctrine* was supported by several different rationales:

1. Deferral to the expertise of administrators: the view that correctional administration is a technical matter best left to the discretion of experts rather than courts.
2. Prisoner grievances were categorized as privileges rather than rights. Naturally, prisoners were deemed to have forfeited privileges by virtue of conviction.
3. The conditions of confinement experienced by prisoners were viewed as matters properly left to the legislative and executive branches of government, which are equipped with superior resources for fact finding, budgeting, and policy.
4. Even slight erosion of the hands off doctrine would invite a tidal wave of litigation that could overwhelm the resources of the judicial branch and drain the energy of states and governmental agencies brought into court to defend their policies and practices (National Advisory Commission 1973, 18).

As the 1960s drew to a close, great turmoil possessed the nation and its court systems. The hands off doctrine appeared to erode rapidly in the face of an avalanche of legal arguments for its abandonment. Federal courts, increasingly activist, became a welcome harbor for the politically disenfranchised. Not surprisingly, prisoners (a bitterly alienated and ever volatile category of citizen) joined other dissident groups in using federal legal remedies, specifically the civil rights statutes.

## MECHANICS OF LITIGATION

Most litigation addressing conditions of confinement or treatment is brought under the federal Civil Rights Act (42 U.S.C.A. §1983) in federal court. *Section 1983 actions* allow an individual to sue a public official for alleged violations of civil rights. They are attractive to prisoner litigants for a number of reasons: the act embraces a wide variety of official misconduct regarding prison conditions and procedures; it offers comprehensive remedies including money damages, injunctive relief, and attorney's fees; and it is a relatively easy cause of action to file. State laws generally do not provide workable and adequate remedies, and history has demonstrated the futility of pursuing civil rights litigation on behalf of convicted persons in state courts (Jacobs 1980, 434). Prisoners' rights claims, while perhaps not receiving a friendly reception in any forum, found a more receptive atmosphere in federal courts, a fact attributable in no small part to the insulation from political retaliation enjoyed by the federal judiciary. The lack of litigation in state courts may change in the future as some progressive jurisdictions adopt statutes that approach the functional equivalent of the federal Section 1983 statute. The increasingly conservative nature of the federal judiciary may also divert some cases into state forums.

## SECTION 1983

The single most important development in the abandonment of the hands off doctrine was the Supreme Court decision in *Monroe v. Pape*, 81 S. Ct. 473 (1961). That case did not deal with the rights of prisoners but rather arose from a claim filed after 13 Chicago police officers allegedly entered the plaintiffs' home and conducted a warrantless search and arrest. The case imposed a revolutionary interpretation of a federal law enacted originally to discourage lawless activities by state officials in the aftermath of the Civil War. The statute states:

> Every person who, under color of any statute, ordinance, regulation, custom, or usage, of any State or Territory or the District of Columbia, subjects or causes to be subjected, any citizen of the United States or other person within the jurisdiction thereof to the deprivation of any rights, privileges, or immunities secured by the Constitution and laws, shall be liable to the party injured in an action at law, suit in equity, or other proper proceeding for redress. (42 U.S.C.A. §1983)

The central issue in the case was the requirement that a person, to be liable, act "under color of" state law. The Supreme Court, in an opinion by Justice Douglas, held that for activities to have taken place under color of state law it was not necessary that the activities be authorized by state law. The statute was intended to protect against "misuse of power, possessed by virtue of state law and made possible only because the wrongdoer is clothed with the authority of state law." 81 S. Ct. at 482. In 1964, the U.S. Supreme Court held that state inmates could file suit against their keepers under Section 1983. *Cooper v. Pate*, 378 U.S. 546 (1964).

States themselves remain immune from liability under the Civil Rights Act, although since 1978 the states' political subdivisions can be successfully sued. In most cases, the named defendants remain individual employees who allegedly harm the claimed right of a person in custody. See generally *Monell v. Department of Social Services of the City of New York,* 98 S. Ct. 2018 (1978).

To be held liable under Section 1983, a defendant must be acting under color of state law as that phrase has been interpreted by the courts. Often private parties who contract with state agencies to provide medical, psychological, or other services will be deemed to be acting under state authority. See *West v. Atkins,* 108 S. Ct. 2250 (1988). In these civil rights cases, there is no basis for any disability other than personal. Master-servant or employer-employee theories are not applicable.

The state of mind of the party allegedly inflicting the injury is extremely relevant to the disposition of these lawsuits; mere negligence, a state of mind usually adequate to impose liability in traditional personal injury lawsuits, is clearly not an adequate foundation in civil rights cases. *Estelle v. Gamble,* 97 S. Ct. 285 (1976). Later cases have emphasized that a standard of *deliberate indifference,* comparable to gross negligence or recklessness, to the inmate's risk of injury is necessary to establish a valid claim. This is consistent with the theory that the statute was intended to protect persons from deprivations associated with an abuse of official power or authority. Thus, its protections are not triggered by the failure to give due care that an ordinary prudent person would provide.

In theory, a state inmate could file a civil rights lawsuit in either a state or federal court. The lack of filings in state courts is well documented and is attributable to several factors. State court judges do not enjoy the insulation from politically explosive rulings that federal judges do, and state court juries, especially those located in counties in which there are significant inmate populations, are believed to be unfriendly to the claims of the prison population. The lack of state court claims is further attributable to the fact that prisoners are not generally required to exhaust available state administrative or judicial remedies before filing a civil rights cause of action. *Morgan v. La-Vallee,* 526 F.2d 221 (2d Cir. 1975).

The doctrine of *sovereign immunity* is a significant shield from liability in suits claiming deprivation of civil rights. Judges, legislators, prosecutors, and parole board members still have almost complete immunity from liability. Members of the executive branch involved in activities such as planning and budgeting are also cloaked with a presumption of immunity. Other officials of state and local governments enjoy "qualified immunity," that is, immunity from liability for actions undertaken in "good faith" with no desire to maliciously deprive an individual of constitutional rights (*Scheuer v. Rhodes,* 94 S. Ct. 1683 (1974)).

A prisoner who is successful in establishing a claim under the Civil Rights Act may qualify for a variety of remedies including monetary damages, injunctive relief, attorney's fees, and relief in the form of a judgment defining the legal rights and responsibilities of the parties to the litigation, known as a declaratory judgment. Three distinct types of monetary damages may be awarded a successful plaintiff: (1) actual damages to compensate for expenses incurred and mental suffering, (2) nominal damages to vindicate the plaintiff's rights even where no actual damages were sustained, and (3) punitive damages if the wrongful acts were done maliciously, intentionally, or with "evil motive or intent." *Smith v. Wade,* 103 S. Ct. 1625 (1983).

*Injunctive relief,* also referred to as equitable relief, is expressed in a judicial order that a person refrain from doing a particular act or that a person perform a particular act. Injunctive relief is a very common and useful remedy in prison litigation because it protects the complaining prisoner and others from continued future deprivations of the rights specifically addressed in the court order. Failure to comply with ordered injunctive relief, which may order sweeping changes in institutional conditions and in extreme cases include mandated closure of severely defective institutions, cannot be justified by the often heard complaint that funds to make required changes are unavailable. *Smith v. Sullivan,* 553 F.2d 373 (5th Cir. 1977).

A failure to comply with an order imposing injunctive relief is punishable under the judicial power of contempt, which may include the imposition of both fines and confinement. A very significant item of money damages that may be imposed on prison official defendants is the cost of the prevailing parties' attorney's fees. Attorney's fees have historically been an element of punitive damages, available only when a party acted in willful disobedience of a valid court order or acted in bad faith. It is a remedy designed to punish those who deliberately impair the functioning of the judicial system. The U.S. Congress, however, has adopted a statute that grants attorney's fees to the prevailing party in various civil rights actions. Civil Rights Attorney's Fees Award Act of 1976, 42 U.S.C.A. §1988. The amount of other damages assessed is only one of several factors in the assessment of attorney's fees, and, in some cases, the award of attorney's fees may exceed other damages. This resulted when Congress found that the private market for legal services failed to provide many victims of civil rights abuse meaningful access to the court system.

## OTHER AVENUES OF ACCESS

One other significant legal tool often employed by persons held in custody or restrained in the exercise of guaranteed liberties is the writ of *habeas corpus*. Since 1944 it has been available to contest not only the legality of confinement itself but also the conditions of confinement. *Coffin v. Reichard*, 143 F.2d 443 (6th Cir. 1944). In fact "the great writ" may be used to challenge the constitutionality of conditions of probation or parole that infringe unnecessarily on protected liberties. In essence, the writ, once properly filed, requires any governmental official holding another person in custody to come forward and show why the person should not be released. In contemporary times this application of the writ has been expanded to include conditions of confinement. Unlike its counterpart found in Section 1983, however, there is a requirement that the prisoner first exhaust available state remedies before eligibility for federal habeas corpus consideration. Exhaustion of state administrative and judicial remedies is not required if the applicant can prove that resort to them would be futile and serve only to prolong the litigation. *Patton v. North Carolina*, 381 F.2d 636 (4th Cir. 1967), *cert. denied*, 390 U.S. 905 (1968). Thus, if there exists an earlier adverse decision at the state level on the identical federal question an inmate seeks to assert, the exhaustion requirement could be waived. The remedies described above are the essential tools most often employed in litigation intended to improve the conditions of confinement experienced by prisoners.

In addition to these civil, or personal, remedies, there are also criminal prosecution alternatives available in both state and federal jurisdictions. Criminal prosecution to enforce the constitutional rights of prisoners is rarely employed. Prosecutorial discretion, the lack of a financial incentive to complain, the credibility of the complainants, jury skepticism regarding the victims, and the paramount requirement that willfulness or intent be proved to gain a conviction are all factors contributing to this fact. State remedies to redress the grievances do exist, and they often appear to parallel federal civil and criminal remedies. Prisoners and their advocates have not elected to use them to any great degree, and the body of law defining the legal status of prisoners has been shaped almost exclusively by the federal civil rights acts, especially the ubiquitous Section 1983, and the federal habeas corpus mechanism.

# CORPORAL PUNISHMENT AND THE USE OF FORCE

Revelations of brutal and inhumane treatment of prisoners served as a catalyst for judicial reform of the institution. It is well documented that physical force has been utilized for legitimate and illegitimate purposes in the past (Clemmer 1958). Legitimate uses of force include self-defense, defense of third parties, enforcement of prison rules and regulations, prevention of escape, and prevention of crime. Illegitimate use of force has come to be understood in the Anglo-American legal system as the implementation of force, beatings, and whippings as retaliation or punishment for inmate misconduct or the use of excessive and unnecessary force in the course of legitimate application of force.

The means of inflicting *corporal punishment* are limited only by the human imagination and have included beatings, use of water torture, electrical shock, suspension from cell bars by handcuffing, and excessive use of punitive isolation.

Corporal punishment was long a feature of some American penal institutions, as observed in the following case in which the court approved the use of force for discipline:

> From time immemorial prison officials were vested with the power and authority of imposing corporal punishment upon prisoners as a part of the discipline and restraint. . . . For centuries whipping or corporal punishment has been a recognized method of discipline of convicts. (*United States v. Jones,* 108 F. Supp. 266, 270 (S.D. Fla. 1952))

Not until 1968, in *Jackson v. Bishop,* 404 F.2d 571 (8th Cir. 1968), did a court specifically hold that whipping a prisoner (a leather strap was used) as a technique of discipline violated the Eighth Amendment prohibition of cruel and unusual punishment. Only three years earlier a federal district court in the same judicial circuit had approved the use of that punishment with the provision that its use be "carefully controlled." *Talley v. Stephens,* 247 F. Supp. 683 (E.D. Ark. 1965). Numerous cases subsequent to *Jackson* have addressed this issue, and there is unanimity in support of it. The American Correctional Association and other professional organizations, such as the American Bar Association, support the prohibition. The American Correctional Association's *Manual of Correctional Standards* states unequivocally that "corporal punishment should never be used under any circumstances" and further elaborates the rationale for such a prohibition.

> Punishments out of all proportion to the offense, employing inhumane and archaic methods and dictated by brutality coupled with ignorance, incompetence, fear, and weakness, are demoralizing to both inmates and staff. Staff punishment substantially increases the chances that the inmates will continue to be disciplinary problems in the institution and will return to crime after release. (American Correctional Association 1966, 417)

Despite the apparent clarity of the prohibition, there are some correctional practices that raise intriguing related issues. These include the use of tranquilizing drugs for punishment purposes, verbal abuse and insults, reckless failure to protect inmates from assaultive conduct by other inmates, and *totality of circumstance* cases in which the cumulative effect of numerous shocking and degrading practices result in findings that the conditions of confinement as a whole constitute cruel and unusual punishment.

The landmark case that determined that a prison system as a whole could be administered in a manner violative of the Eighth Amendment standard was *Holt v. Sarver*, 309 F. Supp. 362 (E.D. Ark. 1970), *aff'd* 442 F.2d 304 (8th Cir. 1971). Among a shocking list of constitutional violations enumerated in *Holt* were the following:

1. a virtual absence of professional staff to supervise the inmate population;
2. a prison system administered primarily by inmate trusties;
3. an atmosphere of hatred and mistrust maintained by brutal use of physical force;
4. an open barracks system that invited physical assault;
5. unsanitary isolation cells;
6. a complete absence of rehabilitation or training programs;
7. inadequate diet and medical care; and
8. access to prison records, prescription drugs, contraband alcohol and drugs, weapons, and vehicles by some inmate trusties.

These factual findings were accompanied by remedial orders, grounded in the belief that the legislative and executive branches of the state would rush to remedy the situation. Sadly, these orders were so ineffective that in subsequent years, as the litigation progressed, reviewing courts concluded that the conditions described by the trial court actually deteriorated. *Finney v. Arkansas Board of Correction,* 410 F. Supp. 251 (E.D. Ark. 1976). Although *Holt* maintains a singular distinction as the nadir of prison conditions within the United States, Arkansas was not that unique. The cumulative substandard conditions of prisons and jails in many states were determined to be cruel and unusual punishment.

In some cases the conditions of confinement experienced by prisoners have provided them with a viable defense to the felony of escape from prison. A criminal defendant charged with escape who claims the defense of duress or necessity must offer bona fide evidence that conditions within the institution constituted an immediate threat of death or serious bodily injury, that the escape was accomplished without threat of force or injury to third parties, and that an effort to surrender to law enforcement authorities was made as soon as "the claimed duress or necessity had lost its coercive force." *United States v. Bailey,* 100 S. Ct. 624, 638 (1980). The recognition of this defense in both state and federal jurisdictions is an implicit acknowledgment that intolerable conditions may exist within penal institutions (Gardner and Anderson 1992).

There is consensus that the Eighth Amendment protects inmates from assault not only by correctional officials but also at the hands of other inmates. Perhaps in part because it is a commonplace occurrence within penal institutions, courts have been reluctant to impose liability on prison officials for the failure to protect inmates from physical and sexual assaults by other inmates. The protective umbrella of conditional "good faith" sovereign immunity has been widespread in these cases. As noted in *Penn v. Oliver,* 351 F. Supp. 1292, 1297 (E.D. Va. 1972):

> It would be fantasy to believe that even the most enlightened prison officials operating with unlimited resources could prevent all acts of violence within the prison. Moreover, even if a prison official fails through his negligence to prevent an act of violence, a violation of constitutional right is not of necessity stated. To the contrary, there must be a showing either of a pattern of undisputed and unchecked violence or, on a different level, of an egregious failure to provide security to a particular inmate, before a deprivation of constitutional right is stated.

State officials' deliberate indifference to a known and substantial risk of violent harm must be demonstrated by the inmate in these cases. However, failure of prison officials to establish procedures to determine compatibility of cellmates was found to constitute deliberate indifference when members of competing criminal gangs were housed together and injury resulted (*Walsh v. Mellas*, 837 F.2d 789 (7th Cir. 1988)).

The failure of jail officials to conduct rudimentary screening to determine the suicidal tendencies of recently arrested individuals is a related area in which there has been much recent wrongful death litigation, some of it successful. A significant explanation of the reasonable expectation of safety and security to which a prisoner is entitled under the Eighth Amendment standard is found in *Whitley v. Albers*, 106 S. Ct. 1078 (1986). The prisoner in that case had been severely injured by a close-range shotgun blast during efforts to quell a disturbance. His position was that the gunshot wound that resulted in a permanent disability constituted cruel and unusual punishment because it was not a justified use of force under the circumstances in which it occurred. The Supreme Court found no Eighth Amendment violation because the Eighth Amendment prohibits only the "unnecessary and wanton infliction of pain" in a prison setting. The application of extreme, even unnecessary, force to restore discipline and order violates the constitutional standard only if "applied maliciously and sadistically for the very purpose of causing harm." *Whitley v. Albers*, 106 S. Ct. 1078, 1084 (1986). Thus it appears that only the *deliberate* application of excessive force for the purpose of maliciously or sadistically causing harm will trigger a remedy under the Civil Rights Act in the context of disturbance of prison order and security.

Some cases have raised interesting issues about the constitutionality of more "advanced" and contemporary applications of force, sometimes clothed as therapy. In *Knecht v. Gillman*, 48 F.2d 1136 (8th Cir. 1973), which was discussed in Chapter 6, the complaint stated that prisoners had been subjected to injections of the drug apomorphine without their consent in an Iowa facility. The evidence demonstrated that the injections were administered as "aversive stimuli." The injections, which were characterized by the state as "therapy" based on "Pavlovian conditioning" techniques, induced vomiting that lasted from fifteen minutes to an hour and changes in blood pressure and heart function. The simple question confronted by the court was whether this process, deliberately administered, constituted an acceptable therapeutic treatment or a cruel and unusual punishment. The practice was enjoined by the court as violative of the Eighth Amendment prohibition, clearly analogous to the infliction of an uncontrolled physical beating. Only with elaborate protection to insure the voluntary consent of the participants could such novel therapy be lawfully employed in the future. The use of involuntarily administered drugs to control prisoner conduct is an intriguing issue for future study and, undoubtedly, for future litigation.

The application of psychotropic, or tranquilizing, medication over the objection of a prisoner, not for punishment but rather to protect the prisoner or others, was challenged in *Sconiers v. Jarvis,* 458 F. Supp. 37 (D. Kan. 1978); *Gilliam v. Martin,* 589 F. Supp. 680 (W.D. Okla. 1984); and *United States v. Bryant,* 670 F. Supp. 840 (D. Minn. 1987). The use of physical force as a method of institutional control and discipline has largely been abandoned in the contemporary American penal institution. Remnants of the use of corporal punishment remain, but only as unsanctioned, informal power by some correctional officers.

## ACCESS TO THE LEGAL SYSTEM

The right of access to the courts is not specifically guaranteed in the federal constitution. The U.S. Supreme Court and the courts below it have nonetheless repeatedly affirmed that it is a fundamental right implied in the *due process clauses* of both the Fifth and Fourteenth Amendments. Prisoners' rights to access were first acknowledged by the Supreme Court in 1941 in *Ex parte Hull,* 61 S. Ct. 640 (1941). State prison regulations that required that all legal documents a prisoner might attempt to file with a court be first submitted to prison officials for examination and censorship were challenged successfully.

Despite the *Hull* case, oppression and interference with the fundamental right of judicial access, consistent with the belief that an "iron curtain" was drawn between convicted offenders and the free world, persisted for decades. The right of access to the courts is problematic because of the peripheral issues related to meaningful exercise of that right. Those issues include the control of prisoners with superior education and legal skills who might exploit their less capable peers, the provision of legal research materials and orderly access to them, correspondence between prisoners and their attorneys and courts, and the provision of equitable legal assistance to a population largely deprived of the advantages of advanced education and sophisticated literacy.

Despite prevailing in a series of legal challenges to official obstruction of prisoners' right of access to the courts, the need for legal services for prisoners in America is largely unmet. Prisoners are often immersed in a variety of legal problems independent of the matter of their criminal conviction. These include domestic relations disputes such as child custody, divorce, and child support actions, disputes over distribution of governmental benefits, and consumer matters.

## JAILHOUSE LAWYERS AND LAW LIBRARIES

The barriers between confined prisoners and the courts have gradually eroded. In 1969, in *Johnson v. Avery*, 89 S. Ct. 747 (1969), the Court declared unconstitutional a Tennessee regulation prohibiting *jailhouse lawyers* (inmates who use their legal knowledge for other inmates) from assisting other inmates in the preparation of habeas corpus petitions (absent any other form of legal assistance offered). Soon thereafter, in the 1974 opinion in *Procunier v. Martinez*, 94 S. Ct. 1800 (1974), the Court invalidated a California regulation that prohibited law students from entering prison to assist in case interviews and investigations. In reaching its decision the Court noted that most prisons are located away from major population centers, handicapping the ability of lawyers to perform those tasks. Similar rules that inhibit attorney-client relationships by excessively restricting personal visits or telephone contact between prisoners and attorneys or their staff members have met a similar fate. Given the significance of the right and the fact that such prison regulations in effect curtailed the jurisdiction of the courts themselves, it is not surprising that the burden is on prison officials to demonstrate that indigent prisoners are given adequate means of obtaining the legal help needed to obtain judicial consideration of alleged grievances cognizable by the courts. *Bounds v. Smith*, 97 S. Ct. 1491 (1977), reinforced the trend by establishing that the Constitution requires that prisoners have access either to adequate law libraries or to legal services to aid them in cases involving their convictions, prison conditions, or other prison problems. Subsequently, in *Smith v. Bounds*, 813 F.2d 1299 (4th Cir. 1987), the federal appellate court required that a prison plan that elects a law library in lieu of the direct provision of legal services must include free photocopy privileges, inmates trained as paralegals, and access to the resource for all inmates.

While affirming the right of representation and self-representation by incarcerated offenders, the Supreme Court was also rendering decisions that some might view as inconsistent. In *Ross v. Moffitt*, 94 S. Ct. 1404 (1974), the Court found that the Fourteenth Amendment due process concept does not entitle indigent appellants to the right of appointed counsel on all appeals of their conviction. In most cases, the right of appeal is restricted to trial and one appellate review. The availability of federal *habeas corpus petition* relief, based in claims of Fourth Amendment violations (unlawful arrest or search claims), was sharply curtailed in *Stone v. Powell,* 96 S. Ct. 3037 (1976). This case denied prisoners the right to seek review in federal court of state court Fourth Amendment decisions in all but a few cases. *Stone* reversed the direction of previous decisions increasing the availability of federal postconviction review of state and federal convictions and may have been an early managerial reaction to the enormous proliferation of criminal appeals in the federal courts.

## LEGAL CORRESPONDENCE

The freedom of correspondence between attorney and client was addressed in *Wolff v. McDonnell,* 94 S. Ct. 2963 (1974), invalidating a Nebraska prison regulation authorizing the inspection of all incoming and outgoing inmate-attorney mail. Finding that inspection for purposes of intercepting contraband is distinguishable from censorship, the Court substituted a practice allowing the opening of letters from attorneys in the presence of the prisoners. Similar results have been reached in cases involving correspondence with other governmental officials in the executive and legislative branches. More recent cases have suggested that the right of the inmate to be present may be overcome by a showing of probable cause or reasonable suspicion that incoming attorney mail contains impermissible material. *Proudfoot v. Williams,* 803 F. Supp. 1048 (E.D. Pa. 1992).

# FIRST AMENDMENT RIGHTS

The following issues have been commonly recognized as engaging the First Amendment: (1) access to prisons and prisoners by the press, and (2) freedom of speech and communication. Freedom of association and visitation and freedom of religion will be addressed separately.

## ACCESS OF PRESS

During the Vietnam War era, federal courts were confronted with a series of challenges to prison rules that barred or curtailed access to the press. Prisons were confronted with mounting pressure for access

by investigative journalists, eager to examine the conditions of confinement supported by tax dollars. The courts were called on to resolve the tension between the press demands, the role of the press
in providing information in a democratic society, and the need for
institutional security. Some inmates, such as draft resisters, were being characterized as political martyrs rather than conventional offenders. Other charismatic inmates, such as George Jackson, a black
militant, and Charles Manson, a notorious murderer, openly courted
and encouraged a high degree of media attention and celebrity.

The Federal Bureau of Prison's regulations, which completely
denied press interviews with individual inmates, withstood a First
Amendment violation challenge in federal appellate court in *Seattle-
Tacoma Newspaper Guild v. Parker,* 480 F.2d 1062 (9th Cir. 1973). The
Supreme Court later used this decision in reaching a similar conclusion regarding state regulations. The Ninth Circuit recognized the
existence of viable alternative means of communication that would
insure that legitimate inmate grievances would not be concealed.
The Court noted that the regulation in question would not interfere
with the inmate's right to visit with relatives and friends, counsel with
clergy, confer with legal counsel, enjoy access to the courts, and engage in correspondence. The Court also noted that free access by
the press to individual inmates could contribute to the evolution of
celebrity status and undermine constructive rehabilitation. Given the
existence of viable press alternatives to personal interviews, the Court
concluded that any burden on the media and the First Amendment
in the challenged policy was justified.

The policy and rationale of *Seattle-Tacoma* were adopted by the
Supreme Court in the companion cases *Pell v. Procunier,* 94 S. Ct.
2800 (1974), and *Saxbe v. Washington Post,* 94 S. Ct. 2811 (1974). The
Court majority held that there was a valid general rule that the press
enjoy no *greater* right of access than the general public. The exceptions to the general rule were limited to the attorney, clergy, relatives,
or friends of the inmate. The authority to grant media interviews with
members of the press was properly vested in the discretionary authority of the prison administration. The principle of these cases was extended to embrace the electronic media and detainees awaiting trial
in *Houchins v. KQED,* 98 S. Ct. 2588 (1978). In that case, the Supreme
Court majority deferred to legislative prerogative and declared that
the degree of openness of a penal institution is properly a matter of
legislative policy that a legislature, not a court, should resolve. The
news media has no right of access to prisons or jails superior to that
of other members of the general population.

## CORRESPONDENCE AND CENSORSHIP

First Amendment protections regarding unrestricted use of the mails historically were not applied to prisoners. That approach began to erode in *Palmigiano v. Travisono,* 317 F. Supp. 776 (D.R.I. 1970), which held that prison officials must employ the "*least restrictive means*" available to deal with the problem. The court held that outgoing mail should not be read or otherwise interfered with absent a search warrant. Incoming mail, unless it was from a public official or attorney, was subject to inspection for contraband. Further, incoming mail that came from sources other than an approved addressee list could be inspected not only for contraband but also reviewed and censored for pornography or highly inflammatory writings. As in other First Amendment cases, the federal courts have struggled with a general standard or test to be applied in First Amendment communication cases. The rehabilitative objectives of incarceration may be undermined by the content of writings. The need to censor may also be linked to the prior criminal conduct of the individual inmate, and the problem is complicated by the fact that restrictions on inmate receipt of ideas also interferes with the freedom of communication rights of the individual writing to the inmate.

Institutional restrictions on correspondence were considered by the Supreme Court in *Procunier v. Martinez,* 94 S. Ct. 1800 (1974). The Court sidestepped a determination of the First Amendment rights of prisoners by focusing its analysis on the rights of citizens with whom a prisoner might correspond. The California regulations under scrutiny in the case prohibited inmate correspondence that "unduly complained of" or "magnified" grievances, two fatally vague standards. The expression of "inflammatory political, racial, religious, or other views or beliefs" in writing was likewise prohibited. Finally, inmates could not mail letters that pertained to criminal activity, contained foreign matter, were lewd, obscene or defamatory or otherwise deemed inappropriate. The sweeping, vague nature of the prohibitions doomed these regulations. *Procunier* declared that restrictions on prisoners' rights of correspondence must demonstrably further a substantial governmental interest: specifically, security, order, or rehabilitation. Any limitation on freedom of expression had to be carefully limited so that it would be no greater than necessary for protection of the governmental interest. Thus, even if a regulation furthers an important, legitimate governmental interest, it is invalid if its coverage is unnecessarily broad. This approach was somewhat relaxed in the subsequent case of *Pell v. Procunier* when the

Court pronounced that First Amendment restrictions must only be demonstrated to be "reasonably related to a legitimate security concern," a standard that indicated a substantial deference to the expertise of prison administrators.

Thus *Martinez* and *Pell* were rather empty, pyrrhic victories for the rights of prisoners. Collectively, they established that prisoners and those with whom they correspond retain First Amendment rights to communicate, but a relatively light burden to justify mail censorship was placed on prison officials. A more thorough reaffirmation of this stance was presented in *Turner v. Safley,* 107 S. Ct. 2254 (1987), in which the Court reviewed Missouri prison regulations conferring discretion on administrators to completely prohibit correspondence among inmates in different prisons. Any correspondence between inmates was prohibited unless the inmates were family members, the correspondence concerned exclusively legal matters, or treatment staff gave it prior approval. The majority accepted the administratively expressed concern about the growing problem with prison gangs and their ability to manage ongoing criminal activities even while incarcerated. Four dissenters, led by Justice Stevens, were unpersuaded that the regulations were not an "exaggerated response" to the problem. The Court, in an opinion rendered by Justice O'Connor, relied on the *Pell* decision in affirming the regulations as reasonably related to legitimate security concerns.

Somewhat distinct from the issue of interpersonal communications addressed in *Pell, Martinez,* and *Turner* is the interception and censorship of publications. It remains commonplace for prison authorities to suppress reading materials unless they come directly from the publisher (the "publisher only rule"). Also censored with regularity are publications deemed inflammatory, obscene, racially divisive, or likely to incite criminal or other inappropriate conduct. The publisher only rule, grounded in a concern about the infiltration of contraband and weapons concealed in books and magazines, was affirmed in *Bell v. Wolfish,* 99 S. Ct. 1861 (1979), a case of great magnitude in regard to the rights of pretrial detainees. It may be safely assumed that any restrictions on the rights of pretrial detainees apply also to the convicted since pretrial detainees, still enjoying the theoretical protection afforded by the presumption of innocence, enjoy more expansive constitutional rights.

Some clarification of the standards in this delicate area were afforded in *Thornburgh v. Abbot,* 109 S. Ct. 1874 (1989). At issue were regulations promulgated by the Federal Bureau of Prisons. Federal administrators attempted to give fair notice to the inmate population of the circumstances under which a publication might be intercepted and withheld. Publications determined to be "detrimental to the security, good order, or discipline of the institution" or that might "facilitate criminal activity" were targeted, but amplification of those standards was provided in the following language:

> Publications which may be rejected by a Warden include but are not limited to publications which meet one of the following criteria: (1) It depicts or describes procedures for the construction or use of weapons, ammunition, bombs, or incendiary devices; (2) It depicts, encourages or describes methods of escape from correctional facilities, or contains blueprints, drawings or similar descriptions of Bureau of Prisons institutions; (3) It depicts or describes procedures for the brewing of alcoholic beverages, or the manufacture of drugs; (4) It is written in code; (5) It depicts, describes, or encourages activities which may lead to the use of physical violence or group disruption; (6) It encourages or instructs in the commission of criminal activities; (7) It is sexually explicit material which by its nature or content poses a threat to the security, good order, or discipline of the institution, or facilitates criminal activity. (*Thornburgh v. Abbot,* 109 S. Ct. 1874, 1883 (1989))

To reiterate the four elements of this test:

1. Is the regulation rationally related to a legitimate governmental objective, and is that objective a legitimate and neutral one, without regard to content?
2. Are there alternative means of exercising the right open to prison inmates?
3. What adverse impact will the asserted right have on guards and other inmates?
4. Is the regulation an exaggerated response to the problem, that is, are less restrictive alternatives available?

This four-pronged approach is the current standard for analysis not only of First Amendment claims of prisoners but other claims of constitutionally based rights as well. Applying the same test, the Supreme Court struck down, for example, the Missouri regulation prohibiting inmates from marriage during their incarceration. This four-part test represents the current state of legal evaluation of these conflicts. Opponents of the majority approach often cite it as evidence of a gradual rediscovery and attraction to the hands off doctrine. At the least the test represents an increased deferral to administrative expertise in correctional facilities. Minimal procedural due process guarantees (notice, opportunity to object, and an impartial decision) do apply to publication censorship.

Interference with and restraints on the ability of inmates to prepare and publish articles and books while incarcerated is another area of dispute. It is unclear what governmental interest is served by preventing the writings of inmates from being consumed by members of the general public. Such censorship would have to be defended on the tenuous ground that the very act of literary creation, and the thought processes that accompany it, are "anti-rehabilitative." Certainly there may be varieties of fiction or quasi-fiction highly reminiscent of the offender's criminal history that would cause concern, but proving that they undermine rehabilitation is a daunting legal challenge and engages larger concerns about the limits of state authority to control the thoughts and beliefs of person. Legislatures in recent years have attempted to remove the financial incentive to inmate literary enterprise by creating statutes that require the proceeds from a contract with a prisoner who had admitted guilt of or been convicted of a specific crime to be placed in escrow with the state and then distributed to the crime victims and other creditors if the depiction was of that specific offense. Any depiction of the person's crime in book, magazine, film, or other medium of communication would be subject to the statutory provisions. Such legislation is known popularly as a "Son of Sam" law after David Berkowitz, a serial murderer convicted in New York.

In *Simon & Schuster v. New York State Crime Victims Board,* 112 S. Ct. 501 (1991), the Supreme Court decided the constitutionality of the New York statute. A publisher who had contracted with an organized crime figure for a book about his life of crime filed suit, challenging the statute on First Amendment grounds. One may surmise that the prospective author's enthusiasm for the autobiography had diminished in face of the legislative action. The Court recognized that the statute in question served two compelling state policies: that criminals not profit from their crimes and that victims of those crimes receive compensation. Balancing the gravity of a substantial interference with freedom of expression and the public's interest in having access to information against those two legitimate interests resulted in a finding of unconstitutionality of the state statute. The statute was determined to be defective because of its sweeping scope and the fact that it would encompass accounts of crime that had occurred many years earlier and against which the statute of limitations had run. States may wish, in the future, to voice the policies of the New York state statute in laws that more precisely and narrowly define the crimes targeted.

Freedom of expression within the institution is an issue separate from issues of extrainstitutional communication addressed above. Severe restrictions on prisoners' freedom of expression within the institution have generally received favorable treatment by the courts. Issues litigated include the use of unsavory language, the right to solicit membership in organizations, the right to solicit funds in support of political agendas, and the right to petition to express grievances to the administration or legislature. Discipline imposed against prisoners for angry racial comments, peaceful work stoppage, and petitions protesting prison conditions are usually sustained. Strong restraints on speech and heavy penalties for violation of those restraints may be necessary in penitentiaries where maintenance of order and security are always a foremost consideration.

In *Procunier v. Martinez*, the Court noted that censorship of inmate expression "simply to eliminate unflattering or unwelcome opinions or factually inaccurate statements" was overly burdensome when the speech sought to be restrained was directed outside the institution. Other cases have implied that prisoners at least have the right to communicate their grievances and request redress from prison officials. Spontaneous colorful speech by inmates remains a different matter as evidenced by *Ustrak v. Fairman*, 781 F.2d 573 (7th Cir. 1986), which sustained prison regulations prohibiting speech that was disrespectful to prison employees or was considered "vulgar, abusive, insolent, threatening or improper language toward any . . . resident or employee."

Attempts by prisoners to communicate with each other and form organizations not approved by prison administrators were addressed definitively in *Jones v. North Carolina Prisoners' Labor Union*, 97 S. Ct. 2532 (1977). Although prisons actively encourage many organizations within their walls (such as Rotary International, the Junior Chamber of Commerce, Boy Scouts, and Alcoholics Anonymous), each has a relationship to a valid penological purpose — rehabilitation. The ability of prisoners to form and maintain organizations that openly challenge conditions of confinement are another matter, a veritable red flag of provocation.

In *Jones,* North Carolina adopted regulations that prohibited inmates from soliciting other inmates to join the union, barred all union meetings, and denied use of the mail to deliver union applications and information within the prison population. The union could continue to exist and prisoners were free to think about the concept even though they were barred from any feasible means to solicit members. The Supreme Court sustained the regulations, finding that First Amendment rights must give way when an association possesses a likelihood of disruption of order or stability or otherwise interferes with legitimate penological objectives. Despite a vigorous dissent by Justice Marshall, the majority's concerns for inmate exploitation, fomentation of power struggles within the prison, and creation of unrealistic expectations in the general prison population prevailed. *Jones* and *Bell v. Wolfish* are widely regarded as the determinative cases in the stifling of the blossoming prisoners' rights movement. The Court rejected a "clear and present danger" test for First Amendment issues in prison matters in favor of a much more elastic "reasonable likelihood of danger" approach.

## VISITATION

It is widely believed that visitation is essential for the offender who at some point will reenter society. The maintenance of social bonds between family, friends, and community are held to be essential elements of successful reintegration into society. There is virtual unanimity on the need for visitation (National Advisory Commission 1973, 17-72; American Bar Association 1981; United Nations 1956; Model Sentencing and Corrections Act 1978). Recognition of a right to visitation and encouragement of its exercise are widely reflected in professional commentary.

Despite these arguments favoring visitation, numerous cases have categorized visitation as a *privilege* that may be curtailed or denied for just cause, rather than a *right*. This categorization is applied to furloughs as well. Justifying this position are concerns for institutional security (weapons and contraband infiltration), for social associations that undermine punishment or rehabilitation, and, often unstated, for the logistical burdens of administering a system of visitation. Limited tolerance of visitation by prison administrators may be an invitation to litigation. *Doe v. Sparks,* 733 F. Supp. 227 (W.D. Pa. 1990), challenged a policy that allowed visits by heterosexual but not homosexual boyfriends and girlfriends, but *Goodwin v. Turner,* 908 F.2d 1395 (8th Cir. 1990), held that a male inmate had no constitutionally protected interest that would give him a right to artificially inseminate his spouse.

Administrative controls over visitation are accepted unless a clear abuse of discretion is shown. The courts have held that a protected liberty interest in visitation occurs only when state regulations or statutes create such an interest with "explicitly mandatory language." The same rationale and approach is applied to another discretionary phenomena — parole. In other words, inmates have no *right* to parole unless there is state authority that creates the right. *Greenholtz v. Nebraska,* 99 S. Ct. 2100, 2106 (1979).

Prison administrators may severely regulate the exercise of visitation privileges by prohibiting physical contact, even between parents and minor children, and requiring intrusive physical searches of inmates before and after a contact visit without probable cause or reasonable suspicion. Since visitation is rarely defined as a right, that the remote locations of many prisons act as a significant barrier to visitation has not been meaningfully addressed. Likewise, the discretionary transfer of inmates to remote institutions and its adverse impact on visitation was determined not to raise a constitutional issue in *Ribideau v. Stoneman,* 398 F. Supp. 805 (D. Vt. 1975). The most significant decisions regarding visitation rights have considered the status of pretrial detainees rather than convicted offenders. *Block v. Rutherford,* 104 S. Ct. 3227 (1984), held that jail inmates could be denied contact visits with spouses, children, relatives, and friends on security grounds, and *Bell v. Wolfish,* 99 S. Ct. 1861 (1979), defined jail inmate search standards before and after receiving a visit. Cases defining the minimum rights of persons held in jail pending trial almost invariably apply to institutionalized offenders, theoretically, a person who has not yet been convicted of a crime should have a greater expectancy of privacy than a person who has been convicted.

Conjugal visitation is not a popular practice within American correctional facilities, although it is widely employed in Europe and Latin America. In *Polakoff v. Henderson,* 370 F. Supp. 690 (D. Ga. 1973), the court held that no constitutional right to such visitation exists; although at least two states (California and Mississippi) have permitted limited conjugal visitation in recent years.

Women who bear children while incarcerated or are the mothers of infants or small children pose different (and difficult) problems for the analysis of visitation rights, although few courts to date have recognized any special or unique rights at stake between a mother and a small child. A humane system of corrections, if for no other reason than its own self-interest in preventing future criminal conduct, should make efforts to minimize the damage to the bond between mother and child. Minimal attention has been paid to this issue by the courts, and it has largely been left to the discretion of administrators working within the confinement of their budgets. In *Women Prisoners of the District of Columbia Department of Corrections v. District of Columbia,* 877 F. Supp. 634 (D.D.C. 1994), the court found an Eighth Amendment (cruel and unusual punishment) violation in the lack of opportunity and appropriate facility for child visitation. It further found that the lack of adequate child placement counseling for female prisoners immediately after giving birth resulted in an unacceptable risk of psychological trauma.

# RELIGIOUS PRACTICES

Freedom of religion is a primary constitutional right guaranteed by the First Amendment. It provides not only a barrier to state regulation of religious beliefs and practices but also to state promotion of religious doctrine. Judicial interpretation of the intent and scope of the First Amendment has resulted in a policy that, while the guarantee of religious *belief* is an absolute, the freedom to *act* in the exercise of religious belief is subject to regulation.

A primary issue in the consideration of prisoner religious practices is the determination of whether the religious practice in dispute is the product of a sincerely held religious belief or an attempt to gain privilege and advantage through subterfuge veiled in the First Amendment. There has been substantial litigation on the issue of freedom of religion within the confines of penal institutions, a significant portion of it revolving around the exercise of religious practices by confined Black Muslims.

The Black Muslim movement within prisons was linked directly to social strife and change external to the prison. The discovery of self and the search for identity and dignity was at the core of the civil rights movement. Many African Americans discovered in the process the attraction of a religious belief system that offered a distinct alternative to Christianity. Some became persuaded that traditional Protestant religious theology was an integral component of the system of social control designed to perpetuate the advantages of the Anglo oligarchy and maintain the subservient position of African Americans.

Demands for separate religious services, special diets, alternative times of worship, specialized religious tracts and books, and alteration of personal appearance were vigorously resisted by prison administrators. Restrictions on religious practices were upheld at first by judicial deference to administrative concern for and expertise in security and discipline. *Ex parte Ferguson,* 361 P.2d 417 (Cal. 1961). The deference to expertise diminished greatly as consideration of prisoner claims progressed. Prisoners prevailed, and religious diversity has been accommodated, within boundaries, in American penal institutions. The legal standard, or test, to be applied in religious freedom cases was announced in *O'Lone v. Estate of Shabazz,* 107 S. Ct. 2400 (1987). That case, in which Muslim inmates challenged work assignments that made it impossible for them to attend Friday evening religious services, resulted in a victory for state interest when the Court applied a test derived from *Turner v. Safley,* 107 S. Ct. 2254 (1987). The majority, in a narrow 5-4 decision, determined that the restrictions were valid because they were "reasonably related to legitimate penological interests." Id. at 2265. The four factors of the test in *Turner* were:

1. a valid, rational connection between a regulation and a governmental interest;
2. alternative means to exercise the right;
3. examination of the adverse effect the inmate request would have on inmates, prison officials, and prison resources; and
4. absence of alternatives to the regulation.

In effect, the majority crafted a rather obscure rule deferring greatly to the need for orderly administration of a bureaucratic institution.

Despite *O'Lone,* major advances in the free exercise of religion have occurred. A summary list of such advances includes:

1. a Buddhist inmate must have a reasonable opportunity to pursue his faith if other inmates are allowed to participate in conventional religious practices;
2. an Orthodox Jewish inmate has the right to a diet that would sustain her in good health and not be offensive to her religious beliefs;
3. a Black Muslim cannot be punished with administrative segregation for his refusal to handle pork;
4. a Cherokee Indian inmate may have the right to have long hair; and
5. the government is required to pay a Muslim minister at the same hourly rate paid chaplains.

A particularly intriguing issue litigated under color of the First Amendment is that of personal appearance. There is disagreement among penologists about the effect of prison regulations that restrict inmate appearance. Perhaps one of the most degrading aspects of prison life is its dehumanization. Prisoners are denied such symbols of their individual identity as clothing, hairstyle, facial hair, and decorative accessories. This stripping away of personality is reinforced by the sterility and lack of decoration in the prison environment. Tolerance of individual diversity in clothing and appearance is largely a matter of administrative discretion and correctional philosophy because courts have generally refused to disturb regulations governing appearance. Although some lower courts have dissolved such regulations when appearance is linked to religious beliefs. *Fromer v. Scully,* 817 F.2d 227 (2d Cir. 1987), the general rule is to the contrary. Restriction on appearance is an example of the many areas in which courts do not generally interfere with administration of the institutions. The theory that appearance is a form of speech entitled to constitutional protection within the confines of penitentiaries has minimum viability.

In summary, the litigation of issues related to the First Amendment have resulted in marginal gains for prisoners in the areas of free expression and communication. Prisoners have been successful in forging rights related to religious practices so long as they are not overly burdensome to accommodate and are based in sincerely held, recognized religious beliefs and practices. The courts have been astute in rejecting prisoner requests where they detect that the prisoner is manipulating First Amendment principles to gain special privilege, mocking institutional authority, or engaging in subterfuge. *Theriault v. Carlson,* 495 F.2d 390 (5th Cir. 1974).

# THE RIGHT TO PRIVACY

The right of privacy, a phrase found nowhere in the Constitution, is a curious alchemy sometimes referred to as a *penumbral right.* It is a phrase derived from the collective interpretation of several explicit constitutional guarantees such as the rights to travel and associate freely, freedom of speech and religion, and the freedom from unreasonable searches and seizures. It symbolizes a respect for individual integrity and minimal state regulation of behaviors, including procreation, reasonably deemed "private." The concept that prisoners might enjoy some vestigial expectation of privacy, a theory associated with the rehabilitative ideal, has been dashed on the rocks of administrative convenience and necessity.

The death knell for even a minimal expectation of privacy in prison cells was sounded in *Bell v. Wolfish,* 99 S. Ct. 1861 (1979), a case in which pretrial detainees (awaiting trial and presumed innocent) had won a lower court victory establishing that they had a right to be present at and observe cell searches and be free from body cavity searches conducted after visitation absent probable cause to believe the inmate was concealing contraband. Those holdings, based in the Fourth Amendment, were reversed by the Supreme Court, which held that institutional security concerns were paramount. The only concession to the right of privacy and freedom from unreasonable search recognized in the majority opinion was that searches could not be used abusively by prison administrators for purposes of harassment and punishment. Many lower courts resisted the *Bell v. Wolfish* holding, and the Supreme Court further clarified its position in *Hudson v. Palmer*, 104 S. Ct. 3194 (1984), maintaining that a prisoner has no "reasonable expectation of privacy" in a prison cell. Searches and seizures of the persons or living quarters of prisoners that inflict injury, are more intense than necessary, or are conducted exclusively for purposes of harassment remain viable civil rights violations, but the presumption is that discretionary searches are valid.

The Supreme Court decision in *Turner v. Safley*, 107 S. Ct. 2254 (1987), inferred that prisoners retain some constitutionally protected privacy interests when it ruled that a regulation restricting inmate marriage violated a fundamental right. The right of marriage and selection of a marriage partner has been recognized as within the boundaries of the right to privacy. Courts may infer that inmates have residual privacy rights, as the Supreme Court did, without specifically identifying the source of the rights.

Several cases have addressed sexually discriminatory search policies in regard to arrestees or those temporarily detained in jails. Prominent among these is *Mary Beth G. v. City of Chicago*, 723 F.2d 1263 (7th Cir. 1983). Although a number of states have placed statutory limits on strip searches of persons arrested for minor offenses, the court's invalidation in *Mary Beth G.* of strip searches and visual body cavity inspections of females arrested for minor infractions rested, in part, on the fact that such inspections were not routinely performed on males arrested on minor charges. There is a presumption against the validity of degrading and humiliating searches of arrestees unless based at least upon reasonable suspicion that reinforces the Fourteenth Amendment equal protection policy against sexually discriminatory treatment of arrestees. This theory should be transferred to any situation in which female prisoners experience greater intrusion of personal privacy than that experienced by their male counterparts.

Substantial litigation has resulted from the collision of rights guaranteed by the Equal Employment Opportunity Act and the privacy interests of prisoners. These challenges have presented difficult problems to the federal judiciary. For instance, in an early case, the court accepted a rationale that justified the exclusion of female guards from contact positions in Alabama's maximum security male institutions. *Dothard v. Rawlinson*, 97 S. Ct. 2720 (1970). Rejecting the female guard's right to equal employment, the Court decided that exposing women guards to the male maximum security prisoner population in Alabama, *under the conditions then existing*, posed an unacceptably high security risk. Concluding that the Alabama prisons were characterized by intolerable levels of rampant violence and disorganization, the Court concluded that male gender was a "bona fide occupational qualification" despite the willingness of some female guards to expose themselves to the risk.

As to the inmates' rights to privacy, courts have generally concluded, as in *Brasch v. Gunter* (unpublished opinion, U.S.D.C. Nebraska 1985), that inmates are protected from unrestricted viewing of genitals or bodily functions by members of the opposite sex in the workforce of the prison. This restriction on the performance of routine duties of guards may impede the advancement of female guards in male penitentiaries and vice versa. Accidental or infrequent observations of private functions and nudity by a member of the opposite sex of the inmate have been classified as a minimal intrusion on privacy interests, inadequate to rise to the level of a constitutional violation. Inmates' constitutionally protected privacy interests are not violated when members of the opposite sex are present in inmate living quarters for a brief and predictable amount of time. *Avery v. Perrin*, 473 F. Supp. 90 (D.N.H. 1979).

In addition to the privacy issues raised by visual observation of inmates, gender issues have been raised about the performance of more intrusive searches of inmates. Pat-down or "frisk" searches of inmates by members of the opposite sex are generally condoned if they are conducted in a manner that does not include touching of genital areas. In *Smith v. Fairman*, 678 F.2d 52 (7th Cir. 1982), the frisk by female correctional officers of male inmates' necks, backs, chests, stomachs, waists, buttocks, and outer legs was approved. Correctional administrators should feel free to structure prudent policies regarding these matters in the female institution where male guards are present.

In bona fide emergency situations, correctional officers of the opposite sex cannot only pat down the genital areas of inmates but also conduct more intrusive strip or body cavity searches. In *Lee v. Downs*, 641 F.2d 1117 (4th Cir. 1981), the court found no invasion of the female inmate's privacy protections when two male correctional officers restrained the arms and legs of the woman while a female nurse conducted a body cavity search for matches after the inmate had set her clothing afire. Whether a bona fide emergency exists when such an incident occurs will continue to be the subject of dispute.

The courts have had to balance the employment interests of correctional officers of opposite sex with inmates' privacy interests. The most thorough analysis of the dilemma is found in *Forts v. Ward*, 621 F.2d 1210 (2d Cir. 1980). In a lengthy decision wherein the court thoroughly discussed the benefits and detriments of various types of sleepwear, including "Dr. Dentons" (pajamas with closed feet usually worn by children), and the advantages and disadvantages of translucent and opaque screening in shower and bathroom areas of a female prison, the appellate court, in a Solomon-like decision, vacated the lower court prohibition on the assignment of male guards to the nighttime shifts in dormitories at the female correctional facility. The court confronted the clash between principles of equal employment opportunity and female inmate privacy interests and fashioned a remedy partially accommodating the competing interests.

There continues to be disagreement on the wisdom of even employing correctional officers of the opposite sex in penitentiaries, an issue that suggests the related concept of sexually desegregated inmate populations. Whether inmate contact with members of the opposite sex, especially when they are in a position of authority, furthers or undermines the rehabilitative process is not definitively understood. Some courts and observers allege that opposite sex correctional officers within a prison contribute to rehabilitation, a view expressed in *Bagley v. Watson*, 597 F. Supp. 1099 (D. Or. 1983). That case discussed the impact of female officers in a male prison environment. In marked contrast is the intriguing perspective offered in *Torres v. Wisconsin Department of Health and Social Services*, 859 F.2d 1523 (7th Cir. 1988). In that case, the court observed that the mere presence of male correctional officers may be anti-rehabilitative. The court relied on a finding that many, probably most, female prisoners were the product of physical, emotional, and sexual abuse by males. Temporary isolation from male authority figures might be necessary to provide a therapeutic setting in which rehabilitation could even be initiated. The proposition that female officers in male penitentiaries enhance rehabilitation by contributing to the "normalcy" of the environment while the corresponding presence of male officers in a female institution undermines the rehabilitative process is symbolic of the lack of knowledge, and need for study, in this area.

## MEDICAL TREATMENT IN CORRECTIONAL INSTITUTIONS

The primary case defining the appropriate level of medical care for prisoners is *Estelle v. Gamble,* 97 S. Ct. 285 (1976). It was preceded by cases, such as those in Arkansas and Alabama, in which grossly inadequate medical care was cited as an element contributing to a finding that penitentiary conditions as a whole violated the Eighth Amendment.

In *Gamble,* the Supreme Court clearly established that there is a right to medical care and a corresponding duty of the state to provide it. The quality of care to be provided was also addressed and a nebulous test established. It was established in *Gamble* that "deliberate indifference to the serious medical needs of prisoners constitutes unnecessary and wanton infliction of pain proscribed (prohibited) by the Eighth Amendment." *Estelle v. Gamble,* 97 S. Ct. 285, 291 (1976). Negligent or careless failure to provide adequate medical care, while far from laudable, would not constitute a viable cause of action under the civil rights statute. Accidents, negligence, or professional disagreement on diagnosis or treatment of illness or injury are not within federal civil rights jurisdiction. Nonetheless, agreed settlements of prison reform lawsuits routinely address and remedy deficiencies in staff and medical facilities, and there has been widespread and systematic improvement in the health care extended to prisoners.

The special issues of women's health services, the needs of disabled and geriatric prisoners, and the provision of care to the terminally ill must be addressed as these issues proliferate when mandatory sentencing schemes are installed. The legal issues of prisoners with AIDS are rapidly emerging. They include the right to treatment, the quality of care to be administered, protection of inmates and staff, the right of HIV-positive individuals and AIDS patients to remain in the general population, mandatory HIV testing, the relevance of medical condition to parole and furlough decisions, and the issue of notification of spouses and sexual partners on release. In *Nolley v. County of Erie,* 776 F. Supp. 715 (W.D.N.Y. 1991), automatic segregation of a female prisoner known to be HIV-positive in a wing otherwise reserved for mentally ill inmates was held to violate the constitutional right to privacy. However, in *Harris v. Thigpen,* 941 F.2d 1495 (11th Cir. 1991), the court found that segregation of all HIV-positive inmates was constitutionally permissible.

Many troublesome policy issues that transcend provision of health care await resolution. For example, what persons, within and without the institutional setting, are entitled to notification of the HIV-positive status of a prisoner? The prevalent theory is that other prisoners and prison staff in non-health-related capacities have no right to notice because the HIV virus is not easily transmitted. It is also current wisdom that family and associates of the inmate have no right to receive notice of the infectious status of an inmate.

# THE RIGHT TO TREATMENT

The decline of the rehabilitative ideal was discussed in Chapter 6. As previously noted, the policies of retribution, isolation, and deterrence are increasingly favored, while treatment and rehabilitation rationales are diminishing in significance. Nonetheless, the courts continue to recognize the dependency imposed by incarceration. Closely related to the issue of adequate medical treatment of physical ailments is that of treatment for emotionally unhealthy inmates. The serious medical ailments implicated in *Estelle v. Gamble* are not restricted to physical ailments. Unattended mental illness may cause pain and suffering that equals or exceeds that attributable to physical injury.

Inevitably a prisoner, by virtue of his status and confinement, will be depressed during some or all of his sentence. Because depression is so common but also not easily measured, issues arise as to when a mental or emotional problem demands a constitutional duty requiring the custodian of the inmate to provide care. In *Parte v. Lane,* 528 F. Supp. 1254 (N.D. Ill. 1981), the court found that the inmate's complaint that he felt depressed and was not receiving adequate attention to his condition did not give rise to a claim of sufficient magnitude. According to the *Parte* case, the constitutional entitlement to psychological or psychiatric care is triggered when a physician or other health care provider concludes with reasonable medical certainty, that: (1) the prisoner's symptoms evidence a serious disease or injury; (2) such disease or injury is curable or may be substantially alleviated; and (3) the potential for harm to the prisoner by reason of delay or denial of care would be substantial. *Parte v. Lane,* 528 F. Supp. 1254, 1260 (N.D. Ill. 1981).

The right to treatment under these circumstances is limited to that which may reasonably be provided under constraints of time and cost. *Bowring v. Godwin,* 551 F.2d 44 (4th Cir. 1977). The Supreme Court extended the "deliberate indifference" standard derived from *Estelle v. Gamble* to include medical, dental, and psychiatric care and defined it rather narrowly. In *Farmer v. Brennan,* 114 S. Ct. 1970 (1994), it was held that a prison official can be liable under the Eighth Amendment for denying an inmate humane conditions of confinement only if the official both knows of and disregards an excessive risk to inmate health and safety. The current posture of the courts appears to be that prisoners are entitled to adequate, rather than exemplary, or even good, health care.

Women's needs for health care may exceed the customary needs of male prisoners. In everyday life women are less reluctant than men to seek medical services; and the same is probably true in institutional settings. Women's needs for medical care exceed those of men because of the more complex biology of their reproductive systems (Pollock-Byrne 1990, 96-97). If greater need is acknowledged and inferior delivery of health care exists, clearly a violation of the principle of equal protection exists.

Growing indications show that the provision of health care in women's prisons is inadequate. Recent literature indicates that substance abuse is more common among women than men, that female arrestees are more likely to test positive for drugs, especially cocaine and heroin, that a greater percentage of women are incarcerated for drug-related offenses, and that women are more likely than men to have been using drugs daily at the time of their arrest (Fletcher, et al. 1993). This implies not only an enhanced need for medical services related to substance abuse but also an increased risk factor for HIV and other diseases associated with drug use (Greenspan 1990).

Successful litigation has already lifted the veil on gender-based discrimination in the area of prison educational and vocational programming. In the institution charged in *Glover v. Johnson,* 478 F. Supp. 1075 (E.D. Mich. 1979), female inmates were provided educational and vocational programs dramatically inferior to those offered their male counterparts. The court, finding an equal protection violation, prohibited such differential treatment as discriminatory. Equal access to educational and vocational programs must be provided unless the state could demonstrate an important, legitimate governmental objective in the provision of inferior treatment to female offenders (Bershad 1985). *Glover* and cases like it have set the stage for other charges of gender-based discrimination.

The American Bar Association Standards Relating to the Legal Status of Prisoners proposes in Standard 26-6.14 that prisoners should be free from discriminatory treatment based solely on race, sex, religion, or national origin. Furthermore, prisoners of either sex may be assigned to the same facility or assigned to separate facilities so long as there is essential equality in living conditions and access to community and institutional programs including education, employment, and vocational training.

A recent class action suit brought on behalf of all female prisoners in the District of Columbia found Eighth Amendment violations in the lack of medical care, sexual harassment, and inferior living conditions. *Women Prisoners of the District of Columbia Department of Corrections v. District of Columbia*, 877 F. Supp. 634 (D.D.C. 1994). The court also found violation of federally guaranteed rights (Title IX of the Civil Rights Acts) in the provision of substandard recreational, educational, and religious opportunities in comparison to those afforded male inmates. After an extensive trial, the court concluded that civil rights violations were established conclusively by the plaintiffs and that prison officials had deviated from the standard of acceptable mental health care for women prisoners, had tolerated deficient gynecological examinations and testing, and had maintained inadequate testing for sexually transmitted diseases. The court, applying the "deliberate indifference" standard, further found liability for inadequate health education, prenatal care, ineffective prenatal education, and overall inadequate prenatal protocol. In a scathing portion of the opinion, the judge found that shackling of female prisoners in the third trimester of pregnancy and immediately after childbirth violated contemporary standards of decency. The belief that adequate medical care exists in women's prisons may be on the brink of serious reexamination in light of the revelations of facts in this case.

# THE RIGHT TO REFUSE TREATMENT

An opposite, and equally intriguing, question is when may an inmate refuse psychological or psychiatric medical care? It is well established that a correctional institution or official may not administer antipsychotic medication for purposes of punishment, but what about for treatment? Therapeutic personality alteration through surgical techniques, electroshock therapy, chemical castration, or administration of psychotropic drugs is, perhaps, a tempting tool of reform. The rights to be different, eccentric, and even antisocial are, however, cherished freedoms at the root of contemporary constitutional theory. The concept that the state has the right to reshape or mold citizens into an ideal of social conformity is associated only with extreme authoritarian regimes. Disillusion with the rehabilitative justification for incarceration aside, the pressure generated by spiraling prison populations only diminishes the possibility of effective treatment in the artificial environment of prison. It has been noted that the combination of treatment and coercion is potentially much more oppressive than unembellished confinement (Kittrie 1971).

From an examination of these issues there has emerged a philosophy that prisoners should have a right to be "free from treatment," especially where behavior modification programs and aversion therapies have been considered. A highly influential case on this topic emerged from a Michigan trial court, *Kaimowitz v. Department of Mental Health for the State of Michigan* (Cir. Ct. for Wayne County, Mich. 1973). The court concluded that an involuntarily confined mental patient did not have the capacity, while confined, to give informed, voluntary, adequate consent to experimental psychosurgery procedures on the brain. The patient in that case had been diverted into the mental health system as an alternative to prosecution for recidivist, highly aggressive sexual offenses.

The issue of the prisoner's right to refuse medical administration of psychotropic drugs was examined by the Supreme Court in *Washington v. Harper,* 110 S. Ct. 1028 (1990). The state's prison policy in that case permitted the involuntary administration of antipsychotic drugs when an inmate, previously diagnosed as mentally ill, "constitutes a likelihood of serious harm to himself or others and/or is gravely disabled." Id. at 1031. Before medication could be administered there must have been a medical finding that a mental disorder likely to cause harm exists, the medication had been prescribed by a psychiatrist, approved by a reviewing psychiatrist, and treatment would be ordered only if in the medical interests of the patient. The majority, per Justice Kennedy, held that the Due Process Clause was not offended by the *Washington* scheme and that substantive due process considerations do not prohibit the state from involuntarily treating a severely ill prison inmate with antipsychotic drugs if the inmate is dangerous to himself or others and the treatment is in the inmate's medical interest. The three dissenting justices were unpersuaded that the state would refrain from using the drug in question for punitive purposes. They also expressed grave concern about the potentially extreme adverse side effects of the drug (prolixin injections) in question. These included substantial risk of permanent injury and premature death.

The concern of the minority opinion in this case was the ability of the inmate to make a voluntary election to refuse the treatment. The majority approved of the administrative procedural due process protections provided by the state of Washington and refused to require judicial review of the process before administration of the drug. In contrast, the American Bar Association Standards Relating to the Legal Status of Prisoners propose that prisoners have a right to decline mental health treatment unless that treatment is (1) required by an order issued by a court of competent jurisdiction, or (2) reasonably believed to be necessary to save the inmate's life or prevent permanent and serious damage to the prisoner's health.

There is virtually unanimous agreement that prison officials, as legal guardians and custodians of the imprisoned, are allowed to impose other emergency medical treatments to save a prisoner's life or prevent irreparable harm, even against the prisoner's opposition. The force-feeding of a prisoner whose health is jeopardized by fasting or starving was addressed in *In re Sanchez,* 577 F. Supp. 7 (D.C.N.Y. 1983), while involuntary kidney dialysis treatment was examined in *Commissioner of Corrections v. Myer,* 399 N.E.2d 452 (Mass. 1979). One may reasonably conclude that the majority of authorities see an analogy between the thrust and logic of these cases and those involving the treatment of mental illness, thus permitting dramatic state intervention in those few cases in which the medically diagnosed and dangerous mentally ill patient refuses treatment.

## RACIAL SEGREGATION AND EQUAL PROTECTION

A study of the legal issues addressed by the courts in regard to the rights of prisoners suggests that virtually all of the dilemmas of the larger society are contained within the unique closed society of the penitentiary. The tensions of life in confinement are exacerbated by the deep-seated animosity and distrust among prisoners of different races. In 1989, one of every four black males in the 20-29 age group and one of every ten Hispanic males in that group were in prison, jail, on probation, or on parole, as compared to one of sixteen white males. More than 55 percent of the nation's prisoners were nonwhite (Mauer 1990). Nothing in the intervening years has impacted this historic fact. Much current literature in criminal justice is preoccupied with the gang phenomena, and gangs, both within

and without the institution, are perceived to exist in strict racial segregation and rivalry. Since maintenance of order and safety is the
highest priority of the prison administrator, officials have segregated
prisoners of different races. Such segregation may appear as a legislative mandate, administrative regulation, de facto phenomena, or as
a temporary response to a disturbance or anticipated disturbance. It
may also assume subtle camouflage in any area of prisoner treatment
such as classification, work assignments, and access to therapeutic
programs.

Statutorily imposed racial discrimination in prison facilities was
first addressed in *Washington v. Lee*, 263 F. Supp. 327 (M.D. Ala. 1966).
Both white and black prisoners filed a complaint alleging violation
of the Equal Protection Clause of the Fourteenth Amendment. The
district court brushed aside the state defense of institutional security
and held the practice unconstitutional. The district court was affirmed *per curiam* by the United States Supreme Court in *Lee v. Washington*, 88 S. Ct. 994 (1968). Three justices wrote a concurring
opinion in which they observed that an extremely narrow exception
to the prohibition on racial segregation might exist where there is a
clear and immediate threat to institutional security in jails or prisons,
a dictum only implied in the main opinion. The lessons of *Washington
v. Lee* have been widely honored by lower federal courts in the years
since. A generalized fear or concern that racial desegregation will
initiate violence does not justify segregation. *Stewart v. Rhodes*, 473 F.
Supp. 1185 (S.D. Ohio 1979), *aff'd* 785 F.2d 310 (6th Cir. 1986). Even
a specific and factually grounded concern for institutional security is
an impermissible reason for racial segregation until other alternatives such as reduction of the prison population, increased supervision of the inmates, and disciplinary action against sources of conflict
have been fully explored. *Blevins v. Brew*, 593 F. Supp. 245 (W.D. Wis.
1984). Claims that inmates prefer racial segregation and that it is thus
a voluntary election by the inmates were characterized as a "gauze for
discrimination" in the Fifth Circuit case *Jones v. Diamond*, 636 F.2d
1363 (5th Cir. 1981).

Regarding First Amendment issues, African American inmates
have been generally successful in gaining access to publications cater-
ing to ethnic issues unless they are extremely inflammatory and
conducive to violence. Courts have not been sympathetic toward demands for accommodation of cultural tastes in food or in popular
entertainment such as movies. *United States v. State of Michigan*, 680 F.
Supp. 270 (W.D. Mich. 1988). While racial tension and friction continue to be society's overriding social problem both within and with-

out the walls of confinement, when called on to address the legal issue of the rights of prisoners the courts have spoken in a clear and unmuffled voice in favor of the principles of desegregation and equal protection of the law.

# PROCEDURAL DUE PROCESS

The federal constitution prohibits both state and federal government authority from taking life, liberty, or property without due process of law. The meaning and scope of procedural due process is a constantly evolving line of demarcation of the rights of citizens. Its most familiar manifestation is in the criminal trial where defendants are guaranteed an impartial trier of fact, a jury, counsel, right to remain silent, the right to confront and cross-examine accusers, and so on. In the last quarter century, governmental agencies have experienced a dramatic "due process revolution" imposed by the courts and designed to curtail the abuses of governmental discretion. The case that initiated this phenomena was *Goldberg v. Kelly,* 90 S. Ct. 1011 (1970), in which the Court prohibited a public assistance agency from terminating benefits without a pretermination evidentiary hearing. Since that time, any allegedly "grievous loss" imposed on a person by state action has been subject to judicial challenge as to the need for and adequacy of procedural due process protection. Prisoners have challenged the adequacy of due process protections in disciplinary hearings with no more than modest success.

In *Wolff v. McDonnell,* 94 S. Ct. 2963 (1974), the Supreme Court imposed a minimal due process model on prison disciplinary proceedings involving punitive isolation or diminished eligibility for early release. Three safeguards to check abuse of discretion were imposed:

1. advance written statement of the claimed violation (24 hours minimum);
2. a written statement by an impartial fact-finder as to evidence relied on and reasons for the discipline; and
3. the right to testify and the right to call witnesses and present documentary evidence unless the fact-finder concludes that these rights would undermine institutional security or valid correctional goals.

The court majority specifically denied appointment of counsel and confrontation or cross-examination, classifying such procedures as hazards to valid correctional goals. Many advocates of correctional reform and other courts' judges were dismayed by the decision, but the Supreme Court has subsequently undermined even the minimal procedural due process requirements of *Wolff.* In 1985 the Court stated in *Superintendent, Massachusetts Correctional Institution, Walpole v. Hill,* 105 S. Ct. 2768 (1985), that disciplinary revocation of a prisoner's accrued good time (which affects date of release adversely) could be based on "some evidence" contained within the administrative record, an extremely relaxed standard. In *Ponte v. Real,* 105 S. Ct. 2192 (1985), the Court continued its reluctance to impose due process burdens on prison officials, determining that it was unnecessary for disciplinary officials to prepare written reasons for refusing to allow the prisoner to call a witness on his behalf unless and until the matter was appealed to the courts. Some states, through statute or regulation, establish more generous procedural safeguards for disciplinary hearings than the minimal standards found in Supreme Court cases (Branham 1990).

Challenges to reclassification or physical transfer of prisoners to other penal institutions have likewise been ignored by the Court. In *Meachum v. Fano,* 96 S. Ct. 2532 (1976), the Court concluded that prisoners had no right to be in any particular prison, and therefore they had no due process protections before transfer from one prison to another, even if the transfer involved substantially inferior living conditions. This has been an important case, frequently cited for the Court's analysis regarding the source of rights, with some justices arguing that if a right is not specifically defined in the Constitution or by state statute, it does not exist. *Meachum* is also a bellwether case because it unequivocally states that the Court would defer to the states in matters of prisoners' rights deemed ephemeral or insubstantial. Not just any deprivation of liberty, but only those deemed significant and in violation of a specific constitutional guarantee, will invoke federal court jurisdiction.

The availability of a due process hearing for prison disciplinary activities was further reduced in *Sandin v. Conner,* 115 S. Ct. 2293 (1995), in which the Court observed that the hearing process is appropriate only when the discipline "imposes atypical and significant conditions on inmates in relation to ordinary incidents of prison life." 115 S. Ct. 2293 at 2302. In that case Conner had been placed in segregated confinement for 30 days without benefit of a hearing. The Court majority reasoned that because the confinement did not inevitably affect the duration of the sentence, no due process rights attached to the prisoner's grievance. The case clearly indicates a return to broadened discretion for state prison administrators and a reluctance to make federal courts available to review prison disciplinary proceedings.

## CONCLUSIONS

The fundamental doctrine that has evolved as the judiciary has examined the conditions of confinement experienced by prisoners in the United States is that they retain all the rights of free people except those which are inconsistent with institutional needs of order, security, and rehabilitation and must, of necessity, be withdrawn or diminished during incarceration. The evolving standards of decency, inside and outside correctional institutions, require constant reevaluation in a dynamic and pluralistic society that purports to value individual integrity and potential. The litigation of the rights of prisoners is the established theater for this continuing dialogue, and there is little reason to believe that, with a burgeoning prison population, the tide of prison litigation is likely to recede.

The concerns of convicted persons struggling to retain or shape their individual integrity and identity are not that much different from those of the unconvicted. Each issue raised in prison litigation has precedent in some other area of civil rights law. The treatment afforded those who have offended society's laws are a fair measure of that society's ethics. Although conviction and incarceration necessarily involve a fundamental change in constitutional status, the belief that a society can be judged by its prisons retains validity now as it has throughout history.

## Vocabulary

| | |
|---|---|
| corporal punishment | least restrictive means test |
| deliberate indifference test | penumbral right |
| habeas corpus | retention of rights theory |
| hands off doctrine | Section 1983 actions |
| injunctive relief | sovereign immunity |
| jailhouse lawyers | totality of circumstances cases |

## Study Questions

1. Until the 1960s, the courts generally followed a hands off philosophy toward prison matters. What factors in society influenced the courts to abandon this policy and intervene in prison administration?

2. Why do many prisoners file suit in federal courts rather than state courts?

3. What are some of the differences in the needs of female prisoners as compared to male prisoners?

4. Should prisons employ male guards in institutions for women? Should prisons employ female guards in institutions for men? How do the courts balance these rights against the inmates' rights of privacy?

5. Should prisons allow conjugal visits? What rights, if any, are at issue?

6. What quality of medical care should be provided prisoners, especially those with terminal illnesses? What is the standard used by the Supreme Court in medical cases, and how is it applied?

7. How important is freedom of religion in penitentiaries, and what accommodations should be made to protect it?

## Sources Cited

— Allen, Harry, and Clifford Simonson. 1982. *Corrections in America*. 5th ed. New York: Macmillan.

— American Bar Association. 1981. *Standards for Criminal Justice*. 2d ed. Chicago: ABA.

— American Correctional Association. 1966. *Manual of Correctional Standards*. 3d ed. Laurel, Md.: ACA.

— American Correctional Association. 1979. *Standards for the Administration of Correctional Agencies.* Laurel, Md.: ACA.

— Bershad, Lawrence. 1985. "Discriminatory Treatment of the Female Offenders in the Criminal Justice System." *Boston College Law Review* 26: 309.

— Branham, Lynn S. 1990. "Out of Sight, Out of Danger? Procedural Due Process and the Segregation of HIV-Positive Inmates." *Hastings Law Quarterly* 17: 193.

— Clemmer, Donald. 1958. *The Prison Community.* New York: Holt, Rinehart and Winston.

— "Confronting the Conditions of Confinement: An Expanded Role for Courts in Prison Reform." 1977. Note. *Harvard Civil Rights Civil Liberties Law Review* 12: 367.

— Crouch, Ben, and James Marquart. 1989. *An Appeal to Justice.* Austin: University of Texas Press.

— Dilulio, John J., ed. 1990. *Courts, Corrections, and the Constitution.* New York: Oxford University Press.

— Fletcher, Beverly R., L. Shaver, L. Dixon, and D. Moon. 1993. *Women Prisoners: A Forgotten Population.* Westport, Conn.: Praeger.

— Gardner, Thomas J., and Terry M. Anderson. 1992. *Criminal Law,* 5th ed. St. Paul: West.

— Greenspan, Judy. 1990. "States Move Toward Mainstreaming of HIV-Infected Prisoners." *National Prison Project Journal* 22: 18.

— Hammett, Theodore M., and Sairi Moiri. 1990. "Update on AIDS in Prisons and Jails." U.S. Department of Justice. Washington, D.C.: GPO.

— Jacobs, James B. 1980. "The Prisoners' Movement Rights and Its Impacts, 1960-1980." In *Crime and Justice, Vol. 2,* ed. N. Morris and M. Tonry. Chicago: University of Chicago Press.

— Jacobs, James B. 1983. *Perspectives on Prisons and Imprisonment.* Ithaca, N.Y.: Cornell University Press.

— Johnson, Robert. 1987. *Hard Time: Understanding and Reforming the Prison.* Monterey, Cal.: Brooks/Cole.

— Kittrie, Nicholas N. 1971. *The Right to Be Different.* Baltimore: Johns Hopkins Press.

— Krantz, Sheldon, and Lynn Branam. 1991. *The Law of Sentencing, Corrections, and Prisoners' Rights.* 4th ed. Minneapolis: West.

— Mauer, Marc. 1990. *The Sentencing Project, Americans Behind Bars: One Year Later.* Washington, D.C.: American Civil Liberties Union National Prison Project.

— McCarthy, C. M. 1989. "Experimentation on Prisoners: The Inadequacy of Voluntary Consent." *New England Journal on Civil and Criminal Confinement* 15: 55.

— National Advisory Commission on Criminal Justice Standards and Goals. 1973. "Report on Corrections." Washington, D.C.: GPO.

— Palmer, John W. 1994. *Constitutional Rights of Prisoners.* 4th ed. Cincinnati: Anderson.

— Pollock-Byrne, J. M. 1990. *Women, Prison, and Crime.* Pacific Grove, Cal.: Brooks/Cole.

— Robertson, James E. 1993. "Fatal Custody: A Reassessment of Section 1983 Liability for Custodial Suicide." *University of Toledo Law Review* 24: 807.

— United Nations. 1956. *Standard Minimum Rules for the Treatment of Prisoners.* First United Nations Congress on the Prevention of Cirme and Treatment of Offenders. Annex I(A); U.N. Doc. A/Conf. 6/1.

# 11

# THE PRIVATIZATION OF PRISONS

## *Ronald Becker*

Arguments against private prisons vary in soundness and plausibility, but in no area have I found any potential problem with private prisons that is not at least matched by an identical or a closely corresponding problem among prisons that are run by the government. (Logan 1989, 303)

## *Chapter Overview*

The United States spends in excess of $20 billion a year to provide necessary facilities for inmates (Bryce 1993, 7). The number of individuals incarcerated grows daily as does the cost of keeping them incarcerated. The United States has more people in prison than any other country. In the midst of this expansion, the United States taxpayers will be asked to spend $10 billion dollars over the next few years to increase prison capacity by 170,000 new beds (Bryce 1993, 7). Each year approximately 800,000 people are arrested in the United States for violent offenses, and 2.5 million more are arrested for serious property crimes. The demand for prison beds is growing at a rate of 1,000 per week (Bowman 1992, 132).

Every state has been touched by prison overcrowding. Most states have felt the impact of that overcrowding in the reality of human numbers, others by court decisions pertaining to inmate rights and prison conditions. It has been estimated that federal and state prisons are being run at 106 to 150 percent capacity, and that percentage is increasing daily (Johnson and Ross 1990, 352). As of this writing, 80 percent of the states in the United States have been the subject of court orders to reduce inmate populations and to improve prison conditions. Efforts to comport with growing populations are varied, and few states are keeping pace with the demand for prison beds. In addition to court orders, states are being confronted with citizen fear and the ever-present, politically expedient "get tough on crime" agenda. Legislative response to citizens' fear has been to pass laws requiring mandatory sentences or sentences without parole for violent offenders.

States have overburdened their penal institutions with no efforts toward addressing the associated costs of the popular "get tough on crime" policy. Much the same is happening on the federal scene. Enacting the Comprehensive Crime Control Act (1984), the Anti-Drug Abuse Act (1986), and concomitant sentencing policies have resulted in placing over 40,000 inmates in the federal detention network, a system that was designed to address 28,000 offenders. Half of the federal districts are operating under serious to critical space-availability conditions, and 16 percent are operating under "emergency" conditions. The U.S. Marshals service, which is responsible for detaining federal pretrial defendants, has been forced to hold 60 percent of them in state and local jails (Bryce 1993, 7).

The anticipated costs of bringing prisons into conformity with court decisions is not included in correctional budgets. Taxpayers are loath to pay another dime for what they often see as only benefiting the criminal; and politicians know the consequences of such taxation (Ellison 1987, 718).

In the midst of this situation comes private industry with its profit and loss ledgers and efficiency managers. Many have embraced private enterprise as the answer to the ever-growing inmate population problem and the court orders mandating compliance to standards. Others see the specter of private enterprise hovering above penal institutions as a harbinger of constitutional deprivation and an obstruction to due process and equal protection under the law.

It is important to note that the entry of private business into the operation of prisons is not an altruistic endeavor. Private enterprise will continue working in corrections only as long as it remains profitable to do so (Kastenmeier 1986, 40). Privatization may breed corruption, touching anyone who is in the process (Stinebaker 1995).

Those who are concerned with the constitutional rights of inmates fear that the profit motive may lead to financial shortcuts at the expense of inmates. This chapter will include a brief history of privatization and discuss some of the arguments proffered against privatization, which include:

1. the constitutionality of private enterprise being delegated a responsibility that has historically been relegated to and belongs to the government;
2. the extent to which a state may be held responsible for the constitutional deprivations endured by inmates incarcerated in privately operated prisons; and
3. the extent to which force may be used by private citizens (private prison employees) against private citizens (inmates).

The age of many prisons, as well as court orders to upgrade existing physical plants, may explain why the private sector has been quick to move into a high-profit enterprise (Kastenmeier 1986, 42). Private enterprise has discovered a market ready for development and has wasted no time in doing just that. Private corporations would not be inclined to invest large sums of money unless they anticipated a reasonable return on their investment. Private prison operation is not a get-rich-quick scheme. Corrections Corporation of America, a private corporation, spent over one and a half million dollars from 1985 to 1987 on marketing and lobbying (CCA Annual Report 1987). In addition to money, considerable time, effort, public relations, and market development are required. It is readily apparent that, with the type of money involved, private prison corporations intend to obtain and hold their share of the correctional market. It is also readily apparent that state governments are willing to assist them in that endeavor.

The concept of privatization is generally understood to refer to five formal arrangements:

1. sale of government-owned assets: for example, opening the Oklahoma Territory to settlers;
2. abolition or relaxation of monopolies held by nationalized industries: for example, the vouchers given to citizens of the former Soviet Union as their share in previously state-owned industries;
3. a build-operate-transfer agreement under which a private company agrees to build a major project and to operate it for an agreed-upon length of time: under this method, portions of world fair exhibitions were built and operated by private industry on land owned by taxpayers with the understanding that, on closing of the exhibition, the exhibit becomes the property of the taxpayers;
4. financing by customer fees "pay for use" rather than by taxes: most tollways apply this method; and
5. the contracting out of public services to the private sector: most commonly seen in municipal waste disposal.

The privatization of prisons usually involves a combination of contracting out (number five above) and build-operate-transfer (number three above) of the penal institution (McCrie 1992, 231). For example, the government might enter into a contract with the proposed corporate operator for the specialized custodial staffing and treatment personnel required to address needs of specialized inmate populations. A separate agreement would be negotiated with the same corporation for building the institution, with a transfer of ownership clause to take effect after a specific number of years. The staffing contract would generally be subject to renewal and revision at various yearly intervals. The transfer contract would not be executable until a date specified in the transfer agreement.

## THE BIRTH OF PRIVATIZATION

During the 1600s, England sent its felons to the American colonies. Merchants transported convicts in exchange for the privilege of selling them as indentured servants. In 1666, Raymond Stapleford agreed to build a prison in the colony of Maryland in exchange for

10,000 pounds of tobacco and the right to be named keeper of the prison for life (Durham 1989).

As discussed in Chapter 2, the original American concept of the penitentiary was as a place for doing penance. At the Walnut Street Jail, and later the Eastern Penitentiary, inmates were put to work within their solitary confines. They were provided raw materials, and basic skills were taught. Inmates manufactured clothing, textiles, furniture and other products that were sold in the community at large. Raw materials and training were provided by private industry, and profits were retained by that enterprise. Supervisory staff were provided and paid by that same entity (Allen and Simonsen 1992, 247). Although built at public expense, the operation of this institution was relegated to what we would call today an independent contractor (Johnson 1988, 110).

In the "industrial prisons" that followed the Auburn model, inmates were provided materials and machinery. Singly or in numbers, inmates turned these materials into a variety of saleable commodities. These early prison "industries" were operated by private individuals with profits retained by the operator (Allen 1989, 247). The National Prison Congress of 1870 held in Cincinnati, Ohio, ushered in a new era in the management of penal institutions that stressed vocational training, inmate labor, and the idea that prisons should be run efficiently and at a profit. One legacy of the First National Prison Congress of 1870 was to establish the idea that prison was an industry and should be operated as such.

It was only a short step to recognize that there was profit to be made providing inmate labor to private industry. Labor inside and outside the penal institution provided supplements to institutional budgets or to the income of those operating the facility. As discussed in Chapter 2 and Chapter 5, the *lease system* allowed businessmen to utilize inmates for contract labor. Of course, the contract was not with the inmates but with the prison administrators. That contract may have been entered into with or without the knowledge of the state. Responsibility for discipline became the province of the independent contractor who leased the inmates. Discipline was often harsh and disproportionate to the offense, but nonetheless accepted as part of the contractor's responsibility. Many southern roads, bridges, dams, drained swamps, cleared fields, and general construction was a product of contracted inmate labor. The inmates were housed, supervised, and disciplined by private contractors. There is little question that incarceration and discipline of offenders has perhaps *never* been the *sole* prerogative of the government.

## *THE SOUTHERN EXPERIENCE*

After the Civil War in the United States, many southern states did not have the resources to operate penal institutions. In 1866, Mississippi awarded a 14-year lease to a private firm to operate its state prison. Georgia was the first state to enact convict leasing legislation. Georgia's experience is fairly representative of convict leasing as practiced throughout the South. It is from this experience that the American people derive their collective memories of "prison privatization" and on which much of the opposition to privatization is based.

The South's response to the emancipation proclamation was to begin filling penal institutions with African Americans who had previously been slaves. The first convict lease was entered into on May 11, 1868, by General Thomas H. Ruger, Provisional Governor of Georgia and William A. Fort of Rome, Georgia. The lease was for 100 black inmates to work on the Georgia and Alabama Railroad for one year with the sum of $1,000 paid to the state of Georgia (Taylor 1987). By 1869, the penitentiary of Georgia, containing 393 inmates, was operated by Grant, Alexander and Company, a construction company engaged in the building of railroads (Executive Minutes 1866, 131). The experience with short-term convict leasing prompted Georgia in 1876 to pass legislation allowing private contracts to endure for a period of 20 years. The legislature was concerned that, on the expiration of short-term leases, the state would become responsible for housing the leased inmates, for whom it had no facilities or budget.

Numerous contracts were canceled because of convict abuse or neglect, but the lease system continued. By 1879, there were 14 convict camps in Georgia operated pursuant to leases. Tales of extreme cruelty and deprivation leaked out from the system. Hygiene, potable water, medical care, beds, and food continued to deteriorate under the token supervision provided by the "keeper of the penitentiary," whose responsibility it was to assure that leasers were neither neglecting nor abusing convicts.

The increasing number of convicts dying from illness gave rise to public concern for the conditions within the various convict camps. Allegations of excessive beatings resulting in loss of sight, limb, and life became common. Public concern was met with additional legislation resulting in the Convict Act, adopted on September 28, 1881, which was to address the evils of the lease system. Joint committees of the Georgia Senate and House launched investigations and reported that the new legislation had in fact remedied prior concerns. By 1895, the House and Senate reported that "with few exceptions we find all the camps in bad condition, and the convicts not well treated, and we most heartily condemn the present lease system" (Taylor 1987, 126). Public sentiment finally brought enough scrutiny and interest to the convict lease system that the Georgia General Assembly finally abolished the system in a special session in 1908.

Huntsville Prison in Texas was at one time leased to a private entrepreneur. As early as 1844, Louisiana had awarded a five-year lease on its prison to a private manufacturer (Durham 1989). Many authors have described the inhumane conditions and treatment suffered by inmates in the South under the lease system (Taylor 1987). In light of the early history of private enterprise in corrections, it is not surprising that states are being counseled to enter cautiously into contracts with private enterprise. It is also important to learn from our mistakes and realize that what is financially expedient is not always consistent with a fundamentally ordered society. Many opponents of privatization claim that prisons and prison operations have historically been the province of the government and should remain so (Evans 1987, 259).

It is contended that prisons are publicly operated as a result of our early experience with private enterprise. The courts are seen as overseers of the states and states' employees, whose responsibility it is to assure that inmates are treated humanely and in a constitutionally permissible fashion. There are grave concerns pertaining to the type of oversight that will be provided for privately operated prisons.

## PRIVATIZATION TODAY

Medical and dental care, school programs, counseling, nursing homes, halfway houses, juvenile facilities, drug treatment facilities and alcohol treatment programs are currently being delivered through contracts between private industry and the state. These contracts allow the state to pay private enterprises to provide specific services — some of which occur within prisons. It is the expansion of this contractual premise that has allowed private enterprise to operate the entire prison.

In considering the effectiveness of private enterprise in providing services to state governments, recent court orders demanding an improvement of living conditions and a reduction of overcrowding may give weight to those who argue that private industry cannot do a worse job than is presently being done (Robbins 1986, 26). Over $200 million is spent yearly by state agencies in contracts with private firms for services provided to prisons. The state agencies reported that these contract services were cost effective, that the agencies could not provide them at a similar cost, and that they intended to continue and expand their use of contract services (Camp and Camp 1985). These experiences with private contracting have strongly suggested that the same level of service provided by government may be provided less expensively by a competitive private enterprise.

In 1986, Kentucky saved $400,000 a year by allowing Corrections Corporation of America to manage the Marion Adjustment Center. The Marion Adjustment Center, originally operated by the state at $40 a day per inmate, was successfully operated by private enterprise for $25 per inmate, without a loss in service or quality (Bryce 1993). Since 1985, there has been a rapid growth in local, state, and federal agencies shifting to private firms for the full-scale operation of correctional facilities. It has been estimated that in 1989 the value of contracts exceeded $250 million. Private corporations are currently operating prisons in 16 states. In Texas alone, there are presently 28 facilities either under construction or operated by private contractors (Corrections Corporation of America 1992).

Proponents of privatization claim that private prisons can be constructed more quickly. This argument may have merit when examined in light of the bidding procedures required by states. Before groundbreaking can begin, the taxpayers must pass a resolution allowing bonds to be sold, the proceeds of which will be used to build a prison. During the planning stage, bids are received from state-approved contractors and a prospective building budget is developed, determining how many bonds need to be sold. After the bond issue is agreed on by the state, it must then be submitted to the voting public. Meanwhile, all the costs have inflated directly in proportion to the length of time that has passed from the receipt of bids to the day the first nail is driven (Logan and Rausch 1985, 313). All estimates of cost using this procedure fall short, and then voters become angry because of cost overrides. This time lag is not altogether seen as an impediment. In the words of M. Wayne Huggins, spokesman for the national sheriffs' group, "Red tape, in a lot of cases, is there to protect the public" (Bowditch and Everett 1991, 184).

Private industry is not bound by a restricted list of bidders. There may be other parties who can provide material and building services more rapidly and less expensively than those nominated by the state as exclusive bidding contractors. There is no need for a bond issue or voter approval. The cost of construction can be deferred through a lease purchase agreement, an agreement whereby private financing is used to build and operate the prison. The state then leases the prison from the private contractor. Pursuant to the same agreement the contractor agrees to provide all services for a fee. At the end of the lease period, the state can purchase the facility from the builder at a fraction of the original construction costs, paying only future operating costs. If the facility was constructed with quality material and provided for expansion, this purchase may be in the interests of the taxpayer; but, if inferior quality materials were used, maintenance of the facility was lacking, or the original design does not allow for expansion, the purchase may not be in the best interests of the taxpayer (Logan and Rausch 1985, 315).

Comparing costs between private and public institutions may disguise important differences in the type and extent of services rendered. When a private corporation takes over a total institution, such as a psychiatric hospital, medical hospital, nursing home, or school, concerns for profitability often restrict, compromise, or eliminate special services. In such instances, public institutions may have to provide the necessary services (Bowditch and Everett 1991, 184).

## DELEGATION OF A UNIQUELY STATE FUNCTION

Opponents of privatization question government's authority to delegate correctional responsibilities to the private sector. While some opponents take this stand based on concern for the constitutionality of such delegation, it should be noted that there may be different motivations involved as well. Just as private enterprise has not been motivated to enter the correctional marketplace out of altruism, many objecting to privatization are less interested in inmate rights than in the self-interest of protecting jobs and power. History shows that government has seen fit to delegate responsibility in the form of privately operated penal facilities, chain gangs, and other forms of contract labor, most of which have now been rendered impermissible as a result of lawsuits and court decisions. These private uses of inmates were abandoned not only because of concerns over the constitutional authority of states to allow private industry to operate penal institutions or discipline inmates, but also because of a populist movement to prohibit state competition with private enterprise (Johnson 1988, 114).

The delegation of authority has been seen by states as unavoidable. State governments do not have the resources to provide the myriad services that citizens need. Some of the services traditionally provided by private contractors include public transportation, ambulance service, garbage collection, sewage processing, and hospital operations. Of the many services delegated by the state to private contractors, in the last 50 years neither the U.S. Supreme Court nor any state supreme court has invalidated a single contract for privatized services (Robbins 1986, 29). There is both statutory and case law that supports the delegation of services by the state to private vendors (Robbins 1986).

On the state level, only Pennsylvania continues to embrace legal impediments to privatization of corrections. The trend today is toward "clarifying and granting statutory authority to state agencies to permit contracting" (Hackett and Hatry 1987, 17). Statutes that permit correctional authorities to delegate are referred to as *enabling statutes*. Numerous states have passed enabling statutes delegating to private contractors authority to operate prisons, including Alaska, Colorado, Florida, Kentucky, Massachusetts, Montana, New Mexico, Tennessee, Texas, Utah, and Wisconsin (Brakel 1992, 263).

Privatization in limited security situations has become a reality in 16 states, Britain, New Zealand, and Australia. Twenty-five states, Washington, D.C., and Puerto Rico have passed enabling statutes to allow private contractors to operate correctional institutions. The debate on whether government can delegate correctional authority is devolving into a question of whether maximum security prisons can be operated by private enterprise. To date, the private sector has not expressed an overwhelming interest in maximum security institutions. But there are some notable exceptions. Corrections Corporation of America's (CCA) Silverdale Detention Center, near Chattanooga, Tennessee, houses 120 felons. CCA's Bay County Jail in Panama City, Florida, houses serious and capital felons. Finally, the Butler County Prison, formally operated in Pennsylvania by Buckingham Security Company, was and is specifically designated a maximum security institution housing state and federal felons. Legal challenges based on security level are spurious. A constitutional challenge must rest on the question of delegation per se. If the delegation of correctional authority is constitutional on any level, it is constitutional on all levels; conversely, if it is unconstitutional on any level, it is unconstitutional on all levels (Brakel 1992, 264).

From a purely legal perspective, the government possesses no authority unless so granted by the people it governs. If the people have delegated authority to the government, then it should be apparent that the concept of delegation is not inherently an anathema to the people. It is not the question of delegation of authority that is in dispute, but rather what accountability is retained by the government for the conduct of those to whom it has delegated the people's authority. In the final analysis, it is the law, not the civil status of the actor, that determines whether any particular exercise of authority is legitimate (Logan 1987, 36).

## THE STATE ACTION DOCTRINE

An additional constitutional concern regarding privatization involves the question of whether the acts of a private entity operating a correctional institution constitute *state action* for the purpose of determining federal civil liability. When a party violates rights guaranteed by the Constitution or federal statutes, in order to prevail, the party who is alleging their rights have been violated must show that the violating party was acting "under the color of law," or in other words, with the power of the federal or a state government. *Lugar v. Edmonson Oil Co.,* 457 U.S. 922 (1982).

As discussed in the last chapter, the federal statutes protecting individual rights and constitutional guarantees for due process contained in the Fifth and Fourteenth Amendments apply only to the acts of government, not private industry. The obvious question is whether the violation of individual constitutional rights by private correctional personnel is "attributable to the state." *Rendell-Baker v. Kohn,* 457 U.S. 830 (1982). Federal courts have applied one of three tests in determining if state action exists: (1) the public function test; (2) the close nexus test; and (3) the state compulsion test. At one time or another, legal commentators have applied all three to the private prison context (Robbins 1986, 813).

*Public Function Test.* Although there is no precise formula for defining state action, the courts have recognized a *public function* concept, which provides that state action exists when the state delegates to private parties a power "traditionally exclusively reserved to the State." *Flagg Brothers, Inc. v. Brooks,* 436 U.S. 149, 153 (1978). It is not simply whether a private group is serving a public function but whether that function has been exclusively the prerogative of the state. *Rendall-Baker v. Kohn,* 457 U.S. 830 (1982). To date, no court has held penal incarceration as "traditionally exclusively" reserved to the state.

*Close Nexus Test.* In applying the *close nexus* test, the courts have been primarily concerned with the nature of the relationship between the state and the challenged action, that is, whether the action of the private actor was so intertwined with the action of the state as to be indistinguishable. *Jackson v. Metropolitan Edison Co.,* 419 U.S. 345 (1974). In *Milonas v. Williams,* 691 F.2d 931 (10th Cir. 1982), a student of a privately operated school for behaviorally disturbed youth brought a cause of action alleging constitutional violations as a result of the behavior modification techniques in use. The student alleged that the school administration violated the cruel and unusual punishment clause of the Eighth Amendment and the due process clause of the Fourteenth Amendment. The unanimous decision by the court of appeals found that the conduct in question was state action, because the state had so "insinuated itself with the school as to be considered a joint participant in the offending actions." 691 F.2d at 934.

In coming to the conclusion that there was state action, the court considered several things: that many of the juveniles had been placed at the school pursuant to court order; contracts were entered into with the local public schools that allowed placement of recalcitrant students; the state paid "tuition" for juveniles placed; and there was significant state regulation of the educational program employed. The court saw these facts, as well as the involuntary nature of the confinement, the detailed nature of the contracts, the level of government funding, and the extent of state regulation, as a sufficiently close nexus between the state and the conduct of the school administration to support a claim of violation of constitutional rights as a result of state action (Robbins 1986).

*State Compulsion Test.*    In applying the *state compulsion test,* it must be determined whether the duty provided is one for which the state is obligated. Opponents of privatization have been concerned that states may attempt to avoid constitutional liability by delegating their correctional responsibilities to the private sector. It is apparent that the courts are not overly receptive to that notion. *Lombard v. Eunice Kennedy Shriver Center,* 566 F. Supp. 677 (D. Mass. 1983), was a case involving a mentally retarded resident of a state institution who had received substandard care from a medical practitioner. The services in question had been rendered pursuant to contract with a private vendor. The state contended that because the private corporation providing all of the medical care was a private entity, the state could not be held accountable. The *Lombard* court said:

> Because the state bore an affirmative obligation to provide adequate medical care to plaintiff, because the state delegated that function . . . , and because [that corporation] voluntarily assumed that obligation by contract, [the private entity] must be

considered to have acted under color of law, and its acts and omissions must be considered actions of the state. For if [the private entity] were not held so responsible, the state could avoid its constitutional obligations simply by delegating governmental functions to private entities. (566 F. Supp. at 680)

It is most likely that, when the courts specifically address deprivation of inmate constitutional rights at the hands of privately operated correctional institutions, one or all of the above tests will be employed in determining whether state action was involved. As a practical matter, however, *indemnification agreements* (an agreement whereby the vendor agrees to pay all costs associated with lawsuits arising out of the operation of the facility) between the state and the private vendor should provide sufficient financial security for the state that delegation of correctional authority to avoid liability ceases to be an issue.

## ENABLING STATUTES

Fundamental to the contracting process is an enabling statute whereby the legislature has authorized the state to delegate by contract its correctional authority. This statute must specifically address rules, regulations, licensing, policies, and procedures pertinent to the operation of private correctional facilities, as well as designate staff, facilities, budgets, and responsible agencies for the oversight of those rules, regulations, licensing, policies, and procedures.

Enabling statutes must grant judges authority to sentence defendants to private institutions; without such legislation, any sentence to a private prison would be subject to a jurisdictional challenge. In those states that allow accrual of good time, enabling statutes must address how that good time is to be calculated and by whom. If correctional personnel in private prisons are to have disciplinary authority, the parameters of that authority must be set out in some detail within the enabling legislation.

## CONTRACT CONSIDERATIONS

To ensure that inmate rights are protected, that taxpayer confidence is not misplaced, and that an accountability mechanism exists, states must provide competent legal expertise in negotiating, drafting, and executing contracts for the operation of correctional facilities. In

Pennsylvania, the Attorney General's office has responsibility for approving private correctional contracts. These contracts minimally include an adequate performance bond, adequate insurance, familiarity with and agreement to abide by all applicable regulations, an operations plan including security features, an annual contract review provision, and a termination for cause clause (Woolley 1985). In addition to specific contractual obligations, the contract must contain indemnification language, by which the contractor assumes all costs incurred in defending against any actions arising out of the operation of the facility, and a promise to obtain insurance to cover such costs. See Highlight 11-1.

---

**HIGHLIGHT 11-1**
**Example of an Indemnification Clause**

CCA shall save and hold harmless and indemnify the [insert name of governmental entity] the members of its governing body, employees, agents, attorneys, legal representatives, heirs and beneficiaries, whether acting in their official or individual capacity, and shall pay all judgments rendered against any and all liability, claims, and cost, of whatsoever kind and nature for physical or personal injury and any other kind of injury, specifically deprivation of civil rights, and for loss or damage to any property occurring in connection with or in any way incident to or arising out of the occupancy, use, service, operation or performance by CCA, its agents, employees or representatives of any of the provisions or agreements contained in this Contract, including any Appendices, for which the [insert name of government entity] or governing body, employees and agents, attorneys, or other persons, as noted hereinabove, whether acting in their official or individual capacity, who may become legally liable resulting in whole or in part from the acts, errors, or omissions of CCA, or any officer, agent, representative, or employee thereof, and for which CCA shall pay all judgments which may be rendered against the [enter name of government entity], employees, and agents, including attorneys, and other persons as noted hereinabove, whether in their individual or official capacity. (Correctional Corporation of America 1987, 32-33)

In 1986, Corrections Corporation of America (CCA) spent $940,000 for $5 million of liability insurance. By 1987, CCA had established a self-insurance trust fund in the sum of $5 million and hired a claims adjusting firm to administer the fund. Most private corrections companies carry large amounts of insurance (Logan 1990).

With appropriate oversight, it should be possible to negotiate and execute contracts that address the needs and interests of all the parties, bearing in mind that the state has the responsibility for representing the interests of all the people of the state, including inmates.

## USE OF FORCE

"The right to use deadly force is widely regarded as an exclusive prerogative of government, but this is a misconception" (Logan 1990, 172). Logan goes on to say that the right to use force lies in the law, not the person or status of the person employing such force. In those states that have a penal code based on the Modern Penal Code (1962), there are provisions that exist for a citizen's use of force and deadly force. Many situations arising in a penal institution that would require the use of force would permit a citizen to use reasonable and necessary force. Most of the language used by states in authorizing public correctional officials to use force can be used for private correctional staff with minor modification (Woolley 1985, 323). From a practical standpoint, private correctional personnel should have training and standards comparable to or in excess of those in the public sector. Training, hiring, and firing issues should be addressed in contract negotiations.

If private correctional institutions are subject to state action constitutional violation causes of action, a failure on the part of the private prison to provide adequate training is actionable. *City of Canton, Ohio v. Harris et al.,* 489 U.S. 378 (1989). It would be foolhardy for private enterprise to subject itself to prospective litigation for failing to provide adequate training. The best approach in dealing with the use of force and use of deadly force issues is to require that correctional staff be "certified" as correctional officers with the same breadth and scope of training as public correctional personnel.

# A Future Perspective on Privatization

Traditionally, states have responded in one of four ways to the housing shortage created by an ever-growing number of inmates:

1. Build more prisons.    Chapter 3 chronicled the expansion of prison construction in this country and the seemingly little effect this expansion has had on crime rates. The costs of such an enterprise are astronomical, and taxpayers may soon decide they cannot afford to continue building more and more prisons.

2. Community corrections (intermediate sanctions).    Many states have developed alternatives to incarceration by attempting to employ community resources to address the low-risk offender. Most intermediate sanctions (for example, house arrest and home monitoring programs) simply widen the correctional net. Individuals who would have been placed on intensively supervised probation status are now being relegated to home monitoring programs. People who would ordinarily receive a prison sentence still go to prison. Those who would have received probation still receive probation except to perhaps more strict conditions, for example, home monitoring. The less harsh alternatives are often reserved for the low-risk white offender, thereby increasing the number of poor men and women of color who fill our prisons.

3. Do nothing.    Ignore the problem and hope that it goes away or at least remains unnoticed. The courts will no longer allow us to pretend that we do not see, hear, or read about constitutional deprivations as a result of overcrowding. Regardless of taxpayer willingness and readiness to address prison expansion, courts are giving municipalities, counties, and states few alternatives. It is expensive to address court orders to provide additional space per inmate; it is potentially more costly not to abide by those court orders. The court can levy direct monetary penalties on the governmental entity, which will ultimately be paid by the taxpayer.

4. Privatization.    Although there are many opponents to privately operated prisons and many realistic concerns about accountability and constitutional issues, until opponents come up with a better short-term alternative, privatization is here to stay.

Privatization is not the answer to crime reduction, but an alternative while we are working on crime reduction. State, federal, and municipal governments have recognized that privatization is an idea whose time has come. Since the word was first used in 1969, privatization has gained broad recognition and widespread acceptance. Recent years have seen a marked trend toward privatization in the United States, primarily in the area of service contracts.

The management of prisons was not and is not the most frequent use of privatization. Services — such as medical care — constitute what is most frequently purchased from private sources. Medical care, mental health, community treatment centers, education, drug treatment, college programs, staff training, vocational training, and counseling ranked numbers one through nine in frequency of purchase from private sources (Demone and Gibelman 1990). Those jurisdictions entering into private contracts for what had historically been public services have been highly satisfied with the performance and quality of those services. That satisfaction laid the foundation for an ever-broadening spectrum of delegation of services culminating in contracts to operate prisons and prison industries (Savas 1987, 892).

The future of prison privatization is here. Fifteen years ago, privately operated prisons were a figment of the imagination. Since 1980, 25 states, the District of Columbia, and Puerto Rico have enacted legislation authorizing private sector operation of correctional facilities. In 1980, no states had legislation allowing the operation of prisons by private enterprise. Today 50 percent of the states have enacted such legislation. The last 16 years have witnessed a substantial growth in the number of states recognizing the potential of privately operated prisons.

The overall prison population is growing at 30 percent a year, a rate that exceeds the taxpayers' inclination to fund. While the demand for incarceration grows, the funds for additional prison space does not. Although the public demands that offenders be incarcerated, the public refuses to pay the associated costs of incarceration. Federal, state, and even foreign governments are looking to the private sector for relief. Internationally, including facilities under construction and facilities operating, there are about 30,000 beds being provided by 21 different private contractors.

Corrections Corporation of America (CCA) controls 41 percent of the private correctional market worldwide and one-third of the domestic market. Established in 1983, CCA manages over 9,000 beds in six states, Britain, and Australia. Company revenues are growing at 30 percent per year. Wall Street views CCA as part of a growth industry (Bryce 1993, 7). Wackenhut, a Coral Gables, Florida-based international private investigation and security service firm, operates 18 percent of all privately run prisons in the United States. Wackenhut Corrections is growing at about 12 percent per year (Bryce 1993, 7).

## PRIVATIZATION AND WOMEN

The first privately contracted state prison holding adults at all levels of security was a facility specifically designed and operated for women (Logan 1990). On July 1, 1988, New Mexico entered into a contract with Corrections Corporation of America for the design, construction, and operation of a prison for 200 women felons. This prison has all levels of internal and external security. Staff for the New Mexico prison were transferred from another state penitentiary that originally had responsibility for the women. All training is provided by the state. Services include education, recreation, counseling, and medical and dental care. CCA operates work, study release, and furlough programs. The New Mexico Corrections Department retains authority over all major decisions including classification, discipline, grievances, good time, parole eligibility, discharge dates, work release participation, study release participation, and furlough participation (Logan 1990). Wackenhut operates a 500-bed facility for women in Lockhart, Texas. This facility is structurally attached to a 500-bed pre-release unit for men but is separated programmatically and through contract (for example, the women cannot participate in the same work programs because they are not designated by the pre-release status).

Actually, private contractors have been involved in corrections for women for a very long time. The earliest halfway houses were established for women and run by private religious organizations. For instance, the Volunteers of America, a nonprofit agency, has been involved in corrections since 1896 (Volunteers of America 1985). Today, the Volunteers of America operates a 42-bed medium security regional correctional facility for women in Rosedale, Minnesota. It has a staff of 17 full-time workers and a number of volunteer workers. All the inmates are women serving sentences of up to one year. Volunteers of America has contracts with other Minnesota counties and the federal government to provide incarceration at the Rosedale facility on an as needed basis (Woolley 1985, 308).

## PRIVATE PRISON FUNCTIONS

The private sector can and will continue to perform several distinct functions with respect to prisons:

1. operate juvenile facilities;
2. finance and construct prisons;

3. provide work for prisoners; and
4. provide specific services for inmates.

Each of these functions continues to draw the attention of state government and is being employed more often in more states (Main 1985, 92).

*Operate Juvenile Facilities.* Citizen concern over random violence, juvenile gangs, drug use, and drug distribution has altered the national perspective from one of protecting the child to protecting the community. A move toward a "due process" perspective and away from the "best interest of the child" perspective based on those concerns guarantees increases in the number of juveniles incarcerated. The private sector entered into the contracting of juvenile services as early as 1987. The move from contracting services to operating juvenile facilities was a logical progression. Private enterprise presently operates over 500 juvenile facilities in the United States (Johnson and Ross 1990, 354).

*Finance and Construct Prisons.* Public interest has focused on the role of private enterprise in the construction and operation of various types of correctional facilities. Interest in prison privatization stems from the public's belief that private industry is capable of providing cost-effective prison operations without the concomitant bureaucratic delays and cost overrides. The costs of publicly operated prisons are said to be 20 to 40 percent greater than private costs; the evidence is not yet persuasive, but taxpayers and state governments are neither willing nor able to wait until all the evidence is in (Savas 1987, 896).

Although opponents voice reasonable concerns over constitutional rights and contract accountability, states are turning to private industry in large numbers for answers to their correctional dilemma. Private enterprise operates over 7,000 jails and prisons nationwide (Johnson and Ross 1990, 354). In 1984, Camp and Camp conducted a poll and predicted that, because private companies target low-risk minimum security inmates, only a small percentage of inmates would be housed in private prisons (Camp and Camp 1984). There are over 15,000 beds under private contract, most of which did not exist at the time of the Camp and Camp opinion poll in 1984. It should be noted that private corrections facilities are not replacing public facilities but are being added to the system.

*Provide Work for Prisoners.* The issues involved in prison industry have been discussed in Chapter 5. Although public opinion favors prisoners working, private interest groups do not want jobs taken from citizens to employ inmates. By 1940, most prisons were involved in some type of prison labor that competed with private enterprise. As a result of labor group lobbying, in 1940 Congress banned all interstate commerce in goods made by prisoners (Acker 1989). This prohibition continued until 1979, when the rapid growth of prison populations, accompanied by new concerns about the high cost of corrections, led to a reappraisal of this ban. Recognizing that no business can operate profitably if it is not allowed to sell its product across state lines, the 1979 Percy Amendment allowed exceptions to the federal prohibition on interstate trade of prison-produced goods. Today, the Department of Justice, through the American Correctional Association, is allowed to grant 20 exceptions per year under the Private Industry Enhancement (PIE) program (Acker 1989, 73). Nebraska is one of the states recognized under PIE. The Nebraska program has generated hundreds of thousands of dollars for the prison system by bringing in outside businesses to employ inmates at minimum wage. Five percent of each inmate's wage is deducted for victims' restitution, and one dollar an hour is deducted for room and board (Acker 1989, 74).

In Florida, a private firm established Prison Rehabilitation Industries and Diversified Enterprise, Inc. (PRIDE) to operate all state correctional industries. In 1988, the company made a $4 million profit and paid 60 percent of inmates' wages to the state to defray correctional costs (Chi 1989, 71). Private industry recognizes the advantages of a captive workforce. There are few problems with alcohol or substance abuse and little inventory loss. There is no need for vacations, health insurance, national holidays, or sick leave. Absenteeism is minimal. The workforce is available 24 hours a day, seven days a week. Although multishift operations have not yet begun, it is reasonable to foresee shift changes and shift workers.

The minimum overhead to private enterprise in operating prison industries has attracted the attention of various labor organizations. Unions in several states have protested the new work programs. Unions are concerned with the impact privately operated prison industries will have on job availability in the marketplace and with the morality of using prison labor to manufacture consumer goods. Critics point to the sanctions imposed by the United States government on China and Korea for using inmate labor. The concerns of labor groups have had little impact on privatization of prison industries. The fact that inmates are contributing to the costs of their upkeep and restitution has not been lost on taxpayers or state officials and policy makers. The goal is not solely to produce a profit, but also to assist prisoners to become, or return to being, productive members of society by having them produce a product or perform a service that can compete in the marketplace (Demone and Gibelman 1990). There are presently 38 states operating prison industries under PIE. Given the movement toward a greater role for the private sector in prison operations, it is likely that prisoners will do more piecework and factory labor in the future (Chi 1989, 72).

***Provide Specific Services for Inmates.***   The use of the private sector to provide various correctional services is not new. Traditionally food service, health care, counseling, education, and transportation have often been provided by private vendors. The rationale for using private contractors has been the belief that these vendors are more economical and efficient in rendering certain services. Over the years, states have been contracting for additional correctional services once exclusively performed by public employees. Such services have included administrative as well as institutional services. Some states contract for rehabilitation and conservation camps. Studies have addressed the feasibility of contracting inmate classification, management of offender data systems, purchasing, payroll, and accounting. New Jersey's Department of Corrections has contracted for data management, and Illinois has contracted with private enterprise to provide parole services (Chi 1989, 71).

Contracting for services can also offer states the ability to meet the needs of atypical inmates. The special health, medical, or psychological needs of certain prisoners could be met by contracting with an appropriately equipped private institution. This raises the possibility of a cottage industry of private prisons designed solely to meet the needs of special-care prisoners. The individual aptitudes of prisoners could be matched with corresponding educational and technical skills programs that specific private prisons could establish as specialties (Evans 1987, 281).

While cost effectiveness of private service contracts should be assessed on a case-by-case basis, it appears that most jurisdictions are contracting, and will continue to contract, selected correctional services.

# CONCLUSIONS

With violence now one of this nation's top concerns, lawmakers have voted on crime legislation that would increase the number of street police by 100,000. The fruits of the efforts of these additional "street police" will be more arrests, prosecutions, and lengthier prison terms (Gest 1993, 6). It is reasonable to presume that inmate numbers will continue to grow as violence, drug abuse, and media coverage of violence continues to grow.

Responding to public pressures to "get tough on crime," legislators have enacted laws that have contributed to the overcrowding problem. These same legislatures often fail to appropriate the additional funds needed to implement these laws. We are confronted with the daily reality of releasing serious offenders before they have served a significant portion of their sentences. They must be released so that we can make room for other offenders. We also find ourselves, pursuant to federal mandatory sentencing schemes for drug offenders, releasing serious offenders who have been sentenced without the benefit of mandatory sentences so that less serious drug offenders who have been sentenced under mandatory sentences can be housed. The squeeze of having to uncrowd correctional facilities quickly while cutting budgets has forced federal and state officials to look with favor on companies that will finance, design, build, and run correctional facilities (Main 1985, 101).

If we revised penal codes to include shorter sentences (admittedly in the face of public pressure for longer sentences), decriminalized the drugs most commonly abused, and addressed social, economic and ethnic inequities, there would still be inmates incarcerated in constitutionally unacceptable conditions, as well as those who would be incarcerated until the enacted changes took effect. It is not likely that sentences are going to be reduced, drugs decriminalized, or social inequities addressed any time in the near future. If taxpayers are unwilling to fund additional prisons or to address constitutionally unacceptable living conditions in presently existing prisons, then privatization becomes the only workable idea proffered. The bottom line is fairly simple: "A well-run correctional facility is a well-run correctional facility, no matter who runs it" (Saxton 1988, 17).

In ten short years, privatization of prisons has gone from a hotly debated idea to a hotly debated reality. Left unattended, the private sector might maximize profits and turn prisons into a growth industry. As long as private industry can finance, build, and administer prisons with relative ease, there may be no impetus for the public to evaluate correctional policies, living conditions, and alternatives to inmate warehousing (DiIulio 1990, 6). The government, as the consumer of the private prison product, can relieve itself of the day-to-day headaches of prison operations. As long as the operation was cost-effective, both government and private industry may be satisfied.

However, without governmental accountability and oversight, a profitable private prison industry could easily become an oppressive private prison industry. Bureaucracies are often criticized for creating nothing but larger bureaucracies. Yet the idea of government oversight through agencies was designed to protect the powerless from the powerful. Much of the very government red tape, redundancy, and inefficiency we so readily criticize was designed to protect workers from the unscrupulous, ruthless, and inhumane pursuit of profit.

We may delegate the authority to incarcerate to the private sector, but we cannot delegate the responsibility for those incarcerated to anyone. If inmates are to receive constitutionally mandated treatment, government must remain vigilant. If inmates are to continue to have redress for constitutional deprivations, courts must remain accessible. If constitutional rights are to be preserved, accountability must be effective.

If the privatization experiences of other fields, ranging from defense to social services, are lessons from which to learn, there are some caveats that must be considered by government and private enterprise. Although the governmental agency will need fewer employees as a result of privatization, they must be better trained. The contract should be clear as to governmental objectives and focus on methods of quantitative and qualitative measurement. Efforts should be made to collaborate with colleges and universities in including prison privatization into the Criminal Justice curriculum. Private contractors must avoid "jumping on the band wagon" in an effort to get in on the profits to be made and bid on privatization contracts only when possessing the necessary resources and competence. Private enterprise should not be bound to the anachronistic, formalistic, and cost-intensive hiring practices of the government. Line item budget vetoes are workable in governmental agencies where budgets can be supplemented by creative bookkeeping; they are not workable in private enterprise without causing organizational problems. Salary structures and benefit programs of the government should not be imposed upon the private sector (Demone and Gibelman 1990).

Much has been written in support of private enterprise operating prisons. More needs to be written opposing the notion. It is only through constant research, questions, and criticism that we can be sure that inmates will not become the invisible victims of an inhumane pursuit of profits. Prisons are a reality of contemporary life as are the costs associated with them.

Regardless of public sentiment, the United States courts will not allow inmates to be housed in deprived and punitive circumstances.

Ever-increasing prison populations are creating a bureaucratic and fiscal nightmare. Much of the bureaucracy and most of the cost of prison operations can be borne by private enterprise. In many states and some foreign countries, privately operated prisons are a reality. There are serious concerns confronting those states that embark on the privatization sea. Constitutional issues that will not lie quietly bloom from the fertile seeds of inhumanity that were sown in the early years of America's infatuation with prison privatization. Greed, racism, prejudice, and insensitivity gave rise to a public outcry against the convict lease system. That concern should serve as a warning for the types of abuses that can arise when profit is the only motive and the government abrogates its supervisory responsibility. The early southern experience should not prevent us from continuing to experiment with penal methodology to discover the most cost-effective, humane, and just method of incarcerating citizens. Yet constant vigilance is required in any penal endeavor, perhaps more so when private enterprise is involved.

The most obvious balance available in the state versus private sector contracting scheme is the contract. Shrewd scrutiny and foresight during contract negotiations will go a long way in reducing many concerns pertaining to private prison accountability. Indemnification agreements, performance bonds, review procedures, and training criteria can provide public accountability to an extent that exceeds what may be presently available in many states.

It is apparent that all aspects of public incarceration have, at times, included private operations: juvenile facilities, community correctional programs, and prisons for men and women. There is every reason to believe that, with recent "get tough on crime" legislation and mandatory sentences, privately operated prisons are a growth industry. Private prisons are not only an idea whose time has come; if those prisons and inmate services being operated by private contractors are successful, private prisons are an idea whose time is unavoidable.

## Vocabulary

| | |
|---|---|
| close nexus test | public function test |
| enabling statutes | state action doctrine |
| indemnification agreements | state compulsion test |
| lease system | |

## Study Questions

1. What are three common arguments opposing prison privatization? What are the arguments in favor of prison privatization?

2. The convict lease system was abandoned for two reasons. What were they?

3. Explain the five formal arrangements between government and private enterprise.

4. What are the four distinct functions the private sector performs with respect to prisons?

5. What constitutional issues are involved with private prisons' use of force, discipline, and good time?

6. What is the state action doctrine and what, if any, impact has it on private prisons?

7. In what way will the Private Industry Enhancement program allow prisons to become self-sufficient?

## Sources Cited

— Acker, Kevin. 1989. "Off with Their Overhead: More Prison Bars for the Buck." *Policy Review* (Fall): 73-76.

— Allen, Harry E., and Clifford Simonsen. 1992. *Corrections in America: An Introduction.* New York: Macmillan.

— American Bar Association. 1990. *Report on Prison Overcrowding.* Submitted to the American Bar Association's House of Delegates by the ABA Criminal Justice Section. February.

— Ammons, David, Richard Campbell, and Sandra Somoza. 1992. "The Option of Prison Privatization: A Guide for Community Deliberations." Athens, Ga.: Carl Vinson Institute of Government, University of Georgia.

— Anderson, Patrick, Charles Davoli, and Laura Moriarty. 1985. "Private Corrections: Feast or Fiasco?" *Prison Journal* 65(2): 32-41.

— Baird, Charles. 1989. "Building More Prisons Will Not Solve Prison Overcrowding." In *American Prisons: Opposing Viewpoints,* ed. S. Tipp, 118-124. San Diego: Greenhaven.

— Bast, Diane C. 1986. *In Defense of Private Prisons.* Chicago: Heartland Institute.

— Becker, Craig, and Amy Stanley. 1985. "Incarceration, Inc.: The Downside of Private Prisons." *Nation* (June 15): 728-730.

— Borna, Shaneen. 1986. "Free Enterprise Goes to Prison." *British Journal of Criminology* 226(4): 321-334.

— Bowditch, Christine, and Ronald Everett. 1987. "Private Prisons: Problems within the Solution." *Justice Quarterly* 4: 441-453.

— Bowditch, Christine, and Ronald Everett. 1991. "Private Prisons Are Not More Efficient Than Public Prisons." In *America's Prisons: Opposing Viewpoints,* ed. S. Tipp, 184-193. San Diego: Greenhaven.

— Bowman, George W. 1992. *Privatizing the United States Justice System.* Jefferson, N.C.: McFarland.

— Brakel, Samuel Jan. 1989. "Privatization in Corrections: Radical Prison Chic or Mainstream Americana?" *New England Journal on Criminal and Civil Confinement* 14 (Winter): 1-39.

— Brakel, Samuel. 1992. "Private Corrections." In *Privatizing the United States Justice System,* ed. G. Bowman, 114-133. Jefferson, N.C.: McFarland.

— Brockway, Zebulon R. 1912. *Fifty Years of Prison Service: An Autobiography.* New York: Charities Publishing.

— Bryce, Robert. 1993. "A Lock on Prisons: Big Business Behind Bars." *Current* (November 4): 6.

— Camp, Camille G., and George M. Camp. 1984. "Private Sector Involvement in Prison Services and Operations." Report to

National Institute of Corrections. Washington, D.C.: National Institute of Corrections.

— Camp, Camille, and George Camp. 1985. "Correctional Privatization in Perspective." *Prison Journal* 65(2): 14-31.

— Chi, Keon S. 1989. "Prison Overcrowding and Privatization: Models and Opportunities." *The Journal of State Government* (Fall): 71-76.

— Cikins, Warren I. 1986. "Privatization of the American Prison System: An Idea Whose Time Has Come?" *Notre Dame Journal of Law, Ethics, and Public Policy* 2(2): 445-464.

— Collins, William C. 1986. "Privatization: Some Legal Considerations from a Neutral Perspective." In *Correctional Law*, 81-93. Olympia, Wash.: William C. Collins.

— Corrections Corporation of America. 1987. *Annual Report.* Nashville, Tenn.: CCA.

— Corrections Corporation of America. 1992. *Annual Report.* Nashville, Tenn.: CCA.

— Demone, Harold W., and Margaret Gibelman. 1990. "Privatizing the Treatment of Criminal Offenders." In *The Clinical Treatment of the Criminal Offender in Outpatient Mental Health Settings*, ed. N. Pallone and S. Chaneles, 37-51. New York: Haworth.

— DiIulio, John J., Jr. 1986. "Prisons, Profits, and the Public Good: The Privatization of Corrections." *Research Bulletin — Sam Houston State University* 1, 6. Rockville, Md.: NIJ.

— DiIulio, John J., Jr. 1988. "What's Wrong with Private Prisons." *Public Interest* 92 (Summer): 66-83.

— DiIulio, John J., Jr. 1990. *Duty to Govern: A Critical Perspective on the Private Management of Prisons and Jails.* New Brunswick, N.J.: Rutgers University Press.

— Dunham, Douglas W. 1986. "Inmates' Rights and the Privatization of Prisons." *Columbia Law Review* 86: 1475-1504.

— Durham, Alexis M., III. 1989. "Origins of Interest in the Privatization of Punishment: The Nineteenth and Twentieth Century American Experience." *Criminology* 27(1): 43-52.

— Ellison W. James. 1987. "Privatization of Corrections: A Critique and Analysis of Contemporary Views." *Cumberland Law Review* 17: 683-729.

— Elvin, Jan. 1985. "A Civil Liberties View of Private Prisons." *Prison Journal* 65(2): 48-52.

— Evans, Brian B. 1987. "Private Prisons." *Emory Law Journal* 36 (Winter): 253-283.

— Gentry, James T. 1986. "The Panopticon Revisited: The Problem of Monitoring Private Prisons." *Yale Law Journal* 96: 353-375.

— Gest, Terrence. 1993. "Violence and Its Terrifying Randomness." *U.S. News and World Report* (December 20): 6.

— Hackett, J., and H. Hatry. 1987. "Issues in Contracting for the Private Operation of Prisons and Jails — Executive Summary." National Institute of Justice. Rockville, Md.: NIJ.

— Johnson, Byron, and Paul Ross. 1990. "The Privatization of Correctional Management: A Review." *Journal of Criminal Justice* 18: 351-358.

— Johnson, Harold A. 1988. *History of Criminal Justice.* Cincinnati: Anderson.

— Kastenmeier, R. W. 1986. "Corrections and Crowding." *Corrections Today* 48: 38-42.

— Kay, Susan L. 1987. "The Implications of Prison Privatization on the Conduct of Prisoner Litigation under 42 U.S.C. Section 1983." *Vanderbilt Law Review* 40(4): 867-888.

— Larson, Erik. 1988. "Captive Company." *Inc.* (June): 86-92.

— Logan, Charles H. 1987. "The Propriety of Proprietary Prisons." *Federal Probation* 51: 36.

— Logan Charles H. 1989. "Proprietary Prisons." In *The American Prison: Issues in Research and Policy,* ed. Lynne Goodstein and Doris L. Mackenzie, 137-147. New York: Plenum.

— Logan, Charles H. 1990. *Private Prisons: Cons and Pros.* New York: Oxford University Press.

— Logan, Charles H., and Sharla Rausch. 1985. "Punishment and Profit: The Emergence of Private Enterprise Prisons." *Justice Quarterly* 2: 303-318.

— Main, Jeremy. 1985. "When Public Services Go Private." *Fortune* (May 27): 92.

— McCrie, R. D. 1992. *Three Centuries of Criminal Justice Privatization in the United States. Privatizing the United States Justice System.* Jefferson, N.C.: McFarland.

— McDonald, Douglas. 1990. *Private Prisons and Public Interest.* New Brunswick, N.J.: Rutgers University Press.

— Quinlan, James M. 1989. "Building More Prisons Will Solve Prison Overcrowding." In *American Prisons: Opposing Viewpoints,* ed. S. Tipp, 112-117. San Diego: Greenhaven.

— Robbins, Ira P. 1986. "Privatization of Corrections." *Federal Probation* 48: 24-30.

— Robbins, Ira P. 1988. "The Impact of the Non-delegation Doctrine on Prison Privatization." *UCLA Law Review* 35: 911-952.

— Savas, E. S. 1987. "Privatization of Prisons." *Vanderbilt Law Review* 40: 889-899.

— Saxton, Samuel F. 1988. "Contracting for Services: Different Facilities, Different Needs." *Corrections Today* (October): 16-22.

— Smith, Paul. 1972. *Pioneers in Criminology.* New York: Montclair.

— Stinebaker, J. 1995. "County Jail Privatization Receives Serious Scrutiny." *Houston Chronicle,* July 15, p. 1, col. 1.

— Taylor, Elizabeth A. 1987. "The Origin and Development of the Convict Lease System in Georgia." In *Police, Prisons and Punishment,* ed. K. Hull, 113-128. New York: Garland.

— Thomas, Charles W., and Linda Calvert. 1989. "The Implications of 42 U.S.C. Section 1983 for the Privatization of Prisons." *Florida State University Law Review* 16(4): 933-962.

— "Volunteers of America." 1985. St. Paul Pioneer Press, Mar. 3, col. 1.

— Woolley, Mary R. 1985. "Prisons for Profit: Policy Considerations for Government Officials." *Dickenson Law Review* 90: 307.

# 12

# JAILS

*Dennis Giever*

A jail is not a prison. A prison houses convicted criminals; no untried people go to prisons. A jail is essentially a pretrial detention center used to hold people until they are tried. But to complicate matters, the jail also has come to be used both as a short-term correctional institution for misdemeanants, and a way station for a random melange of other defendants. Sometimes people are lost and forgotten in the jails for weeks and months after they could have been legally released. Men convicted but awaiting sentence or appeal, defendants being moved from one institution to another, immigrants awaiting deportation, military arrestees, people held as material witnesses to a forthcoming trial also crowd the jails, adding to the confusion and the bedlam and complicating the mission of these institutions. (Goldfarb 1975, 2-3)

---

*Chapter Overview* ——————

—— **HISTORY OF JAILS**
        History of Jails in England
        History of Jails in America
—— **THE TWENTIETH-CENTURY JAIL**
        Functions of Jails
                *Pretrial Detainees*
                *Misdemeanants*
                *Felons*
                *Others*
                *Juveniles*
        Population Characteristics
        Architecture
                *Traditional Jails*
                *Second Generation Jails*
                *New Generation Jails*
—— **JAIL OPERATIONS AND ADMINISTRATION**
        Jail Personnel
        Legal Issues
        Jail Standards
        Overcrowding
        Special Needs Inmates
                *The Mentally Ill*
                *Alcoholics*
                *Drug Addicts*
                *Sex Offenders*

The quote above is as timely today as it was 20 years ago. Jails play a unique role within the criminal justice system. While they are unquestionably important, jails remain one of the most understudied and widely misunderstood agencies within the system. Adding to this plight is the fact that jails are almost totally dependent on other agencies within the criminal justice system and have little control over their own destiny (Thompson and Mays 1991b, 1). The population that enters and is housed in our jails is diverse; it includes pretrial detainees (those who have not been convicted of any crime) and those convicted of a misdemeanor who are serving a short sentence (usually under one year). Jail inmates have been described by Irwin (1985, 2) as society's *rabble*. The rabble, according to Irwin, are those individuals who are perceived by society as "irksome, offensive, threatening, capable of arousal, even proto-revolutionary" (1985, 2). Jails house inmates with a wide array of problems including mental illness, alcoholism, and homelessness (Klofas 1990, 69). Since jails often house individuals that no other agency within the criminal justice system will take, they are often referred to as the "dumping ground" for society's problems (Moynahan and Stewart 1980, 104).

Jails suffer from an identity crisis as well. Often the words "jail" and "prison" are used interchangeably by the public and the media alike. When the media does pay homage to a local jail, it is usually after some major event such as a riot, a fire, or a death has occurred within its walls. This chapter will examine the unique role that jails play within the criminal justice system. We will begin by addressing a number of unique features of jails that distinguish them from other places of confinement.

Jails must not only be distinguished from prisons, but also from lockups. *Lockups*, also known as *police lockups*, are facilities authorized to hold persons awaiting court appearance for periods that usually do not exceed 48 hours (Clear and Cole 1994, 144). Such facilities include drunk tanks and holding tanks, which are usually administered by local police agencies. According to Moynahan and Stewart, a clear distinction occurred between jails and lockups sometime early

in the development of American confinement (1980, 71). According
to these authors, "the lockup ... is a municipal institution that is
generally administered by the city police. Held in lockups are usually
those confined for less than forty-eight hours and quite often those
charged with offenses to be heard in lower court" (Moynahan and
Stewart 1980, 71). Lockups are found in most police stations and
serve the purpose of holding individuals during questioning and intake until they can be transported to the local jail. These facilities
may be little more than a steel cage set up inside the police station
offering no toilet facilities or beds.

Jails are distinguished from prisons by a number of factors. First,
the vast majority of prisons in the United States are designed as single
gender institutions that house only adults convicted in a court of law
of a crime, except that they may also now house juveniles waived to
the adult system. Jails have a very heterogeneous population made
up of both males and females, adults and juveniles, who are often
housed within the same facility. Women account for about 10 percent
of the jail population in the United States today, up from about 7.1
percent in 1983 (Bureau of Justice Statistics 1995, 5). While there is
a mandate in the federal Juvenile Justice and Delinquency Prevention Act calling for the removal of all juveniles from adult facilities,
approximately 100,000 juveniles are incarcerated in adult jails each
year (Schwartz 1991, 216-217). As pointed out above, jails house both
convicted criminals as well as those who have not been convicted of a
crime, adding to the heterogeneity of the population.

Although jails house a very diverse group of individuals, the jail
population is characterized by a number of commonalities. With only
a few exceptions, the individuals housed in jails are poor, underedu-
cated, unemployed, and disproportionately a member of a minority
group (Irwin 1985, 2). Later in the chapter we will look at the jail
population in more detail.

A second distinguishing factor between jails and prisons is how
the facilities are administered. Jails usually are locally administered
by elected county sheriffs, while prisons are state institutions (Zupan
1991, 47-48). Often, jails play a secondary role to the law enforcement responsibilities of the local sheriff. In six states — Alaska, Connecticut, Delaware, Hawaii, Rhode Island, and Vermont — jails are
administered by state officials rather than by county sheriffs (Mays
and Thompson 1991, 12; Zupan 1991, 47). In only a small number
of other jurisdictions are jails administered by a specific local department devoted to corrections. The fact that most jails in the United
States are administered by county sheriffs is an important one. Most
sheriffs have law enforcement backgrounds with little or no correc-

tional management experience. There are a number of problems related to this factor, all of which will be covered in detail later in this chapter.

Within the United States there is a small number of federal detention facilities that function as jails (Bureau of Justice Statistics 1995, 12). According to the Bureau of Justice Statistics, these facilities in 1994 housed 5,899 persons who were either awaiting adjudication or serving a sentence of less than one year (1995, 12). The federal government relies on contracts with local jail facilities for the vast majority of its short-term needs, representing about 12,000 persons in 1993, half of whom were unconvicted (Bureau of Justice Statistics 1995, 12).

The third factor that distinguishes jails from prisons is the term of confinement. Jails are institutions for short-term confinement, usually under one year. Prisons are places of long-term confinement, ranging from one year to life, and house those awaiting a death sentence as well. As such, jails have a large turnover in population. While the number of persons being held in jail at any one time is smaller than the prison population in this country, about 17 million persons pass through our nation's jails each year. Prisons, by contrast, have a rather stable population. While jails, by definition, do not house those sentenced to longer terms of confinement, many jails find themselves holding convicted felons for increasingly longer periods of time due to overcrowding within state and federal prison facilities.

Another important distinction between jails and prisons is the type and number of programs that are available to the inmates. While many prisons have only limited programs, they are far more prevalent than those offered in jails. Much of this is related to a number of the factors mentioned above. Due to a large turnover, it would be difficult to offer classes or technical training to many inmates in jail. However, as jails house more and more inmates awaiting transfer to prison facilities, the need to keep such individuals busy has become a concern to administrators.

Finally, jails are most often located in or near the central business districts of most cities. Often, these jails are located in the same building as the county courthouse. Such an arrangement facilitates the quick transfer of the pretrial detainees to court hearings. Prisons are, in most cases, located in remote locations.

Just as there are a number of unique features that distinguish jails from prisons, their history is in stark contrast as well. In the section that follows, we will take a brief look at the history of jails, both in Europe and the United States. Only then can we begin to fully grasp the current situation we find ourselves in.

# HISTORY OF JAILS

## *HISTORY OF JAILS IN ENGLAND*

The development of jails in America can be traced to our ancestory with England. In fact, the American jail has been classified as a "curious hybrid between the tenth century gaol with its principal function being to detain arrested offenders until they were tried, and the fifteenth and sixteenth century houses of correction with their special function being punishment of minor offenders, debtors, vagrants, and beggars" (Flynn 1973, 49). The term jail comes from the English term *gaol* (pronounced jail), which can be traced back to the year 1166 when King Henry II ordered the reeve (the official law enforcement officer for the crown) of each shire (county) to establish a place to secure offenders until the next appearance of the king's court. The shire reeve (sheriff) had a variety of law enforcement responsibilities, only one of which was to maintain a jail. These jails fulfilled a single function of detaining the accused until such time as a trial could be held. While the original purpose of the jail was for this single function, there is evidence that, in some instances, these jails were used to house those convicted of crimes as well (Moynahan and Stewart 1980, 13). Prisoners had to wait for long periods of time, often years, before a trial was held. The conditions of these early jails were dismal at best, and frequently the sheriff would utilize existing structures such as dungeons, cellars, or towers to serve the county's needs (Moynahan and Stewart 1980, 15). In other cases, jails were constructed of wood and amounted to little more than a shed set under the city wall (Zupan 1991, 11). At this time in the history of jails, no real attempt was made to separate prisoners by gender, age, or seriousness of offense. The young were housed with the hardened criminals, and women were often housed in the same cells as men. No provisions were made for either the construction or the operation of the facilities. As such, the sheriff relied on the *fee system* for income. Prisoners were often charged a fee on entering the jail. If they were unable to pay, "other prisoners would literally strip the clothes from the back of the new inmate" (Zupan 1991, 12). Prisoners or their families had to pay for the privilege of being housed in such a facility, and if prisoners did not have the resources, or at least friends or relatives who would provide the monies for such necessities as food, they would often perish long before a court appearance was made.

Real change in the conditions of these early jails did not occur until the beginning of the sixteenth century, and even then such change was due more to economic conditions than to any real attempt to rectify the many problems. During that time period, a large number of people were moving to the cities often looking for work. This influx of vagrants and beggars caused an economic strain on these cities. Louis Robinson listed five conditions which he felt brought about this change: "(1) The breakup of the feudal system which did away with the employments of war and service; (2) the growth of large-scale manufacturers which rendered employment less stable; (3) the rise of prices brought about by sudden increase in the world's supply of silver, increasing the hardships of the laboring class; (4) the enclosures which drove the people from the land. A fifth reason may be found in the whole system of poor relief which had been woefully lacking in constructiveness" (Robinson 1922; quoted in Moynahan and Stewart 1980, 17). Largely as a result of this influx and the failure of more serious measures such as branding and mutilation in controlling the masses, houses of corrections or *bridewells* were established. The first, St. Brigit's Well (Bridewell) was established in London in 1553 in a mansion that was originally built to house royal visitors. As discussed in a previous chapter, these houses of corrections, or workhouses, were for sentenced criminals and provided places for inmate labor.

Further attempts to improve the conditions of these jails did not occur until the eighteenth century. Although attempts were made as early as 1702, such efforts were never published and had little, if any, impact (Moynahan and Stewart 1980, 21; Zupan 1991, 14). It was not until the publication of John Howard's *The State of the Prisons in England and Wales with Preliminary Observations and an Account of Some Foreign Prisons* (1777) that true reform began. Howard, who was at that time the sheriff of Bedford County, wrote about the deplorable conditions of jails in Europe in the latter half of the eighteenth century. In 1779, Howard, along with Sir William Blackstone and William Eden, drafted the Penitentiary Act that was passed by Parliament. This act enumerated four principles of reform: secure and sanitary structures, systematic inspections, abolition of fees, and a reformatory regime. Even after stepping down as sheriff, Howard continued touring confinement facilities throughout Europe. It is ironic that Howard, who worked so tirelessly to improve the sanitary conditions in jails, died of a disease (jail fever or typhus) that claimed the lives of many who either worked or were housed in these facilities (Moynahan and Stewart 1980, 22). Although many of the reforms Howard recommended did not take shape until long after his death, his contribution had a vast impact on the condition of facilities in Europe as well as those in the American colonies.

## HISTORY OF JAILS IN AMERICA

Jails in colonial America were basically an extension of those found in England. As had been the case in England, jails remained the responsibility of the local government, most notably the sheriff. The fee system was retained as well, and the deplorable conditions found in England were also common in the colonies. The first such jail was thought to be in Jamestown, Virginia, and was established in the early part of the seventeenth century. A number of important issues were prevalent in the New World. As new communities began to spring up, each began establishing punishments for those who committed criminal acts. Some of the more common methods of punishment were stocks, pillories, dunking stools, and whipping posts. Stocks were little more than a bench or stump to which the offender was shackled; they usually were located in a public area where the townspeople could jeer and throw garbage.

The *pillory* was a wooden structure in which the offender had to stand and place both the head and hands through holes that were clamped down. Once again, such punishment was usually within public view so townspeople could wreak their vengeance on the offender. While the pillory was still allowed in Delaware by statutes until 1905, its common usage began to fade by 1839 (Moynahan and Stewart 1980, 26).

The dunking stool was also used as punishment in colonial America. The stool or chair in which the offender was tied was attached to a long lever. The offender was dunked into a body of water, the number of times and duration of which were dependent on the sentence or seriousness of the offense.

Moynahan and Stewart claim that two important practices emerged from colonial times (1980, 27). First, the colonies used the most direct and least expensive form of punishment possible. Second, the punishment imposed in the colonies was more humane than that found in Europe. The latter fact was due to economic conditions. Unemployment was high in Europe, and often death sentences were imposed for rather minor offenses. In contrast, the colonies were still growing and were in need of labor; the citizens were reluctant to execute anyone except those who committed the most serious or heinous crimes.

The jails in colonial America, as in Europe, were used largely to house those awaiting trial. It was not until the use of corporal punishment came under fire that we began using these facilities to house those convicted of offenses (Moynahan and Stewart 1980, 32). The first real attempt at such a reform in America occurred in Pennsylvania under the direction of William Penn, a leader of the Quakers. The cornerstone of the Quaker movement in America was penal reform. Penn and his followers believed that hard labor in a house of corrections, rather than corporal or capital punishment, was more effective in handling crime. In 1682 the Quaker code or "great law" was enacted in Pennsylvania. It emphasized fines and hard labor in a house of correction as punishment for most crimes. At the same time, the first jail designed exclusively to house convicted offenders serving a sentence was opened in Philadelphia. The reforms established by Penn and his followers were idealistic at best, for soon after the High Street Jail was built in Philadelphia, it too became overcrowded and deteriorated to deplorable conditions. The reforms did not last, for in 1718, when William Penn died, so did the great law. Pennsylvania reverted back to using whipping, mutilation, branding, and other forms of corporal punishment for criminal offenses. The conditions and role of the jails in America remained largely unchanged until about the time of the American Revolution.

Soon after the end of the Revolutionary War, a number of reformers, Benjamin Franklin among them, led a movement to change the English criminal code of 1718, which had been in effect since the death of William Penn. The new law enacted on September 15, 1786, allowed prisoners to be put to work out in the streets cleaning and repairing roads. Prisoners had their heads shaved to distinguish them from others and were encumbered with iron collars and chains (Takagi 1975, 20). Shortly after this law was enacted, the Quakers formed the Philadelphia Society for Alleviating the Miseries of Public Prisons. The society's main goal, aside from introducing religious services in the Walnut Street Jail, was to amend the new law (Takagi 1975, 20). The society felt that a more private or solitary labor would be more successful.

In 1790, the Society for Alleviating the Miseries of Public Prisons was able to pass legislation that was almost identical to the Penitentiary Act of 1779. Many of the efforts of the Quakers were centered on the Walnut Street Jail. The society was able to get females segregated from the male population and was able to abolish the fee system at the Walnut Street facility. They provided food and clothing for all inmates, and medical care was offered weekly (Zupan 1991, 18). As was previously the case, while the reforms were widely heralded, the conditions soon began to deteriorate. By 1816 the conditions in the Walnut Street Jail had deteriorated back to the conditions found before the reforms. The only exceptions were that inmates were still segregated by sex and offense, and liquor was still prohibited (Zupan 1991, 19).

In the late 1700s and early 1800s, jails began to be used not only to detain those awaiting trial, but also to hold those who had been convicted (Moynahan and Stewart 1980, 41). If available, those sentenced for more serious crimes were sent to the newly developed state prisons. States that did not have prisons either executed those convicted of serious crimes or confined them to time in the county jail (Moynahan and Stewart 1980, 41). The whipping post, stocks, and pillory had begun disappearing from the American scene. These changes did not occur overnight and did not take place in all jails at the same time. Jails then, as they are now, were locally operated, and the speed in which changes occurred was due largely to the local climate. Some jurisdictions brought about change rather quickly, and others took decades (Moynahan and Stewart 1980, 41).

During the mid-nineteenth century, the jailing of persons for debt was generally abolished (Moynahan and Stewart 1980, 43). At about this time in our history, new facilities dedicated to housing juveniles were opening around the country. A number of private houses of refuge had opened in Boston in 1826 and in Philadelphia in 1828, but not until 1847 did the first state — Massachusetts — establish a reformatory. (For a discussion on the plight of juveniles in such early institutions, see Platt 1969.) There was no typical jail in the United States during the nineteenth century, just as there is no typical jail today. Their sizes and purposes varied greatly (Moynahan and Stewart 1980, 46).

## THE TWENTIETH-CENTURY JAIL

The growth of jails in America through the twentieth century is sketchy at best. In 1880, the census bureau began compiling information on individuals housed in jails, workhouses, and prisons. During this time, and to a certain degree today, the definition of a jail was ambiguous. While the data are open to question, one can look at the trend in confinement by studying the population trends. Champion (1990) compiled data collected from a number of sources and developed a table of jail populations. The figures he developed are given in Table 12-1.

**TABLE 12-1**
**Jail Population**

| Year | Number of jail inmates |
| --- | --- |
| 1880 | 18,666 |
| 1890 | 33,093 |
| 1940 | 99,249 |
| 1950 | 86,492 |
| 1960 | 119,671 |
| 1970 | 129,189 |
| 1980 | 163,994 |
| 1983 | 223,551 |
| 1986 | 274,444 |

*Sources:* Cahalan 1986 and Kline 1987; quoted in Champion 1990, 164-165.

As Table 12-1 shows, the jail population in this country almost doubled from 1880 through 1890. The population is still exploding with the latest survey of jails estimating 490,442 incarcerated in jails (Bureau of Justice Statistics 1995, 1).

About 85 percent of the jails in America today are operated by local county governments. In most cases, jails that are not operated by county governments are operated by large municipalities. The federal government, through the Federal Bureau of Prisons, operates a number of pretrial detention facilities that house those awaiting trial on federal charges.

While the number of inmates housed in jails is on the rise, the number of jails is actually declining. In 1983, there were 3,338 local jail facilities. By 1988, that number dropped to 3,316; by 1993, it had further declined to 3,304. Much of this decline can be attributed to the concept of regionalization, whereby two or more governments join forces to build one regional jail serving multiple jurisdictions (Mays and Thompson 1991, 13; Cox and Osterhoff 1991, 237-238). Many jurisdictions, faced with the need to build a new facility to either alleviate overcrowding or to replace a physical plant that is old and deteriorating, find it cost effective to pool resources with a neighboring county to build one facility. In some areas, as a way to encourage regionalization, the state will reimburse a large portion of the construction cost of the new jail when three or more jurisdictions are involved in such a joint venture (Leibowitz 1991, 42-43). There are a number of problems associated with these arrangements, for example, transportation of inmates (most notably pretrial detainees) and multijurisdictional problems associated with both the funding of the facility and the determination of a location and management of the facility (McGee 1975, 11). Given the number of benefits of multi-jurisdictional jails, many communities have been able to work through these problems and to develop solutions allowing them to take advantage of these benefits.

## FUNCTIONS OF JAILS

As was discussed above, jails were originally conceived as places to hold pretrial detainees until their appearance in court. This single purpose has evolved into a multitude of differing roles, which often cause a strain on the system. Jails are often thought of as the criminal justice agency of last resort and, by default, deal with a large number of individuals that no other agency can handle. Jails house a wide variety of sentenced and unsentenced persons. According to the Bureau of Justice Statistics, jails perform the following functions:

1. receive individuals pending arraignment and hold them awaiting trial, conviction, and sentencing;
2. readmit probation, parole, and bail-bond violators and absconders;
3. temporarily detain juveniles pending transfer to juvenile authorities;
4. hold mentally ill persons pending their movement to appropriate health facilities;
5. hold individuals for the military, for protective custody, for contempt, and for the courts as witnesses;
6. release convicted inmates to the community on completion of sentence;
7. transfer inmates to state, federal, and local authorities; and
8. relinquish custody of temporary detainees to juvenile and medical authorities. (Bureau of Justice Statistics 1990, 2)

*Pretrial Detainees.*  About half of all people housed in jails are *pretrial detainees* (Bureau of Justice Statistics 1995, 5). These individuals are arrested for a wide assortment of offenses and, for one reason or another, are either unable to afford or are denied bail. As a result, they are housed in jails until their trial. As the jail population increases and administrators are faced with lawsuits, they are constantly searching for ways to relieve the crowding. With little control over the number of convicted misdemeanants sent to their facilities, jail administrators are faced with the challenge of decreasing their population by reducing the number of pretrial detainees held or by reducing the time they spend in jail. Several issues have had an effect on the number of pretrial detainees who were housed in jails in the last three decades. First, attempts have been made to limit the amount of time pretrial detainees have to spend in jail. In 1974, Congress passed the Speedy Trial Act, which mandated that federal charges must be filed against a defendant within 30 days of the arrest. A preliminary hearing must be held within 10 days of that date, and the trial must begin within 60 days of the arraignment. While the states are not specifically bound to the Speedy Trial Act, the Sixth Amendment of the Constitution claims that "the accused shall enjoy the right to a speedy and public trial."

Of obvious concern is who is held as a pretrial detainee. The Eighth Amendment to the Constitution states that "Excessive bail shall not be required. . . ." The purpose of setting bail is to ensure that the defendant will appear for trial. The obvious consequence of this is those who can afford bail will pay it, while those unable to pay will have to wait in jail. In reality, while the purpose of bail is to ensure appearance at trial, often those who are forced to stay in jail until trial are the individuals who possess the least risk of flight.

A study undertaken in 1960 by Louis Schweitzer addressed this very issue. He discovered that of the 115,000 people detained before trial in New York City, only about 31,000 were later convicted and sentenced to incarceration (Goldfarb 1975, 40). Schweitzer's personal attempts to address this problem included, first, trying to generate donations from the public to bail out the poor who were of little risk of flight and, when that failed, bringing light to the problem. As a result of his efforts, the Manhattan Bail Project was conducted by the Vera Institute of Justice in New York City from 1961 through 1964. Law students would interview defendants before their arraignment, ask questions about the defendants' ties to the community and then assign points based on the defendants' responses. If a defendant obtained a sufficient number of points, the Vera Institute would recommend to the court that he be released on his own recognizance (Goldfarb 1975, 40). It was found that those released on the recommendation of the Vera Institute returned to trial in greater numbers than those who were released on bond through a bail bondsman. This project evolved into the practice of "Release on Recognizance" (ROR).

The Bail Reform Act of 1984 has also had an impact on the number of pretrial detainees. One of the provisions in the Bail Reform Act permitted judges to deny bail to those charged with a violent crime, to those charged with crimes that carried a possible life sentence, to those charged with crimes that carried a possible death sentence, to those charged with some major drug offenses, and in those cases in which the defendant is charged with a felony and has a serious past criminal record (Bureau of Justice Statistics 1988; 1994a; 1994b).

*Misdemeanants.* A second function of jails is to house offenders serving short-term sentences. Those convicted of misdemeanors and sentenced by the local courts to incarceration for a period of less than one year typically serve their sentences in jails. However, in North Carolina, jails house misdemeanants for up to two years (Brannon 1977, 8). Almost half of all inmates in jail are serving sentences, the number only fluctuating in the past ten years from a low of about 47 percent in 1986 to a high of about 49 percent in 1994 (Maguire and Pastore 1995, 533).

The average length of the sentences that misdemeanants are given does not seem to be increasing to any drastic extent. Data available from 1983 and 1989 surveys of inmates in local jails show that of those serving a sentence (both felons and misdemeanants), the mean length of their sentence had increased in the six-year period from 14 to 17 months, but there had not been a change in the median (midpoint of sentence range). The change in the mean (average) is most likely due to a small number of relatively long sentences. In both years, about half of the inmates had received sentences of six months or less (Bureau of Justice Statistics 1991, 7).

*Felons.* Jails must also house inmates convicted of felonies who are awaiting transfer to a state or federal prison. Some of these inmates are waiting for the court to sentence them; in some cases, a separate sentencing hearing is held once a presentence investigation (PSI) is undertaken. In such cases, the jail is usually reimbursed by either the state or federal government for housing the individual.

As previously discussed in Chapter 3, jails in a number of jurisdictions find themselves housing convicted felons due to overcrowding in either state or federal prisons. If sufficient bed space is not available to accommodate an inmate, the state or federal government enters into a leasing agreement with the local jail to house the inmate. According to the Bureau of Justice Statistics (1995, 14), in 1993 approximately 34,200 jail inmates were being housed in local facilities due to crowding in state or federal prisons (up from 23,186 in 1988). This number represented about 7.4 percent of all jail inmates. Once again, when the local jurisdictions house such inmates, they are reimbursed by the state or federal government.

Jails are increasingly being used by the courts as their sentencing option for convicted felons. Between 1986 and 1992, the number of convicted felons who were sentenced to confinement in local jails almost doubled (Bureau of Justice Statistics 1995, 13). Convicted felons sentenced to jail amounted to 26 percent of all convicted felons in this country in 1992, up from 21 percent in 1986 (Bureau of Justice Statistics 1995, 13).

D'Alessio and Stolzenberg (1995) looked at the effect of determinate sentencing laws on jail use and found that the implementation of such guidelines increased the judicial use of jail sanctions. Due to overcrowding in state prisons, judges will often circumvent these new laws as a mechanism to shift the burden of incarcerating offenders from the state to the local level (D'Alessio and Stolzenberg 1995, 283). In fact, in the state of Minnesota, such guidelines have increased jail use in that state by as much as 26 percent (D'Alessio and Stolzenberg 1995, 297). The authors caution policy makers against just developing guidelines aimed at only reducing prison population because such guidelines will often shift the burden from the prison to the local jails.

***Others.***    According to Irwin, "the vast majority of the persons who are arrested, booked, and held in jail are not charged with serious crimes" (1985, 18). Examples of such are the mentally ill or homeless, who are housed in jails often for their own protection and welfare. Such inmates are the "rabble" of society, meaning the "disorganized" and "disorderly," the "lowest class of people" (Irwin 1985, 2). There is a growing number of mentally ill inmates who are incarcerated in jail (Gibbs 1986; Senese, Kalinich, and Embert 1989). Jails are ill-equipped to handle the unique needs of such inmates. Many smaller jails do not provide full-time medical staff to deal with ongoing problems but have only doctors on call. Jails hold a large array of other inmates who do not fit the above classifications.

Jails hold persons wanted for crimes in other states. If a warrant is issued in another jurisdiction and the person is detected or stopped for a traffic violation, she is arrested and held until extradition proceedings can take place. Jails hold alleged probation and parole violators. Such individuals are entitled to a hearing to determine whether their probation or parole should be revoked, but if suspected of committing a serious crime, they are often held in jail. Such violators share many of the characteristics of the pretrial detainee.

Finally, jails hold a number of inmates who do not fit neatly into any of the above categories. They may be material witnesses who are reluctant to testify, or possibly a witness in need of protection. As

Goldfarb stated, "American jails operate primarily as catchall asylums for poor people" (1975, 27). It is only rarely that they hold a person who fits the popular image of a criminal, one who is a serious threat to society (Irwin 1985, 1).

*Juveniles.* Jails may house juvenile offenders when no juvenile detention facility is available in a jurisdiction. These juveniles are often housed in adult facilities despite a mandate in the federal Juvenile Justice and Delinquency Prevention Act that banned the jailing of juveniles (Schwartz 1991, 216-217). Many such youths are incarcerated for relatively minor offenses.

The law requires that any juvenile being housed in a jail receive sight and sound separation from the adult population. The requirement stems from the Juvenile Justice and Delinquency Prevention Act of 1974, which states that juveniles "shall not be detained or confined in any institution in which they have regular contact with adult persons incarcerated because they have been convicted of a crime or are awaiting trial on criminal charges" (U.S. Department of Justice 1980, 400). This provision was interpreted to mean that juveniles could be held in adult jails as long as they had sight and sound separation from the adults, which meant that juveniles would often find themselves housed in solitary confinement away from everyone. Juveniles who are out of sight and sound from the general population are often out of sight and sound (and sometimes mind) of the jail personnel. Such an arrangement can have an impact on the number of suicides in jails, as we will see below. Another impact of juveniles being housed in adult jails is the trend of lawsuits being filed to control the practice (Soler 1988). For example, in 1985 a coalition of public interest law offices and private law firms in California launched a litigation offensive to end the jailing of children in that state. Within 18 months these advocates had won three lawsuits against local jurisdictions totaling close to half a million dollars (Soler 1988, 204). The success of the California initiative prompted advocates from other states to take similar steps (Soler 1988, 205).

In 1991, there were over 60,000 juvenile admissions and over 56,000 juvenile releases from jails. Males made up 53,257 of the admissions, while females accounted for 6,954. As for releases, males made up 49,571, while females accounted for 6,728 (Bureau of Justice Statistics 1992, 2). It is ironic that even while we have a critical shortage of jail space for adult offenders, we persist in confining juveniles in these facilities (Schwartz 1991, 216). Despite a mandate in 1980 in the Juvenile Justice and Delinquency Prevention Act, it is estimated that over 6,500 juveniles were housed in local jails in 1994 on an average day (Bureau of Justice Statistics 1995, 15). Of these juveniles, 76.4 percent were being held as adults, and approximately 23.6 percent were held as juveniles. These numbers represent a one-day total and tell nothing of the thousands of juveniles who pass through adult jails each year. The average number of juveniles (those under the age of 18) held in local jails on any given day in 1994 was 1,586 (Bureau of Justice Statistics 1995, 3). A statistic that has become available in the last couple of years is the number of juveniles held in jails as adults. Such juveniles await trial or have been tried already as adults. According to the annual survey of jails in 1994, there were 5,139 juveniles who were being held in jails as adult inmates. In 1993, there were only 3,300 such juveniles. Thus in 1994, there were 1,586 juveniles held in adult jails with an additional 5,139 defined as "adults," for a total of 6,725 children in jail.

In light of the many problems of jailing juveniles, Schwartz (1991, 225-226) makes the following recommendations:

1. The most effective way to eliminate the jailing of juveniles is to enact legislation prohibiting the practice under any circumstances. Such legislation, as was the case in Pennsylvania, should include a grace period so that the deed could be accomplished within a reasonable time period.

2. Experience has shown that there are a variety of policies and community-based alternatives to jailing that can be implemented without significantly increasing the risk to the community. Also, many of these options can be implemented at relatively low cost. For example, one of the most effective strategies for limiting juvenile jailing would be to develop and utilize objective detention intake criteria, particularly those recommended by the National Juvenile Justice Advisory Committee. In addition, such programs as home detention, family-operated shelter care, report centers, and staff-operated shelter care have proved to be effective options.

3. There are some juveniles who need to be detained pending their court appearance. Experience has demonstrated that the number of youth who fall into this category are relatively small. Because of this, and because secure detention facilities are costly to build and operate, a careful and comprehensive needs assessment should be completed to determine how many secure beds may be needed in a particular jurisdiction or jurisdictions, and how those needs can be met best.

Schwartz and his colleagues have also advocated passing legislation that would make the jailing of juveniles a crime (1988, 146). The same group of researchers also recommended the development of alternatives to adult jails for female juveniles. In many areas females account for as many as one-quarter of the juveniles admitted to adult facilities, but the vast majority of them are of no risk to the community (Schwartz, Harris, and Levi 1988, 148).

## POPULATION CHARACTERISTICS

Of the 455,500 inmates housed in American jails on June 30, 1993, 228,900 or 50.25 percent were unconvicted or pretrial detainees (Bureau or Justice Statistics 1995, 5). As Table 12-2 shows, 44,100 or 9.66 percent were female. The female population in American jails is on the rise. As mentioned previously, females accounted for 7.1 percent of the adult population in jails in 1983, and by 1994 that number had risen to 10.1 percent representing over 33,000 additional female jail inmates.

Women in jail face a number of problems. According to the Bureau of Statistics, about 68 percent of women in jails have children under the age of 18 (1992, 9). Two-thirds of these women were living with their children before entering jail. Table 12-3 shows the number of children and their living arrangements before their mothers entered jail based on a 1989 jail survey. In addition to facing the shock

**TABLE 12-2**
**Number and Average Daily Population in Local Jails**

|                          | June 30, 1983 | June 30, 1988 | June 30, 1993 | June 30, 1994 |
|--------------------------|--------------:|--------------:|--------------:|--------------:|
| **Number of inmates**    |               |               |               |               |
| All inmates              | 223,551       | 343,569       | 459,804       | 490,442       |
| Adults                   | 221,815       | 341,893       | 455,500       | 483,717       |
| Male                     | 206,163       | 311,594       | 411,500       | 434,838       |
| Female                   | 15,652        | 30,299        | 44,100        | 48,879        |
| Juveniles                | —             | —             | 4,300         | 6,725         |
| Held as adults           | —             | —             | 3,300         | 5,139         |
| Held as juveniles        | 1,736         | 1,676         | 1,000         | 1,586         |
|                          |               |               |               |               |
| **Average daily population** |           |               |               |               |
| All inmates              | 227,541       | 336,017       | 466,155       | 479,757       |
| Adults                   | 225,781       | 334,566       | 462,800       | —             |
| Male                     | 210,451       | 306,379       | 418,200       | —             |
| Female                   | 15,330        | 28,187        | 44,600        | —             |
| Juveniles                | 1,760         | 1,451         | 3,400         | —             |

*Source:* From Bureau of Justice Statistics (1995), *Jails and Jail Inmates, 1993-1994*, 5. Washington, D.C.: GPO.

**TABLE 12-3**
**Children of Female Jail Inmates, by Race, 1989**

| Characteristic | Percent of female inmates | | |
| --- | --- | --- | --- |
| | *All* | *White* | *Black* |
| **Have children** | | | |
| No | 26.2% | 28.6% | 23.3% |
| Yes | 73.8 | 71.5 | 76.7 |
| Any under age 18 | 67.9 | 64.9 | 71.3 |
| Adult only | 5.9 | 6.6 | 5.4 |
| Number of inmates | 37,071 | 19,306 | 16,513 |
| **Number of children under age 18** | | | |
| 1 | 37.8% | 38.9% | 35.5% |
| 2 | 33.4 | 37.0 | 31.3 |
| 3 | 17.9 | 14.9 | 21.1 |
| 4 | 6.4 | 5.3 | 7.9 |
| 5 or more | 4.4 | 3.9 | 4.2 |
| **Lived with children under 18 before entering jail** | | | |
| No | 32.8% | 35.9% | 27.7% |
| Yes | 67.2 | 64.1 | 72.3 |
| **Where children under 18 live now** | | | |
| Child's father | 23.5% | 30.1% | 15.8% |
| Maternal grandparents | 41.6 | 34.9 | 50.0 |
| Paternal grandparents | 8.7 | 9.3 | 7.1 |
| Other relative | 22.9 | 18.6 | 27.0 |
| Friends | 4.3 | 4.2 | 4.5 |
| Foster home | 6.5 | 7.2 | 6.1 |
| Agency/institution | 1.6 | 2.2 | 0.9 |
| Other | 4.0 | 5.0 | 1.9 |
| **Plan to live with children under 18 after release from jail** | | | |
| Yes | 84.5% | 77.7% | 91.7% |
| No | 12.4 | 18.1 | 6.3 |
| Don't know | 3.1 | 4.3 | 1.9 |

*Source:* From Bureau of Justice Statistics (1992), *Women in Jail, 1989,* 9. Washington, D.C.: GPO.

of incarceration, another problem that women face in jail is the loss of contact with their children. While the vast majority of these children are placed with either their father or a close relative, almost 10 percent are placed in foster care or some other institutional setting (Bureau of Justice Statistics 1992, 9). Many women worry about the arrangements available for their children, and their ability to cope in a jail environment may depend on whether they know their children are being cared for. Another concern for many mothers is the ability to keep in contact with their children, either through the mail or by periodic visits. The children too must deal with the loss of their mother. Whether the children are placed with relatives or in foster care, the sanctions imposed on their mothers may act as punishment for them as well.

With females accounting for over 10 percent of the jail population, a number of questions have been raised about the criminal justice system's response to female offenders. Ralph Weisheit (1987) looked at whether females were afforded preferential treatment within the criminal justice system. By looking at a number of legal factors, such as the number of charges filed by law enforcement officials and the number of prior incarcerations between male and female offenders, Weisheit found that males and females are jailed for similar types of charges and are equally likely to have multiple charges lodged against them (1987, 50).

The relatively small number of women housed in jails presents a second set of more ominous problems. Jails rarely have programs and services for females to the extent offered to males. Women spend an average of 17 hours per day in their cells, and are less likely than their male counterparts to have work assignments (Bureau of Justice Statistics 1992, 8). Because women only represent a small number of the total inmates, their medical needs are often not adequately addressed. As the American Correctional Association points out, "There is a lack of gynecological care for jailed women and seldom any special health care for pregnant women; use of contraceptive pills is often interrupted because they are not available in jail" (1985, 24).

Most women serving sentences in jail serve their sentences in facilities that also house male inmates. In a study done to examine jails that are exclusively women's facilities, Gray and her colleagues identified 18 jails in the United States that house only women (Gray, Mays, and Stohr 1995). In their study, they collected data (surveys and interviews) from 5 such facilities to explore the extent to which these jails meet the particular needs of women. With the exception of treatment programs for drug and alcohol abuse, they found that the programming in these women's jails was "woefully inadequate" (Gray, Mays, and Stohr 1995, 199).

Another important population characteristic is the racial composition in American jails. Jails house a disproportionate number of black inmates compared to the distribution of blacks in the general population. Almost 44 percent of the inmates housed in jails in 1994 were black, with Hispanics accounting for an additional 15 percent (Bureau of Justice Statistics 1995, 5). In the last 10 years the gap has widened, with the incarceration rate for blacks climbing from about 400 black inmates per 100,000 black residents in 1987 to almost 700 black inmates per 100,000 in 1995.

This explosion in jail population is apparent in the number of inmates and in the building trends. The percentage of inmates grew over 106 percent in the 10-year period of 1983-1993; during the same period, jail capacity grew only 82 percent. The percentage growth in the inmate population has far outpaced that in the general population, with the number of jail inmates per 100,000 residents almost doubling from 96 in 1983 to 188 in 1994 (Bureau of Justice Statistics 1995, 2).

Jail population numbers represent a one-day census undertaken on June 30th of each year. Such numbers do not represent the many individuals who pass in and out of jail each year, some only staying for a few hours. Much of the turnover is concentrated during peak periods, such as Friday and Saturday evenings. In 1993, there were over 13 million people booked into jails. This number represents an increase of 63.8 percent from 1983. The vast turnover of inmates each year represents an administrative burden on the staff of jail facilities.

## ARCHITECTURE

There are two distinct designs present in American jails today: the traditional or linear design and what is now being characterized as new generation or podular jails. Each of these designs is based on a number of underlying philosophies and presents a number of important distinctions. Note, however, that most U.S. jails are small. Over 55 percent of American jails house fewer than 50 inmates (Bureau of Justice Statistics 1995, 5). About 10 percent of the nation's jails house 10 or fewer inmates (Mays and Thompson 1988, 437). While we address the differences in architectural styles of jails, it is important to remember that alternative approaches are limited in many jurisdictions due to these size restrictions.

*Traditional Jails.*    Most jails in America are traditional in design. This design, also referred to as the *linear design,* has a long history dating back to the time of the Walnut Street Jail in Philadelphia. In the linear design, inmate cells are situated along corridors. The staff monitors the cells of these traditional jails by walking the corridors. The staff cannot monitor all of the inmate housing units at one time; they can only provide intermittent surveillance (Nelson 1988, 2). During the period when staff is not in the corridor, the inmates enjoy a free rein in what is occurring in their cells. Most behavior problems occur between the intermittent patrols. The familiar image of inmates holding mirrors from their cells to observe the corridor is a striking example of this reality. Often, inmates watch out for the jailer and warn others when he is coming. The linear design presents a number of security issues; the most important is graphically shown in an account by a female inmate in the Cook County Jail in Illinois. In this account, inmate Dorothy West was labeled a snitch by other inmates. West, fearing for her safety, asked for protective custody, but the matron only laughed at her. Later that night, West was attacked by eight other inmates.

> Ruby's first blow caught me on the side of my head. As soon as she hit me, a scream went up from the others. "Kill the stool-pigeon bitch." All eight of them fell on me at once. Somebody set fire to my skirt, and my nylon petticoat went up in flames. I tried to beat at my burning legs, but they were banging my head against the bars. I felt my nose crumple, and start to gush blood. I fell and they kicked me repeatedly in the left eye. They kicked my breasts and jumped up and down on me. Then somebody pulled off my panties, thrust them into my mouth as a gag, and I was raped. My hair was burning and I could feel the skin on my forehead crack and begin to peel. I'm told the beating went on for an hour. (West 1972, 157; quoted in Zupan 1991, 20)

Traditional jails are built to last. Inmates, even with time on their hands and very little supervision, can cause very little damage to the physical structure. The toilet facilities and beds are designed to hold up to the most intense punishment and, as such, are costly to purchase. They are not designed for aesthetics, but rather for function. Therefore, traditional jails are noisy, with concrete floors and walls that do not absorb sound. The metal doors clang shut, causing the sound to reverberate throughout the facility. Lighting fixtures are either encased in metal or outside the actual cell to keep inmates from having access to them.

The lack of supervision combined with the noise level adds to the stress inmates face. Inmates are already experiencing stress and when they find themselves locked up in a noisy and often hostile environment, they frequently exhibit signs of psychopathology soon after their arrival in jail (Gibbs 1987, 308).

*Second Generation Jails.* A second generation of jails has been designed and put into use in many areas. In this design, jail personnel have what is termed remote or indirect surveillance of inmates. Under the *remote design,* cells are situated around a central dayroom, and jail personnel occupy a secure control room that overlooks the dayroom and also the individual cells. While such a design actually increases the visual surveillance by jail personnel, it limits verbal interactions between inmates and jail personnel, who often communicate through an intercom. While the inmates are more closely monitored in second generation jails, most such jails still employ high security fixtures, furnishings, and finishes (Nelson 1988, 2).

*New Generation Jails.* New generation jails stand in stark contrast to the more traditional linear jails and their new cousin the remote supervision jails, both in design and in their philosophy of operation. A number of important distinctions must be made between the new generation jail and its traditional counterpart. First, traditional jails, by design, require the staff to constantly patrol inmates' cells, usually only offering intermittent supervision at best. Under the new generation design, the jail staff is in direct contact with the inmates. Jail personnel actually occupy a space within the dayroom or housing pod (Nelson 1988, 170). The fundamental goal of the new generation jail is to provide a safe, violence-free environment for both inmates and staff that treats inmates in a humane fashion (Zupan 1991, 73).

This style of architecture originated with an effort by the U.S. Bureau of Prisons to open three federal detention facilities in Chicago, San Diego, and New York City in the mid-1960s. The government commissioned three architectural firms to design these new facilities and gave only three stipulations: single cells for inmates, direct supervision by staff, and functional living units (Zupan and Menke 1991, 185). The concept of *functional living units* places all sleeping, food, hygiene, and recreational facilities in a self-contained unit. A number of advantages to these new designs have added to their appeal. First, the concept of direct supervision, where staff and inmates share a common area, has a very practical significance. No longer are inmates locked in cells with other inmates out of sight from jail personnel. In the new generation jail, inmates and staff share the facility, with staff members in constant contact with the inmates. It forces the staff to run the facility rather than allowing the inmates to do so.

Another advantage of the new generation design is that furnishings, fixtures, and finishes of these jails are of normal commercial grade, as opposed to high-priced security fixtures. This can result in a substantial savings in the cost of building such a facility. For example, Nelson determined that the savings in building costs for a single unit housing 48 inmates would be over $200,000 compared to a traditional jail. There are savings in the initial construction of the facility and substantial savings in operating expenses and upkeep. With inmates in constant contact with jail personnel, incidences of vandalism and graffiti are greatly decreased. An example is Contra Costa County Detention Center in California, the first local jail facility to incorporate the new generation design. Administrators there claimed that the county's old facility needed to be painted every year, while the new facility only received a fresh coat of paint after five years of operation (Nelson 1988, 6). The new generation design also incorporates carpeting and acoustical tile to reduce the noise level and to add to the aesthetics of the environment. Instead of gates and steel bars, solid walls and doors with impenetrable glass are used. Once again, this adds to the aesthetics and reduces the noise of metal clanging against metal often found in traditional jails.

Another important issue with new generation jails is staffing. Do new generation jails require a larger staff than their traditional counterparts? There is no definite answer to this important question, since often it is dependent on the level of staffing present in the other facilities. In some states with jail standards, the inmate to staff ratio is set, and little savings will be found. In Dade County, Florida, it was found that only about half the staff was required to operate the new direct supervision facility as compared to the older linear jail (Nelson 1988, 4). Much depends on the efficiency and size of the traditional jail. The working conditions are another important factor. The new generation concept is, without question, a quantum leap, with jail personnel now occupying living space with the inmates. How do jail personnel feel about such an arrangement? One way of measuring this is to look at the number of sick days taken by the staff. In one study reported by Nelson, the National Institute of Corrections found that sick leave in the new generation jails was significantly less than the average in the four other houses of detention. The savings amounted to 1,810 staff days, or the equivalent of eight full-time positions. This number could have amounted to one-quarter of a million dollars in overtime expenditures if overtime was used to fill the vacancies (Nelson 1988, 4).

Another concern with staffing is that to effectively manage inmates in a new generation jail, the correctional officers must be trained to use a number of sophisticated human relations skills, ranging from conflict management, to problem solving, to interpersonal community (Zupan and Menke 1991, 193). Such training is in stark contrast to the traditional custodial skills now taught, such as physical control techniques and firearms usage. Zupan and Menke (1991, 193) recommend that, for the new generation philosophy to really succeed, we must also develop the correctional officer's career orientation. The costs of such an orientation and of training officers in conflict management have not been fully assessed, but the literature available on new generation jails seems to indicate that such an effort will have a substantial savings over the long run, both in operating costs and in the reduction in the number of lawsuits.

New generation jails offer an opportunity for cost savings, and an improvement in the working environment for jail personnel, and an improvement in the environment for the inmates. As of 1991, there are about 80 direct supervision jails that incorporate podular designs (Stohr, et al. 1994, 473). Once we begin looking at a number of concerns that jail administrators must face, the benefits of the new generation philosophy will become more apparent.


# Jail Operations and Administration


## Jail Personnel

Personnel represent the single largest expenditure in local jails. Total operating expenditures, which include salaries, wages, employer contributions to employee benefits, food, supplies, and contractual services, accounted for 71.3 percent of the total expenditures for local jails in 1993 (Bureau of Justice Statistics 1995, 8). Personnel expenditures only represent one-half of the puzzle. When asked, jail administrators rank personnel concerns as second only to crowding as the major obstacle facing them (Guynes 1988). Staff shortages are one problem that jail administrators face; they often result from the "poor image of jail work and inadequate career incentives" (Poole and Pogrebin 1991, 163).

As pointed out above, in many jurisdictions the local jail is operated by the county. The person most often responsible for the jail's operation is the sheriff. In most jurisdictions the sheriff is an elected official who may or may not have law enforcement experience. The local sheriff has a large number of responsibilities, only one of which is the administration of the local jail. For the most part, the public has one of two attitudes toward jails: at best indifference or, at worst, a strongly negative view (Mays and Thompson 1991, 10). As such, jails often find themselves at the bottom of the newly elected county sheriff's list of priorities. As might be expected, the local sheriff, as an elected official, wants to appease the residents of his or her jurisdiction, and the most visible way to do this is by putting more deputies out on the street, patrolling the neighborhoods, making arrests, and answering citizens' calls for service. As long as there are no major problems in the jail, such as a riot or escape, the public is often unwilling to put forth any efforts for jail improvements.

The local sheriff will appoint a jail administrator, or deputy sheriff, to oversee the jail's day-to-day operation and to supervise the jail staff. Often, such staff consists of individuals who, looking to move into the more lucrative and much higher status deputy position, are seeing the job in the jail as only a temporary position. In some cases, the jail is staffed with deputies who are being punished for violating a departmental rule (Champion 1990, 173). Sometimes the correctional officer on the night shift also has to handle incoming calls and dispatch officers.

In some jurisdictions a second career track has been initiated exclusively for correctional officers. There are a number of problems with this approach as well. Many times these officers are paid less than their counterparts in the sheriff's office and, as such, are often considered second-class citizens. Adding to this lack of stature is the fact that jail personnel often receive less training, and the environment in which they work is often less than desirable. The jail employee suffers from a lack of potential advancement as well. Correctional officers account for over 76 percent of all jail personnel, with promotions to supervisory positions highly competitive and often nonexistent.

The National Sheriffs' Association reported in 1982 that "Jail officer careers will never achieve the status they deserve so long as counties continue to pay jail officers less money than the officers assigned to police duties" (1982, 151). Salaries in law enforcement and corrections vary greatly from jurisdiction to jurisdiction, but data available on a national level by the U.S. Department of Labor found that the average starting salaries of state corrections officers are about $18,600 a year. They found that "Salaries generally were comparable for correction officers working in jails and other county and municipal correctional institutions" (U.S. Department of Labor 1994, 296). The same report indicated that sheriffs' deputies had a median annual salary of about $25,800 (U.S. Department of Labor 1994, 303).

From 1988 to 1993, the female staff at local jails almost doubled (from 16,545 to 28,500), but this increase only represents about a 3 percentage point increase in the proportion of female staff (from 22.6 percent to 24.2 percent of all officers). The race and ethnic origin of jail staff has changed very little in the same time period; in fact, the actual proportion of minority personnel has slightly declined in the five-year period from 1988 to 1993 (from 24.1 percent to 23.2 percent for blacks and from 7.1 percent to 6.7 percent for Hispanics). The number of inmates per jail employee has dropped in the last 10 years by about 25 percent from 3.5 to 2.8, with the total number of inmates per jail correctional officer dropping as well from 5 in 1983 to 3.9 in 1993 (Bureau of Justice Statistics 1995, 9).

The problems with jail staff cannot be understated. Poor working conditions affect employees' morale and, consequently, affect the treatment of those under their care. Efforts must be made to bring about a number of changes for jail personnel. As Poole and Pogrebin have pointed out, we must "examine ways of maximizing the use of employee talents, skills, and abilities, thus enhancing both staff and program development" (1991, 164). If changes are made in the training and enrichment of the correctional officer's job, it will also enhance the environment in which we house inmates.

Another important factor in improving the working conditions of jails is in the philosophy of the new generation jail. As pointed out above, some of the end results of the direct supervision models are improved staff morale, decreased staff tension, reduced sick leave, improved treatment of inmates by staff, decreased staff-inmate conflicts, and reduced employee misconduct (Nelson 1988, 4). New generation jails offer correctional officers greater control of inmate behavior and, as such, much more interaction and control over what happens. They must actively supervise the inmates, resulting in more responsibility and job satisfaction.

## LEGAL ISSUES

While jail administrators are wrestling with personnel problems, an even bigger concern looms on the horizon — that of inmate lawsuits. Inmate lawsuits have the potential of costing the local government millions of dollars. Inmates are filing lawsuits in record numbers for such things as overcrowded conditions, damage to personal property during shakedowns, and injuries received from other inmates and staff. Local jurisdictions do not have the same immunity from civil liability and the collection of damages that states usually enjoy (McCoy 1982).

Champion (1991, 205) lists three major avenues that jail inmates follow for filing lawsuits: civil rights violations, habeas corpus petitions, and mandamus actions. The Civil Rights Act of 1871 (often referred to as 42 U.S.C. §1983 or simply Section 1983) stipulates that governmental officials can be held legally liable for their actions or failures to act within their official capacity. As discussed in an earlier chapter, the specific provisions of the Civil Rights Act claim that any public officer who violates any person's constitutional rights under the color of law or custom can be held liable for action in lawsuits (42 U.S.C. §1983). Not only can an inmate file suit against an individual employee for a violation of civil rights, but in many cases a suit is filed against the jail administrator (the sheriff in many cases), the county, and, quite possibly, the county commission.

The rationale for such suits is that administrators at all levels are responsible for the actions of subordinates. If it can be shown that either through neglect in hiring, training, or retention, the administrator or county officials should have been aware of inappropriate actions by their subordinates, then they too can be held liable. The jail administrator hires and is responsible for the training and supervision of all subordinates. If something happens, both the jail employee and the supervisor are responsible. *Section 1983 suits* are the most prevalent jail inmate litigation mechanisms (Champion 1991, 206).

*Habeas corpus lawsuits* are the second most prevalent form of inmate suits filed. Under habeas corpus lawsuits, inmates challenge either their confinement or the conditions of confinement (Champion 1991, 206). A person who is confined can use this writ to obtain a hearing as to the legality of her detention. In the case of *Coffin v. Reichard*, 143 F.2d 443 (8th Cir. 1944), the court ruled that inmates are entitled to habeas corpus relief, even though they are lawfully held, if it is shown that they have been deprived of some right to which they are entitled (Champion 1991, 206).

*Mandamus actions* are often filed to compel jail personnel to perform their administrative duties. If the court orders a jail to provide a service or reduce overcrowding and the jail fails to carry out that order, a mandamus action can be sought. The problem with such actions in a jail is that often the inmate filing the action has been released from confinement, or is no longer in the facility when the case finally reaches the court. As such, lawyers will often file class action suits rather than individual suits.

The best approach to the litigation crisis is to avoid the conditions in which lawsuits are brought. Jail administrators should design and run their facility in a "preventative" fashion (Sechrest and Collins 1989, ix). Sechrest and Collins (1989) offer jail administrators and jail personnel an alternative to simply dealing with lawsuits as they occur. They recommend that steps should be taken to avoid the possibility of lawsuits. They offer both recommendations to the administrator, as well as security checklists which should be used to head off problems.

As discussed in Chapter 10, in *Bell v. Wolfish,* 441 U.S. 520 (1979), the Supreme Court ruled on a number of issues dealing with crowding, health care, and the rights of pretrial detainees. As to the latter, the court ruled that a pretrial detainee may not be punished prior to adjudication of guilt. However, they held that double-bunking and other practices that were necessary to manage the institution and maintain security were not punishment. If a jail shows that its conditions are designed to maintain security or to manage the institution, they are not considered to be punishing the inmate.

One positive effect of inmate litigation has been that local jurisdictions have had to take a serious look at the facilities and training afforded their staff. While large settlements are not the norm, such threats have forced local jurisdictions to look very seriously at both their physical plants and their training procedures. In fact, one of the best mechanisms to head off litigation is in the development of jail standards, which includes a procedure for monitoring compliance (Thompson and Mays 1988).

## JAIL STANDARDS

The implementation of jail standards has been hailed as potentially the best way to correct many of the deficiencies found in American jails (Mays and Thompson 1991, 15). The implementation of such standards is seen as one of the best defenses against inmate litigation. A number of agencies have developed and disseminated model standards for jails (American Correctional Association 1981; National Advisory Commission on Criminal Justice Standards and Goals 1973). Although these standards are readily available, their implementation has been slow at best. Mays and Thompson (1991) have pointed to three possible reasons why these standards have not made a significant impact on the conditions of American jails. First, they point out that adopting these standards may require major capital expenditures (Mays and Thompson 1991, 15). In many jurisdictions such large capital outlays are just not possible. The local jurisdictions must also deal with public pressure to put tax money into more popular public programs such as education and recreational programs.

A second concern is a major problem for smaller jails. Smaller jails cannot provide the level of service advocated by the jail standards. Many treatment programs are just not feasible in such small jails. Small jails also suffer from the problems of economies of scale (Mays and Thompson 1988). The rationale behind economies of scale is that the cost of services and products can be greatly reduced if larger quantities are purchased at one time. The cost to provide medical care in a small jail must be divided by only a small number of inmates, while in large metropolitan jails such as Cook County, which can house over 9,000 inmates, the relative cost per inmate is small. The same rationale holds for other services such as food, supplies and, to a certain extent, labor costs. The obvious solution to this problem is to eliminate smaller, economically inefficient jails and consolidate them into regional detention facilities (Mays and Thompson 1991, 16). This trend is already taking place, with the number of small jails (fewer than 50 inmates) declining and the number of large jails (over 1,000 inmates) increasing. In 1993 there were 1,874 small jails, which compares to 2,844 in 1978; and in 1993 there were 76 large jails, compared to only 10 in 1978 (Bureau of Justice Statistics 1990).

The concept of regional jails is not new; in fact, Goldfarb proposed such facilities in the mid 1970s. He envisioned the elimination of jails as we now know them, and the creation of regional detention centers to house pretrial detainees. Those convicted of crimes would serve their sentences in a separate community correctional facility (Goldfarb 1975, 419).

The third and final reason that progress has been slow is because even if the standards are put in place, rarely do mechanisms exist to enforce those standards (Mays and Thompson 1991, 16). Without an effective enforcement body with authority to force compliance, true change is unlikely to take place.

The obvious trend is for jail administrators to move toward the implementations of jail standards on a local level or face the possibility that the court would force compliance. An even better approach would be to develop standards at the state level. In 1991, about 27 percent of the jurisdictions surveyed had at least one jail under court order to limit crowding, and 30 percent were under court order to improve one or more conditions of confinement (Bureau of Justice Statistics 1992, 1).


## OVERCROWDING

In Chapter 3, the overcrowding of this nation's prisons was described. The situation is similar for jails as well. The dilemma facing jails and prisons is that while they must react to overcrowded conditions, they have little or no control over their populations (Kalinich 1986, 85). In the past ten years alone, jail populations have doubled. This trend is tantamount to a crisis, and efforts have been made to build jail space to keep up with the increasing number of inmates. The rated capacity of local jails in this country has risen from 261,432 in 1984 to 504,324 in 1994, an increase of almost 93 percent (Bureau of Justice Statistics 1995, 6). Despite this stepped-up attempt to build our way out of a problem, our nation's jails are still overcrowded. In fact, "overcrowded penal facilities represent the single largest dilemma facing modern American penology." About 27 percent of the jurisdictions had at least one jail under court order to limit their population (Welsh, et al. 1991, 131).

Even though we are adding between 25,000 and 30,000 new bed spaces each year, capacity continues to hover very near the 100 percent mark. The Bureau of Justice Statistics defines rated capacity as "the number of beds or inmates assigned by a rating official to facilities within each jurisdiction" (1995, 6). The obvious implication here is that we find bed space for all those held in jail, and the rated capacity tells us little about crowding. In fact, it may just be an indication of the number of beds in a jail rather than an indication of crowding. If this is the case, and there is every indication that it is, then a number of states are beyond the crisis point. In eight states and the District of Columbia, the percent of capacity occupied is above 100 percent, and figures for 1993 indicate that Virginia jails are at 160 percent of their rated capacity (Bureau of Justice Statistics 1995, 6-7).

A number of states are well below their rated capacity. Nine states had a combined average rated capacity below 75 percent for the year 1993. The state with the lowest occupancy rate was North Dakota at 43 percent (Bureau of Justice Statistics 1995, 6-7). All of these figures may be somewhat deceiving because occupancy fluctuates throughout a week or month in most jurisdictions. These numbers represent averages, and the actual numbers may increase drastically on a Friday or Saturday evening and drop off during the week. Sometimes people serving sentences for minor offenses are given their sentence during the weekend so they can continue to hold down a job during the week.

A second major concern also indicates the above numbers may be misleading. Due to classification problems, many jails, even if they are below their rated capacity, may be very crowded due to the housing of females and juveniles at the same facility. Federal law mandates that there be sight and sound separation of the sexes and between juveniles and adults. In many small jails, if space is needed to house a female or juvenile, a whole wing of the jail must be emptied to accommodate this person. In a sense, you have one or two individuals staying in an area that is designed to hold 50 inmates, while the other displaced inmates occupy a much smaller area.

In an attempt to deal with the crowding problem, policy makers have decided to house many jail inmates in what have been called makeshift jails (Welch 1991). These makeshift jails may range from converted gas stations or motels to barges or ferry boats converted to floating detention facilities. New York City has taken a lead in the use of decommissioned ferry boats and military troop transports as makeshift jails. The first two such floating detention centers were moored at Rikers Island to add much needed jail capacity (Welch 1991, 151). Others have been added to the fleet as well, with the largest holding over 800 inmates.

Although it seems that the only approach being undertaken to control the crowding problem is to build or fabricate additional beds, on other fronts attempts are being made to reduce the actual number of individuals housed in jails, for example, by home confinement and monitoring. A number of factors must be considered when addressing the problem of crowding. Removing juveniles from adult facilities would reduce crowding, and it would also bring many jails into compliance with the amended Juvenile Justice and Delinquency Prevention Act of 1980. A second widely mentioned solution is to reduce the number of pretrial detainees in jail. Since they account for about 50 percent of the jail population, reducing their number would substantially reduce crowding. Much of this could be accomplished if we eliminated or completely overhauled the antiquated and biased bail system (Welch 1991, 155). Bail was established to insure that the charged individual showed up for a court hearing, but it has become a system in which only those who are poor or disadvantaged are held. Those with the means to offer bail will be released. A word of caution. Even with the new provisions of the Bail Reform Act, about 14 percent of those on pretrial release are rearrested, 71 percent of whom were rearrested for a felony (Bureau of Justice Statistics 1994b).

The courts could also rely more heavily on alternatives to incarceration for many individuals found guilty of nonviolent offenses. The use of fines, community service and such could be expanded. Where the public demands jail time, such as in the case of driving while intoxicated or while under the influence, alternative forms of incarceration could be employed. Many such offenders are in little danger of escape and, as such, can often be punished using a less restrictive and costly approach. The maximum security jails that we spend millions of dollars to build should be reserved for those who possess the greatest risk to society. Whenever possible, alternatives should be used for all other offenders.

## SPECIAL NEEDS INMATES

There are a large array of inmates who present unique problems to jailers. Many jails are just not equipped to meet the special needs of these inmates. Inmates with special medical needs or those suffering from mental illness create additional sets of burdens on an already overtaxed system. In many cases, the physical plant is not equipped to handle those who are visually or hearing impaired. Older inmates who have trouble walking may find the maze of corridors and stairs insurmountable. In the sections that follow, we will look at a number of these special needs inmates.

*The Mentally Ill.* The treatment of mental illness has become an increasingly complex problem for jails in this country (Gibbs 1986). Much of the problem today is related to the fact that the courts have ruled that mental hospitals must either treat their mental patients or release them (*Wyatt v. Stickney*, 325 F. Supp. 781 (M.D. Ala. (1971)).

The proverbial flood gates were opened as previously institutionalized patients were released onto the street. Many such individuals become public nuisances, and the police have few alternatives to deal with such individuals. With a lack of other public facilities to house them, they subsequently end up in jail. Even if a public or private facility is available, often the mentally ill are housed in jail for short periods of time until they can be committed to such institutions. Studies have found that as many as thirty percent of all jail inmates show some signs of mental disturbance (Guy, et al. 1985, 29).

The question then becomes how to deal with mentally ill persons in jail. Among the number of studies that addressed this issue, Gibbs (1987) recommended a careful look at both the mentally ill inmates and the jail environment. The actual environment in which we lock up individuals can have a profound effect on the symptoms of psychopathology. When inmates were given a battery of tests to measure symptoms of psychopathology, both at the time of arrest and then again after five days of confinement, it was repeatedly found that the symptoms of psychopathology had increased (Gibbs 1987).

In dealing with this ever-increasing demand, jail administrators must make major operational changes in the delivery of mental health services (Kalinich, et al. 1991, 86). Screening mechanisms must be put in place with highly trained personnel conducting the intake process. When a need is identified, appropriate mental health care must be provided. If such care is not available in the community, then the jail must take the lead in providing the service within the facility. Jail personnel must also be trained to recognize the symptoms of mental illness and follow the course recommended by Gibbs in making every effort to reduce the environmental effects that can cause or add to the problem.

A direct supervision design may offer a partial solution. New generation jails that employ direct supervision offer inmates a less stressful environment because they feel less threatened from predatory attacks and because the noise level in these facilities is greatly reduced. A study by Zupan that compared the stress levels between a traditional jail and a direct supervision facility found that inmates in the direct supervision facility reported fewer symptoms of psychological and physical stress than those inmates housed in the traditional designed jail (1991, 161-162).

*Alcoholics.* One of the most pressing problems of jail management is what to do with individuals taken into custody who are under the influence of alcohol. The number of individuals arrested who are under the influence of alcohol has grown rapidly in the past decade, due largely to the efforts of public interest groups such as Mothers Against Drunk Drivers (MADD). Public awareness of the risks drivers present who are under the influence of alcohol has forced courts to place more emphasis on this behavior. In some cases, mandatory jail time has been legislated for those convicted of driving under the influence (National Institute of Justice 1984). The impact of alcohol-related arrests is "immense," especially in terms of cost and jail space (Zupan 1991, 28). While the increasing number of individuals housed in jails for alcohol-related charges has added to the crowding problem, an even greater concern is the number of problems that can occur during the first few hours of confinement. Sickness, vomiting, and the possibility of slipping and falling are all very real concerns to jail personnel. Such individuals may become despondent and try to commit suicide or may have compounding health problems that simply go unrecognized when they enter the jail. It is not uncommon for individuals who seem drunk and are placed in a cell to later fall into a coma and, in some cases, die. As the number of persons who are housed in jails increases and, more importantly, as the number who flow through jails increases, usually during peak periods such as Friday and Saturday evenings, such problems only compound themselves.

*Drug Addicts.* Persons who use and abuse drugs present a special problem to jail personnel. Those who have a long history of drug use will often appear normal when they arrive at jail. The actual physical and medical problems do not begin to materialize until they begin coming off the drugs. The withdrawal symptoms may be very severe and require the assistance of medical personnel. A study undertaken in 21 large city jails in 1989 found that as many as 66 percent of all persons arrested during that year tested positive for some drug at the time of their arrest (National Institute of Justice 1990). This is not only a big city problem. Drug use is a problem in all communities. In some cases, the drug users may be so strung out on drugs that they have to be restrained to insure that they do not hurt their captors or themselves.

Jail personnel must be trained to look for signs of drug use and be prepared to assist the inmates during withdrawals. Jail personnel should be familiar with the side effects of a large number of differing types of drugs so that appropriate action can be taken. When medical treatment is needed, it is often up to the jailer to administer medication prescribed by doctors.

Another pressing problem in jails is control of the distribution of illicit drugs within the institution. Inmates will often go to extraordinary means to obtain drugs within a jail. Jail and support personnel may be bribed or coerced into supplying drugs, or whenever contact visits are allowed, the potential exists for drug smuggling to occur.

*Sex Offenders.* Another type of offender that can present problems in jail is the sex offender. It is impossible to lump all sex offenders into one category, since a wide range of offenses fall under this classification. The jail is often faced with holding a person accused of molesting a child or indecent exposure. Such an offender is often quite passive in a correctional environment and may become a victim of predatory crime within the jail. In fact, other prisoners look down on many sex offenders (especially child molesters) and often will go to great lengths to injure or even kill them. Such offenders may need to be separated from the general population for their own protection. Such arrangements often have an adverse effect because many such offenders become depressed and suicidal, and segregation affords the opportunity to carry out these suicides.

*Suicide.* The high rate of suicides in jail can largely be attributed to the type of offenders that are housed there. Studies have found that the suicide rate is five to six times higher among jail inmates than that of comparable free world individuals (Winfree 1988). In 1993, 36.2 percent of deaths in local jails were attributed to suicides (Bureau of Justice Statistics 1995, 11), while only 4.9 percent of the deaths in state correctional institutions were attributed to suicides (Bureau of Justice Statistics 1994c, 585). Much of this can be attributed to the fact that jails service an at-risk group of individuals, for example, young men abusing drugs or alcohol (Winfree and Wooldredge 1991, 77).

In looking at data collected on 344 of the 419 suicides that occurred in jails in 1979, Hayes (1980) identified a number of important victim characteristics. Hayes found that almost 97 percent of suicide victims are males and about 68 percent are white. Even more startling is the fact that about 92 percent were unconvicted pretrial detainees, and over half committed suicide during the first 24 hours of incarceration. Twenty-seven percent had taken their life within three hours of being locked up. Sixty percent of those who took their life were being held in isolation (Hayes 1980). Hayes offers a profile of the typical jail suicide.

> An inmate committing suicide in jail was most likely to be a 22-year-old, white, single male. He would have been arrested for public intoxication, the only offense leading to his arrest, and would presumably be under the influence of alcohol and/or drugs upon incarceration. Further, the victim would not have a significant history of prior arrests. He would have been taken to an urban county jail and immediately placed in isolation for his own protection and/or surveillance. However, less than three hours after incarceration, the victim would be dead. He would have hanged himself with material from his bed (such as a sheet or pillowcase). (1983, 467-468)

Some words of caution should be issued: First, a reliance on such a profile might cause jail personnel to overlook other inmates who may take their lives (Kennedy and Homant 1988, 452). Second, the use of profiles may allow lawyers to attach tort liability to jail personnel when a death occurs if the individual who committed suicide fits the profile. Due to these concerns, Kennedy and Homant have suggested alternatives to profiles that should be employed by jails (1988, 453). They suggest that we should first develop jails that are suicide-resistant. By developing new designs that allow more careful monitoring and the use of hardware that does not facilitate hanging, we could reduce the opportunity of suicide. There are a number of potential problems with such an approach, such as the dehumanization of the jail environment, which might just shift the suicides to prisons. The best approach is the direct supervision design, where inmates are under continuous supervision. Not only are they afforded little or no opportunity to commit suicide, but jail personnel would be more likely to notice warning signs and could offer assistance.

A second alternative is to extend extra awareness of inmates' needs during the first critical 24 hours that they are in custody (Kennedy and Homant 1988, 453). Whether inmates fit the profile or not, realizing that those first few hours are the most critical and providing additional care during that crucial time period can reduce a substantial number of suicides. It was also noted by Kennedy and Homant that often jail suicides are nothing more than suicides that occurred in jail, meaning that presence in jail was not directly tied to the individual's decision to commit suicide (1988, 454).

During the year ending June 30, 1993, there were 647 inmate deaths that occurred in local jails. This number is somewhat conservative, with about 10 percent of the nation's jails (which housed about 7 percent of the total jail population) unable to report data on deaths within their institutions. Over 36 percent or 234 of those deaths were attributed to suicides. Suicide deaths per 100,000 jail inmates has dropped by over 58 percent in the last ten years, due largely to the increased awareness of the problem and a concern for the possibility of lawsuits.

*Juveniles.*   In 1988, a total of 33 juveniles died while being held in public custody facilities: 17 were by suicide, 6 were homicides, and the remainder can be attributed to illnesses and other causes (Allen-Hagen 1991, 3). Suicides are just one of many problems jails face with juveniles. A study undertaken by the Department of Justice on juvenile suicide in adult jails, lockups, and juvenile detention centers found that the incidence of juvenile suicide is 7.7 times greater in adult jails than in juvenile detention facilities, and 1.4 times greater in adult lockups than in juvenile detention facilities (Flaherty 1980, 10). The incidence of juvenile suicides for adult jails and lockups is 4.48 times greater than the risk among juveniles in the general population.

An even more pressing problem is the fact that half of the children who committed suicide while in adult jails or lockups in 1978 had not committed a felony and appeared to present no real danger to society (Flaherty 1980, 12). These youthful offenders may become victims of abuse or sexual assault by older more hardened criminals housed in jails. Such factors can only add to the shock of incarceration. Juvenile females seem especially at risk. Those girls who have a history of sexual or physical abuse are especially vulnerable to suicide and depression (Chesney-Lind 1988, 161-162). Chesney-Lind warns that juvenile girls are vulnerable to sexual assault by jail personnel (1988, 163). These girls suffer from a "doubly disadvantaged status" being both female and juveniles (Chesney-Lind 1988, 164).

## JAIL SOCIALIZATION AND SUBCULTURES

Little research has been undertaken addressing the role of subcultures within local jails. In fact, there is some question that subcultures exist within the jail environment. Stojkovic argues that inmates move in and out of jails with such "rapidity that it is difficult for an identifiable subculture to develop" (1986, 32). On the chance that a subculture is found, it is probably "imported" into the facility by those who have experienced prison incarceration (Stojkovic 1986, 32). Garofalo and Clark (1985) draw similar conclusions, claiming that if a subculture does exist in jails, it can be attributed to more experienced inmates who are able to readapt when they find themselves confined in jail again. As early as 1986, Stojkovic brought to light the dearth of research and literature on jail subcultures and recommended a thorough investigation of all elements of subcultures such as violence and stress adaptation, sexual relations, race relations, contraband markets, and power relations within the jail setting. To date, little effort has been made toward this effort.

"If the prisoner subculture of the jail is crucial to our collective understanding of the environment of jail, it is essential that more data be gathered on how the socialization of jail inmates influences jail operations" (Stojkovic 1986, 24). Once again, there is a dearth of information on the socialization process facing inmates confined to jail. Much of this oversight may be due to the transitory nature of the jail confinement. In 1993 alone, over 13 million people passed in and out of local jails; many of those stayed for only a short period of time. As such, for the vast majority of jail inmates, there is little or no opportunity for the socialization process to take place.

This is not to claim that socialization does not take place, and we must look at an important factor that is involved here. Jails act as the entry point for virtually all persons entering the correctional system. Almost everyone who is going to serve time in a state or federal prison will begin the process in a jail. As such, jails act as one's first taste of confinement, and it can be argued that jails begin the actual inmate socialization process. This process of socialization within a jail is evident in the story told by a 20-year-old who, after being arrested for the first time on a commercial burglary charge, began his journey into the criminal justice system within a county jail.

> My first few months within the county jail can be compared to boot camp in the army. I basically followed the county jail staff's orders and learned to keep my eyes to myself and my mouth shut. I survived through this wicked transition from free-world society into this jungle-like surrounding by adjusting to not only the whims of the jail administrators, but also to the jail inmate code of conduct. I was exposed to many different walks of life: from gang bangers to sex offenders, wealthy inmates to winos, and questionable heterosexuals to full-blown transsexuals. I remember getting initiated into the system my first night by a group of inmates who beat me down to the ground for the sole purpose of stealing my sneakers. (Wooden and Ballan 1996, 8)

According to Wooden and Ballan (1996) socialization begins with jail confinement, where inmates move from the relative freedom of life on the streets to their first encounter with the correctional system. This important first step in the socialization process was described as a school with inmates and correctional officers serving as teachers.

> Day and night I observed the transactions and trends within my world behind bars. I often hid behind a mask to camouflage my true feelings, acting like a chameleon in order to blend into the background. I constantly found myself adapting to fit the rules of each situation. I remember I'd be resting on my bunk late at night and watching inmates quietly move around the bunk area like shadows. A few times I actually caught a glimpse of these shadows stealing, or raping and/or beating other inmates for their own personal gain. I had been a victim to these predators, also, so I used this daily knowledge to protect myself. Almost instantaneously, I learned to sleep with both eyes open. (Wooden and Ballan 1996, 9-10)

This first stage of inmate socialization — learning the system — leads inmates into the second stage in which dysfunctional roles are assumed. This stage takes place when inmates enter prison. Inmates at this stage take on what Goffman has called "impression management," where inmates attempt to control the impressions that others have of them (Goffman 1959, 208-237). This coping mechanism is part of the adaptation process to the new surroundings.

It seems that as we rely more and more on jails to handle the overflow from state and federal prisons and to house convicted persons ordered to serve their sentences in jail, subcultures similar to those found in prisons will begin to form. Recent data show that in 1993 about 53,900 or 11.7 percent of all inmates housed in jails are held for either state or federal authorities. A vast majority of these individuals, 34,200, were held due to crowding in the prison systems (Bureau of Justice Statistics 1995, 14). In addition, it may be that persons are serving longer sentences in jails. Between 1983 and 1989, the average sentence served by convicted inmates in jails increased from 14 months to 17 months (Bureau of Justice Statistics 1995, 13-14). With longer sentences, jail inmates will inevitably be more subject to the jail version of prisonization.

## *A DAY IN THE LIFE*

A common phrase mentioned by scholars is that "jail time is dead time." Many jails just do not have the resources to provide inmates with meaningful activities. Part of this problem lies in the high turnover in population that jails experience. The Bureau of Justice Statistics found that approximately two-fifths of jail inmates are released after spending only one day or less in jail, and three-fifths spend only four days or less (1990, 5). The median time that inmates spend in jail was found to be only three days (Bureau of Justice Statistics 1990, 5). But "without appropriate programs that focus on changing the criminal behavior of inmates, the jail becomes a 'revolving door,' releasing individuals into the community simply to readmit them in a few months, weeks, days, or even hours, when they are arrested for another crime" (Lightfoot, Zupan, and Stohr 1991, 50).

There is no typical day in jail, but a common theme seems to be inmate idleness. On a typical day, inmates might be awakened at 6:00 A.M. when they are to clean up their cells and make their bunks. They have breakfast and can then take showers and, when necessary, get ready for court appearances. After 8:00 A.M. the inmates might take part in programs or attend a bible study or job skills class, provided that their facility offers these activities and space is available. If they choose not to attend or no such program is available, inmates will often spend the morning in the dayroom of their cell block. At about 11:00 A.M. the jail might be closed down so an inmate count can be taken. When the jail is closed down, visitation is halted, including visits by attorneys, and inmates are required to return to their cells or bunks for a head count. Once the count is complete, lunch is served. At about 1:00 P.M. the jail is once again open for visitation. If available, inmates can take part in jail programs in the afternoon.

While each jail is different, most inmates are allowed a limited number of personal visits per week, although unlimited visits are usually allowed with their attorneys. Generally, the only exception is during times when counts are taken or meals are served. During shift change in mid-afternoon, the jail is once again shut down and another count is made. Once this is accomplished, the jail is reopened. At about 5:00 P.M., the jail is shut down for another count and for dinner, then reopens again at 6:00 P.M. The final shutdown may occur as late as 10:00 P.M.

During the week, inmates are also given some form of recreation time. The American Correctional Association recommends at least four hours of recreation time per week for jail inmates, although the actual time fluctuates from institution to institution. Even with programs and recreation time, inmates have an abundance of idle time on their hands. The challenge for jail administrators and personnel then becomes what to do to reduce this inmate idleness.

One possible solution was addressed in a report developed through the Jail Industries Initiative (Miller, Sexton, and Jacobsen 1991). The purpose of the report was to look at ways to make jails more productive. Four objectives were mentioned:

1. the development of inmate work habits and skills,
2. the generation of revenues or reduction of costs for the county,
3. the reduction of inmate idleness, and
4. the satisfaction of community needs (Miller, Sexton, and Jacobsen 1991, 2).

While such programs might seem prohibitive to many smaller facilities, the report mentions a continuum of tasks that might fit within any jail. At one end of the continuum, the inmate might simply cut the grass in front of the jail, earning little more than the privilege to watch television for an extra hour. At the other end of the continuum, the jail inmate might work for private-sector industry to earn real dollars that could be used to offset the cost of confinement (Miller, Sexton, and Jacobsen 1991, 2). In both cases, "the elements of labor, service provision, value, and compensation are all present"

(Miller, Sexton, and Jacobsen 1991, 2). The ultimate goal for any such program is to reduce idleness among jail inmates. Beyond this, such programs can both improve work habits as well as defray the cost of housing inmates.

# THE FUTURE OF JAILS

The importance of jails within the criminal justice system is growing. Jails act as the entry point of the criminal justice system. All those convicted of a crime and sentenced to time in a prison pass through the local jail's doors. With prison overcrowding, jails have been saddled with the additional burden of housing convicted felons for longer periods of time until prison space opens up. Increasing conservatism has added jail time to many offenses that just a few years ago would have been diverted with a fine or community treatment program. The future of jails is largely dependent on how we address the concerns mentioned above.

In looking at the jail crisis, Thompson and Mays (1991) place much of the blame on the states (244). They make four very specific recommendations. The first recommendation deals with states providing the necessary resources for new jail construction or renovation (Thompson and Mays 1991, 244). States, not local governments, have the ability to finance large capital outlays. Many communities that need to build jails are the very ones that do not have the resources to do so. The states can take the lead, using their superior resources to finance the construction or renovation of jails in small communities.

The second and third recommendations address the problem of mandatory jail standards and their enforcement. According to Thompson and Mays, states should develop mandatory jail standards and the mechanisms to enforce them (1991, 244). This should be done at the state level, removed from local politics. The fourth recommendation is for states to adopt legislation that enables local jurisdictions to engage in cooperative agreements to build regional jails (Thompson and Mays 1991, 245). As mentioned above, in many jurisdictions such arrangements are cost effective because duplication of services is not a problem.

Local governments must also take the lead in a number of areas. Thompson and Mays list four recommendations that local officials might employ to handle the jail crisis (1991, 245-246). The first deals with a community awareness program, with the goal of informing the community both of the jail's functions and the conditions. Citizens must realize that "jails are not prisons" and become aware of the jail's unique legal and financial problems (Thompson and Mays 1991, 245). In those communities where the jail is run by the sheriff's department, increased emphasis should be placed on that role during campaigns and elections. If the sheriff has a dual role, then that individual should provide the expertise in both roles, not just in law enforcement.

Once greater public awareness is established, the local community must develop long-term financial plans for jail construction or renovation, staffing, and operation (Thompson and Mays 1991, 245). The management-by-crisis philosophy of the past must be replaced by a careful examination of long-term needs and fiscal responsibility. Local officials must realize that there is a cost benefit in building a new facility. The alternative is to continue housing inmates in facilities that may violate constitutional rights and therefore face losing rather substantial lawsuits.

The third recommendation at the local level deals with requiring local officials to have written policies and procedures (Thompson and Mays 1991, 245). Having written policies and procedures and following them is at the heart of mandatory state jail standards. Local governments must have explicit guidelines for the jail to follow, and those guidelines should follow the standards adopted by the state. If such policies and procedures are implemented and followed, they can be used to prevent lawsuits.

The final recommendation offers probably the greatest hope for the condition of jails today. Communities should look at alternatives to incarceration (Thompson and Mays 1991, 246). To paraphrase a National Institute of Justice report on alternative sentencing, we cannot "build our way" out of the current jail crisis; we must instead develop sensible sentencing policies that offer a wide range of sanctions, while at the same time implementing an aggressive public education program (Castle 1991, 5).

As early as 1974, Hans Mattick was recommending alternatives to jail incarceration: "the simplest sentencing alternatives for reducing jail populations are suspended sentence, summary probation, and probation without verdict" (1974, 825). Local communities might look into other alternatives to jail incarceration such as the use of fines (citation and release), community service, electronic monitoring, day reporting centers, specialized treatment facilities, and the use of work-release and weekender sentences (Mattick 1974, 827-828). Local communities might also use early release or furlough programs that allow the jail to release early those inmates who show the most promise and who are unlikely to commit further crimes. As noted previously, jails suffer from the fact that they do not have control over their populations: Outside forces control the flow of inmates in and out of the facility. By implementing furloughs or good time options (which in the past have been in the domain of prisons), jail officials would have a release mechanism similar to that which is available for prisons (Mattick 1974, 828-830).

The future of American jails clearly lies in our ability to adapt to the changing needs of the criminal justice system. In the past two decades, we have attempted to build our way out of the current predicament, and as new jails are built, more and more prisoners are held. The inmate litigation explosion has forced us to take a careful look at what has been a persistent problem. The conditions in today's jails are not new, nor are the solutions something we can implement in the short term. If we are to truly control the jail crisis, we must make a concerted effort to allocate the necessary funds to renovate or replace old and deteriorating facilities. Funds must also be made available for the hiring, retention, and training of correctional personnel. And finally, we must make a concerted effort to clearly define the role and function of jails in the United States. "The challenge for the twenty-first century will be to develop, implement, and monitor jail policies that will bring about fundamental changes to the jail's organizational and operational world" (Thompson and Mays 1991, 246).

## Vocabulary

bridewells
functional living units
gaol
habeas corpus lawsuits
linear design
lockups

mandamus actions
pillory
pretrial detainees
rabble
remote design
Section 1983 suits

## Study Questions

1. What groups of people are incarcerated in jails? What are the differences between jails and prisons (for example, in function, management, population characteristics)?

2. Why are juveniles housed in adult jails?

3. What are new generation jails?

4. What are some of the problems of managing a jail?

5. Discuss suicide in jail. How often does it occur? Why?

# Sources Cited

— Allen-Hagen, B. 1991. *Public Juvenile Facilities: Children in Custody 1989.* Washington, D.C.: U.S. Government Printing Office.

— American Correctional Association. 1981. *Standards for Adult Local Detention Facilities.* Rockville, Md.: ACA.

— American Correctional Association. 1985. *Jails in America: An Overview of Issues.* College Park, Md.: ACA.

— Brannon, J. G. 1977. *The Judicial System in North Carolina.* Raleigh, N.C.: Administration Office of the Courts.

— Bureau of Justice Statistics. 1990. *Census of Local Jails 1988.* Washington, D.C.: GPO.

— Bureau of Justice Statistics. 1991. *Profile of Jail Inmates, 1989.* Washington, D.C.: GPO.

— Bureau of Justice Statistics. 1992. *Jail Inmates 1991.* Washington, D.C.: GPO.

— Bureau of Justice Statistics. 1994a. *Pretrial Release of Federal Felony Defendants.* Washington, D.C.: GPO.

— Bureau of Justice Statistics. 1994b. *Pretrial Release of Felony Defendants, 1992.* Washington, D.C.: GPO.

— Bureau of Justice Statistics. 1994c. *Sourcebook of Criminal Justice Statistics — 1994.* Washington, D.C.: GPO.

— Bureau of Justice Statistics. 1995. *Jails and Jail Inmates, 1993-1994.* Washington, D.C.: GPO.

— Cahalan, M. W. 1986. *Historical Corrections Statistics in the United States, 1850-1984.* Washington, D.C.: U.S. Department of Justice.

— Castle, M. N. 1991. *Alternative Sentencing: Selling It to the Public.* Washington, D.C.: GPO.

— Champion, D. J. 1990. *Corrections in the United States: A Contemporary Perspective.* Englewood Cliffs, N.J.: Prentice-Hall.

— Champion, D. J. 1991. "Jail Inmate Litigation in the 1990s." In *American Jails: Public Policy Issues,* ed. Joel A. Thompson and G. Larry Mays, 197-215. Chicago: Nelson-Hall.

— Chesney-Lind, M. 1988. "Girls in Jail." *Crime and Delinquency* 34: 150-168.

— Clear, T. R., and G. F. Cole. 1994. *American Corrections.* 3d ed. Belmont, Cal.: Wadsworth.

— Committee on Education and Labor. 1980. *Juvenile Justice Amendments of 1980.* Hearing before the Subcommittee on Human Resources of the Committee on Education and Labor, House of Representatives.

— Cox, N. R., Jr., and W. E. Osterhoff. 1991. "Managing the Crisis in Local Corrections: A Public-Private Partnership Approach." In *American Jails: Public Policy Issues,* ed. Joel A. Thompson and G. Larry Mays, 227-239. Chicago: Nelson-Hall.

— D'Alessio, S. J., and L. Stolzenberg. 1995. "The Impact of Sentencing Guidelines on Jail Incarceration in Minnesota." *Criminology* 33(2): 282-302.

— Embert, P. S. 1986. "Correctional Law and Jails." In *Sneaking Inmates Down the Alley: Problems and Prospects in Jail Management,* ed. David B. Kalinich and John Klofas, 63-83. Springfield, Ill.: Charles C. Thomas.

— Federal Register. June 20, 1985. 50(119), 25551.

— Flaherty, M. G. 1980. *An Assessment of the National Incidence of Juvenile Suicide in Adult Jails, Lockups, and Juvenile Detention Centers.* Washington, D.C.: GPO.

— Flynn, E. E. 1973. "Jails and Criminal Justice." In *Prisoners in America,* ed. Lloyd E. Ohlin, 49-85. Englewood Cliffs, N.J.: Prentice-Hall.

— Frazier, C. E., and D. M. Bishop. 1990. "Jailing Juveniles in Florida: The Dynamics of Compliance with a Sluggish Federal Reform Initiative." *Crime and Delinquency* 36(4): 427-442.

— Garafalo, J., and R. Clark. 1985. "The Inmate Subculture in Jails." *Criminal Justice and Behavior* 12(4), 415-434.

— Gibbs, J. J. 1986. "When Donkeys Fly: A Zen Perspective on Dealing with the Problem of the Mentally Disturbed Jail Inmate." In *Sneaking Inmates Down the Alley: Problems and Prospects in Jail Management,* ed. D. Kalinich and J. Klofas, 149-166. Springfield, Ill.: Charles C. Thomas.

— Gibbs, J. J. 1987. "Symptoms of Psychopathology among Jail Prisoners: The Effects of Exposure to the Jail Environment." *Criminal Justice and Behavior,* 14: 299-310.

— Gibbs, J. J. 1991. "Environmental Congruence and Symptoms of Psychopathology: A Futher Exploration of the Effects of Exposure to the Jail Environment." *Criminal Justice and Behavior* 18(3): 351-374.

— Goffman, I. 1959. *The Presentation of Self in Everyday Life.* Garden City, N.J.: Anchor.

— Goldfarb, R. 1975. *Jails.* New York: Anchor.

— Gray, T., G. L. Mays, and M. K. Stohr. 1995. "Inmate Needs and Programming in Exclusively Women's Jails." *The Prison Journal,* 75(2): 186-202.

— Guy, E., J. Platt, I. Zwelling, and S. Bullock. 1985. "Mental Health Status of Prisoners in an Urban Jail." *Criminal Justice and Behavior* 12: 29-33.

— Guynes, R. 1988. *Nation's Jail Managers Assess Their Problems.* Rockville, Md.: National Institute of Justice.

— Hayes, L. M. 1980. *And Darkness Closes In, A National Study of Jail Suicides.* Alexandria, Va.: National Center on Institutions and Alternatives.

— Hayes, Lindsay M. 1983. "And Darkness Closes In . . . A National Study of Jail Suicides." *Criminal Justice and Behavior* 10: 461-484.

— Howard, J. 1777. *The State of the Prisons in England and Wales.* London: W. Eyres.

— Irwin, J. 1985. *The Jail.* Berkeley, Cal.: University of California Press.

— Kalinich, D. 1986. "Overcrowding and the Jail Budget: Addressing Dilemmas of Population Control." In *Sneaking Inmates Down the Alley: Problems and Prospects in Jail Management,* ed. David B. Kalinich and John Klofas, 85-100. Springfield, Ill.: Charles C. Thomas.

— Kalinich, D., P. Embert, and J. Senese. 1991. "Mental Health Services for Jail Inmates: Imprecise Standards, Traditional Philosophies, and the Need for Change." In *American Jails: Public Policy Issues,* ed. Joel A. Thompson and G. Larry Mays, 79-99. Chicago: Nelson-Hall.

— Kennedy, D. B., and R. J. Homant. 1988. "Predicting Custodial Suicides: Problems with the Use of Profiles." *Justice Quarterly* 5(3): 441-456.

— Kennedy, S., and K. Carlson. 1988. *Pretrial Release and Detention: The Bail Reform Act of 1984.* Washington, D.C.: U.S. Department of Justice, Bureau of Justice Statistics.

— Kline, S. 1987. *Jail Inmates 1986.* Washington, D.C.: GPO.

— Klofas, J. M. 1990. "The Jail and the Community." *Justice Quarterly* 7(1): 69-102.

— Leibowitz, M. J. (1991). "Regionalization in Virginia Jails." *American Jails* 5(5): 42-43.

— Lightfoot, C. A., L. L. Zupan, and M. K. Stohr. 1991. "Jails and the Community: Modeling the Future in Local Detention Facilities." *American Jails* 4(4): 50-52.

— Maguire, K., and A. L. Pastore, eds. 1995. *Sourcebook of Criminal Justice Statistics.* Washington, D.C.: GPO.

— Mattick, H. W. 1974. "The Contemporary Jails of the United States: An Unknown and Neglected Area of Justice." In *Handbook of Criminology,* ed. Daniel Glaser, 777-848. Chicago, Ill.: Rand McNally.

— Mays, G. L., and J. A. Thompson. 1988. "Mayberry Revisited: The Characteristics and Operations of America's Small Jails." *Justice Quarterly* 5(3): 421-440.

— Mays, G. L., and J. A. Thompson. 1991. "The Political and Organizational Context of American Jails." In *American Jails: Public Policy Issues,* ed. Joel A. Thompson and G. Larry Mays, 3-21. Chicago: Nelson-Hall.

— McCoy, C. 1982. "New Federalism, Old Remedies, and Corrections Policy-Making." *Policy Studies Review* 2 (Nov.): 271-278.

— McGee, R. A. 1975. "Our Sick Jails." In *Jails and Justice,* ed. Paul F. Cromwell, 5-18. Springfield, Ill.: Charles C. Thomas.

— Miller, R., G. E. Sexton, and V. J. Jacobsen. 1991. *Making Jails Productive.* Washington, D.C.: GPO.

— Moynahan, J. M., and E. K. Stewart. 1980. *The American Jail: Its Development and Growth.* Chicago: Nelson-Hall.

— National Advisory Commission on Criminal Justice Standards and Goals. 1973. *Report on Corrections.* Washington, D.C.: U.S. Department of Justice.

— National Institute of Justice. 1984. *Jailing Drunk Drivers: Impact on the Criminal Justice System.* Washington, D.C.: U.S. Department of Justice.

— National Institute of Justice. 1990. *Drugs and Crime 1989.* Washington, D.C.: GPO.

— National Sheriffs' Association. 1982. *The State of Our Nation's Jails, 1982.* Washington, D.C.: National Sheriffs' Association.

— Nelson, W. R. 1988. *Cost Savings in New Generation Jails: The Direct Supervision Approach.* Washington, D.C.: GPO.

— Platt, A. M. 1969. *The Child Savers: The Invention of Delinquency.* Chicago: University of Chicago Press.

— Poole, E. R., and M. R. Pogrebin. 1991. "Changing Jail Organization and Management: Toward Improved Employee Utilization." In *American Jails: Public Policy Issues,* ed. Joel A. Thompson and G. Larry Mays, 163-179. Chicago: Nelson-Hall.

— Robinson, L. N. 1922. *Penology in the United States.* Philadelphia: John C. Winston.

— Rowen, J. R. 1989. "Suicide Detection and Prevention: A Must for Juvenile Facilities." *Corrections Today* 51(5): 218-220.

— Schwartz, I. M. 1988. *(In) Justice for Juveniles: Rethinking the Best Interest of Children.* Lexington, Mass.: Lexington.

— Schwartz, I. M. 1991. "Removing Juveniles from Adult Jails: The Unfinished Agenda." In *American Jails: Public Policy Issues,* ed. Joel A. Thompson and G. Larry Mays, 216-226. Chicago: Nelson-Hall.

— Schwartz, I. M., L. Harris, and L. Levi. 1988. "The Jailing of Juveniles in Minnesota: A Case Study." *Crime and Delinquency* 34(2): 133-149.

— Sechrest, D. K., and W. C. Collins. 1989. *Jail Management and Liability Issues.* Miami: Coral Gables.

— Senese, J. D., D. B. Kalinich, and P. S. Embert. 1989. "Jails in the United States: The Phenomenon of Mental Illness in Local Correctional Facilities." *American Journal of Criminal Justice* 14(1): 104-121.

— Soler, M. 1988. "Litigation on Behalf of Children in Adult Jails." *Crime and Delinquency* 34(2): 190-208.

— Steinhart, D. 1988. "California Legislature Ends the Jailing of Children: The Story of a Policy Reversal." *Crime and Delinquency* 34(2): 169-189.

— Stohr, M. K., N. P. Lovrich, Jr., B. A. Menke, and L. L. Zupan. 1994. "Staff Management in Correctional Institutions: Comparing DiIulio's 'Control Model' and 'Employee Investment Model' Outcomes in Five Jails." *Justice Quarterly,* 11(3): 471-497.

— Stojkovic, S. 1986. "Jails versus Prisons: Comparisons, Problems and Prescriptions on Inmate Subcultures." In *Sneaking Inmates Down the Alley: Problems and Prospects in Jail Management,* ed. D. Kalinich and J. Klofas, 23-37. Springfield, Ill.: Charles C. Thomas.

— Takagi, P. 1975. "The Walnut Street Jail: A Penal Reform to Centralize the Power of the State." *Federal Probation* (December): 18-26.

— Thompson, J. A., and G. L. Mays. 1988. "State-Local Relations and the American Jail Crisis: An Assessment of State Jail Mandates." *Policy Studies Review* 7(3): 567-580.

— Thompson, J. A., and G. L. Mays. 1991a. "Paying the Piper but Changing the Tune: Policy Changes and Initiatives for the American Jail." In *American Jails: Public Policy Issues,* ed. Joel A. Thompson and G. Larry Mays, 240-246. Chicago: Nelson-Hall.

— Thompson, J. A., and G. L. Mays. 1991b. "The Policy Environment of the American Jail." In *American Jails: Public Policy Issues,* ed. Joel A. Thompson and G. Larry Mays, 1-2. Chicago: Nelson-Hall.

— U.S. Department of Labor. 1994. *Occupational Outlook Handbook.* Washington, D.C.: GPO.

— U.S. Department of Justice. 1980. *Indexed Legislative History of the Juvenile Justice Amendments of 1977.* Washington, D.C.: GPO.

— U.S. Department of Justice. 1981. *Indexed Legislative History of the Juvenile Justice Amendments of 1980.* Washington, D.C.: GPO.

— Weisheit, R. A. 1987. "Sex Differences in the Jail Population: Competing Explanations." *Criminal Justice Review* 10(1): 47-51.

— Welch, M. 1991. "The Expansion of Jail Capacity: Makeshift Jails and Public Policy." In *American Jails: Public Policy Issues,* ed. Joel A. Thompson and G. Larry Mays, 148-162. Chicago: Nelson-Hall.

— Welsh, W. N., M. C. Leone, P. T. Kinkade, and H. N. Pontell. 1991. "The Politics of Jail Overcrowding: Public Attitudes and Official Policies." In *American Jails: Public Policy Issues,* ed. Joel A. Thompson and G. Larry Mays, 131-147. Chicago: Nelson-Hall.

— West, D. 1972. "I Was Afraid to Shut My Eyes." In *Criminal Life: Views From the Inside,* ed. D. M. Petersen and M. Truzzi. Englewood Cliffs, N.J.: Prentice-Hall.

— Winfree, L. T. 1988. "Rethinking American Jail Death Rates: A Comparison of National Mortality and Jail Mortality, 1978, 1983." *Policy Studies Review* 7: 641-659.

— Winfree, L. T., Jr., and J. D. Wooldredge. 1991. "Exploring Suicide and Death by Natural Causes in America's Large Jails: A Panel Study of Institutional Change, 1978 and 1983." In *American Jails: Public Policy Issues,* ed. Joel A. Thompson and G. Larry Mays, 63-78. Chicago, Ill.: Nelson-Hall.

— Wooden, W. S., and A. O. Ballan. 1996. Jail/Prison Inmate Socialization: One Man's Journey. Paper presented at the Annual Meeting of the Academy of Criminal Justice Sciences. Las Vegas, Nev.

— Zupan, L. L., and B. A. Menke. 1991. "The New Generation Jail: An Overview." In *American Jails: Public Policy Issues,* ed. Joel A. Thompson and G. Larry Mays, 180-194. Chicago: Nelson-Hall.

— Zupan, L. L. 1991. *Jails: Reform and the New Generation Philosophy.* Cincinnati: Anderson.

# CHAPTER

## 13

# THE FUTURE

*Joycelyn M. Pollock*

[T]he prison of the future will be small. There will be many institutions, of diverse custodial levels, within any metropolitan area. . . . The prisons of the future, because they will be small, can be highly diverse, both in architecture and in program. . . . In the prison of tomorrow there will be much concern with utilizing the personal relationships between staff and inmates for rehabilitative purposes. . . . The prison of the future, clearly, will be part of a society in which rationality is institutionalized, and goodness, truth, and beauty are cardinal goals. (Glaser 1970, 261-266)

---

*Chapter Overview*

—— D**RUG** L**AWS**, O**VERCROWDING**, **AND** R**ACE**
—— P**RISONER** "R**IGHTS**" **AND** P**RISON** V**IOLENCE**
—— I**NDUSTRY**, P**ROGRAMMING AND** C**ORRECTIONAL** P**ROFESSIONALS**
—— C**ONCLUSIONS**

The opening quote illustrates the pitfalls of writing a chapter predicting the "future" of prisons. Glaser's predictions were made during the optimism of the rehabilitative era when it seemed possible, at least to some, that institutions of incarceration could be positive places of change. The future looked bright, given the right resources and the proper frame of mind. Obviously the firestorm of the Martinson report (1974), the disillusionment with rehabilitation, and the tremendous increase in prison populations were yet to be realized. In fact, the entire history of the prison can be characterized as cycles of optimism and despair. The 1870 Prison Congress was a high point in a swing of correctional optimism, yet the 100 years that followed produced so little progress that the principles pronounced by the participants at the 1870 Congress were endorsed again in 1970. Considering recent history, one safe prediction may be that in 2070, these principles will be dusted off once again and upheld as objectives for the future.

In this last chapter, we will take a brief look at some selected issues of this nation's prisons and attempt to make some projections of what might happen in the future. These projections are appreciably less optimistic than Glaser's above.

## Drug Laws, Overcrowding, and Race

As discussed in Chapters 3 and 11, prisons are full, and most states are struggling with ever-increasing numbers of prisoners sent to them by courts. The largest single contributor to the increase of prison populations is drug laws. As Alida Merlo cited in Chapter 3, almost a third of prison commitments are for drug crimes. This single crime category is approaching property crimes in level of frequency of commitment. With projections of the prison population reaching two million by the year 2000, it is ironic that the news is (and has been for several years) that crime rates are going *down*. Serious crimes dropped across the country for the fourth year in a row, with homicide leading the decline at a drop of 8 percent (Butterfield 1996). Explanations for the decline identify tough drug laws, increased enforcement, the reduction of turf wars between drug dealing gangs, and a reduction in the number of people in the crime-prone age groups, but no one really can prove why crime rates decrease any more than one can prove why crime rates increase. Further, incarceration rates do not seem to correlate with crime rates at all — the rate of imprisonment is still going up! The United States has the dubious distinction of now having the highest incarceration rate in the world.

Another issue is that the public's fear of crime does not correlate with their risk of being victimized. Most people think that crime is a serious problem in the nation and that they have a greater chance of being a victim of violent crime today than in years past. The truth is that the homicide rate today is about the same as it was in 1974 (Butterfield 1996), and, in fact, is going down. If victimization rates are further analyzed, it is apparent that certain groups in this society bear most of the risk, specifically young black males — exactly the same group who have the highest incarceration rate.

One thing is true, however: Crime, criminals, and how they should be punished is an ever-popular political platform. The myth that we "coddle" criminals is still around, even though the rehabilitative era has been over for several decades. The "get tough on criminals" message is so tempting that both Democrats and Republicans use it to get elected. It is a stand that has the attraction of no detractors — the argument that longer sentences and tougher laws are not the way to solve crime is so unpopular that no one dares express it and hope to get elected. Privately, though, many legislators will admit that they have doubts that the present incarcerative approach to drug control is working and, even more important, that the nation can afford to continue down the path of incarcerating everyone who sells or uses drugs for increasingly longer prison sentences. As Merlo points out in Chapter 3, the estimates of drug users in the country exceed two million. Obviously, we cannot imprison everyone who chooses to use drugs.

One effect of the "drug war" has been that incarceration rates for African Americans, and to a lesser extent Hispanics, are rapidly outpacing the rate for whites. For instance, Merlo cites the statistic that the three strikes law in California was used for African American defendants 17 times more often than for whites. The crackdown on crack cocaine has been described by some as thinly disguised race politics because crack is used more often than powdered cocaine in urban ghettos and receives incredibly more severe sanctions for its sale. Congress recently refused to adjust federal laws to more evenly distribute the punishments attached to the two types of cocaine, so there seems to be no indication on the horizon that the current pattern of sentencing will abate.

African American men are now the majority in prison. As stated in Chapter 2, it is the only place in this country where African American males clearly have power, albeit the power of race-based gangs.

Prison subcultures have become the subculture of race. As discussed in Chapter 7, race determines almost everything that happens to an individual sent to prison — from where he lives, to his job, to who he associates with, to his risk of victimization. Women in prison form more integrated social groupings, but some researchers find ominous trends that race is becoming a more powerful factor in the social culture of prisons for women as well. The dramatic increase in the numbers of women sent to prison over the last decade is largely due to the increase of African Americans imprisoned.

The "build your way" out of the overcrowded prison problem has few winners. More individuals will be sent to prison — despite dismal recidivism rates — and, when they have accumulated their three strikes, may make prison their home for life, with the public bearing the cost. Obviously, less money will be available for higher education and social programs. Thus, the truism that prisoners are living "better" in prison than they lived on the outside will continue to be factual, at least economically speaking. Interestingly, no one seems to notice that the statement that prison is better than the street says as much about our society's ability to care for its free citizens as it does about its places of confinement. No one seems to conclude that perhaps if we made the streets better than prison, some individuals would end up making choices that kept them out; instead, the conclusion is that we should make prisons worse. If the streets get worse, evidently, prisons need to get "worser."

Some states have managed to build enough prison beds to meet the demands of sentencing practices. Texas, for instance, now has enough beds for its own prisoners and, in fact, is "selling" their spares to other states. Some of these beds are in county jails rather than prisons. As described in Chapter 12, jails are not prisons, are not designed for long-term confinement, and have separate and distinct management and legal issues. Yet increasingly, the lines between jail and prison populations are blurring. Some prisoners are spending short sentences in prison and then being released to probation (under shock probation or boot camp sentencing alternatives); some felons are serving their entire sentence of several years in a jail facility, either in their own state or one far away. The practice of transferring large numbers of inmates across states has outpaced the ethical and legal analysis of such practice.

Another alternative to state-built prisons is to contract with private companies like Wackenhut and Corrections Corporation of America. As discussed in Chapter 11, these companies have moved from obscurity to having enviable growth and profit statements. Imprisonment truly has become big business. Again, the practice has outpaced the analysis of legal and ethical issues regarding its use. One advantage of privately run institutions may be that innovative programming is more likely, however, the standard practice has been for the state to oversee such contracts through byzantine rules and regulations. While no one can question the need for careful monitoring, one would hope that states will allow these private institutions to attempt innovations that can be done more quickly than perhaps is possible in state bureaucracies. Another issue that has been raised is the tendency of private contractors to "skim" the "best" inmates, leaving the state to take care of the most violent, the most intractable, and the most needy offenders.

What predictions can one make for the future? First, that eventually lower crime rates have to penetrate the nation's consciousness and the zeal for longer prison sentences will subside. This will reduce the numbers coming from state courts, and thus, reduce the need for more construction. Those states that have built institutions will continue to maintain them, however. First, there have been, thus far, no successful legal challenges to the practice of interstate transfer of prisoners, thus, some states may continue to be the vendors of prison beds. A second possibility is that since the projected large group of "crime prone" teenagers is imminent and many states have passed harsher juvenile laws, some facilities will be turned over to juvenile authorities to house juvenile offenders. At least some of these young people, already becoming the state-raised youth discussed in Chapter 7, may spend their entire lives in an institution — perhaps in the same institution because, as this group matures, the need for adult beds will again grow, and it is likely that the institutions transferred to juvenile authorities will be taken back again by state prison systems. It rarely occurs that prisons, once built, ever close. Only the individuals inside change.

## PRISONER "RIGHTS" AND PRISON VIOLENCE

The limitation on the current enthusiasm to bring back the chain gang (literally in some southern states) is the thin line of legal rights laid down by the Warren Court, even though most recent prison cases have been exercises in reducing those rights. As discussed in Chapter 10, many recent court decisions have followed the principles of the hands off era and defer to prison administrators' expertise and the states' interest in running safe and orderly institutions. Thus, segregation evidently no longer requires much due process (*Sandin v. Conner,* 115 S. Ct. 2293 (1995)), state court remedies must be exhausted before federal courts will entertain such suits, and the only prisoner rights cases that seem to be successful are those that spell out clear violations of equal protection (for example, where treatment of women offenders is markedly different than that of male offenders). Equal protection analysis might also result in institutions for women becoming more like institutions for men in negative ways. For instance, women's institutions have had more flexible visitation and privacy, but these differences may fall under the same legal equity model that has brought women more equal programming.

Section 1983 cases have been successful tools in sanctioning clear abuses of power, for example, incidences of officer brutality. Thus, prisoners today have less to fear from official misuse of power. Ironically, however, prisoner rights litigation may have led to a situation where they have more to fear from each other. As Chapters 2 and 7 discussed, the prison of today is filled with "prowling" predators who victimize each other, are freer in movement, and are safer from informal sanctions than in the past.

There does seem to be a recent reduction of such violence, however, and prison homicide rates have dramatically declined compared to the years when the vacuum of power led to turf wars between rival gangs. Inmates who kill in prison or who are convicted of multiple homicides outside of prison will probably find themselves in the new "maxi-maxi" prisons, which from all accounts, are a Quaker's nightmare of space-age solitude through technology untouched by objectives of redemption. Courts, thus far, have been unwilling to define such conditions as unconstitutional.

## INDUSTRY, PROGRAMMING AND CORRECTIONAL PROFESSIONALS

Chapter 5 discussed the potential of correctional industry. It may be that this area has the greatest possibility for transforming prisons into productive places of change. Programs that emphasize accountability, responsibility, and, perhaps most important, saving taxpayers' money have the greatest chance of acceptance. If private industry can be sold on the idea that partnerships with prisons are good business, then all parties can benefit from such enterprise. American labor will probably eventually mount a more concerted attack on such programs, yet labor unions have lost power over the last several decades and may be unable to prevent the increase of using prisoners in private enterprise. Obviously this is not a new concept, and, hopefully, these partnerships will not bear any resemblance to the lease labor systems in use after the Civil War, as described in Chapters 5 and 11.

Arguably, work is rehabilitative as well as productive. "Talking" treatments do not alone solve problems of housing, employment, and self-esteem. A paying job can contribute to the cost of running the prison, as well as provide a savings account for the inmate's release. Many examples exist across the country of how these programs can work. Further, as discussed in Chapter 6, most evaluations of rehabilitation show that the most successful programs are those that have pragmatic elements. Continued exploration of prison programming may show that cognitive and behaviorally based programs, combined with work opportunities, carried through to release do have appreciable effects on recidivism. Thus, another prediction is that these programs will increase in number and variety. The impetus for such programs is management-related, as Stone points out in Chapter 5: "Hundreds of thousands of inmates in a state of forced idleness is a very dangerous combination for inmates and correctional employees." But these programs also may have positive effects on individual change.

Another prediction is that correctional professionals may expand their role. Many agree that the purely custodial role is not one that contributes to self-esteem or professionalism. Once treatment staff developed, custodial officers found their role further reduced to mere key turning. As argued in Chapters 8 and 9, correctional professionals who perceive their role as having more complexity and one that requires human relations skills and expanded goals are more likely to have positive self-esteem and a more professional orientation. The trend toward greater professionalism in corrections is continuing. Two possible avenues may emerge: First, some correctional officers may find their niche in work-industry programs, providing not only security but also having more management-related tasks. Second, therapeutic communities may become more popular avenues of treatment and a way of providing niches that offer positive alternatives to the negative subculture of the general population. In these protected living units, correctional professionals find expanded roles that allow them to interact in more meaningful ways with the inmates they supervise.

## CONCLUSIONS

Despite Glaser's predictions in the opening quote, we have seen growth in numbers as well as size of prisons. Instead of increasing sophistication and individualization of treatment programs, prisons turned once again to "warehousing," struggling to find room for the ever-increasing numbers of prisoners. Changes occurred in the internal management of prisons: Legal suits resulted in the dismantling of the building tender system in Texas and the improvement of some of the terrible conditions in such prisons as the Tucker and Cummins prison farms. The worst prisons got appreciably better. Prisoners now enjoy increased rights of mail, movement, and due process protections before punishment. However, along with these changes, inmates arguably became less safe from each other as gangs and violent inmates took advantage of the vacuum of power to advance their self-interest. If current trends continue, this violence should continue to abate, although prisons will never be completely safe places to live. Rehabilitative programs decreased, but education and work programs continued. There are still some rehabilitation efforts as well as some success in prison change efforts. As the prison overcrowding crisis dissipates, perhaps these programs will become more popular.

In conclusion, prisons will probably continue on pretty much the way they have since their inception. They have always been the repository for the disenfranchised. They have endured several cycles of overcrowding and corruption, followed by optimism and enthusiasm for their capacity to change the individuals incarcerated within. Their management and objectives continue to be the hostage of politics and public sentiment, influenced more by general economics and human caprice than crime rates or the needs of those incarcerated. Change can and does occur in prison. In some cases it is positive change, influenced by a teacher, a sympathetic correctional officer, a work foreman, or a chaplain; in some cases it is negative change, incurred through a prison rape, a mental breakdown, or the constant belittlement that all prisoners endure when they receive the pervasive message that "you are nothing and you are not wanted in our community." Those who choose to work in prisons have a worthy goal: Soften that message by treating those inside with basic human kindness and respect.

## Study Question

Present your own predictions of the future of American prisons.

## Sources Cited

— Butterfield, Fox. 1996. "Major Crime Rates Drop for Fourth Year." *Austin American Statesman,* Dec. 5, A1, A5.

— Glaser, Daniel. 1970. "The Prison of the Future." In *Crime in the City,* 261-266. New York: Harper and Row.

— Martinson, Robert. 1974. "What Works? Questions and Answers about Prison Reform." *Public Interest* (Spring): 22-54.

# GLOSSARY

**AIMS:** the Adult Internal Management System, also known as the Quay system, looks at the inmates' behavior during their entry into the prison system and their life history. An analysis is done on this to develop five factors, or dimensions, for the purpose of classification.

**Alienation:** a state of mind vis-à-vis the individual's relationship with others. The five types of alienation are powerlessness, normlessness, meaninglessness, social isolation, and self-estrangement.

**Argot:** the language of the prison subculture.

**Argot roles:** social roles that are discrete types in the subculture, each with attached values and behavior systems.

**Aversive conditioning:** the attempt to control behavior through the use of negative reinforcement and punishment.

**Bridewells:** a cross between a workhouse and a prison. Designed to provide vocational and moral reformation for minor offenders, debtors, homeless children, and other public charges so that they would be fit for city life.

**Building tenders:** system that involved some of the most violent and physically intimidating inmates being chosen as "building tenders" by officers who then controlled their tier or work group through fear and coercion.

**Chain of command:** a way of organizing staff along rigid paramilitary lines. Each person is responsible for those directly beneath him or her and each person is responsible to those directly above him or her.

**Classical conditioning:** utilizing the autonomic nervous system to induce a "conditioned response" to a stimulus.

**Classification:** the assessing of offenders' risks and needs so that they can be assigned to an institution and a custody level according to those risks and needs.

**Close nexus test:** the courts are primarily concerned with the nature of the relationship between the state and the challenged action, that is, whether the action of the private actor was so intertwined with the action of the state as to be indistinguishable.

**Coercive power:** the ability to make an individual act against free will.

**Congregate system:** system introduced at Auburn Prison (often called the Auburn system). The prisoners of this system slept in solitary cells, congregated for work and meals, but did not share any interactions.

**Consensus model:** an explanation of the evolution of law that considers law to be the formalized views and values of the people, arising from the aggregate of social values and developing through social interaction.

**Contraband:** items that are illegal to import, export, transport, or possess.

**Control group:** in an experiment the control group is similar to the experimental group on all important factors but is not introduced to the experimental variable.

**Control model:** emphasizes the internal environment of inmate obedience, work, and education, and largely ignores the external environment.

**Corporal punishment:** physical punishment.

**Counseling:** a "helping" relationship, characterized by good, productive communication, goals, and the use of techniques to further personal growth.

**Custody classification:** the classification assigned to an inmate to designate the security precautions that must be observed when working with that inmate.

**Custody-oriented officer:** a correctional officer who maintains control by enforcing the rules and who possesses the legitimate, coercive, and reward power to do so without fear of contradiction.

**Deliberate indifference test:** phrase describing the legal test used to determine if medical care (to prisoners) reaches the level of "cruel and unusual punishment." Must show more than negligence or poor care; must constitute deliberate indifference to the pain and suffering of an inmate.

**Determinate sentencing:** a sentencing system where the length of the sentence is determined by the legislature with no range (that is, no minimum or maximum).

**Deterrence:** preventing individuals (specific) and others (general) from committing future crimes through the use of punishment.

**Disparate impact:** although procedures as written do not distinguish between inmates of different genders, the practical results are that the sexes are treated differently.

**Disparate treatment:** people of different genders are treated differently in an obvious, intentional manner.

**Eclectic:** means that many different treatment modalities may be brought together in a professional treatment program.

**Enabling statutes:** laws that grant new powers to do something, usually to a public official, a county, or a city.

**Expert power:** compliance based on a perception of some special skill, ability, or expertise on the part of another.

**Ex post facto laws:** "After the fact." A law that attempts to reduce a person's rights based on a past act that was not subject to the law when it was done.

**External environment:** consists of a variety of outside forces that may interact with, and have a dramatic impact on, the internal environment.

**Functional living units:** used in the federal correctional system. This type of facility places all food, sleeping, hygiene, and counseling services in a self-contained unit.

**General deterrence:** the belief that the punishment of one individual inhibits others from committing the offense.

**Habeas corpus:** "You have the body." A judicial order to someone holding a person to bring that person to court. It is used to force a captor to bring the person being held to the court for a decision on the legality of the confinement.

**Hands off doctrine:** a doctrine used by federal courts to justify nonintervention in the daily administration of correctional facilities.

**Hedonistic calculus:** Jeremy Bentham's concept that mankind was essentially rational and pleasure-seeking and would seek to maximize pleasure and reduce pain in all behavior decisions. Also, that a legal system could accurately determine exactly what measurement of punishment was necessary to slightly outweigh the potential pleasure or profit from any criminal act.

**I-level:** Interpersonal Maturity Level system. An internal classification system based on intellectual development.

**Incapacitation:** the removal or restriction of freedom to prevent criminal behavior.

**Indemnification agreements:** an agreement by which one party agrees to pay all costs associated with lawsuits arising out of the actions of another party.

**Indeterminate sentencing:** a type of sentencing system in which the sentence is a range with a minimum and a maximum sentence; the length of the sentence is determined by professionals at the institution or by the parole board.

**Injunctive relief:** also referred to as equitable relief, is expressed in a judicial order that a person (or agency) refrain from doing a particular act or perform a particular act.

**Inmate code:** the Magna Carta, so to speak, of the prison subculture. The code describes a world where "cons" leave one another alone, shun guards, and never lose their "cool" even in the face of great provocation.

**Internal classification:** the means of augmenting the initial management determination of an inmate's classification.

**Internal environment:** a small environment that consists of the inmate social culture, a physical environment of walls, fences, cells, bars, and a prison staff culture.

**Jailhouse lawyer:** a name for a prisoner who helps other prisoners with legal problems and files writs (often called "writ writers").

**Judicial discretion:** the right of a judge to have great leeway in making decisions, so long as he or she follows the law and proper procedure and refrains from arbitrary action.

**"Just deserts" model:** the idea that offenders should be punished because they deserve to suffer from the harm they have caused and that they are not being held for the purpose of treatment.

**Lease labor system:** the earliest form of prison privatization. A winning bidder would become the leaseholder and gain almost total control over prisoners' labor.

**Least restrictive means test:** a legal test in which the governmental action must be the "least intrusive" to an individual's liberty interests while still accomplishing the governmental objective.

**Linear design:** jails that are designed so that inmate cells are situated along corridors and the staff has to walk the corridors to monitor what is occurring. It is impossible for staff to monitor all the inmate housing units at one time under this design. Also referred to as traditional design.

**Lockstep:** used in Auburn Prison; a means of movement where inmates walked (shuffled) with their hands on the shoulder of the prisoner in front. Allowed guards to control large numbers of prisoners.

**Lockups:** a temporary place of detention in a police station or courthouse.

**Mandamus actions:** used to compel officials to perform their administrative duties.

**Mandatory sentencing:** a specified number of years of imprisonment provided for particular crimes.

**Matron:** female officers in women's correctional institutions.

**Medical model:** views criminal behavior as a symptom of an underlying pathology that can be treated. Causes of disorder may be sociological or psychological.

**MMPI:** the Minnesota Multiphasic Personality Inventory, a "true" or "false" paper-and-pencil test. The scores are used for clinical scales to describe a particular psychological characteristic.

**"Net widening":** the phenomena of increasing the correctional clientele by diversion programs; for example, when diversion programs are created those who might have received no official sanction are placed in them rather than those who were intended to be diverted from more serious sanctions.

**Niches:** jobs or positions that are fairly safe, away from the mainstream, and relatively comfortable for the individual to spend his or her time.

**Objective classification:** a classification system for inmates based on objective criteria such as the inmate's criminal history and institutional behavior.

**Operant conditioning:** relies on the fact that behavior can be shaped through the use of rewards and that the rewards are most effective when they are important to the client.

**Override:** the ability of a classification analyst to change the outcome of an objective evaluation.

**Paradigm:** a way of seeing the world or of organizing and making sense of knowledge.

**Penance:** the aim of punishment in the separate system that was to result in purity and personal reform. Prisoners' labors were intended to focus their minds on the simple things of nature and hence to bring ever to their thoughts the image of the Maker.

**Penumbral right:** a right not specifically mentioned or guaranteed in the constitution but implied from other guarantees.

**Phenomenological approach:** a therapist attempting to see the world through the eyes of the client.

**PIE program:** the Private Sector Prison Industry Enhancement Certification Program, which permitted certified states to sell goods on the open market. States had to meet certain conditions to be certified.

**Pillory:** a wooden structure that held the offender's head and hands through holes which were clamped down. Such punishment was usually held in public view so townspeople could wreak their vengeance on the offender.

**Presumptive sentence:** sentencing in which the legislature determines a sentence range for each crime.

**Pretrial detainees:** individuals arrested for a wide assortment of offenses who, for one reason or another, are either unable to afford or are denied bail, and are housed in jails until their trial.

**Prisonization:** the process by which a prison inmate assimilates the customs, norms, values, and culture of prison life.

**Pseudofamilies:** make-believe family systems in women's prisons that include all the familial roles including grandparents, parents, daughters, sons, cousins, aunts, and so on.

**Psychotherapy:** a self-enlightenment and development of individual responsibility through a process of developing a relationship with a therapist and discussing issues of the past and present, as well as utilizing more specific methods to induce discovery. From this an individual develops self-awareness of motivations for his or her behavior.

**Public function test:** states that state action exists when the state delegates to private parties a power "traditionally exclusively reserved to the state."

**"Rabble":** those individuals who are perceived by society as "irksome, offensive, threatening, capable of arousal, even proto-revolutionary."

**Random assignment:** used to ensure nonbiased sample for statistical purposes; every individual in the "universe" (the population studied) has an equal chance to be selected for a sample.

**Recidivism:** the repeating of criminal behavior.

**Reclassification:** the taking into account of an inmate's behavior since his or her last classification cycle.

**Referent power:** personal authority; the ability of managers to deal with personnel in a fair, evenhanded manner that respects the dignity of the individual and operates without malice or partiality.

**Reform:** monitors external behavior: success is defined as conformance of behavior to expectations.

**Reformatory movement:** a movement where incarceration facilities added goals of reform to punishment, penance, and deterrence.

**Rehabilitation:** the restoration of criminals to a law-abiding way of life through treatment; the result of any planned intervention focused on the offender that reduces criminal activity.

**Reintegration:** the process of rebuilding and establishing new community ties following release from prison.

**Remote design:** cells are situated around a central dayroom and jail personnel are in a secure control room that overlooks the dayroom and the individual cells.

**Responsibility model:** deemphasizes paramilitary structure and stresses inmate classification and elaborate grievance procedures.

**Retention of rights theory:** a prisoner retains all the rights of an ordinary citizen except those expressly, or by necessary implication, are taken from him by law.

**Retribution:** the idea that offenders should be punished because they deserve to suffer from the harm they have caused.

**Returnees:** those who commit crime and are returned to prison as parole violators.

**Reward power:** entails the ability to issue rewards and privileges.

**"Right guy":** the "old style con," respected for his criminal professionalism — he is a thief, bank robber, or organized crime figure. He would be a leader in the yard and not afraid of violence.

**Section 1983 suits:** allow an individual to sue a public official for alleged violations of civil rights.

**Security classification:** has to do with the degree of physical separation from the outside world that the structure of the institution imposes on the inmate.

**Sentence disparity:** the difference in the criminal sanctions that are handed out to people who are convicted of similar offenses and who have similar criminal records.

**Sentence enhancements:** added time to a sentence based on certain, specified factors, for example, use of weapon during the commission of a crime.

**Sentencing guidelines:** guidelines that provide ranges of sentences for most offenses based on the seriousness of the crime and the criminal history of the offender.

**Separate system:** a system that originated in Philadelphia at the Walnut Street Jail where the regime was one of solitary confinement and manual labor. It was a simple monastic existence in which the prisoners were kept separate from one another as well as from the outside world.

**Shot-drill:** a form of unproductive labor consisting of repetitively picking up and setting down large cannon balls.

**Social contract:** an imaginary agreement entered into by persons who have sacrificed the minimum amount of their liberty necessary to prevent anarchy and chaos.

**Sociopath:** a chronic personality disorder, not a mental illness, that often appears in offender populations. Two major themes are lovelessness or inability to feel affection and impulsivity.

**Sovereign immunity test:** the government's immunity from being sued. The U.S. government may waive immunity by a statute such as the Federal Tort Claims Act.

**Special needs inmate:** the growing number of inmates who require a disproportionate share of limited resources. These groups include the elderly, mentally ill, retarded, handicapped, and HIV-positive inmates.

**Specific deterrence:** the effect of a penalty that causes a person who is punished for a crime not to commit that crime again because their reward/risk calculation has been altered by the punishment.

**State action doctrine:** states that when a party violates rights guaranteed by the U.S. Constitution or federal statutes, in order to prevail, the party who is alleging their rights have been violated must show that the violating party was acting "under the color of the law," or in other words, with the power of the federal or state government.

**State compulsion test:** determines whether the duty provided is one for which the state is obligated.

**State-use laws:** provided that goods manufactured with prison labor could not be sold to the open market.

**Subculture:** the social world inside the prison, including argot values, attitudes, behavioral norms, and beliefs.

**Theory X:** a theory of human behavior by Douglas McGregor that assumes that the average person has an inherent dislike of work and will avoid it whenever possible, that people must be coerced, controlled, directed, and threatened with punishment if they are to be motivated to achieve organizational objectives, and that the average person likes to be directed, avoids responsibility, has little ambition, and prizes security.

**Theory Y:** a theory of human behavior by Douglas McGregor that postulates that people represent a potential that can and must be realized by administrators. The leader will view change as positive and seek out opportunities to challenge subordinates to use their potential to address and solve critical issues confronting corrections as it moves into the next century.

**"Three strikes law":** law that states that an individual receives a life sentence after committing any three felonies.

**Tips:** cliques that are largely defined in racial and ethnic terms.

**Title VII of the 1964 Civil Rights Act:** extended the prohibition of employment discrimination to public employees at the state, county, and local levels.

**Totality of circumstances cases:** the cumulative effect of numerous shocking and degrading practices resulting in findings that the conditions of confinement as a whole constitute cruel and unusual punishment.

**Treadmill:** or treadwheels, originally designed as a source of industrial power but were later converted to provide forced unproductive labor.

**Treatment ethic:** states that crime is a symptom of an underlying pathology that can be treated.

**UNICOR:** the Federal Bureau of Prisons manufacturing industry that produces such goods as office furniture, dormitory furniture, metal storage cabinets, and general office supplies.

**Utilitarianism:** the philosophy that makes the happiness of the individual or society the end and the criterion of the morally good. The greatest good for the greatest number is the sole rationale for all public action.

# TABLE OF CASES

# Name Index

# SUBJECT INDEX